Baedeker's

GREEK ISLANDS

W9-BHV-574

How to use this book

Following the tradition established by Karl Baedeker in 1844, sights of particular interest and restaurants of particular quality are distinguished by either one ★ or two ★★ stars.

To make it easier to locate the various places listed in the Sights from A to Z section of the guide, their coordinates on the large city map are shown in red at the head of each entry.

Coloured lines down the right-hand side of the page are an aid to finding the main headings in the guide: blue stands for the Introduction (Nature, Culture, History), red for the Sights from A to Z section, while yellow indicates Practical Information.

Only a selection of hotels and restaurants can be given. No reflection is implied, therefore, on establishments not included.

In a time of rapid change it is difficult to ensure that all the information given is entirely accurate and up to date, and the possibility of error can never be completely eliminated. Although the publishers can accept no responsibility for inaccuracies and omissions, they are always grateful for corrections and suggestions for improvement.

Nature, Culture
History

Facts and Figures

There is no generally accepted system for the transliteration of modern Greek place names and personal names into the Latin alphabet, and the visitor to Greece will find much diversity and inconsistency of spelling, for example on signposts and in guidebooks and other literature in English. The situation is still further complicated by changes in pronunciation that have taken place since antiquity, so that many familiar classical names sound very different in modern Greek.

In this guide modern Greek place names and personal names are transliterated in a form approximating to their pronunciation – though you will encounter many variant spellings in Greece itself. Classical names are generally given in the normally used Latin form rather than the less familiar "Greek" transliteration (e.g. Polycleitus rather than Polykleitos); and where there is a generally accepted English form (e.g. Athens, Crete, Delos) this is, of course, used.

In the transliterated forms of Greek names – and of Greek words used in the text – the syllable on which the stress falls is indicated by an acute accent.

In the headings of the entries in the Sights from A to Z section of the guide the name of the island or town in its transliterated or English form is followed by the name in Greek script.

General

The Greek Republic lies in south-eastern Europe on the southern extremities of the Balkan peninsula, which reach out into the south-eastern Mediterranean. To the west, south and east it is bounded by the sea; on the north it is bordered by Albania, Macedonia, Bulgaria and Turkey.

The country's territory consists of the Greek mainland and some 3050 islands, large and small, of which only 167 are inhabited. It has a total land area of around 131,900 sq. km (50,900 sq. mi.), of which the islands account for 24,700 sq. km (9500 sq. mi.), or 19 per cent. Including sea areas, the total extent of Greek territory is around 400,000 sq. km (55,000 sq. mi.). Greece, including the mainland and the islands, has a total coastline of 15,000 km (9300 mi.); the islands alone have a total coastline of 11,000 km (6800 mi.)

The Greek islands are scattered over a wide area between 41°45′N (with Thásos as the most northerly) and 34°48′N (the little island of Gávdos, south of Crete, being the most southerly point in Europe), and between 19°22′E (the island of Othóni, north-west of Corfu) and 29°38′E (the islet of Strongylí, south-east of Kastellórizo).

Island groups

The broadest classification of the Greek islands is into the Ionian Islands to the west and the Aegean islands to the east and south-east. More exactly, they can be divided into seven regions, six of them in the Aegean.

The Ionian Islands lie off the west coast of Greece at the mouth of the

◀ *The most easterly of the Greek islands is Kastellórizo, which lies only 2.5 km (1½ mi.) off the Turkish coast.*

Greece

Adriatic, between Corfu in the north and Kýthira, far to the south-west off the southern tip of the Peloponnese.

The Northern Sporades lie off the east coast of central Greece, with Skópelos, Skíathos, Alónnisos and Skýros to the north and Euboea to the south.

Northern Sporades

The Saronic or Argolic islands of Aegina, Hydra, Póros, Salamis and Spétses lie in the Saronic Gulf between Attica and the Peloponnese, south of Athens.

Saronic islands

Along with the Saronic and Argolic islands the thirty or forty islands, large and small, of the Cyclades group (so-called because the islands lie in a ring round the sacred island of Delos), including Mýkonos, Páros, Náxos and Santoríni, occupy the southern part of the Aegean, forming in effect a south-easterly continuation of Euboea and Attica.

Cyclades

Widely dispersed in the north-eastern Aegean are the four large islands of Chíos, Lésbos, Lemnos, Samothrace and Thásos.

Islands of the northern and eastern Aegean

Off the south-west coast of Asia Minor, strung closely together in a chain extending from Sámos to Rhodes, are the Southern Sporades, most of which belong to the twelve-island Dodecanese. The best known of these islands, in addition to Rhodes, the largest in the group, are Pátmos, Kálymnos and Kos.

Dodecanese

Kýthira, lying to the south-east of the Peloponnese, points the way to Crete, the largest of the Greek islands (disregarding the independent island of Cyprus in the eastern Mediterranean), forms the southern boundary of the Aegean. Some 300 km (185 mi.) long, it is about the same distance from Attica as from the North African coast, and is at no great distance from Asia Minor.

Crete

Geology

The Ionian Islands off the west coast of Greece are part of the ranges of

Ionian Islands

11

mountains that run through the Balkan peninsula from north-west to south-east and are still on the continental shelf, with the sea ranging in depth between 100 and 600 m (330 and 2000 ft) – though to the west of the islands the shelf plunges steeply down into the Inoussai Trench, which is up to 4150 m (13,600 ft) deep. The much fissured profile indicates that this is the result of a fault fracture. During the folding of the Alps and the Balkan range in the Tertiary era the margins of the land-mass broke up into separate blocks, and the junctions between them are still in motion. Evidence of this is provided by the frequency of severe earthquakes in these areas (more than 30 recorded since the 15th c.); the Ionian Islands are the focal point for earthquakes in the Balkans. An earthquake in 1953 lasted from August 9th to 12th, the heaviest damage being caused on Zákynthos, Kefaloniá, Lefkás and Ithaca; the level of Kefaloniá was raised between 30 centimetres and a metre (12 and 40 inches), leaving some of the famous Argostóli watermills high and dry.

Aegean islands

The Aegean islands are a continuation of the mountains of central Greece, which in the Mesozoic period, some 170 million years ago, were linked with Asia Minor. This is reflected in the rock of which they are composed, mainly crystalline rocks and sediments. In the Palaeozoic period these slates, together with limestones and sandstones partly metamorphosed into marble, granites and gneisses, created what is known as the Cycladic landmass. In subsequent ages these mountains were worn down by erosion and in some areas subsided, when rift and erosion valleys were flooded by the sea. Thereafter there were further deposits of limestones and sediments.

In the later Pliocene the folded Aegean mountains underwent further upthrusts, mainly as a result of the drifting of continental plates. Thus the African Plate, moving northward, was the cause of the folding of the Alps and the Carpathian mountain arc. The upthrust of the moun-

Spring in the Lassíthi plain on Crete; in the background the Dikti range

Preface

This guide to the Greek islands is one of the new generation of Baedeker guides.

These guides, illustrated throughout in colour, are designed to meet the needs of the modern traveller. They are quick and easy to consult, with the principal features of interest described in alphabetical order, and the information is presented in a format that is both attractive and easy to follow.

The present guide is concerned with the whole of the Greek island world, in both the Aegean and the Ionian Sea, and also includes the Greek capital, Athens, and the port of Piraeus, through which most visitors to the islands will pass.

The guide is in three parts. The first part gives a general account of the Greek islands, their geological structure, climate, flora and fauna, population, religion, economy, history, famous people, art and culture. A selection of quotations and some suggestions on island-hopping lead to the second part, in which the individual islands with their principal

Picturesque harbours, like that of Sámos town, and whitewashed houses climbing up the slopes of a hill, as here on Sífnos, are typical features on many islands.

sights are described. The third part contains a variety of practical information. Both the Sights and the Practical Information sections are in alphabetical order.

Baedeker guides are noted for their concentration on essentials and their convenience of use. They contain many coloured illustrations and specially drawn plans, and at the back of the book will be found a fold-out map, making it easy to locate the various islands with the help of the coordinates given at the head of each entry.

Contents

Nature, Culture, History
9–67

Facts and Figures 10
General 10 · Geology 11 · Climate 14 ·
Island Groups 15 · Flora and Fauna 19 ·
Environment 21 · Population 22 ·
Religion 24 · Economy and Transport 25

History 29

Sights from A to Z
70–325

Island-hopping 70

Aegina 75 · Alónnisos 79 · Amorgós 80 ·
Anáfi 83 · Ándros 83 · Astypálaia 88 ·
Athens 89 · Chíos 113 · Corfu 122 ·
Crete 130 · Delos 153 · Erimonísia 161 ·
Euboea 161 · Folégandros 167 ·
Hydra 168 · Ikaría 170 · Íos 172 ·
Ithaca 174 · Kálymnos 177 ·
Kárpathos 183 · Kásos 187 ·
Kastellórizo 188 · Kéa 190 ·

Practical Information from A to Z
328–374

Air Travel 328 · Antiquities 328 ·
Beaches 329 · Camping 330 ·
Cruises 331 · Currency 331 · Customs
Regulations 331 · Diplomatic
Representation 332 · Electricity 333 ·
Emergencies 333 · Events 334 ·
Ferries 335 · Food and Drink 337 · Getting

Glossary 379

Index 385

Source of Illustrations 389

Imprint 390

Principal Sights 391

Large map of Greek Islands at end of book

Famous People 41

Culture 46
Art and Architecture 46 · Music 60 · Folk
Traditions 60

Quotations 63

Kefaloniá 192 · Kímolos 198 · Kos 199 ·
Kýthira 205 · Kýthnos 207 · Lefkás 209 ·
Lemnos 214 · Léros 216 · Lésbos 218 ·
Lipsí 228 · Melos 229 · Mýkonos 232 ·
Náxos 235 · Nísyros 240 · Páros 242 ·
Pátmos 245 · Paxí 251 · Piraeus 253 ·
Póros 255 · Rhodes 256 · Salamis 270 ·
Sámos 271 · Samothrace 282 ·
Santoríni 285 · Sérifos 293 · Sífnos 295 ·
Síkinos 296 · Skíathos 297 · Skópelos 299 ·
Skýros 301 · Spétses 304 · Sými 306 ·
Sýros 307 · Thásos 310 · Tílos 314 ·
Tínos 316 · Zákynthos 319

to the Greek Islands 339 · Health 342 ·
Hotels 343 · Information 353 · Island-
hopping 355 · Language 355 · Manners and
Customs 361 · Media 362 · Motoring 362 ·
Nightlife 363 · Opening Hours 364 ·
Photography 364 · Post 364 · Public
Holidays 364 · Restaurants 365 ·

Sailing 372 · Self-catering 373 ·
Shopping 374 · Sport 375 · Taxis 376 ·
Telephone 376 · Time 377 · Tipping 377 ·
Travel Documents 377 · When to Go 378

Baedeker Specials

The Kafeníon 23
Icons – Sacred Images 59
When Zorba Dances the Syrtáki 134
The God of Wine 154
In the Wake of Odysseus 178
Island of the Poets 220

Beauty in Marble 231
The Revelation of St John 246
A Despot with a Philosophical Turn 278
Santoríni – the Legendary
   Atlantis? 286
Dining Greek Style 340

Come to

You do not need to go to the South Seas or the Caribbean to find a multitude of islands, large and small, within a relatively small compass. Greece has more than 160 inhabited islands offering attractions for every taste. If you are looking for lush green landscapes you must visit the islands in the spring or choose one of the more northerly Aegean islands. Sámos and Thásos are covered by dense forests; on Skíathos and Skópelos pinewoods reach right down to the coasts; and millions of olive trees flourish on Lésbos. The Ionian islands of Corfu, Zákynthos and Paxí also have lush green vegetation, with slender cypresses and pines perfuming the air. Very different are the bare and arid islands of the Cyclades (except Náxos and Pátmos) and Kárpathos and Kálymnos in the Dodecanese and, at the other extreme, the rocky island of Samothrace with its many waterfalls flowing throughout the year.

The architecture of the islands – the way they build their houses – also varies widely. On the islands in the northern Aegean and the Ionian Islands the houses are mostly built of the local stone with gabled roofs, while in the Cyclades and on Pátmos and Kálymnos in the Dodecanese the narrow and winding streets of the villages are lined by dazzling whitewashed houses with blue-, red- and green-painted doors and shutters, while a profusion of flowers provide marvellous colour contrasts.

The spectrum of Greek islands extends from peaceful islands like Ikaría and Chíos, still almost untouched by tourism, to such major tourist centres as Crete, Rhodes, Kos and M[y]konos.

Traditional

costumes are worn everyday at Ólympos on Kárpathos

Picturesque harbours

like Yialós on Ios appeal to many visitors, not only sailing enthusiasts

Excavation sites

like the Asklepieion on Kos are to be found on many islands.

A green "oasis" and a stony desert on the north-east coast of Chíos – a landscape typical of the Greek islands

tains led to further faults. Then in the early Pleistocene, some 2.6 million years ago, the rump mountains, now much ruined, subsided again and were mostly engulfed by the sea. This subsidence led to the formation of the central and northern Aegean, from which the peaks of the sunken mountain ranges and new summits created by volcanic action emerged as islands. The violent folding movements to which the mountains had been subjected led to further fracture and corrosion of the limestones, producing the karstic landscapes found on all the islands.

Throughout the Mediterranean the earth's crust has still not settled down. Earth tremors in varying degrees of strength are almost a daily occurrence, and sometimes they have catastrophic effects. They result from the continuing movement of continental plates. In the case of Greece the tremors are caused by the African Plate, moving north at the rate of about 2.5 cm (1 in.) a year and thrusting under the Aegean Plate – part of the great Eurasian Plate – in a zone of increased volcanic activity. The islands of Aegina, Melos and Santoríni were brought into being by this volcanic activity, which at the moment is probably only dormant (see Baedeker Special p. 286).

Earthquakes and volcanic activity

In a violent volcanic eruption in 1628 BC huge quantities of pumice, volcanic tuffs and ash were ejected. The volcanic activity was accompanied by severe earthquakes, which were particularly destructive in Crete and brought about the collapse of Minoan civilisation. A final lava flow was identified in 1950. There have also been devastating earthquakes in the Aegean Sea in modern times (Crete 1856, Rhodes 1926).

Climate

Like mainland Greece, the Greek islands have really only three seasons – a relatively short spring (March to mid-May) during which there is a veritable explosion of vegetation, a long, hot and very dry summer (mid May to October) and a cool winter rainy season that lasts from November to March. The Greek islands are noted for their abundance of sun: the average duration of sunshine over the year ranges between 2500 and 3000 hours. In many areas the sun shines on 300 days in the year. The average temperature in the hottest month (July/August) ranges between 26° and 30°C (79°and 86°F), but temperatures of up to 40°C (104°F) are not infrequent. Temperatures and summer aridity increase from north to south. Although winters in the Greek islands are rainy, particularly in the months of December and January, most of the rain comes down in heavy showers that do not last long; and even in winter there are many days on which the sun shines.

Ionian Islands

Thanks to their westerly situation and the moderating influence of the sea, the Ionian Islands have a more even temperature pattern (rather warmer in winter and not so hot in summer); but above all they differ from the rest of Greece in having more rain. The "bad" weather, however, is concentrated in a relatively small number of days with heavy rain, so that the Ionian Islands have more sunny days and less cloud cover than Greek territory further east. This is particularly true of Corfu, which has an average annual rainfall of 1137 mm (45 in.), and in spite of four months with little or no rain is, for Greece, uncharacteristically green.

Although summer temperatures may range up to 40°C (104°F), they are made tolerable by the *maístros,* a north-west wind that blows most of the time, sometimes very strongly. Water temperatures rise to a maximum of 24°C (75°F). The pleasantest times for a visit to the Ionian Islands are from April to the end of June and September/October; but, except in the dry months between the end of May and the end of August, rainproof clothing should be included in your luggage.

Aegean islands

The Aegean islands lie in a area of transition between the Mediterranean climatic zone and the steppe climate of Eastern Europe and the Near East. The characteristics of this area are the aridity and subtropical temperatures of the summer months, its relatively mild and rainy winters and the northerly winds that blow almost throughout the year.

The Aegean islands are famed for their springs. After the abundant rain of the winter months (December to March) there is for a few weeks a dazzling show of blossom.

Summer begins at the end of April or early May and lasts until October. During this period there are only sporadic showers of rain, and between June and September there is practically none. This is a time of extreme drought, when long periods of heat with temperatures of up to 40°C (104°F) weigh heavily on man and beast.

From the second half of September or in October thunderstorms, which can locally be very violent, may bring welcome rain.

The rainy period lasts from November to March. The coldest months are January and February, with average afternoon maximum temperatures around 15°C (59°F), while on particularly cold days the temperature can fall to around freezing point. At higher altitudes in the hills there are flurries of snow or snowstorms. Then in March the cold period comes to an end.

Winds

In the summer months strong dry north winds often blow over the Aegean. These are the winds known (after the classical Greek term) as the etesians or as the **meltémi**, whose origins are closely connected with the arrival of the monsoon over the Asian landmass. The winds increase in strength until the early afternoon and die down towards the evening. Over the sea they may produce a heavy swell. These winds were much feared by sailors in antiquity. In more recent times they served to drive large numbers of windmills, which were used to grind corn and draw water for use in elaborate irrigation systems.

In winter and spring the **sirocco**, a moist, warm southerly wind, blows over the southern Greek island world (the Cyclades and Crete), bringing an oppressive sultry air. Sometimes it carries dust from the Sahara that falls on the islands. The sirocco originates at the front of an area of low pressure moving westward over the Mediterranean.

The temperature of the sea falls during winter and only reaches a temperature for suitable for bathing of around 18°C (64°F) in May. Thereafter it rises steadily to 25°C (77°F) in August and then starts slowly to fall again. Surface water in the eastern Mediterranean is still relatively warm until the late autumn, and remains agreeable even in the "cold" season; in October the temperature is still around 20°C (68°F).

Water temperatures

Island Groups

This section brings together information on the characteristics, history and tourist interest of the various island groups. The corresponding information for Crete, which belongs to none of the groups, is given in its entry in the Sights from A to Z section of the guide.

Ionian Islands

The chain of the Ionian Islands, also known as the Eptanisos ("Seven Islands"), extends down the west coast of Greece from the Albanian frontier in the north and far to the south. The main islands are Corfu, Paxí, Lefkás, Ithaca, Kefaloniá and Zákynthos. Kýthira, far to the south-east at the tip of the Peloponnese, also belongs to this group (although for administrative purposes it is attached to Attica). With completely different conditions for tourism, it is excluded from the following description.

The islands in the Ionian Sea have a mild, rainy climate and luxuriant Mediterranean/subtropical vegetation. This gives them an "unGreek" character: they have more of an Italian feeling – a feeling reinforced by their architecture, which bears the mark of several hundred years of Venetian influence. The period of British rule (from 1815 to 1862) has also lefts its mark on the islands' culture and cuisine. Only Lefkás and to a lesser extent Kefaloniá, Zákynthos, Paxí and Ithaca belonged for a time to the Ottoman Empire, so that, particularly on Lefkás and Kefaloniá, some trace of Oriental influence can still be detected.

All the islands are involved, in varying degree, in **tourism**. In the late 19th c. Corfu and Zákynthos were already frequented by the European nobility, and they are now major tourist areas, catering particularly for British visitors. The other islands are less frequented. Lefkás, which has excellent facilities for bathing, seems to have been overlooked by island lovers; while Ithaca has been overshadowed by other islands regarded as more attractive, though it is still a good place for a restful holiday.

History The Ionian Sea – equated by ancient writers with the Adriatic and now regarded as the southern continuation of that sea – and its islands are named after the wanderings of Io (according to Aeschylus) or, according to later sources, the Illyrian hero Ionius, whose name is spelt with an omicron (the short Greek o). There is thus no connection with the Ionian Greeks, derived from an ancestor called Ion (spelt with omega, the long o), who left Greece in the 11th–10th c. BC and colonised the Anatolian coast, which was thereafter known as Ionia.

Excavations have brought to light material dating back to the Mycenaean period, but the Ionian Islands first appear in history in 734 BC, when Corinth founded a colony that was named Korkyra, later Kerkyra. In the 5th c. BC the islands came under Athenian influence, and in the 2nd c. BC they became Roman. After the Byzantine era, during which the islands fell to the Normans (1085), the Fourth Crusade (1203–4) brought a further change in the islands' destinies. New rulers from Italy took over from the Byzantines, and Venice gradually gained control of the islands: in 1363 Kýthira, in 1386 Kérkyra (now renamed Corfu), in 1479 Zákynthos, in 1500 Kefaloniá (after 21 years of Turkish rule) and finally, in 1684, Lefkás, which had been in Turkish hands since 1467. The islands remained under Venetian rule until the fall of the Republic of St Mark in 1797. During this period many people fleeing before the Turks had found refuge in the islands, including artists from Crete who established a distinctive school there. In general the Ionian Islands enjoyed a richer cultural life during these centuries than the rest of Greece; for example the traditions of icon painting were maintained. After interludes of French (Napoleon, 1797–9 and 1807–10) and Russian occupation (1800–7) the young Republic of the Seven United Islands became a British protectorate in 1815. Although colonial rule was felt to be high-handed and repressive, it did give the islands a modern infrastructure (roads, hospitals). In 1864 they were returned to Greece. During the Second World War Corfu was occupied by the Italians and after their surrender in 1943 by the German army.

Othonian Islands   The Othonian Islands, which form part of the Ionian group, are a small archipelago in the northern Ionian Sea (at the point of junction with the Strait of Otranto and the Adriatic), north-west of Corfu (from which there are ferry services to the islands). The group consists of the islets of Othóni (known in Italian as Faro; lighthouse at eastern tip; area 10 sq. km (4 sq. mi.); pop. 150), Erikoúsa (Italian Merlera; area 4.4 sq. km (1½ sq. mi.); pop. 200; boat trips from Corfu), Mathráki and Diaplo, one of which is supposed to be the legendary island of Calypso.

Saronic islands

This group takes in all the islands in the Saronic Gulf between Athens and the Argolid, including Salamis, Aegina, Angístri and Póros, together with numerous smaller islands, islets and stacks, as well as the Argolic Islands. The Argolic Islands, the farthest west and south of the Saronic islands, includes all the islands off the coast of the Argolid and in the Argolic Gulf, notably Hydra, Dokós, Spétses, the smaller islands of Tríkeri, Spetsopoúla, Psilí and Platía, and innumerable isolated stacks. Climatically the islands lie in the arid region of the Aegean, but in spite of their low rainfall they have remarkably luxuriant vegetation. The island of Salamis is famed as the scene of the naval battle in 480 BC in which the Athenians inflicted an annihilating defeat on the Persian fleet. There are important remains of ancient buildings in the islands, most notably on Aegina.

Tourism Lying so close to Athens and the port of Piraeus, the islands, with their idyllic little port towns, attract large numbers of visitors from Athens at weekends.

Sporades

Northern   The name Sporades (the "scattered" islands) was applied in antiquity
Sporades   to all the islands lying round the Cyclades. A distinction is now made

between the Northern Sporades or Magnesian Islands and the Southern Sporades. The Northern Sporades lie north-east of Euboea, the second largest Greek island after Crete, and east of the Magnesian peninsula (Mount Pelion). They include Skópelos, Skíathos, Alónnisos and Skýros, together with some 75 smaller islands. There are few historic buildings in the Northern Sporades, but they offer instead beautiful scenery and marvellous beaches, still relatively unspoiled by mass tourism.

The Southern Sporades, lying off the south-western coast of Asia Minor (Turkey), include Pátmos, Lipsí, Kálymnos, Léros, Kos, Nísyros, Tílos, Sými, Foúrni and Ikaría. Lésbos, Chíos and Sámos are also sometimes regarded as belonging to this group.

Southern Sporades

Dodecanese

The Dodecanese, the group of "Twelve Islands" lying off the south-western coast of Asia Minor, is the most southerly part of the Southern Sporades. It includes the 14 larger islands of Lipsí, Pátmos, Léros, Kálymnos, Kos, Astypálaia, Nísyros, Sými, Tílos, Rhodes, Khalkí, Kárpathos, Kásos and Kastellórizo and around 40 smaller islands, islets and stacks. The islands in the group have a total land area of 2714 sq. km (1048 sq. mi). The administrative centre of the Dodecanese is the town of Rhodes. Linked with Greece by culture but with Anatolia by geology, the islands of the Dodecanese, with the exception of Rhodes, are arid and largely barren. The inhabitants live mainly by the tourist trade; other sources of income are agriculture, pottery, tanning and carpet weaving.

One of the most popular islands in the Dodecanese is Pátmos. From the Khóra there is a view of the whole island

Tourism The islands of the Dodecanese, particularly Rhodes, Kos and Pátmos, are among the most popular tourist areas in Greece. Visitors looking for a quiet holiday in unspoiled country should look to one of the smaller islands.

History In Greek and Roman times the Dodecanese was never a separate political unit. It was only when they were incorporated in the Turkish empire in the 16th c. that the islands were given a common political status by the grant of extensive rights of self-government in domestic affairs. In 1912 Italy occupied most of the islands as security against Turkish-occupied Libya, and under the treaty of Lausanne in 1923 Turkey ceded the whole of the Dodecanese to Italy. After fighting and German occupation during the Second World War the islands were returned to the kingdom of Greece in 1947.

Islands of the northern and eastern Aegean

The islands of Sámos, Chíos, Lésbos, Lémnos, Samothrace and Thásos, scattered about in the northern and eastern Aegean, are not a group in any real sense and have very individual characters. They are very different from other Greek islands: their history has been completely different, and they are greener and more fertile than the other Aegean islands. Most of the islands in the eastern Aegean lie within sight of the Turkish coast.

This region has a long **history**. Thermí on Lésbos was established around 2700 BC, and Polyókhni on Lémnos is older than its near neighbour Troy. During the Greek colonisation movement Aeolians came to Lésbos about 1100 BC, Ionians to Chíos about 1000 and to Lemnos about 800. Around 700 Thásos (from Páros) and Samothrace were colonised. The islands enjoyed a great flowering in the 7th and 6th c., when Lesbos produced the poets Terpander and Arion, Sappho and Alcaeus and a great school of sculptors flourished on Chíos. After a period of Persian rule (546–479 BC) and membership of the first Attic maritime league the islands came from the 4th c. onwards under Macedonian, Ptolemaic and Roman influence. After the Fourth Crusade (1204) they were ruled by Venice and later by Genoa. Then followed the Turkish period, which lasted until 1912. In 1922–3, after the Greek debacle in Asia Minor, Lésbos and Chíos took in many refugees, and after the Second World War many Greeks returned from Egypt to Lemnos. In recent years Turkey, partly with an eye to local deposits of oil, has put forward claims to the Anatolian continental shelf, on which Chíos and Lésbos lie.

Cyclades

The Cyclades represent the prototype of a Greek island: bare rocky islands with characteristic whitewashed houses huddled close together and tiny churches with blue domes, surrounded by the deep blue of the sea and bathed in dazzling light. The name Cyclades was given in antiquity to the circle (Greek *kyklos*) of islands round the sacred island of Delos. According to the legend Poseidon cast the mountains with his trident into the sea, where they took root.

The archipelago consists of 23 large and around 200 small islands, all of them mountainous. None of them except Náxos have any perennial rivers nor, because of the sharp prevailing winds (the meltémi) any trees.

The 1970s saw the beginning of the upsurge of **tourism**, now the islands' main source of income. Mýkonos, Íos and Santoríni are crowded with visitors during the main holiday season, while other islands closer to Athens attract large numbers of weekend visitors. The smaller islands, particularly those to the east of Náxos, are still relatively quiet. Tínos draws many visitors to Greece's most important place of pilgrimage.

History The earliest inhabitants of the Cycladic islands are believed to have been Carians, bearers of the early Bronze Age Cycladic culture (3200–2000 BC), whose "Cycladic idols" have been found on all the islands. Towards the end of the 2nd millennium BC they were supplanted by Ionians on the northern islands and by Dorians on the southern islands. Most of the islands joined the first, and later the second Attic maritime league. In the second half of the 1st millennium BC they were partly under Macedonian and partly under Ptolemaic control. Later they were incorporated in the Roman Empire, and after the division of the Empire came under Byzantine rule. Under Venetian and Frankish rule they enjoyed a flowering of art and intellectual life. Even under Turkish occupation (1579 onwards) they largely maintained their religion and culture. In 1834 they became part of the new kingdom of Greece.

Flora and Fauna

Flora

The flora of Greece is one of the most interesting in Europe, bringing together as it does plants of south-east European, Near Eastern and North African origin; and the Greek islands too have a particularly varied and luxuriant vegetation.

The vegetation of the Greek islands is of typically Mediterranean character, with sclerophyllous (leathery leaved) plants and succulents and trees of only medium size. In fertile depressions and coastal areas, up to a height of around 800 m (2600 ft), mixed forests of oaks, planes, Aleppo pines and carob trees, alternate with a macchia (Greek longos or phrygana) of holm-oaks, kermes oaks, strawberry trees, mastic bushes, laurel, broom, oleander and wild olive trees. In the moister west (the Ionian Islands) this pattern reaches up to 2000 m (6500 ft).

Phrygana, longos

Further south the phrygana becomes scantier. On the more arid islands in the south-eastern Aegean it degenerates into a sparse cover of drought-tolerant plants, consisting almost entirely of junipers, thistles, thyme, dill, peppermint, spurges and water-storing succulents (cactuses, agaves, opuntias). This dry macchia provides only meagre grazing for sheep and goats.

Visitors to the Greek islands in spring are overwhelmed by the profusion of blossom, for almost all the buds burst into flower almost simultaneously – mimosas, hibiscus, oleanders, magnolias, anemones, bougainvilleas, a variety of orchids, narcissi and poppies.

As a result of the ruthless destruction of the islands' forests over millennia many of them are now left with only a sparse growth of trees or none at all. The natural vegetation cover of forest and macchia has been eaten away since antiquity by agricultural use of the land and continued overgrazing and replaced at best by olive groves, plantations of figs and vineyards. Some of the agricultural land has been worked since ancient times and is still under cultivation; but since nowadays wine, olive oil and figs are not particularly profitable crops more and more land is being left fallow, and the wasteland thus created is taken over by phrygana. Recently attempts have been made to reafforest such land.

Forests, olive groves, vineyards

Typical features of the landscape are cypresses and eucalyptus trees. All over the islands, too, are such imported plants as agaves and prickly pears from Central America and date palms from North Africa, originally brought in as ornamental trees but now also growing wild.

Important crops, in addition to the olive and the grape (used for making wine and producing table grapes, raisins and sultanas), are citrus fruits (particularly oranges and mandarines), and cereals. In recent years the

Useful plants

production of vegetables (early potatoes, cucumbers, tomatoes, onions), fruit (apricots, peaches, apples, melons, sweet chestnuts, bananas, figs, almonds) and flowers has flourished.

Fauna

The isolation of the Greek islands from the mainland at an early stage in geological history and the extensive devastation of the natural plant cover have left them with a very limited range of animal species. In addition to sheep, goats, donkeys and mules that have gone wild there are rabbits and hares, preyed on by foxes, badgers, martens and wild cats. On Crete there are still a few wild goats (Capra aegarus), ancestors of the domestic goat.

Reptiles

Reptiles too are increasingly losing ground. This is particularly the case with the common (Greek) tortoise and the loggerhead turtle, which buries its eggs on sandy beaches, to be incubated by the sun. In recent years the few remaining sites where they lay their eggs have been threatened, and only international protests have saved the famous turtle beach in Laganás Bay on Zákynthos from being taken over completely and developed for tourism. Geckos and various species of lizards (including the emerald lizard), however, are very common. Snakes are to be found not only in the scrub of the phrygana but in gardens and other cosy corners. Visitors should beware particularly of the poisonous and very aggressive viper and the Levantine adder, now a protected species.

Birds

Birds have also been reduced in numbers. In the mountains peregrine falcons and hawks can still be seen, and occasionally also lammergeiers, kestrels and buzzards. Grouse and quails, peewits and magpies are common. Near the coast can be seen black and white oystercatchers, terns, common rollers and various species of gull. Common too are nuthatches (particularly the dwarf nuthatch), buntings and the colourful bee-eaters. Pelicans are now to be found only in a few remote spots. Some species of birds that have long been endangered and are included in the famous "Red List" are nevertheless still being hunted by sportsmen.

Insects

The insect life of the islands offers a wide range of species. This is particularly evident in spring, when myriads of butterflies and bees cluster round the flowers and the chirping of the cicadas fills the air. The only insects to beware of are the poisonous rogalida spider and the scorpion with its poisonous sting.

Marine animals

There are surprisingly few species of fish and marine animals in Greek waters – largely the result of overfishing, but in recent years also of pollution of the water. Catches of fish are barely sufficient to meet the needs of the population. Among the relatively common species of fish are grey mullet, red mullet, mackerel, dentex, bass, hake, sardines, anchovies. gurnards and tunny. Also numerous are squid, octopus, various species of shellfish, lobsters, crayfish, prawns and shrimps. Water sports enthusiasts should beware of sharks and moray eels, while sea urchins and stinging jellyfish are hazards for bathers.

Dolphins can occasionally be seen, particularly out at sea. The monk seal, which can sometimes be seen on remote stretches of rocky coast, is threatened with extinction, and banks of coral and colonies of sponges have also declined as a result of water pollution.

Sponge fishing, which was formerly practised all over the Aegean, is now confined to North African coastal waters. The only island on which sponge fishing is of any importance is Kálymnos, which for many generations has produced the best sponge divers.

Environment

There is as yet little consciousness on the Greek islands of the need for effective protection of nature and the environment. Many places have bins for waste paper and rubbish, but sewage is still for the most part discharged into the sea completely unpurified; sewage and waste disposal plants are the exception rather than the rule. There are, however, some positive signs, such as the increased use of wind turbines and solar panels for the production of electricity.

There has never in the past been any great concern for the environment in Greece. The stark beauty of the bare limestone hills, for example, is the result of the destruction of the native forest cover over millennia. Trees were felled not only to win land for cultivation but also to provide timber for the construction of houses and ships and charcoal for the working of metal. Much of the secondary vegetation that replaced the trees (macchia, phrygana) was also taken into cultivation. The destructive forces of erosion were thus given free play. In recent years attempts have been made to stem the process by reafforestation.

Deforestation

Large numbers of sheep and goats have been grazing on the islands for many centuries, and as a result the development of any considerable areas of woodland is prevented, since the animals relish the young shoots as a particular delicacy.

Overgrazing

Nowadays land speculation not infrequently leads to the clearance of woodland by fire. Every year several thousand hectares of woodland or scrub are destroyed by fires started either intentionally or by accident, and very little is replaced by reafforestation. The consequences are erosion by wind and rain and disturbance of the water balance.

Forest and bush fires

Agriculture, particularly the intensive cultivation of fruit and vegetables with much use of fertilisers and pesticides, has contributed to a worrying deterioration in soil and water quality.

Erosion

The explosive growth of tourism has also played a part in aggravating existing ecological problems. A visible sign of this development is the alarming drop in the numbers of plants and animals in coastal areas, affecting particularly the sponge and coral populations.

So much water is consumed in the summer months, particularly on the most popular tourist islands, that the water table is steadily sinking. In coastal areas seawater is increasingly seeping into the subsoil. Some islands have had to install costly desalination plants to meet the demand for water.

Water supply

The increasing pollution of the land and of water has stimulated action by interested citizens and organisations concerned with the environment. Attempts have been made in recent years to deal with the problem of water shortage by strict regulations on building development and the use of water. All hotels of any size are now required to have their own purification plants. Water treated in this way is used for watering gardens and fields, and thereafter reenters the natural cycle.

Protection of the environment

On Zakynthos a watch is being kept on the beaches used by the loggerhead turtles for laying their eggs. The government for its part is planning to reafforest areas that have been cleared of trees. On some of the Cycladic islands the inhabitants are reverting to traditional and sustainable methods of agriculture, for even tourist interests have recognised that an unspoiled natural environment adds to the attractiveness of a place for visitors.

Visitors should therefore set a good example of respect for the environment and thus encourage the local inhabitants to continue the good work.

Population

Of the total number of Greeks (10.6 million in 1997) only about 1.5 million live on the islands. With an average density of population of 84 to the sq. km (218 to the sq. mi.) the Ionian Islands are well above the average density for the whole of Greece (79 to the sq. km, or 205 to the sq. mi.), the Aegean islands well below it, with only 35 to the sq. km (91 to the sq. mi.). Most of the islands show a steady decline in population, and several of them are verging on complete depopulation.

Ethnic groups

The population of the islands, most of whom live on the land, are of Greek origin. After the large-scale exchange of populations in 1922–3 there are only small Turkish minorities on Rhodes and Kos. Some groups of Albanians, particularly on Hydra and Spétses, who had shown themselves during the struggle for liberation from the Turks to be active Greek patriots, are now largely assimilated; only a few older people still speak or understand Albanian. Since the disturbances in Albania in recent years the wave of refugees has reached even some of the remoter islands.

In the Dodecanese centuries of rule by the Turks and Italians have left their mark on the local population, as have the years of British rule in the Ionian Islands, giving them firm links with western European culture. There are also a few nomadic family groups of gypsies.

The uniformity of Greek population today was brought about by political events after the First World War, when some 1.5 million refugees from Asia Minor returned to their homeland and 518,000 Turks and 92,000 Bulgarians left the country.

Emigration

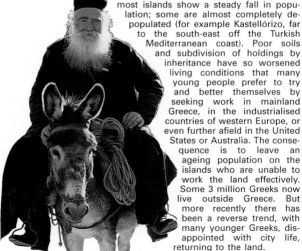

In contrast to the towns on the mainland, most islands show a steady fall in population; some are almost completely depopulated (for example Kastellórizo, far to the south-east off the Turkish Mediterranean coast). Poor soils and subdivision of holdings by inheritance have so worsened living conditions that many young people prefer to try and better themselves by seeking work in mainland Greece, in the industrialised countries of western Europe, or even further afield in the United States or Australia. The consequence is to leave an ageing population on the islands who are unable to work the land effectively. Some 3 million Greeks now live outside Greece. But more recently there has been a reverse trend, with many younger Greeks, disappointed with city life, returning to the land.

The popular image of a Greek countryman

The Kafeníon

The habit of dropping into the *kafeníon*, the traditional Greek café, in the morning or afternoon for a chat with friends is general among older men in the country but is also common in towns. In the kafeníon they exchange the news and gossip and there is much lively discussion, particularly when elections are pending. Here too they play for hours with their *komboloi*, the "worry beads" inherited from Islam. Others prefer to play with their key-ring as a means of preventing themselves from smoking too many cigarettes. Pastimes found in the kafeníon include cards and *tavli*, the Greek form of backgammon. And of course there is Greek coffee (*kofes ellinikon*), which is served in tiny cups – without sugar (*sketos*), with a little sugar (*metrios*), or sweet (*glikos*).

Much attention is made to the proper preparation of the coffee. In order to bring out its full flavour it must be brought briefly to the boil over a low flame twice or even three times. The sign of a good cup of coffee is the thick creamy foam that tops it – increasingly seldom seen now that coffee is heated rapidly on an electric cooker. Greek coffee is drunk in sips – often spread over so long a period that the coffee is completely cold. If the last sip is taken too quickly it will include a mouthful of not very tasty grounds. Those who don't want coffee can drink ouzo, beer or *gliko tou koutallou*, a syrupy concoction with preserved fruit (cherries or quinces, or sometimes pistachios or walnuts), which is served on a small plate with a teaspoon. There is no obligation to order anything in a kafeníon, and a customer will not be looked at askance if he spends hours over his coffee and the newspapers.

Almost every village has its kafeníon, usually very simply – if not shoddily – furnished. Cigarette smoke hangs in the air, the large window panes are clouded, the chairs and tables are rickety. The atmosphere of the kafeníon is appealing mainly to pensioners and

In the kafeníon the men of the village meet and set the world to rights

passionate devotees of cards or tavli. Younger men in particular feel more at home in rather smarter cafés or bars equipped to western standards.

And yet there are certain kafeníons, though they are less well known, where families and friends – men and women, young and old – can gather in the evening, have something to drink and nibble appetisers (*mezedakia*). Not all kafeníons are simply male preserves

Religion

As in other southern European countries, the traditional patriarchal society in Greece is in process of radical change. For centuries the extended family has been the most important economic and emotional unit, which provides the individual with social security and in which he in turn recognises his responsibility for the care of the old and the sick and the support of the unemployed. Nowadays, particularly in towns, this form of communal life is increasingly giving place to the single family with one or two children. This also involves a change in the traditional view of a woman's role, which confined her to bringing up children and running the household. This process is promoted by political reforms. Greek women have had the vote since the early 1950s, and their equality of rights with men was established by law in 1975. Legislation in the 1980s made substantial changes in marriage, family and divorce law – a further important step in the direction of equal rights. The reality, however, is often very different, particularly in the country. Thus it is still expected that when a woman gets married she will bring a dowry with her, in spite of the fact that the obligation to do so was abolished in 1983. A man and his wife still spend their leisure time separately. While he goes to the kafeníon, she sits with other women outside their houses discussing the events of village life.

In spite of changing trends, however, all members of a family still have a strong feeling of community. Thus many Greeks will travel from Athens and other mainland towns, or even from overseas, at Easter, for some particular family occasion or on holiday on their native island.

Religion

Almost the whole Greek population belongs to the Greek Orthodox church, for every child of Greek Orthodox parents automatically becomes a member of the church, and it is not possible to leave it. The small minority of other denominations is made up of Protestants, Roman Catholics (a heritage of Venetian rule in the Cyclades), Muslims and Jews.

Greek Orthodox
church

*Offerings are
always
welcome*

In spite of regional differences resulting from differences in history and wide geographical fragmentation the Greek population of the islands have preserved a profound national consciousness. A strong unifying force, particularly in difficult times, has been the Greek Orthodox church, which has maintained its influence in both public and private life. The Greek church has been autonomous since 1833. In 1850 it was recognised by the Oecumenical Patriarchate in Constantinople (Istanbul) as an independent ("autocephalous") church; and in 1864 it became the state church. The church is headed by the Archbishop of Athens. Only the islands of the Dodecanese, which were united with Greece only in 1912–13, and the autonomous monastic republic of Athos are directly subject to the spiritual jurisdiction of the Patriarchate in Constantinople and not to the Orthodox church of Greece. Crete is in a special position as a semi-autonomous province of the Greek Orthodox church.

The Greek priest, with his black cassock and long hair and beard, is a familiar figure in every Greek village. They are allowed to marry, but only before being ordained as priest (*pappas*), and if a priest's wife dies he may remarry. Married priests may not, however, become monks, and they are not eligible for higher offices in the church. Bishops (metropolitans) normally come from the monastic profession.

Since the Orthodox church is the state religion, the priest is in effect a state employee – though with a very modest salary. He can also earn some extra money by way of offerings or charges for particular services (baptisms, marriages, burials). Frequently he must take on some other employment to make both ends meet.

Social work, such as the care of the young or the old, is not the priest's responsibility. He intervenes in social life only when someone strays from the traditional norms or comes into conflict with the law.

The Orthodox church still sticks to the Julian calendar, so that the dates of church festivals vary from those of the Roman Catholic church, which are determined by the Gregorian calendar. For feast days see Practical Information, Events.

Church festivals

The most important religious festival in Greece, apart from the Dormition (see below), is Easter, which is of much greater significance than Christmas. Like Christmas, it is a family festival. The Easter ceremonies begin with processions on Good Friday that in effect re-enact the Entombment (*epitaphios*) of Christ. The faithful, carrying candles, accompany the supposed coffin of Christ, which is decked with flowers and embroidery. The high point of the festival is reached on the night before Easter Day, when the congregation assembles in the church about an hour before midnight. When the priest proclaims the Resurrection of Christ the worshippers light a candle from the Easter candle in the church and pass the light on from candle to candle. There are special candles for children (*lambades*), decorated with ribbons, animals or other kinds of toys, usually given them by their godparents along with a gift. There are firework displays, firecrackers and in many villages bonfires on which Judas is symbolically burned. After the midnight service families gather to eat their first Easter meal after the period of fasting. This usually consists of *mayiritsa,* a soup of lamb innards with egg, lemon and abundance of dill. On Easter Day the lamb that had been prepared the day before is grilled. There is also a custom involving eggs that have been hard boiled and dyed red: the eggs are knocked against one another, and if your egg has the hardest shell and remains unbroken then, it is said, you will be lucky for a whole year.

Easter

The Dormition of the Mother of God – the equivalent of the Assumption of the Virgin in the Catholic church – is celebrated on August 15th. The main centre of the celebrations is the church of the Panayía Evangelístra on the Cycladic island of Tínos, where thousands of believers gather on that day, after forty days of fasting, in fulfilment of a vow or to seek the intercession of the Panayía. Some of them make their way from the harbour to the church, situated on higher ground, on their knees and then light a candle in front of the wonder-working icon of the Mother of God. The festival is celebrated all over Greece, and many Greeks return to their home village for the occasion.

Dormition

Economy and Transport

In spite of the great progress made by the Greek economy since Greece became a member of the European Community in 1981, Greece remains one of the "problem children" of the European Union, and cannot yet meet the "convergence" criteria for entry to European Monetary Union. Agriculture is still a major element in the economy, though its contribution to the country's gross domestic product has been falling for years. The islands are among the least developed areas in Greece: they have practically no industry, and their trade is centred on agriculture, which remains the main source of income apart from tourism. While the smaller islands produce only enough for their own consumption, the larger ones are able to sell their surplus output to mainland Greece and other countries.

Agriculture

Important agricultural products since antiquity have been olives (both for eating and for the production of oil), wine and honey or wax, and in more recent times melons and early vegetables, cucumbers (Crete), tomatoes (Cyclades; mainly for the production of tomato puree), sultanas, almonds and groundnuts (Crete), table grapes and currants (Ionian Islands), cotton, tobacco, mastic (Chíos), peaches, apricots, apples and pears (canning factory on Crete). In the upland regions there is extensive stockbreeding, though the scanty growth of vegetation means that in most cases only sheep, goats and other small animals (particularly poultry) are reared. The main products are, of course, meat, milk and cheese, together with wool, skins and leather. In some areas beekeeping flourishes, producing honey, propolis and beeswax. On some islands mules and donkeys are still indispensable as working and pack animals.

Fishing

The Greek fishing industry is faced with major problems as a result of overfishing and water pollution, which have led to drastic reductions in catches over the last 20 years. The annual catch of sea fishes (mainly sardines and anchovies) is now only around 100,000 metric tons. In consequence there are now many large companies running fish farms (particularly bass and monkfish, as well as molluscs and crustaceans). The productivity of the Greek fisheries, as a result of the low rate of regeneration of the food chain and continued overfishing, is now much reduced, and it has become necessary to import fish to meet domestic demand.

Sponge-fishing

The sponge fisheries, once one of the most important and most productive industries of the eastern Aegean, are now steadily shrinking in face of competition from synthetic sponges. The Greek sponge-fishing fleet, traditionally based in the Dodecanese, is now to be found in any numbers only on Kálymnos. It is now concentrated mainly in North African coastal waters.

Mining

The mining industry (consisting only of small and medium-size firms with a maximum of 400 employees) is confined to small deposits of iron, manganese, nickel, chromium, zinc, lead and molybdenum (Euboea and Melos). World-famous marble has been quarried since ancient times on Tínos, Chíos, Náxos and Páros. Pozzolana, a type of volcanic ash found on Santorini and Melos, has been prized since ancient times as a mortar that sets under water and can be used in the construction of port installations.

Oil

Since 1981 Greece has been a member of the exclusive club of oil-producing countries, deposits of this "black gold" having been found two years before off the northern Aegean island of Thásos. Natural gas is also being extracted. Other lucrative deposits of oil and gas have since been found on the Asiatic continental shelf of the Aegean. Both Greece and Turkey lay claim to these sites, and there have in consequence been considerable tensions between the two countries in recent years. The most important source of fossil fuel is lignite (brown coal), which is worked on Euboea.

Greece's oil and natural gas make only a modest contribution of some 5 per cent of the country's energy supply. This could change if Greece and Turkey reach agreement on the working of the deposits of oil and natural gas off the coast of Asia Minor.

Greece's craft products are based on the working of clay (pottery and ceramics) and the rearing of sheep and goats (woollen carpets, textiles, leatherworking).

Craft production

The most important sector of the economy, by a long way, has for many years been the service industries, which provide employment for rather more than half the working population. The Greek islands are among the classic holiday destinations of the world, and tourism has long been a major earner of foreign currency. Over the last thirty years considerable sums have been invested in the improvement of the tourist infrastructure. Over 11 million visitors come to Greece every year, two-thirds of them from the countries of the European Union, particularly from Britain and Germany. An agreeable climate, good beaches, scenic beauty and a wealth of historical and architectural attractions offer a promising future for the development of tourism, which is actively promoted by the government.

Service industries; tourism

Transport

Most of the islands have road systems that range between good and adequate. The most important means of mass transport on the islands is the bus. Bus services are run by the state and a host of private companies.

Road transport

Over the last twenty years air services have developed into an important form of inter-island transport. The foundations of Greek air services were laid in the 1950s by the far-seeing shipping magnate Aristoteles Onassis with his Olympic Airways, which has now developed into the all-powerful Greek national carrier. The most important air traffic hub is Athens's international airport of Ellinikon, which is used by numerous international airlines and charter companies. It handles well over 8 million passengers a year and around 85,000 metric tons of air freight. From Ellinikon, too, Olympic Airways, using smaller aircraft, flies to even the remotest islands in the Aegean. There are other international airports on Corfu, Crete (Iráklion), Kos, Lemnos and Rhodes. It is planned to construct a large new international airport 20 km (12½ mi.) east of Athens to relieve the pressure on Ellinikon.

Air services

Ships still remain the most important means of transport between the mainland and the islands and between the various islands. In the seventies and eighties, when the numbers of tourists and the mobility of the Greek population were both increasing, there grew up alongside the traditional ferry services a whole new system of coastal shipping using hydrofoils and catamarans, which could put in anywhere. The largest and most important Greek port is Piraeus, which has been since ancient times Athens's gateway to the world. Other important mainland ports are Salonica, Patrás, Vólos, Kavála and Igoumenítsa. The most important ports on the islands are Kérkyra (Corfu town), Iráklion (Crete) and Rhodes. The ports of Rhodes and Mýkonos are at present in course of improvement.

Shipping

Efficiently functioning ferry services are of great economic importance to Greece and its islands, both for domestic traffic and for the country's links with leading countries of the European Union. The importance of these services was emphasised by the outbreak of hostilities in former Yugoslavia, when land routes to Greece were for all practical purposes

Ferries

"Flying dolphins" – the fast boats that ply between the islands in summer

cut off and Greece's export trade was threatened with strangulation. The Greek reaction was prompt; and there are now modern express ferry services between Patrás and the Italian ports of Brindisi and Ancona, which cover the 500 sea miles in less than 24 hours – much faster than conventional ferries. Recently, too, more modern and faster ferries between Piraeus and the Aegean islands, Rhodes and Crete have been coming into service.

Greece is one of the leading shipping nations in the world, largely because is one of the "cheap" flags and because many Greek shipping lines sail their ships under even cheaper flags (e.g. Liberia, Panama). Some 2200 vessels under the Greek flag, including 900 freighters and 400 tankers, are constantly at sea all over the world's oceans.

History

Archaeological finds show that the Greek islands have been occupied by man since the 7th millennium BC. Common characteristics point to links with Near Eastern cultures, so that it is legitimate to talk of a wider neolithic cultural region. On the mainland finds of axes, knives and pottery have revealed a Chalcolithic culture centred in the Argolid (eastern Peloponnese) in the 3rd millennium BC.

The Minoan culture – named after the mythical King Minos – grew up on Crete, centred on large palace complexes. Material dating from the early 3rd millennium BC found in the port towns of eastern Crete and in the Mesará plain includes seals, copper and bronze daggers and gold jewellery.

In the first flowering of Minoan civilisation, known as the Proto-Palatial or First Palace Period after the palaces of Knossos, Mália and Phaistós, an urban culture was centred on the ruler's court. The economic bases of this civilisation were the intensive production of wine and oil and metalworking. In this phase of the settlement of Crete Minoan society seems to have been relatively autonomous and self-sufficient, with few contacts with other peoples. It was clearly not found necessary to fortify the palaces and towns. The so-called Kamáres ware (after its original findspot) – thin-wall vases painted in bright colours – shows a high level of artistic achievement.

The Cretan palaces were destroyed, probably by an earthquake, around the middle of the 18th c. BC. Their rebuilding in the Neo-Palatial or Second Palace Period marked the beginning of the Late Minoan period. Knossos in particular was splendidly rebuilt. Minoan society was now more outward looking, establishing contacts with Mycenaean culture on the Greek mainland and even more actively with the New Kingdom in Egypt. During this period the Cyclades came under Minoan influence, as evidenced by important excavations at Akrotíri on Santoríni and Fylakopí on Melos. Trade and interchange with neighbouring peoples brought the Linear B script to Crete, replacing the older pictographic script. The religion and social structure of this period showed matriarchal features. In Knossos there was a great flowering of pottery and fresco painting in the so-called Palace style.

Around 1410 BC Mycenaean conquerors landed on Crete. With the final destruction of Knossos in 1400 BC Minoan civilisation came to an end – whether by some natural catastrophe or at the hands of foreign invaders is not known.

Around the middle of the 2nd millennium BC new ethnic groups arrived on the Greek mainland and established a number of principalities, the most powerful of which was based on Mycenae. In contrast to Crete with its originally peaceful and self-sufficient society there developed in Mycenae, in conditions of competition for power and for land, a hierarchically organised warrior aristocracy ruled by a king. In the 15th c. BC the Greeks of the Peloponnese extended their authority as far afield as Asia Minor, Crete and Melos. The mingling of Greek and Minoan culture in particular led to the production of magnificent works of art in the Late Mycenaean period (1400–1150 BC), evidence of which is provided by tholos tombs with their grave goods and powerful fortifications.

Archaic Greece

Dorian migration

Towards the end of the 2nd millennium BC, under pressure from the Illyrians, there was a great migration of the Dorians. Faced with this threat, the peoples of Greece sought refuge in Asia Minor and the islands of the Aegean, where, under influences from the East, they enjoyed a first cultural flowering. The Ionian school of the Pre-Socratics became the cradle of western philosophy. Rhodes, too, flourished economically and culturally as a staging post in the long-distance trade between East and West.

9th–5th c. BC

After the violence of the Dorian migration Greece enjoyed a relatively peaceful period of 500 years between the 9th and the 5th c. BC, allowing the first germs of western culture to develop. Around 850 BC the Greek alphabet came into being, enabling all the major sounds of speech to be written down individually. The Homeric epics, composed in the 8th c., completed the transition from oral tradition to literature and were also the forerunners of historical writing. The art of this early period also developed a distinctive style, now labelled geometric.

The further development of Greece was conditioned by the limited scope for development of the existing cities and the restricted areas of fertile land available to them. The inability of many cities to offer their citizens enough land led to a great wave of **colonisation** and to numerous wars between individual cities. The urge to establish colonies made the Greeks a people of seafarers – a development vividly reflected in Homer's "Odyssey". The acquisition of new territories started on the coast and moved inland only very cautiously: as a rule the colonies occupied only the coastal areas where the new settlers landed. Among the most important new foundations were Kyme (later Roman Cumae), the most northerly Greek city in Italy; Taras (Roman Tarentum), founded by Sparta c. 700 BC; Syracuse, founded by Corinth, 730 BC; and Massilia, founded by Phocaea, 600 BC. By the end of the colonisation movement the Greeks had established some 700 new cities, ranged round the Mediterranean, in Plato's apt and much quoted phrase, "like frogs round a pond".

Greek polis

When, in the early 1st millennium BC, the Greek cities developed from tribal into community-based organisations their political systems were inspired by new collective ideals. The development of cities began with the Mycenaean stronghold, which was both the residence of the ruler and a cult centre. The population of tillers of the soil settled round the palace and under its protection. Thus the authority of the Greek city, the *polis*, extended not only over the town itself but also over the land round it. Gradually the governmental structure of the city evolved from a monarchy by way of an aristocratic oligarchy and a "tyranny" (the rule by a single ruler that was long the pattern for many Greek cities) into democracy. The city itself was divided into the acropolis (the "crown" of the city) and the *asty*, the residential and commercial quarters. The largest cities were Athens, Sparta, Argos, Syracuse and Akragas (later Roman Agrigentum). Essential features of the city were the rule of law *(nomos)*, autonomy (political freedom) and autarky (economic self-sufficiency).

But if the full citizens of the city were to exercise their rights in the agora, the open space in which the popular assembly met, they required to have the necessary leisure. This was provided for them by the slaves without which the polis could not function. In the time of Pericles the population of Athens showed a striking disproportion between some 100,000 slaves and 40,000 adult male citizens. Thus the often proclaimed harmony of the Greek city was a community of privileged citizens – though it was a community that from the colonisation period into Hellenistic times made possible the development of a unique culture and a very varied intellectual life.

The territory of Attica was unaffected by the Dorian migration. From the early 1st millennium BC the government of the city was in the hands of officials known as archons, who until the end of the 6th c. BC were recruited from the aristocracy, owners of almost all the city's land. Then in 594 BC, in order to bridge the gap between the aristocrats and the workers on the land, who were in effect serfs, and avoid a threatened civil war, Solon was appointed archon with special dictatorial powers as a "reconciler". His aim was to reduce social inequalities and inculcate a sense of community in the citizens. From his period of rule dates the earliest code of laws, written on tablets and publicly displayed, which has come down to us.

City state of Athens

A recovery of power by the aristocracy led to further unrest, and in 560 BC Peisistratus seized power and ruled as a tyrant (i.e. as a single absolute ruler, not necessarily in a pejorative sense). This form of rule was the extreme form of aristocratic power, which prevailed in most Greek cities as well as Athens from the mid-7th to the 5th c. BC. The fate of the city, for good or ill, now depended on the character of the tyrant, who might rule harshly like Polycrates on Samos or with moderation like Peisistratus in Athens.

Tyranny to democracy

Then Cleisthenes, the head of a long exiled aristocratic family, led a popular rising against the tyranny of Peisistratus's sons, with proposals for reform. In 511–510 BC, with help from Sparta, he drove out Hippias, Peisistratus's second son and reorganised the territorial and political structure of Athens. Citizens now enjoyed their civic rights on the basis of their membership of an administrative unit, the *phyle* or "tribe", rather than on their allegiance to a noble family.

Classical Greece

In the course of the campaigns of the first Great King of Persia, Cyrus, the whole of the west coast of Asia Minor had fallen into his hands by the middle of the 6th c. BC. At the beginning of the 5th c. the Persians called on the Greek city states to recognise their predominance. Athens and Sparta in particular firmly refused to do so. Thereupon the Persians launched a fleet against Attica, and their advance was stopped only by the hoplites (heavily armed foot soldiers) of Athens in the battle of Marathon in 490 BC. In the autumn of 481 Sparta finally succeeded in forming a military alliance of the city states, which were now fully prepared for war. The Persians had thrust far into Thessaly and Attica, however, before the Greeks, withdrawn to their final defensive line, won the naval battle of Salamis in September 480 BC, annihilating the Persian fleet off the promontory of Mykale and thus securing Greece from further attack. Some of the Cycladic islands sent ships to join the Greek fleet, while others, under Persian occupation, were obliged to supply ships to the enemy. Rhodes, too, was compelled to fight on the Persian side, and after the Greek victory had to submit to Athens.

Persian wars

After the defeat of the Persians Athens within a few years established its position as the leading state of the ancient world. The main bases of its predominance were its decision to build a fleet and the formation of a maritime league of all the major Greek cities to continue the campaigns against the Persians. Sparta had no interest in pursuing a war of revenge against the Persians, and this enabled Athens to take the initiative in continuing the war and thus bring the Greek cities and the states that had previously been dependants of Persia under its own authority. Thus there came into being an empire that took in almost all the Greek cities in the Aegean and much of the Mediterranean and around the Black Sea.

Athens

History

Around 450 BC there was a major change in Athenian policy. Under the newly elected *strategos* (general) Pericles the city turned away from its expansionist policy to a concern with domestic policy and the democratisation of its system of government. The first step was to destroy the power of the aristocracy, who had hitherto dominated the Areopagus, the Council of Elders. Then in 462/461 BC the powers of the Areopagus itself were reduced, leaving control of the executive to the popular assembly. Almost all power was now vested in the popular assembly, which acted in association with a Council (Boule) of 500 members, elected annually, and controlled an army of public officials. The democratic principle of equality – which never applied to women, slaves or foreigners – was given its clearest expression in the system of drawing lots by which the nine archons, the city's highest officials, were appointed. In spite of these provisions, however, there was an elite of politicians drawn from the ranks of the aristocracy and great landowners. One of the most important of these men was Pericles, whose historical significance lay in a balanced policy that gave equal weight to the security of the Athenian empire – in 460 BC the city and its port of Piraeus were fortified to form a single great stronghold – and the promotion of the arts and sciences.

The city's expansionist external policy and democratic domestic policy led to an extraordinary **cultural flowering**. Craft production and trade developed on an unprecedented scale, and Attic products were exported all over the Mediterranean world. In Athens itself magnificent buildings, some of them still to be seen today, were erected on the Acropolis. The Parthenon and the Propylaia were built in the time of Pericles, from 450 BC onwards. During this period, too, the greatest sculptor of classical Greece – Pheidias, creator of two monumental statues of Athena and Zeus, was at work in Athens. Intellectual life was dominated by the school of sophists, but other schools of philosophy independent of official culture also developed. The most prominent representative of unorthodox thinking in this period was undoubtedly Socrates, who was regarded by almost all later Greek philosophers as their spiritual father. Even when Athens lost its political predominance after its defeat by Sparta the intellectual flowering continued. In the 5th c. BC Aeschylus, Sophocles and Euripides carried the tragic drama to new heights, and at the turn of the 5th/4th c. Aristophanes achieved similar success in the field of comedy. In the 4th c. BC Plato and Aristotle dominated the city's intellectual life. The writing of history, too, had its first important representatives in Herodotus and Thucydides.

In the 5th c. BC tensions between Sparta and Athens increased, and in 432 BC Sparta declared war on Athens. In a naval battle at Syracuse in Sicily Sparta – now allied with the Persians – inflicted a heavy defeat on Athenian forces, and in 404 BC Athens itself was besieged and compelled to surrender. The Peloponnesian War, which had thus lasted for almost 30 years, was followed by a period of peace treaties between the Greek cities and with the Persians. Then in 370 BC Theban forces put an end to Sparta's almost 300 years of predominance in the Peloponnese.

Hellenistic age

In the 4th c. BC there were still farming peoples in northern Greece ruled by kings. One of these tribal leaders, Philip II, expanded his territory and made Macedonia a powerful kingdom. In 340 BC the Macedonian army thrust into central Greece and in the summer of 338 defeated a coalition of the larger Greek cities, led by Athens, in the battle of Chaeronea. Philip then established the League of Corinth, in which the Greek cities were allowed domestic freedom but external policy remained firmly in his hands. With his power thus established, Philip crossed the

the Islands!

Until the 1980s the main problem on many of the smaller islands was a continuous loss of population; but since then the growth of the tourist trade has drawn many young people back to the islands. In summer the coastal resorts are now places of bustling activity with a lively night life; but if you explore the interior by car or make your way on foot, following old mule tracks, to remote monasteries and churches you will come on places that are still conscious of their traditions and customs, where the black-clad priests with their abundant beards still maintains their authority. In the mountain village of Ólympos on Kárpathos the women still wear colourful traditional costumes, and not only on festivals and holidays.

The remains of ancient buildings erected in honour of the gods of Greece bear witness to past glories. On Sámos, birthplace of Pythagoras, there is the Heraion; on Delos a sanctuary of Apollo; on Kos, home of Hippocrates, the Asklepieion, dedicated to the god of healing. From later periods there are the castles, watchtowers, fortified villages and mosques that bear witness to periods of foreign rule – by the Knights of St John, the Venetians, the Genoese, the Ottomans.

Then, when you have had your fill of sunbathing and sightseeing, you can stroll round the narrow streets of the village and relax at a café in the market square or on the harbour, watching the fishing boats and yachts swaying at anchor; and finally, in the evening, settle down in a modest taverna to enjoy the local cuisine.

Windmills
are now operated solely for the bene of tourists

A symphony of colour:
whitewashed churches with blue domes, which vie with the blue sky and sea. Myrtidiótissa monastery on Chíos

Hellespont in the spring of 336 BC and set out to conquer the East. Soon afterwards, however, he was assassinated in the Macedonian royal city of Aegae.

Philip was succeeded by his son Alexander, who continued the campaign that his father had begun. When he died in 323 BC he left to his successors, the Diadochoi, territories that extended from the Danube to the Nile and from the Adriatic to the Indus. The countless legends associated with Alexander reflect the reputation acquired in his lifetime by this royal warrior. Alexander's quest to conquer the world left him little time to shape his conglomeration of conquered lands into a unified state. Even though his empire was fragmented after his death by the conflicts between his successors, his campaigns disseminated Greek culture and the Greek language over the whole of the Near East and Egypt. The culture of the Hellenistic period, characterised by refinement in the arts and specialisation in the sciences, left its mark on the ancient world.

336–323 BC
Alexander the Great

One of the great cultural centres of this period was Rhodes, which withstood a siege by Demetrius Poliorcetes, one of the Diadochoi, and commemorated its victory by erecting a 32 m (105 ft) high statue of the sun god Helios – the Colossus of Rhodes, one of the seven wonders of the ancient world. As a trading centre for the whole of the eastern Mediterranean, the island enjoyed a period of great prosperity and became a centre of art and science.

Rhodes

Roman rule and the Byzantine Empire

After a series of victories in the Adriatic Rome, now a rising power, sought a diplomatic rapprochement with Greece. It could not, however, tolerate an attempt by King Perseus of Macedon at the end of the 3rd c. BC to re-establish Macedonian hegemony over Greece, and the conflict ended in the Roman conquest of the Macedonian kingdom, which in 148 BC became a Roman province. Only two years after the defeat of Macedon a Roman victory over the Achaean League decided the destiny of the whole of Greece.

3rd–2nd c. BC

The aim of Rome's policy was now to occupy neighbouring independent states and make them Roman provinces. In 63 BC the Roman consul and general Pompey took his victory over Mithradates VI, king of Pontus in Asia Minor, as the occasion for declaring the whole of Greece a "province of the Roman people", with an appropriate administrative infrastructure. The Greek cities now came under the jurisdiction of the Roman provincial administration in Macedonia. Thus for the next few centuries Greek history was merely a part of Roman history. The Ionian Islands, however, were an important naval base and preserved a degree of independence during the 500 years of Roman rule.

63 BC
Roman province

In the 4th c. AD the Roman Empire was divided into two. When Constantine I, the first Emperor of the Eastern Roman Empire and the first Christian Emperor, chose the ancient city of Byzantium as his capital under the name of Constantinople in AD 330, Greece became part of the Eastern Empire and remained so until the end of the 14th c. In 391 Constantinople, now asserting its separateness from Rome, made Christianity the state religion. The final division of the Empire by the Byzantine Emperor Theodosius marked the end of a single Roman Empire, and thereafter the Latin language and Roman ideas of empire lost ground, while Constantinople defined itself as the successor to ancient Greek culture.

AD 330 to c. 400
Division of the Roman Empire

The attacks by Germanic tribes that were destroying the Western Empire also threatened the Byzantine Empire at the beginning of the 5th c. The

527–565
Justinian I

33

situation was stabilised only in the reign of Justinian I, who succeeded in strengthening the defences of the Byzantine Empire and in domestic matters sought to combine Christianity with government policies of Roman origin. He codified Roman law in *the Corpus iuris civilis,* closed the Platonic Academy in Athens and built the great church of Ayía Sofía in Constantinople. During his reign the Byzantine Empire reached its greatest extent; but within a few years of his death this period of splendour came to an end.

c. 600–1204
Early and middle
Byzantine periods

In the 7th c. the Arabs thrust into the Near East, occupied large tracts of the Byzantine Empire and advanced as far as Crete, which remained in Arab hands for a century and a half. In 1054 came the final schism between the Orthodox and the Roman Catholic churches. With the death of the Empress Theodora, the last ruler of the Macedonian dynasty, in 1054 the Byzantine Empire was plunged into a major crisis, accompanied by civil wars. It was also crumbling on its frontiers: Asia Minor was now in Turkish hands, while Normans conquered southern Italy and crossed into Epirus.

1204–1453
Late Byzantine
period

In 1204 Constantinople was taken by Crusaders and Venetians, ending the Byzantine Empire, whose territory was now divided into a number of smaller areas ruled by the conquerors, among them the kingdom of Salonica and various principalities (Achaea, Athens) ruled by western noble families. Among larger units was the Empire of Nicaea, ruled by Theodore I. Around 1254 extensive territories round the Aegean were incorporated in this successor state to Byzantium, and in 1261 Michael VII recovered Constantinople itself. Once again, briefly, there was a Byzantine Empire; but it was weakened by disputes over succession to the throne and civil wars and had little power to oppose external threats.

Venetian rule in the islands; the Knights of St John

Crete and the
Cyclades

In 1204 Crete and the Cyclades came under Venetian rule. At first the new masters ruled in a high-handed fashion, but over the centuries they became more moderate, and the islands under their control, notably Crete, enjoyed a cultural and intellectual flowering in the monasteries, in art, particularly in literature and painting, and in scholarship. The famous painter El Greco (Domenikos Theotokopoulos; see Famous People) was probably born in a village on Crete.

But the Venetians were unable to hold on to all their islands in face of expanding Ottoman power. In 1537 they lost the Cyclades, in 1669 Crete.

Ionian Islands

The Venetians had more luck in the Ionian Sea. In 1386 they took Kérkyra, which thereafter was known as Corfu, and between 1482 and 1684 they gained control of the other Ionian Islands. Venetian rule in these islands lasted until the fall of the Republic of St Mark in 1797, and Italian remained the official language on Corfu until 1852. The Turks remained for many years a permanent threat to the Ionian Islands, but they never managed to capture the whole archipelago: Corfu and Paxí were the only parts of present-day Greece never occupied by the Turks.

During the period of Venetian rule many merchants, artists and craftsmen sought refuge in the islands from the Turks. The important Ionian school of painting was founded by Cretan artists who came to the islands from 1669 onwards. During the centuries of Venetian rule the Ionian Islands enjoyed a richer cultural life than the rest of Greece; in particular the traditions of icon painting were carried on.

Rhodes and the
Knights of St
John

In 1306 the Knights of St John, the oldest religious military order (founded in the 11th c.), with the approval of the Pope and the help of Genoese pirates, expelled the Byzantine governor of Rhodes and conquered the island in a three-year war against bitter resistance. The order then changed from a knightly army into a naval power that sent regular "caravans", as their expeditions were called, to capture Muslim warships and trading vessels. Under knightly rule the island of Rhodes, which since the 7th c. had been on the periphery of historical events, increased in importance. It became a military outpost of the West and an important staging post for the trade between Europe and the East. The Knights had repeatedly to beat off Turkish attacks, until in 1522 they were finally compelled to surrender to a huge Turkish besieging army and hand over to the Ottomans Rhodes and some neighbouring islands that they had ruled for more than 200 years.

Ottoman rule

In the 14th c. the Ottomans made a dramatic appearance on the European stage when they occupied almost the whole of the Balkan peninsula. Between 1394 and 1402 and again in 1422 they had stood at the very gates of Constantinople, and finally, in 1453, the capital of the Byzantine Empire fell to Sultan Muhammad II.

1453
Fall of
Constantinople

The expansion of Ottoman Turkey transformed the Islamic and Aegean world, hitherto broken up into a number of small and medium-size states, into a unified Turkish empire. Not for the first time, the use of new weapons and military techniques – the Ottomans were the first power to use firearms on a large scale – had enabled a nation to achieve the status of a world power. By the 14th c. large areas of Greek territory were held by the Ottomans. The fall of Athens in 1456 was the final stage in the conquest of Greek lands that had begun with the taking of Adrianople in 1362.

Conquest of
Greece

The most important opponent of the Turks in the Mediterranean was Venice, with whom they vied for predominance in seaborne trade and for Greek territory for a century. Although an annihilating defeat was inflicted on the Turks in the naval battle of Lepanto in 1571 by a combined Venetian and Spanish fleet, the victorious allies were disunited and Venice manoeuvred with great caution, enabling the Sultan to maintain his hold on the whole of Greece under a treaty of 1573.
   Like other peoples ruled by the Ottomans, the Greeks were semi-citizens. This allowed them extensive religious freedom and enabled them to maintain their cultural identity. The regular draft of Christian boys into the elite military force of the janissaries and into the administrative apparatus of the empire enabled the Sultan to integrate the conquered peoples into the Turkish state.

1571
Battle of Lepanto

During the early decades of Ottoman rule the economy prospered; but in the 16th c. domestic crises in the Turkish empire led to steep increases in the burden of taxation. To escape the increasing exploitation of the Greek rural population by the Muslim governing class many peasants and landless men joined bands of robbers. In the 17th c. there was a period of renewed prosperity as a result of maritime trade. Greek merchants dominated the Black Sea trade and brought to Greece not only western products but also the ideas of the Enlightenment and of western nationalist movements.

16th and 17th c.

Resistance to the Turkish regime, now increasingly rigid, was organised in secret societies. Supported by Greek merchants in Constantinople, the Phanariots, and the Orthodox church, they instigated popular risings against the Turks. The Greek rebellion was promoted in particular by the Philiki Etaireia ("Friendly Society") founded in Odessa in 1814 under the leadership of Prince Alexandros Ypsilanti, who in 1821 crossed the river Pruth with his irregular forces, giving the signal for a national rising against the Sultan. The Cyclades were involved in the rebellion from an

1821–7
Greek struggle for
liberation

early stage, taking in large numbers of refugees from the islands off the coast of Asia Minor, and increasing the population of the thinly settled islands by more than 20,000.

In spite of initial failures the movement was able in January 1822 to hold a national assembly at Epidavros and issue a declaration of independence. The resonance throughout Europe was considerable, for the Greeks' resolve to secure national self-determination struck a chord in the Romantic feeling of the time, and many people in the west, such as Byron (see Famous People), King Ludwig I of Bavaria and the German writers Jean Paul and Hölderlin actively supported the Greek independence movement in word and deed.

The decisive factor in the struggle for Greek independence was the intervention of Britain, Russia and France. In the battle of Navarino in 1827 the alliance inflicted an annihilating defeat on the Ottoman and Egyptian fleet. Count Kapodistrias, who had served in the Russian diplomatic service, was elected first ruler of independent Greece and, based at Nauplia (Náfplion), began to build up an administrative structure for the country. In 1830, at the London Conference, the Ottoman Empire recognised the independent existence of the kingdom of Greece. Two years later the Cyclades were incorporated in the new Greek state.

1827–30

Monarchy and dictatorship

The new state established in 1830 as a hereditary monarchy consisted of southern and central Greece, including Euboea and the Cyclades, but not Crete, the Ionian Islands and the greater part of Thessaly and the archipelago. When Kapodistrias was killed in 1831 in a family feud the great powers, whose aim was to europeanise the country, which had been subject to Oriental influences for centuries, on the western model, appointed Prince Otto of Bavaria king of Greece in 1835. Since he failed to endear himself to the Greek people as their ruler he was compelled in 1843, after a bloodless coup d'état, to summon a national assembly.

*1831–62
Otto I*

For the Greek population the continuation of foreign rule under a Bavarian king became increasingly difficult to reconcile with the ideas of the struggle for liberation. The fall of the king, however, was finally brought about by British intrigues. In October 1862 all the major military garrisons rebelled against the king, and in order to prevent a civil war Otto went into exile. The protecting powers thereupon agreed to appoint in his place the anglophile Prince Wilhelm Georg of Sonderburg-Glückstein. In 1864 the Greek National Assembly adopted a new constitution that significantly reduced the king's powers and established a parliamentary monarchy, based on the sovereignty of the people and universal suffrage (for men only: women did not get the vote until 1952).

*1862–1923
Parliamentary
monarchy*

In 1864 Britain finally returned to Greece the Ionian Islands, which had been a British protectorate since 1815 and had given the Royal Navy a useful base. The effects of this were not wholly positive, for it meant that the centre of political, economic and cultural activity was now transferred to Athens. However a new branch of the economy – now the most important – opened up when the popularity of the islands as a holiday resort began to grow, the way being led by such prominent figures as the Empress of Austria and the German Kaiser.

◀ *The Turkish conquest of the Greek islands began in the middle of the 15th c. The town of Rhodes was taken by storm in 1522*

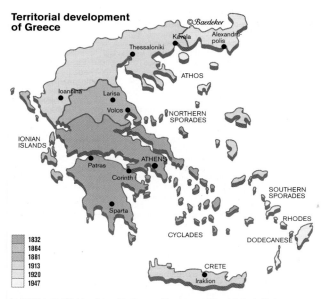

Territorial development of Greece

©Baedeker

Kavala
Alexandrópolis
Thessaloniki
ATHOS
Ioannina
Larisa
Volos
NORTHERN SPORADES
IONIAN ISLANDS
Patras
ATHENS
Corinth
SOUTHERN SPORADES
Sparta
RHODES
CYCLADES
DODECANESE
CRETE
Iraklion

1832
1864
1881
1913
1920
1947

1910–35
Venizélos

In 1897 a conflict broke out between Greece and its old rival, Turkey, over the possession of Crete, and within a few months Turkish troops were at the gates of Athens. The intervention of the great powers led to the treaty of Constantinople, which imposed severe conditions on Greece.

In 1905, supported by the nationalist feeling that had been whipped up in the mass of the population, the army seized power and in the following year handed the government over to the leader of the Greek Liberal Party, Eleftherios Kyriakos Venizélos, who had put himself at the head of the Greater Greece movement with his proclamation in 1908 of the reunion of Crete with Greece (officially achieved only in 1913).

First World War

There was much controversy over Greece's entry into the First World War, and only massive intervention by the western powers prevented the outbreak of civil war over the issue. In 1917 they compelled King Constantine I to abdicate. After the war Greece gained large extensions of its territory, and the vision of a united Greece within its ancient boundaries (Enosis) seemed to have become reality. Five years later, however, after losing a war with Turkey, Greece had to give up much of this new territory.

In 1920 Greek public opinion swung back to the royalists. Venizélos was soundly defeated in a general election and King Constantine returned to the throne from his exile in Switzerland.

1921–2
War with Turkey

Embarking on a war with Turkey in 1921, without the backing of the great powers, Greece was defeated, lost the territory in Asia Minor that had been occupied by Greeks since ancient times, and was faced with the problem of accommodating a vast flood of refugees. This social catastrophe could be dealt with only by land reform. The country's new frontiers were established in the treaty of Lausanne in 1923. The territory in Asia Minor was assigned to Turkey, and the island of Rhodes and the Dodecanese to Italy, which had won them in 1912 in a war with Turkey and had since continued to occupy them.

In 1924 radical elements in the Venizelist party brought about the abolition of the monarchy, and Greece was declared a republic in March of that year. The new regime, however, proved as unstable as the monarchy, and the world economic crisis of the 1920s hit Greece particularly hard. In 1935, with the help of a rigged referendum, General Metaxas restored the monarchy, and King George II returned to the throne after 12 years' absence.

Abolition and restoration of the monarchy

With the outbreak of the Second World War Greece came under pressure from the Axis powers, Germany and Italy. In November 1940 Corfu was bombarded and occupied by the Italians, and remained in Italian hands until September 1943. In May 1941 the bloody battle for Crete began. After the German occupation of Greece British forces had withdrawn to Crete, and German forces now mounted the largest airborne attack in history, using paratroops and trained mountain troops and suffering heavy losses, to secure this strategically important island. The Cyclades were also occupied by German forces, but saw little fighting. After Italy signed an armistice with the Allies the Germans began to take countermeasures. In September 1943 Corfu was bombed by the Luftwaffe and occupied, suffering considerable damage in the process. In December 1944 the last German units left Greece, which was now cleared of enemy forces except on Crete and a few other islands. As a result of naval battles in the Mediterranean German troops on Rhodes were unable to withdraw, and in May 1945 surrendered to the British.

Second World War

At the end of the war the long smouldering conflict between the old political caste and the communists led to open confrontation. The civil war that now broke out reached its climax in the street fighting of December 1944. Again British forces intervened, enabling the conservative National Guard to win. In an election in 1946 the royalists gained a majority and after a national referendum restored the monarchy. King George II now returned to the throne for a second time.

1944–5 Civil war

In 1947 the Treaties of Paris regulated the various claims to territory in the Balkans. Italy was compelled to cede the Dodecanese, which had been occupied by Greek forces at the end of the war, to Greece, which now reached its present territorial extent. From 1952 until the crisis of 1967 Greece had stable governments. In 1952 it became a member of NATO, and its economy, with financial help from the United States, returned to its pre-war level. In 1961 Konstantin Karamanlis signed a treaty of association with the EEC.

1950s and 1960s

On April 21st 1967 the army mounted a coup d'état. Two colonels, Papadopoulos and Pattakos, established a dictatorial regime that led to mounting protest both within Greece and internationally. In 1973, contrary to the provisions of the constitution, Papadopoulos decreed the abolition of the monarchy, proclaimed a republic and appointed himself President. The economic upswing that had begun was brought to a halt in 1973 by the oil crisis and the worldwide recession. Violent disturbances in Athens marked the beginning of the end for the dictatorship.

1967–74 Dictatorship of the Colonels

An attempt by the Colonels to take over the whole of Cyprus led to Turkish intervention; and, under the threat of war, the military regime gave way. On July 24th 1974 Prime Minister Karamanlis return from exile in Paris to take over the government.

Republic

Under the "government of national unity" headed by Karamanlis political conditions returned to normal. The 1952 constitution was reactivated, with the exception of the provisions laying down the form of

1974 National referendum

government. This was followed by a national referendum on December 8th 1974 in which the Greek people decided in favour of a republic. In the same year Greece left NATO on the ground that it had not prevented the Cyprus conflict. In June 1975 a new democratic constitution came into force, establishing the basic rights of the population. In 1979 the Greek government signed a treaty with the European Community on joining the Community, and this came into effect in 1981. In 1980 Greece rejoined NATO as a full member.

1981
PASOK

A general election in 1981 was won by PASOK, the Pan-Hellenic Socialist Movement headed by Andreas Papandreou. The new government at first operated a policy of national independence, leaning towards the non-aligned states. Its foreign policy was centred on the Mediterranean. In the late 1980s Greece's problems with the open EEC market gradually disappeared, and the country's economy settled down with the help of a flourishing tourist trade and merchant fleet.

1990s

After four years of transitional governments headed by the second largest party, New Democracy, PASOK returned to power in an election in 1993. In January 1996 Prime Minister Papandreou resigned on health grounds, and in an election in the autumn of 1996 his successor Konstantinos Simitis again gained a majority for PASOK. The Greek parliament then elected a non-party President, Konstantinos Stephanopoulos.

The central problem of Greek foreign policy was the country's relationship with Turkey: the main points of conflict were Cyprus and the boundaries of the Aegean continental shelf. The most recent dispute over territorial rights in the Aegean was the Imia crisis in January 1996.

In August 1964, in a reaction to the trial in Tirana of Albanians of Greek origin charged with spying, Greece expelled more than 25,000 Albanians who had neither work permits nor work; but after the alleged spies were released diplomatic relations with Albania were resumed in March 1995.

In spite of great efforts Greece has still not been able to meet the criteria for admission to the European Monetary Union established in January 1999.

Famous People

The Greek poet Alcaeus, a contemporary of the poetess Sappho and, like her, a native of Mytilene on Lesbos, ranks after Sappho as the greatest lyric poet of his day. A scion of an aristocratic family, he was passionately involved in the struggle against the tyrants (sole rulers) of Lesbos, Myrsilos and Pittakos. In his poems, of which only fragments survive, he is concerned mainly with this political struggle, but also sings of love and of wine.

Alcaeus gave his name to the alcaic stanza, used by Horace and some Italian Renaissance poets and occasionally experimented with by English poets.

Alcaeus (c. 620 BC)

The lyric poet Anacreon was born in the Ionian city of Teos (near present-day Izmir). About 545 BC he fled to Abdera to escape the advancing Persians; later he moved to the court of Polycrates on the island of Samos, and after Polycrates' murder in 522 BC went to Athens.

Anacreon's poems, composed for a luxurious aristocratic society, celebrate pleasure, gaiety, wine and love. Only a few of his poems have survived complete, in addition to numerous fragments.

Anacreon (c. 580 to c. 495 BC)

The lyric poet Archilochus is one of the earliest figures in the ancient world about whose life we have any reliable information. Born on the island of Paros, the son of a local aristocrat and a slave girl, he was excluded from his inheritance, lived an unsettled life as a soldier and an itinerant minstrel and was killed in a battle with the Naxians. His poetry, which has survived only in fragments, centres on his unhappy love for Neoboule, daughter of Lycambes, whom he was not permitted to marry because of his birth. He wrote poems of great delicacy and tenderness, but also verses of extreme eroticism and vigorous satire. He is thought to have originated iambic verse, and was a strong influence on Alcaeus, Anacreon and Simonides, and later on Horace (see Baedeker Special p. 220).

Archilochus (c. 700 to c. 645 BC)

George Gordon Noel Byron wrote his first poems while still at school. After taking his seat in the House of Lords but failing to make any impression in politics he travelled extensively in Europe and Asia Minor. The publication of the first two cantos of "Childe Harold's Pilgrimage" brought him sudden fame. After a brief and unhappy marriage, outlawed by society, he left England for ever. He went first to Italy and then to Greece, where he became a vigorous supporter of the Greek struggle for independence, and equipped a force of some 500 men at his own expense for an attack on Lepanto. He died of malaria at Mesolóngi in April 1824, aged only 36.

Lord Byron (1788–1824)

The Greek physician Diocles was born at Karystos on the island of Euboea. An adherent of the Sicilian school of medicine, he lived in Athens and was second only to Hippocrates in fame. He wrote works – preserved only in fragments – on human anatomy and women's diseases, the symptoms of disease and herbal medicine.

Diocles (4th c. BC)

Famous People

Empress Elizabeth of Austria (1837–98)

Elizabeth, daughter of the Duke of Bavaria, who married her cousin the Emperor Franz Joseph of Austria, was one of the most striking and unusual women of the 19th c. She was devoted to her husband but was unhappy with her role as Empress and with the life of the Austrian court. She was beautiful, intelligent and cultivated, athletic, but also sensitive and shy of people – a combination which created problems for her entourage and caused her to be regarded as eccentric. She was an excellent horsewoman and installed a gymnasium in the Hofburg, the imperial palace in Vienna. She was interested in literature – she loved Byron and Heine – and herself wrote poetry. She learned Hungarian, then ancient and modern Greek, and translated Shakespeare and Schopenhauer into modern Greek.

When her doctors recommended a warmer climate for a mysterious illness from which she suffered this fell in with her own inclinations, and she was frequently absent from Vienna for months at a time. She came to Corfu for the first time in 1861 and at once fell in love with it. She went there again in 1876 and 1885, and in 1887 asked the Austrian consul on Corfu to find a house for her on the island. He eventually found the Villa Braila at Gastouri, which she altered and rebuilt as the Achilleion from 1889 onwards. Thereafter she frequently stayed in the villa until her death in 1898, when she was assassinated in Geneva by an Italian anarchist.

Epicurus (342/341–271 BC)

The philosopher Epicurus was born on the island of Samos in 341 BC and taught in Mytilene (Lesbos) and Lampsacus (on the east side of the Dardanelles) before going to Athens, where he established his own school in a garden (the "Garden of Epicurus") in 306 BC. His doctrine, which has come down to us in three letters and numerous fragments, is concerned with man's life in this world, defining philosophy as the attempt to achieve happiness by discussion and reasoning. He divided it into three parts – the theory of knowledge (the basis of which is sense perception), physics (based on Democritus's doctrine on the movement of atoms) and ethics (with virtue and a peaceful state of mind as the basic principles). Epicurus died in Athens in 271 BC. Epicureanism, as further developed by Zeno and Demetrius, became a popular philosophy in late antiquity, but increasingly degenerated into a superficial hedonism. In Roman times the term "epicurean" had already acquired the connotation of a thoughtless quest for pleasure.

Euripides (c. 485–406 BC)

The great tragic dramatist Euripides, born on the island of Salamis, was the founder of the psychological drama, the tragedy of character. His main theme was Protagoras's maxim "Man is the measure of all things". In his tragedies the fate of men is no longer controlled by the gods: they act independently, live their own lives and fight their own personal battles.

Of the more than 70 (according to some sources over 90) plays he wrote 18 have been preserved complete and are still performed (among them "Alcestis", "Medea", "Electra" and "Orestes"). His works have been a major influence on the development of drama throughout Europe. Almost all his great dramas have inspired modern versions of their themes – by Corneille and Racine, Goethe, Schiller and Grillparzer, down to Sartre in our own time.

Odysseas Elytis (1911–96)

The poet Odysseas Elytis (real name Alepoudelis) was born in Iráklion (Crete) and spent his early years in Athens, where he studied law. He was associated with Yeóryios Seféris, who gave modern Greek literature a fresh lease of life in the 1930s. In 1979 Elytis was awarded the Nobel Prize for Literature, which Seferis had received in 1963. His poetry shows a strong love of nature. His principal work "To axion esti", a volume of poems published in 1959, was set to music by Mikis Theodorakis.

The Italian writer and literary historian Ugo (Niccolò) Foscolo was born on Zante (Zákynthos), the son of a Venetian father and a Greek mother. A philhellene, an Italian patriot and cosmopolitan, he led an unsettled life. His work was wholly devoted to the Risorgimento, the political rebirth of Italy, showing a remarkable fusion of political zeal and Romantic feeling. He was unsparing in his attacks on Napoleon, who had at first been hailed in Italy as a liberator, and on the Austrians, and in consequence was compelled in 1808 to give up his chair as professor of rhetoric at Pavia and in 1815 to leave Italy. He died in exile at Turnham Green, near London, leaving 12 volumes of odes, sonnets, hymns, tragedies and novels.

Ugo Foscolo
(1778–1827)

El Greco (Spanish, "the Greek") was born Domenikos Theotokopoulos at Fódele, near Iráklion (Crete). As a boy he learned the craft of icon painting; then as a young man he went to Venice, where he was trained in Titian's studio, and later to Rome. From 1577 he lived and worked in Toledo, where he sought commissions from King Philip II and from the Church. Although mainly devoting himself to religious themes, he also painted some striking portraits and landscapes. Characteristic features of his work are the elongated and contorted figures, the unnaturally pale colouring and the unreal light effects, which create an impression of spiritualisation and the transcendental. El Greco died in Toledo in April 1614.

El Greco
(c. 1541–1614)

The mathematician Hippocrates of Chios taught in Athens in the second half of the 5th c. BC. He created the first comprehensive system of geometry and, while seeking to square the circle, discovered the "lunulae Hippocratis" (the "little moons" of Hippocrates) on a right-angle triangle, showing that the sum of the crescentic areas bounded by semicircles on the three sides of the triangle equals the area of the triangle.

Hippocrates of Chios
(c. 450 BC)

Hippocrates, the most celebrated physician of ancient times, was born on Kos, the son of a respected doctor, and died, after a long and eventful life, at Larissa in Thessaly. He is honoured as the founder of scientific medicine, which seeks to establish the principles of health and disease by critical observation and analytical reasoning. To Hippocrates disease was an imbalance in the vital forces resulting from external influences. He attached great importance to the natural healing processes, regarding these processes and prophylactic measures as preferable to therapeutic treatment. His numerous writings covered a wide range of basic medical problems. The Hippocratic oath that is still binding on all medical practitioners was probably not formulated by Hippocrates himself.

Hippocrates of Kos
(c. 460 to c. 370 BC)

Famous People

Homer
(c. 8th c. BC)

The town of Smyrna (now Izmir) in Asia Minor claimed, probably with justice, to be the birthplace of Homer, the legendary earliest epic poet of the western world. It is still not known with certainty whether the author of the "Iliad" and the "Odyssey" was a historical figure or whether the name Homer was a kind of collective designation for the earliest Greek epics. The prevailing view now, however, is that there was a historical Homer, who lived and composed his poems on the west coast of Asia Minor. In writing his great works he probably based himself on earlier and shorter popular epics. The "Iliad" is thought to have preceded the "Odyssey"; but both works underwent much alteration and expansion after Homer's time.

Homer is also credited with the authorship of a number of hymns and epigrams and two comic epics, "Margites" and the "Batrachomyomachia" ("War of the Frogs and Mice").

Nikos Kazantzákis
(1883–1957)

The writer Nikos Kazantzákis was born in Iráklion (Crete) in February 1883, and from his earliest youth was interested in the intellectual movements of the day. After taking a law degree in Athens in 1906 he went to Paris, where he studied philosophy and political science. Returning to Greece, he became a civil servant and in 1945–6 a government minister.

His writings – accounts of his many travels, short stories, novels, poems – are notable for their vigorous narrative power, fresh language, lyrical abundance and philosophical profundity. His novel "Zorba the Greek" (1946), which is set in his native Crete, brought him world-wide fame (see Baedeker Special p. 134). He was also active as a translator, rendering works by Homer, Dante, Goethe, Shakespeare, Darwin, Nietzsche, Rimbaud and Lorca into modern Greek.

Pythagoras
(c. 570–497/496 BC)

Little authentic information has come down to us about the Greek philosopher Pythagoras. He himself left no writings, and his pupils were sworn to secrecy. He was born on Samos about 570 BC, left the island about 530, apparently to escape from the arbitrary rule of Polycrates, and founded at Croton in southern Italy a philosophical and religious community of Pythagoreans. Even during his lifetime he was revered by his disciples as a man of perfect wisdom. After repeated attack and persecution, however, he left Kroton and died at Metapontion in southern Italy, probably between 500 and 480 BC. The Pythagoreans saw number as the basis of all things, a principle of universal harmony and thus applicable also to music.

The doctrine of the transmigration of souls is believed to have been developed by Pythagoras himself. The geometrical theorem that bears his name, however – the proposition that the square on the hypotenuse of a right-angle triangle is equal to the sum of the squares on the other two sides – was probably known before his time.

The Greek poetess Sappho, born on the island of Lesbos about 600 BC, was the greatest lyric poet of classical antiquity. Plato called her the tenth Muse, and Horace named the sapphic stanza after her. She was the head of a community in Mytilene, the capital of Lesbos, in which she instructed young girls until their marriage in the art of poetry and in ritual dances in honour of Aphrodite, goddess of love. After the expulsion of aristocrats from Lesbos Sappho lived for some time in Sicily. She is said to have thrown herself to her death from the Leucadian Rock when her love for the handsome Phaon was unrequited.

Sappho (7th/6th c. BC)

Sappho's rich output of lyric poetry is unfortunately known to us only in fragments. It consists mainly of hymns to the gods and marriage and love songs in simple, vivid language (see Baedeker Special, p. 220).

The lawyer and statesman Eleftherios Kyriakos Venizélos was born at Mourniés (Crete) in 1864. He founded the Greek Liberal Party and became prime minister for the first time in 1912, carrying through far-reaching reforms and laying the foundations of the modern Greek state. In foreign policy he sought the unification of all Greeks and the extension of Greek territory by military means. The two Balkan wars (1912–13) brought considerable territorial gains and the incorporation of Crete in Greece, but later attempts to expand were frustrated by Turkish resistance under Mustafa Kemal Pasha (Atatürk). After an unsuccessful *coup d'état* against the Tsaldaris government Venizélos went into exile in Paris, where he died in March 1936.

Eleftherios Kyriakos Venizélos (1864–1936)

Culture

For a glossary of technical terms used in this section see p. 379.

Art and Architecture

Art, poetry and philosophy were the three fields of ancient Greek achievement that have endured down the ages and won the designation of "classical". While in the 18th c. Johann Joachim Winckelmann, the founder of the study of antiquity, saw the classical period as falling within the 1st millennium BC, the epoch-making discoveries of Schliemann, Evans and others in the latter part of the 19th c., revealing the Mycenaean and Minoan civilisations, have taken our horizons far back into the 2nd and indeed the 3rd millennium BC.

Prehistory

The earliest artistic products in Greece date from the neolithic and the Bronze Age. They come from two cultural regions: one to the south-east, taking in Crete, the Dodecanese, the Cyclades and Samos, and the other in northern and central Greece, known as the Sesklo culture after its most important find-spot at Sesklo in Thessaly. Characteristic of this culture are its polished black and red pottery, sometimes with incised patterns, painted ware and terracotta or, more rarely, stone idols with exaggerated female genitals. In the Dimini culture that appeared after 2900 BC and shows evidence of close links with the Danubian countries the vases take on a more rounded form and spiral patterns appear in the decoration.

Cycladic culture

During the period of transition between the neolithic and the Bronze Age, between 3200 and 2000 BC, an independent and highly advanced culture developed in the Cyclades. The best-known products of this early Cycladic culture are its marble idols, characterised by their slender bodies and much simplified and geometrically styled features. They have been found not only in the Cyclades but in other parts of Greece, to which they were evidently exported.

Minoan art on Crete
(c. 3300–1400 BC)

The advanced Bronze Age culture of Crete takes its name from the legendary King Minos. Among the most important cultural achievements of the Early Minoan period (down to 2100 BC) were bronze working and the introduction of the potter's wheel. The great flowering of Minoan art came with the building of great palaces. Far-reaching political and economic changes on the island and the development of a system of priestly kings were the social prerequisites for the building of these monumental structures, still to be seen at Knossos, Phaistós, Mália and Káto Zákros. The upper floors of the palaces, which in the case of Knossos and Phaistós were laid out in terraces on a hillside, were reached on monumental staircases. The state apartments were decorated with fine wall paintings depicting festivals and cult games, scenes from court life and paradisiac landscapes filled with exotic animals.

In addition to the palaces the Minoan culture is represented by splendid villas, probably designed as summer residences, and shaft, passage and chamber tombs, like the two-storey "temple tomb" near Knossos and the royal tomb at Isopata. Widely distributed, too, are pottery vessels, goldsmith's work, ivories, cut gems and seals. The potter's

An amphora of c. 450–440 BC: the classic vase of ancient Greece ▶

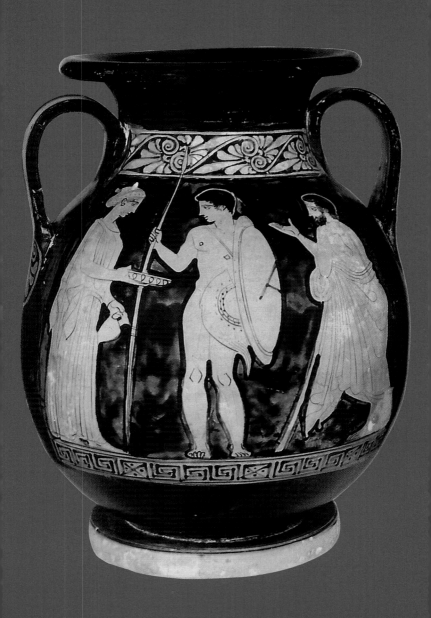

wheel – imported from Anatolia – and new firing techniques made it possible to produce jugs with beak spouts, which were decorated with painted patterns or reliefs. The Kamáres style that predominated at the beginning of the Proto-Palatial period (from 2100 BC onwards), decorated with abstract designs of spirals and stylised leaf forms, gave place around 1700 BC to a richly decorated style with naturalistic representations of plants and marine motifs such as reeds.

Mycenaean art
(c. 1600 to c. 1150 BC)

While the Minoan civilisation on Crete was at its highest point the Peloponnese was following a distinctive course of its own. Mycenae, a fortified town on the northern edge of the Argolid, was the predominant power in the Peloponnese from around 1600 BC. The Mycenaean culture, first revealed by the excavations of Heinrich Schliemann, gives evidence of influences from Egypt and close relations with the Minoan culture of Crete. The most important Mycenaean sites after Mycenae itself (with its palace, its royal tombs and the Lion Gate) are Tiryns, Argos, Asine and Pylos, but there are also Mycenaean sites in northern Greece.

Geometric art
(1050–700 BC)

Greek art in the narrower sense developed in the "dark" centuries after the coming of the Dorians (c. 1200 BC). During this period the Geometric style – named after the linear patterns with which vases were now decorated – came into being. Typical of the Proto-Geometric phase are bands of ornament consisting of concentric circles or semicircles drawn with dividers. Later came bands triangles, lozenges and meanders, which became the most important ornamental motifs. In the course of the 8th c., in the Late Geometric style, figures of human beings and animals increasingly appeared between the geometric patterns and gradually superseded them. The commonest themes were scenes connected with death (burials, lamentations for the dead), but there were also hunting scenes and gymnastic, dancing and musical performances.

The types of vessel – amphoras, craters (wine-mixing jars) – also changed in the Geometric period. More emphasis was given to particular parts of the vase (the foot, the belly, the neck), the varying proportions of which gave an element of tension to the design (for example, amphoras with a big belly and a slender neck; see p. 380). The finest vases were produced in Attica, particularly in Athens.

To the Geometric period also belong small, early temples such as the Heraion on Samos.

Archaic art

Sculpture

The Archaic period (c. 700–500 BC) saw the introduction of live-size statuary in marble or limestone, either in relief or free-standing, and usually coloured. Greek sculptors found models for this work in Egypt and the eastern countries, with which the Greeks had trading connections. The fine marble used mostly came from quarries on the islands of Naxos and Paros. In the Archaic period two particular types of figure predominated: a statue of a clothed female figure, the *kore,* and the naked figure of a youth, the *kouros.* Characteristic features of the early kouros type are the frontality of the figure and the stylised attitude of the body, giving particular emphasis to the joints. The presentation of the body later became more plastic and anatomically correct, though the frontal pose of the figure, with arms hanging by the sides and clenched fists, and with one foot in front of the other, remained obligatory until the 6th c. A particularly impressive kouros can be seen in the Archaeological Museum in Sámos town.

In the 7th c., when stone became the regular building material for temples and treasuries, large-scale relief figures began to appear on **pediments** and entablatures. The Temple of Artemis on Corfu (600 BC), one of the earliest temples to be built wholly of stone, had sculptured figures on its two pediments and metopes decorated with relief carving.

At the beginning of the Archaic period a very varied range of black-figure ware was produced. The main centres of pottery manufacture and vase painting were the Cyclades, the islands in the eastern Aegean, Rhodes and Athens. The details and the outlines of the figures, sometimes very delicately drawn, were incised with a hard point; painted in black, they stood out against the clay ground. There were regional differences in the themes depicted, but as a rule scenes from Greek mythology took a central place. In representations involving numbers of figures the individual scenes are set side by side as if in a frieze, with the heads of all the figures on the same level. In the vase painting of the eastern Aegean islands friezes of animals predominate, and the general effect is more ornamental and flatter than in the rest of Greece.

The red-figure technique was a later development. It worked with the same colour contrasts as the mature black-figure ware, but in reverse: the ground was painted black, while the figures retained the reddish colouring of the clay. The outlines were no longer incised but painted in brilliant black or matt lines. The figures now gained in plastic quality as compared with the silhouette figures of the black-figure technique.

Greek temple

The monumental stone temple ranks as one of the supreme achievements of ancient Greek architecture. It was not designed as a meeting place of the faithful, but as the home of the cult image, and thus of divinity itself. The earliest temples were built in the 9th c. BC. The simplest form of the temple was derived from the basic type of a Greek house, the megaron. In the early temples the main chamber, rectangular and windowless, known in Greek as the naos and in Latin as the cella, stood on a base of undressed stone. The entrance to the temple was normally at the east end, with the divine image facing it against the west wall of the naos. It was only in the second half of the 7th c. BC that marble or limestone began to be used for all parts of the temple.

Different types of temple began to develop from the earliest times. The simplest form is the temple in antis, in which the naos is preceded by an antechamber (the pronaos) flanked by antae (forward projections of the side walls of the naos). Between the antae are two columns supporting the pediment. A temple with a second antechamber (the opisthodomos) at the far end is known as a double anta temple (Temple of Aphaia, Aegina). Where there is a row of columns in front of the antae, supporting the projecting pediment, the temple is known as prostyle (eastern temple in the Erechtheion, Athens). If there is a similar row of columns on the rear end of the temple it is known as amphiprostyle (Temple of Nike, Acropolis, Athens).

The most striking form of the Greek temple from the second half of the 7th c. onwards was the **peripteral temple**, in which the naos was surrounded on all four side by a colonnade (peristasis). At one end was the entrance, with the pronaos; at the other was the opisthodomos. In the 5th c. the classical proportions of the temple were developed, in which the sides have twice the number of columns on the ends plus one. In the Parthenon in Athens the proportion is 17:8.

If the temple has a double row of columns on all four sides it is known as dipteral (Olympieion, Athens). If the inner row of columns is omitted to leave room for a wider naos, the temple is known as pseudo-dipteral.

A less common type of temple is the **tholos**, on a circular plan, with a ring of columns round the naos.

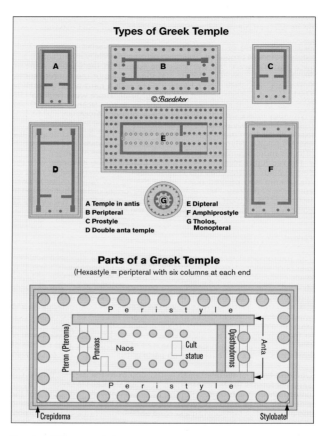

Types of Greek Temple

©Baedeker

A Temple in antis
B Peripteral
C Prostyle
D Double anta temple

E Dipteral
F Amphiprostyle
G Tholos, Monopteral

Parts of a Greek Temple

(Hexastyle = peripteral with six columns at each end

Peristyle

Pteron (Pteroma)

Pronaos

Naos

Cult statue

Opisthodomos

Anta

Peristyle

Crepidoma

Stylobate

Classical orders

Temples differ not only in plan but also in the form and proportions of the columns and entablature.

The earliest stone temples in Greece, such as the Heraion in Olympia (c. 600 BC), are of the **Doric order** (see illustration, p. 383). Temples of this type have a rather heavy, solid air, due mainly to the fact that the columns are relatively thick and that the shafts of the columns, which taper towards the top and have between 16 and 20 flutings, stand directly, without a base, on the stylobate above the triple-stepped substructure. The capital consists of the echinus, curving up from the shaft, and the square abacus. It carries the architrave with its frieze of triglyphs and metopes, which may be either plain or with relief ornament. The triangular pediment (tympanon) is enclosed by the horizontal cornice and the oblique mouldings that form an angle with it. The sculptured decoration normally consists of the relief carving on the metopes and the pediment.

Where limestone and not marble was used in the construction of the temple it was faced with a coat of stucco and painted in colour. Since little of the colouring had survived the centuries, the idea grew up, after the rediscovery of Greek art in the 18th c. that Greek temples were "classically" white.

The Ionic temple, which originated in the Greek settlements in Ionia, was particularly suitable for large temples, like the huge temples on Samos and in the Greek cities of Ephesus, Sardis and Didyma (now in Turkey). Temples of the **Ionic order** have slenderer and more elegant forms than those of the Doric order. This is due to the fact that the columns stand on a base and the flutings of the columns are separated by narrow ridges, emphasising their vertical character. The characteristic feature of the capital is the spiral volute on either side. The architrave is not flat but is made up of three sections, each projecting over the one below. The frieze is continuous, without triglyphs to divide it up.

The **Corinthian order** is similar to the Ionic except in the form of the capital. The characteristic feature of this is the acanthus leaves that enclose the circular body of the capital, with tendrils reaching up to the corners of the concave architrave. The Corinthian order was much favoured under the Roman Empire, which also evolved the "composite" capital out of a marriage of Ionic and Corinthian forms and developed ever more elaborate decorative schemes.

Early classical art

The Archaic period ended with the fall of the Peisistratids (510 BC) and, even more decisively, with the Persian Wars (490–479 BC). The "Archaic smile" disappears, giving place to a more serious expression, as in the "Critian Boy" and the "Fair-Haired Youth", two characteristic works of the early 5th c. (Acropolis Museum). This was the century of classicism, the supreme period of Greek culture, which in the fields of art, poetry and philosophy was now increasingly centred on Athens. Tragedy was a purely Attic creation.

The first phase of classical Greek art is also known as the "severe" style – a name derived from the characteristics of the sculpture of the period. Since most of the large-scale sculpture of the classical period has come down to us only in the form of Roman copies – sculpture in bronze having been melted down and works in marble broken up and used as building material or burned to produce lime – smaller works of sculpture, in particular the numerous bronze statuettes, are of great importance to our understanding of the severe style. The "Critian Boy" also illustrates its new features, relieving the heaviness of earlier work.

Sculpture

By the early 5th c. Attic red-figure pottery had almost completely displaced the earlier black-figure style. During the 5th c. Athens was the undisputed centre of Greek ceramic production. The painted vases produced in Attic workshops were exported throughout the whole of the ancient world. Red-figure ware gave far more scope than the traditional black-figure ware for the delicate modelling of the figures, which thereby gained in plastic effect. Important vase painters of the early classical period were the Cleophrades Painter and the Brygos Painter.

Pottery

High classical art

The extent of Athens's predominance in the Greek world in the mid-5th c. BC is illustrated by the concentration of skills in the Periclean building programme on the Acropolis. The Doric and Ionic orders are found side by side (Temple of Nike, Erechtheion) or even in the same building

Architecture and sculpture

(Propylaia). Under the political leadership of Pericles there was a great flowering of art in many fields.

The naos of the Parthenon (447–438 BC), built to house the gigantic chryselephantine (gold and ivory) cult figure of Athena Parthenos, was designed by the great Athenian sculptor and architect **Pheidias**, widely famed even in his lifetime. He had been entrusted by Pericles in the forties of the 5th c. with the general direction of the construction of the Parthenon, for which he designed the whole sculptural decoration – 92 metopes, a 160 m (525 ft) long frieze and the mighty reliefs in the pediments. Pheidias achieved his greatest fame, however, with the monumental cult figure of Zeus in the Temple of Zeus at Olympia – one of the seven wonders of the ancient world – and his Athena Parthenos in the Parthenon. Both of these works are lost, but Roman copies of the figure of Athena have survived. Successors of Pheidias were responsible for the korai on the Erechtheion (421–415 BC) and the graceful figures of Nike on the balustrade of the Temple of Athena Nike (410 BC).

The second great sculptor of the high classical period was **Polycleitus of Argos**, known mainly for his bronze figures of athletes, surviving only in Roman copies, of which 40 survive, including his famous "Spear-Bearer" (Doryphoros) and the figure of an athlete binding his hair (Diadymenos). Other notable sculptors of this period were Myron, Cresilas and Alcamenes. Many works of sculpture were cast in bronze and are now lost, so that we have to depend on later marble copies. The National Archaeological Museum in Athens has a number of fine bronze originals, outstanding among them the figure of Zeus or Poseidon found in the sea off Cape Artemision (c. 460 BC; probably from the island of Salamis).

Pottery

In vase painting the Attic red-figure technique continued to predominate in the high classical period. The themes included both mythology and genre scenes.

Late classical art

Sculpture

In the late classical period (c. 400–330 BC), both in sculpture and in vase painting, the representation of the human figure became more differentiated. Idealisation and monumentality now gave place to an increase in spiritual and intellectual expression. A good example of the so-called "picturesque style" is provided by the works of Praxiteles, who worked as a sculptor between 360 and 330 BC. Only Roman copies of his sculpture have survived apart from one work – the original of his "Hermes carrying the infant Dionysus" from the Temple of Hera at Olympia (c. 330 BC). Both in the form of his sculpture and in the interpretation of his themes Praxiteles went his own way. His Aphrodite of Cnidus (of which more than 50 copies have survived) was the first representation in Greek art of a naked goddess. Other major sculptors of the period were Timotheus, Bryaxis, Scopas (Stele of the Ilyssus in the National Archaeological Museum, Athens) and Leochares.

Lysippus (c. 395–300 BC) marked the culmination of late classical sculpture and prepared the way for Hellenistic art. He is credited with the remark that a sculptor should copy nature and not the work of a master. He is said to have created more than 1500 works of sculpture, but only Roman copies survive – for example the "Apoxyomenos" (Rome, Vatican Museums), the figure of an athlete scraping himself with a strigil after a contest. Lysippus depicts not the glorious victor but the exhausted fighter, with a melancholy expression.

Pottery

Attic red-figure vase painting continued to be popular in the 4th c., but alongside it there developed a new technique, known as Apulian after the main find-spot in southern Italy. Characteristic of this technique is the use of opaque white, red and a yellowish lapis lazuli. This work shows more of the "picturesque" style developed in monumental painting than does Attic vase painting. With the increasing importance of panel painting and monumental painting the star of vase painting began to sink, and by the end of the 4th c. it had almost completely disappeared.

Architecture

The characteristic type of temple in the late classical period was the tholos (see Greek temple, above). The earliest known is the one at Marmaria, Delphi (380 BC), which was followed by the Thymele at Epidaurus. In both these temples the Doric order is used in the outer ring of columns and the Corinthian order in the inner ring.

During this period the Greek theatre reached its final form (Athens).

Greek theatre

The first stone theatres in Greece were erected in the period of transition between the late classical and the Hellenistic period (Theatre of Dionysus, Athens; c. 330 BC). Until then theatres in Greece had been merely temporary wooden structures.

The origins of the European theatre lie in ancient Greece. The first dramatic performances were associated with the cult of Dionysus, in which a choir performed round dances, accompanied by singing, in honour of Dionysus, god of fertility and of wine.

The central feature was the **orchestra**, a circular "dancing place", on which originally ritual dances in honour of Dionysus were performed. Here too there probably stood the altar of Dionysus (Thymele). The siting of the orchestra on a eloping hillside or in a natural depression

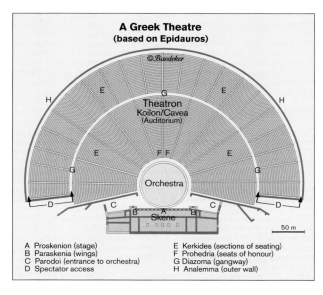

**A Greek Theatre
(based on Epidauros)**

© Baedeker

Theatron
Koilon/Cavea
(Auditorium)

Orchestra

Skene

50 m

A Proskenion (stage)
B Paraskenia (wings)
C Parodoi (entrance to orchestra)
D Spectator access

E Kerkides (sections of seating)
F Prohedria (seats of honour)
G Diazoma (gangway)
H Analemma (outer wall)

made it possible to replace the seating of the audience on wooden stands by a semicircular auditorium with tiers of seats rising above the orchestra. The largest Greek theatres of antiquity could seat an audience of more than 10,000 (Epidaurus 12,000, Dodona 18,000). Opposite the auditorium, on the far side of the orchestra, was the stage building (*skene*), several storeys high. This was originally a timber structure, which in the post-classical period was elaborated into a palatial edifice in stone. The skene was then supplemented by the proscenium (*proskenion*), an additional stage raised above the orchestra. Between the stage and the auditorium, which extended slightly beyond a semicircle, were the *parodoi,* the entrances for the chorus.

The classical form of Greek theatre developed in Athens and spread from there throughout the whole Greek world. Most of the ancient Greek theatres, the largest of which could accommodate many thousand spectators (Theatre of Dionysus, Athens, 17,000; Epidaurus 14,000), have now been either completely or partly excavated; some are excellently preserved, and some have been restored. Some of them are now again in use for the performance of plays, both ancient and modern, and musical works, such as the theatres of Epidaurus, Philippi, Thasos and Dodona and the Odeion of Herodes Atticus in Athens.

Roman theatres

The Romans at first used simple wooden structures, with or without a cavea (auditorium), for their theatrical performances, but later followed the Greek example and built large stone structures. These were no longer built into a hillside like the Greek theatres but were free-standing, with entrances and exits for the spectators on staircases in the outer walls. A Roman innovation was the amphitheatre, a long oval structure with no stage and a central arena that was used for wild beast shows and gladiatorial contests. The best known example is the Colosseum in Rome. The basic idea of the Greco-Roman theatre was taken up and developed at the Renaissance; but theatres were now always roofed and the auditorium constantly more elaborate in form. The type of auditorium with boxes came into vogue only in the Baroque period.

Odeion

The odeion was a small roofed theatre mainly used for musical performances (e.g. the Odeion of Pericles in Athens, near the Theatre of Dionysus). Numbers of these ancient concert and lecture halls were built in the Hellenistic and Roman periods (Latin odeum). The name lives on outside Greece in its application to music halls and cinemas.

Hellenistic art

The cultural epoch between the death of Alexander the Great (323 BC) and the establishment of the Roman province of Achaea (27 BC) is known as the Hellenistic period. During these three centuries Greek culture extended into the Orient and was itself imbued with Oriental influences. New artistic centres now arose alongside the cities in the Peloponnese and the Greek colonies on the coast of Asia Minor – the capitals of the parts of Alexander the Great's empire that had become independent, in particular Alexandria and Pergamon.

Architecture

Architecture now had a new role: the creation of splendid building complexes to satisfy the Hellenistic rulers' love of magnificence. The markets in their towns – the focal points of civic life – were now laid out on a regular plan and decked with new public buildings. Private houses as well as palaces were decorated with sculpture, wall paintings and mosaics. The temples that were now built favoured the Ionic and Corinthian orders. The building of the Asklepieion on Kos began soon after 300 BC,

The Asklepieion on Kos was greatly enlarged in the 3rd c. BC

and the sanctuary was extended in the course of the 3rd c. into a large complex laid out in terraces. The temple of Athena Lindia on Rhodes developed into an elaborate composition of staircases and colonnaded halls.

In sculpture the change from the late classical to the Hellenistic style was accomplished by Lysippus and his school. A typical example of early Hellenistic sculpture is Polyeuctus's portrait statue of Demosthenes (190 BC; Vatican Museums). In the course of the 3rd c. BC sculpture showed greater psychological insight and stronger dramatic effect, with diagonal tensions and complicated turning attitudes, observed with extreme anatomical accuracy.

Sculpture

The expression of movement is particularly vivid in the **"Victory of Samothrace"** (190 BC; Louvre, Paris), probably created to commemorate a Rhodian victory over Antiochus III of Syria. The forward movement of the winged goddess of victory is accompanied by a spiral turning movement of the body that, as it were, carries the spectator's eye round the figure.

The frieze on the Great Altar of Pergamon marked a climax and a turning point in Hellenistic sculpture. Two world-famous works represent its later development: the "Aphrodite of Melos", better known as the **"Venus de Milo"** (end of 2nd c. BC; Paris, Louvre), and the **"Laocoon"** group, which is preserved only in a marble version by the Rhodian sculptors Hagesandrus, Polydorus and Athenodorus (Rome, Vatican Museums). The "Venus de Milo" represents the neoclassical style, while the "Laocoon" combines classical principles with the external dynamic and internal dramatic force characteristic of Hellenistic sculpture.

55

Culture

Mosaics

There was a great development of mosaic art in the Hellenistic period. This field of art had begun in the 5th and early 4th c. BC (Athens, Olynthus) with pebble mosaics, which reached their full flowering in the time of Alexander the Great (Pella) and thereafter. Coloured tesserae began to be used in the 3rd c. BC, for example in dwellings on Delos. Some idea of the artistic possibilities of Hellenistic painting can be gained from the mosaics of Dioscurides of Samos.

Roman period

Sculpture

In Roman times (2nd c. BC–4th c. AD) a new element was added to the Hellenistic school of sculpture: the personalisation of portraiture and the historical relief (Arch of Galerius, Salonica). The Greek portrait had hitherto usually been a full-length statue that depicted its subject in idealised form. Sculptors now aimed at the most individual and realistic representation of the subject's features. In the 4th c. AD strict frontality became the rule in relief sculpture (base of the Egyptian obelisk in the Hippodrome in Constantinople) – a characteristic that was also to predominate in Byzantine art, particularly in icons.

Architecture

In the Roman period some building types were modified – for example the odeion was developed out of the Greek theatre – and some typically Roman types were adopted (triumphal arches, aqueducts, bathhouses). The use of the Roman technique of vaulting made possible the construction of larger and more daring buildings than in Hellenistic times. There was a revival of interest in the architectural forms of the Greek classical period: thus the Olympieion in Athens was completed in the reign of Hadrian (2nd c. AD).

Mosaics

Magnificent Roman mosaic pavements have been preserved both in mainland Greece and on the larger islands; most of them are now to be seen in museums. Since the wall paintings of the period have been lost, only the mosaics can give us some impression of the interiors of Roman town and country houses.

Byzantine period

The foundation of Constantinople in AD 330 and the division of the Roman Empire 65 years later into a Western and an Eastern (Byzantine) Empire led to a new cultural flowering, particularly in the eastern Mediterranean, which was brought to an end by the fall of the Byzantine Empire in 1453. The art of Greece was now informed by the Christian faith. Not surprisingly, therefore, the architects, painters and sculptors of this period sought their models not in ancient Greek art but in the Christian art of late antiquity. Along with the churches and monasteries that have survived and numerous smaller collections, the Byzantine Museum in Athens presents a comprehensive survey of this cultural period.

Painting and mosaics

Byzantine painting covered a wide range of techniques, from monumental to miniature works, from the fresco by way of the icon (see Baedeker Special p. 59) to the mosaic and woven textiles. From the outset Byzantine painting was closely involved in the practices of the Christian faith, concentrating particularly on the representation of human figures, in which the heritage of late antiquity is unmistakable in the attitudes, clothing and movement of the figures. In the 4th c. AD the principle of strict frontality became established. In the representation of groups the heads of all the figures were shown on the same level, and the principal figures were larger than subsidiary ones. In the 8th/9th c. the Iconoclastic movement broke away from this tradition, and the ban

Wall painting in the Monastery of St John on Pátmos

on the depiction of Christ and the saints meant that art was restricted to purely ornamental patterns.

When Christianity became the state religion in the 4th c. the first churches on Greek soil were built. The predominant type of church in the early period was the basilica, a form modelled on the Roman secular basilica that served civic and commercial purposes. In the basilica the central nave was flanked by either one or two lateral aisles. At the east end was the altar, at the west end the entrance, preceded by the narthex (frequently with an atrium).

Architecture

Over the centuries the form of the church increasingly developed from the rectangular form of the basilica towards a centralised structure. In the 9th c. this development culminated in a new type of church that soon became established throughout the area of Byzantine culture: the **domed cruciform church**. Over the intersection of the four arms of the cross, which were usually of equal length, with barrel vaulting, was the central dome, borne on piers or columns. The sanctuary was separated from the body of the church by a stone screen, out of which the iconostasis later developed. Flanking the sanctuary were two small rooms, the prothesis and the diakonikon, which served liturgical purposes. As a result the east end of the church normally had three apses. The narthex at the west end of the church was often preceded by an outer porch or exonarthex. The wall and ceiling paintings in the interior of the church were regulated by an iconographic programme, based on the idea that the church was to be a representation of the heavenly hierarchy.

Turkish rule (15th–19th c.)

Four hundred years of Turkish rule in Greece began with the conquest of

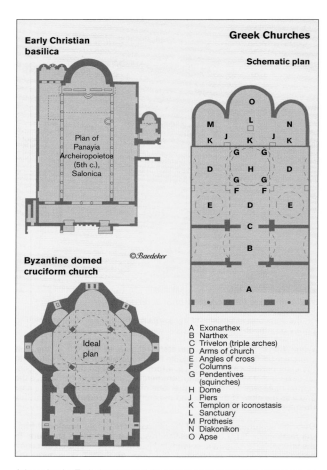

Greek Churches

Schematic plan

Early Christian basilica

Plan of Panayia Archeiropoietos (5th c.), Salonica

Byzantine domed cruciform church

©Baedeker

Ideal plan

A Exonarthex
B Narthex
C Trivelon (triple arches)
D Arms of church
E Angles of cross
F Columns
G Pendentives (squinches)
H Dome
J Piers
K Templon or iconostasis
L Sanctuary
M Prothesis
N Diakonikon
O Apse

Athens by the Turks in 1456 and the subsequent occupation of the whole of the Peloponnese. Post-Byzantine art on the Balkan peninsula fell well below the standard of earlier centuries, but Turkish rule allowed sufficient scope for the traditions of Byzantine art to be carried on. On Crete, which was held by Venice from 1204 to 1669, secular buildings in particular (port and defence installations and imposing mansions) show Venetian influence. In the 16th c., thanks to the Venetians, the art of Crete was brought into contact with the Renaissance.

Architecture

Traditional Greek architecture was shaped mainly by climatic conditions and locally available building materials. Typical of the Cyclades, for example, are their whitewashed houses, while Lindos (Rhodes) has its square flat-roof houses. Architecture was also influenced by the various foreign rulers of the islands. On the Cycladic island of Naxos the influence of its one-time Frankish rulers is still visible, while the Ionian

Icons – Sacred Images

Icons are portable images of saints and Biblical scenes that down the centuries have played an important part in Orthodox worship and belief. Icons are found not only in churches but also in many private homes and in vehicles. They are carried on journeys and are the object of pilgrimages. They may be decorated with precious metals and precious stones, rings and watches and screened by costly curtains. Icons bring the saints close to men and are therefore the subject of great veneration. This veneration is addressed not to the icon but to the saint with whom it is equated.

In churches the icons are arranged in a particular order on the iconostasis, a high screen, usually of wood, which separates the sanctuary from the body of the church. On a stand in the centre is displayed the icon of the saint or the festival of the particular day.

Icon painting is regarded as a liturgical act, which originally could be performed only by a priest. The composition, colouring and materials of an icon are precisely regulated, so that the painter is left with little freedom in the shaping of his picture and cannot develop any individual style. He may not give an icon any personal expression, and he remains nameless. His task is to maintain the established tradition. As a result icons tend to be very similar to one another, no matter in what century they are painted.

A characteristic feature of icons is that the natural and architectural settings, treated abstractly, are played down, so as to emphasise the timeless divinity or holiness of the figures. Icons appeal to the spectator with their richness of colour, achieved through a complicated process of preparation. They are usually painted on wood with mineral colours and then covered with a coat of boiled linseed oil. This ensures the extraordinary durability of

Icons are frequently offered for sale

icons, which are not only contemplated but kissed and touched.

There are numerous stories of wonderworking icons. Thus the icon of the Panayía Evangelístria on the island of Tínos was discovered after a nun had visions in which the Mother of God told her to dig at a certain point in a field. The icon was 800 years old, and it was not known how it had found its way to the field. The largest church in Greece was then built on the spot, and the icon, which is credited with many miraculous healings, is now the object of a pilgrimage that annually attracts hundreds of thousands of worshippers from all over Greece.

Islands – particularly Corfu – show the influence of Italian and British architecture.

Music

The roots of modern Greek music lie in Byzantine church music and in the folk songs that took on many different forms during the centuries of Turkish rule. An example of this variety is the melancholy klepht songs ("robbers' songs") that give expression to the Greeks' longing for freedom and the hardships of the resistance fighters in the mountains. The singers of the klepht songs were accompanied by a lyre or a shepherd's flute.

Italian influences

A strong influence on musical development in the 18th and 19th c. was Italian opera, which was brought to Greece in the early 18th c. by the Italian occupation of the Ionian Islands (Corfu, Kefaloniá, Zákynthos). This later gave rise to the Ionian school, the spiritual father of which was Nikolaos Mantzaros (1795–1872), the first considerable modern Greek composer. Mantzaros, who wrote the music of the Greek national anthem, sought to combine the folk song tradition with features of Byzantine church music in a distinctively Greek form of serious music. The Ionian school produced a number of significant composers, among them Spyridon Xyndas (1812–96), who in 1867 produced the first purely Greek opera with a modern Greek libretto.

Folk music

At the beginning of the 20th c., with the spread of urbanisation, western influences increasingly began to make themselves felt in light music. The music that now became popular was a mingling of folk songs, Byzantine and Turkish music, the *kantades* of the Ionian Islands, which showed Italian influence, and imports from other countries such as the Latin American tango that became popular in the 1920s.

Rembétiko

The *rembétiko* is a type of song that originated in the 1920s in the slums and tavernas of Piraeus. The themes of these songs were the life of social outcasts, pickpockets, their use of drugs, the difficulties of their lives, their loves and sorrows. They were accompanied on a home-made bouzouki, the *baglama,* formed from a hollowed-out pumpkin, a piece of wood and a few wire strings.

At first the rembétiko was officially banned and could be heard only in a few place in the suburbs of Athens. Finally, however, the recording industry took it up (the "Greek blues") and made it socially acceptable. It is now a leading element in Greek folk music. Among the commonest accompanying instruments, in addition to the widely popular bouzouki, are the santouri, a trapezoid stringed instrument, and various woodwind instruments.

Folk Traditions

Costumes

Although in recent years Greek traditional costumes have largely disappeared from everyday life, they can still occasionally be seen on festive occasions in country areas, worn mainly by elderly people. Men wear the fustanella, a white knee-length skirt decorated with bells and coins, usually accompanied by a white shirt and an embroidered jacket. On Crete men can sometimes be seen wearing the traditional *vraka* (baggy black breeches) and black head scarf. Traditional costumes can also be seen on the island of Kárpathos, in the southern part of Rhodes and on

Bright colours, embroidery and spangles give the traditional costume worn on festive occasions on Kárpathos its particular charm

Corfu. The colourful uniform of the Evzones ("finely belted"), the former royal bodyguard, is derived from a traditional Albanian costume. It is still worn by soldiers mounting guard at the National Monument in front of the Parliament Building in Athens.

Dancing and music have been associated in Greek tradition since time immemorial. Ancient vases depict dancers performing round dances, and according to Greek legend Rhea, mother of Zeus, herself taught her priests the original dances. As a result of varying cultural development in different parts of Greece there are now something like 150 local dances, though they are now less and less performed. Two different types of dance can be distinguished, the measured tread of the *syrtos* dances and the impetuous movements of the *pidik* dances – though every island and every part of mainland Greece has developed its own style and its own variations. The traditional dances are preserved by folk-dancing societies and groups and are performed on festive occasions. The ring dances, in which the dancers hold each other's hands or are linked by handkerchiefs, are now danced by men and women together, though originally they were usually danced by the sexes separately.

Dances

A very popular dance is the *syrtos,* which is danced with sliding steps. Also popular are the *tsamikos,* a war dance from Thessaly that is danced with much stamping of the feet, and the *kalamatianos,* which goes back to ancient times. Another well-known dance, both in mainland Greece and on the islands, is the gay *ballos,* which is danced by couples.

Many people believe that the **syrtáki** is the Greek dance par excellence, but in fact it is a product of Hollywood. It was devised in 1964 during the

61

A Rhodian folk dance

shooting of the film "Zorba the Greek". Since the *khasapiko* ("butcher's dance"), a dance of Anatolian origin, was too difficult for Anthony Quinn, a simpler version, the syrtáki, was created, to the music of Mikis Theodorakis (see Baedeker Special, p. 134).

Quotations

Thus we to Tenedos, of home full fain,
Came; but for all our sacrifices slain
Stern Zeus ordained not our return, but there
Stirred evil discord up yet once again.

Then they that had with lord Odysseus gone,
The wise of heart, the subtle-minded one,
Swung round their ships and hastened back to make
Their peace with Agamemnon, Atreus' son.

But I with all the ships that round me drew
Fled in close order: for full well I knew
That God was wroth at us; and with me fled
The valiant son of Tydeus and his crew.

And fair-haired Menelaus late that day
Followed and caught us up in Lesbos bay
Pondering the long sea passage, whether we
Straight for the Psyrian isle our course should lay.

With craggy Chios low on our left hand,
Or coasting Mimas by the windy land
Keep Chios on our starboard; then we prayed
God for a sign that we might understand.

And sign he showed, that bade us cut the sea
Straight forward toward Euboea, so to flee
Quick from destruction; and a wind arose
Shrill-blowing, and before the wind went we.

Swift through the fishes' tracks our ships ran on,
And made Geraestus ere the morning shone:
Where to Poseidon many bulls we slew,
Because we safe through the great deep had gone.

"Odyssey", iii, 159–79; translation by J.W. Mackail

Round the moon, the glorious,
The stars hide their clear light
When the full moon sheds it radiance
Over the earth below ...

The moon and the Pleiades have set;
Midnight is past; and I – I lie alone.

Two fragments of poems

Wine is a mirror to men ...
Sometimes it is sweet as honey; sometimes the wine you pour is
sharper than thorns.

Slight is the strength of men, fruitless their strivings.
In their brief existence trouble is heaped on trouble.
Inescapably death hangs over them –
An equal share failing both to the good and to those who are evil.
Death catches even the man who flees from the battle.

From his fragmentary "Dirges"

Homer
(c. 8th c. BC)

Sappho
Greek poetess
(7th–6th c. BC)

Alcaeus
Greek lyric poet
(c. 620 BC)

Simonides
Greek poet
(6th–5th c. BC)

Quotations

Bacchylides
Greek choral poet
(6th–5th c. BC)

Lachon has won from Zeus the Almighty the highest praise as victor in the race run to the sound of Alpheios' flutes; thus in the past vine-growing Keos celebrated him, richly decked with garlands, as victor at Olympia in wrestling and running ...

Aeschylus
Greek tragedian
(525–456 BC)

(First verse of a short ode of 452, probably composed to celebrate the return to Keos (Kéa) of the Olympic victor Lachon.)
... And swiftly their whole battle hove in view.
Their right wing in good order led the way,
Then all their navy followed; then one heard
A cry that grew: "Sons of Hellenes, on!
Save Hellas, save your children, save your wives,
Your fathers' graves, the temples of their gods
From slavery! Fight, to defend your all!"
Then from a sea of Persian voices roared
The counter clamour. For the hour was come.
Now ship smote ship with brazen-pointed prow.
A Greek began that onslaught, tearing off
All the ornature from a Sidonian hull.
Then on and on, with ships for spears, they fought.
The Persian fleet, in a perpetual stream,
At first appeared invincible; but when
Their numbers in the narrows packed and hemmed
Grew dense, they cracked their oarage in the crowd,
And smote each other with their beaks of brass,
And none might help his fellow. Ware of this,
The Grecian shipmasters with cunning skill
Jostled us round and round, till hulls capsized,
And all the sea was hidden from our sight,
With wrecks and human carnage covered o'er.
The cliffs and jutting reefs were thronged with dead,
And every vessel left in the Asian fleet
Rowed hard for safety in disordered rout.

From the Persian messenger's account at the Persian court in Susa of the naval battle of Salamis (480 BC), in "The Persians" by Aeschylus (who had himself taken part in the battle), which was first performed in the Theatre of Dionysus in Athens in 472 BC. Translation from the Greek by Lewis Campbell, 1890.

Herodotus
Greek historian
(5th c. BC)

... The whole [Persian] fleet amounting in all to six hundred triremes, made sail for Ionia. Thence, instead of proceeding with a straight course along the shore to the Hellespont [Dardanelles] and to Thrace, they loosed from Samos and voyaged across the Icarian sea through the midst of the islands, mainly, as I believe, because they feared the danger of doubling Mount Athos, where the year before they had suffered so grievously on their passage; but a constraining cause also was their former failure to take Naxos.

When the Persians, therefore, approaching from the Icarian sea, cast anchor at Naxos, which, recollecting what there befell them formerly, they had determined to attack before any other state, the Naxians, instead of encountering them, took flight, and hurried off to the hills. The Persians however succeeded in laying hands on some, and them they carried away captive, while at the same time they burnt all the temples together with the town. This done, they left Naxos, and sailed away to the other islands.
    While the Persians were thus employed, the Delians likewise quitted Delos, and took refuge in Tenos. And now the expedition drew near, when Datis sailed forward in advance of the other ships; commanding them, instead of anchoring at Delos, to rendezvous at Rhênea, over against Delos ...

"History", v, 95–7; translation by George Rawlinson

There is good reason for believing that the city [Athens] lies roughly in the centre of Greece, and indeed in the centre of the world. The further you go from Athens the more unbearable is the heat or the cold; and a man travelling from one end of Greece to the other must inevitably go by way of Athens, as of the centre of a circle.

Xenophon
Greek writer
(5th/4th c. BC)

"Poroi"

... In my opinion Neleus' cattle mostly grazed outside the borders [of his land], because the countryside at Pylos is all rather sandy and incapable of producing enough grass for that herd. I can bring Homer as my witness; he always calls Nestor king of sandy Pylos.

Pausanias
Greek writer
(AD 144–170)

The island of Sphakteria lies opposite the harbour, just as Reneia lies opposite the anchorage at Delos. Human fortunes seem to make places famous which were hitherto quite unknown; for example Kaphareus in Euboia where a storm hit Agamemnon and the Greeks on the journey home from Troy, and Psyttaleia at Salamis, which we know only because the Persians perished on it.

"Description of Greece"; translation by Peter Levi

On the island of Lesbos is Mytilene, a large and beautiful city. It is traversed by channels flowing in from the sea and has handsome bridges of smooth white stone: it seems not so much a city as a world of islands. Some 200 stadia from this city of Mytilene was the estate of a wealthy man, a fine property indeed: mountains full of game, fields of wheat, hillsides covered with vines, grazing for sheep and goats. And the sea washed against the soft sand of a long expanse of shore.

Longus
Greek writer
(2nd–3rd c. AD)

A goatherd named Lamon who was grazing his flock there found a baby boy who was being fed by one of his she-goats. The child lay on soft grass amid trees and thorny scrub and a rampant growth of ivy. The goat kept running up to the child, disappearing and returning again, while her kid was left to look after himself. Lamon watched this coming and going closely, for he was concerned for the abandoned kid; and when the sun stood high in the sky at midday he followed the goat and saw it standing over the child, its legs spread wide so as to avoid trampling or injuring the boy, who was sucking the goat's milk as if from his mother's breast. Full of astonishment, as well he might be, he went closer and saw that the child was well grown and fair, clad in swaddling clothes which bespoke a better origin than a poor foundling – a purple over garment with a golden pin and a small sword with an ivory haft.

The goatherd's first impulse was to take these things and concern himself no more with the child; then, feeling ashamed at the thought that a she-goat had more care for the child than he, took him up and returned, along with the goat, to his wife Myrtale. When she, in surprise, asked whether a goat could bring a child into the world he told her the whole story – how he had found the child, left there by his parents, how he had seen the she-goat suckling him and how he had been ashamed to leave him to die. Then they hid the objects found with the child, took him as their own and allowed the goat to continue suckling him. And in order that he might have a name such as a herd might bear they called him Daphnis ...

Then when autumn was at its fairest and it was almost time for the vintage everyone was busy in the fields. One prepared the wine-presses, another cleaned out the casks, another wove baskets. Still another procured a sickle-shaped knife for cutting off the bunches of grapes, another sought a stone for pressing the grapes, another collected pieces of dry wood so as to have light for carrying in the grape juice at night. Daphnis and Chloe now concerned themselves less with their sheep and goats and helped one another with the vintage. Daphnis brought in the grapes in a basket, threw them into the wine-press and trod them, and then filled the wine into the casks. Chloe prepared food for the workers and dispensed older wine for them to drink, and also gathered the lower bunches on the vines. For the vines on Lesbos are low-growing: they do not reach up high or cling to the stems of trees, but spread out their shoots low down, creeping like ivy: even a child whose hands have just been freed from its swaddling clothes can pick grapes on Lesbos.

"Daphnis and Chloe"

Lord Byron
(1788–1824)

The isles of Greece, the isles of Greece!
  Where burning Sappho loved and sung,
Where grew the arts of war and peace,
  Where Delos rose, and Phoebus sprung!
Eternal summer gilds them yet,
  But all, except their sun, is set.

"Don Juan", iii, 86,1

Norman Douglas

I found it a fantastic spot. Picturesque, or romantic, is too mild a term; the cliff-scenery and the colours of the sea and land made one catch one's breath. Under a bleak northern sky it would be a horrific kind of place; drenched in the glittering light of May it was fabulously beautiful … Santorin is surely a vision which can disappoint nobody.

"Looking Back" (1933)

Henry Miller
American writer
(1891–1980)

Next morning I took the bus in the direction of Knossus. I had to walk a mile or so after leaving the bus to reach the ruins. I was so elated that it seemed as if I were walking on air. At last my dream was about to be realised. The sky was overcast and it sprinkled a bit as I hopped along. Again, as at Mycenae, I felt that I was being drawn to the spot. Finally, as I rounded a bend, I stopped dead in my tracks; I had the feeling that I was there. I looked about for traces of the ruins but there were none in sight. I stood for several minutes gazing intently at the contours of the smooth bills which barely grazed the electric blue sky. This must be the spot, I said to myself, I can't be wrong. I retraced my steps and cut through the fields to the bottom of a gulch. Suddenly, to my left, I discovered a bald pavilion with columns painted in raw, bold colours – the palace of King Minos. I was at the back entrance of the ruins amidst a clump of buildings that looked as if they had been gutted by fire. I went round the hill to the main entrance and followed a little group of Greeks in the wake of a guide who spoke a boustrophedonous language which was sheer Pelasgian to me.

There has been much controversy about the aesthetics of Sir Arthur Evans' work of restoration. I found myself unable to come to an conclusion about it; I accepted it as a fact. However Knossus may have looked in the past, however it may look in the future, this one which. Evans has created is the only one I shall ever know. I am grateful to him for what he did, grateful that he had made it possible for me to descend the grand staircase, to sit on that marvellous throne chair, the replica of which at the Hague Peace Tribunal is now almost as much of a relic of the past as the original.

Knossus in all its manifestations suggests the splendour and sanity and opulence of a powerful and peaceful people. It is gay – gay, healthful, sanitary, salubrious. The common people played a great role, that is evident …

Greece is what everybody knows, even *in absentia,* even as a child or as an idiot or as a not-yet-born. It is what you expect the earth to look like given a fair chance. It is the subliminal threshold of innocence. it stands, as it stood from birth, naked and fully revealed. It is not mysterious or impenetrable, not awesome, not defiant, not pretentious. It is made of earth, fire and water. It changes seasonally with harmonious, undulating rhythms. It breathes, it beckons, it answers.

Crete is something else. Crete is a cradle, an instrument, a vibrating test tube in which a volcanic experiment has been performed. Crete can hush the mind, still the bubble of thought.

"The Colossus of Maroussi" (1941)

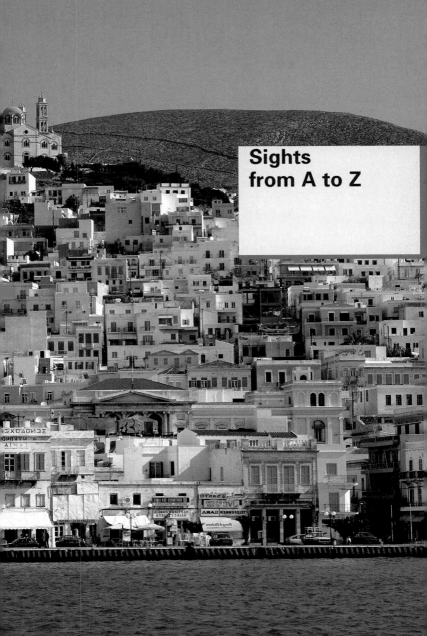

Sights
from A to Z

Island-hopping

A certain amount of organisation is necessary for exploring the Greek island world, for not all the islands are linked with one another by ferry services and there are few direct flights between them: as a rule it is necessary to fly via Athens. But since each island has its own individual character it is very rewarding to visit a number of neighbouring islands. In this section, therefore, we offer some suggestions on "island-hopping" routes. All the places mentioned are described in the Sights from A to Z section of the guide and can be readily found by reference to the Index.

1. Corfu to Zákynthos

The best starting points for a tour of the Ionian Islands are the most northerly and the most southerly of the islands, Corfu and Zákynthos, both of which are easily reached on charter flights. Visitors travelling on a car ferry from one of the Italian Adriatic ports will come first to Corfu. At least two weeks should be allowed for the following tour.

Corfu

Around three days should be allowed for seeing Corfu. The first overnight stop could be in ★★Corfu town, in which Italian influence is very evident. Other good bases for excursions on the island are the holiday resorts on the west coast with their beautiful beaches, for example Glyfáda or Palaiokastrítsa. A visit to the ★★Achilleion, one-time residence of two crowned heads, is almost obligatory. A full day is required for a trip through northern Corfu to the picturesquely situated little town of ★★Palaiokastrítsa, the remains of the once mighty fortress of ★Angelokástro and, at the north-western tip of the island, ★Cape Drastis and the ★Canal d'Amour, where wind and water have carved out bizarre shapes from the light-coloured sandstone. The route continues down the coast to ★Kassiópi. If time permits an excursion can be made to ★Mount Pantokrátor, the highest point on the island; otherwise good speed can be made back to Corfu town on the coast road.

Lefkás

From Corfu town there is a ferry to Igoumenítsa on the Greek mainland. From there E 55 runs down the coast, with fine views of the picturesque coastal scenery. 20 km (13 mi.) south-west of Préveza a causeway and a bridge lead to the "island" of Lefkás. Except for bathing enthusiasts – along the west coast are beautiful and largely unspoiled sandy beaches – one or two days should suffice to explore Lefkás. The main tourist centre is Nydrí, on the east coast, though Áyios Nikítas and Vasilikí are nearer the beautiful beaches. Attractive excursions are to the unspoiled village of Karyá and ★Cape Lefkáda on the south-western peninsula. On the way a stop should be made at the magnificent beach of ★★Pórto Katsíki.

Kefaloniá

From Nydrí and Vasilikí on Lefkás there are ferries to the neighbouring island of Kefaloniá to the south. The ferries sail to ★Fiskárdo, one of the

◀ *From a boat entering the harbour of Ermoúpoli on the island of Sýros there is a striking view of the little town with its brightly coloured houses*

Island-hopping routes

* of particular interest
** of outstanding interest
R1 Route

prettiest places in the Ionian Islands, where an overnight stop is recommended. There are also ferries from here to Ithaca. From Fiskárdo a road runs by way of the picturesque village of Ásos and ★Mýrtos Bay, enclosed by sheer white cliffs, to the island's capital, Argostóli, and then cuts across the island to Sámi. The principal sight here is the ★Melissáni Cave with its shimmering play of blue and violet colours. Then via Póros to Skála, now gradually falling a prey to tourism. It is worth pausing to see the commandingly situated Kástro and the monastery of Áyios Andréas, which has an important museum. Then via Metaxáta back to Argostóli.

From Pesáda on the south-west coast of Kefaloniá there is a ferry to Áyios Nikólaos in the north-east of Zákynthos. From here a boat trip should be taken round the coast to the ★Blue Grotto and ★★Shipwreck Beach. Another rewarding excursion is to the mountain village of ★Anafonitria, with the monastery of the same name. From here the route runs south on a road parallel to the west coast, from which a side trip should be made to the picturesquely situated mountain village of Kerí, to reach the island's lively capital, ★Zákynthos town. From Mount Bokháli there is an impressive view of the town.

Zákynthos

2. Rhodes to Sámos

The Aegean islands of Rhodes, Kos and Sámos can all be reached by charter flights. In summer hydrofoils ply twice daily between these islands, calling in at the smaller islands between them. Since the boats travel at a speed of 60 km (37 mi.) an hour, the distances between the islands, which are sometimes considerable, are not a problem. If you concentrate on the most important sights the tour suggested here, travelling by hydrofoil, can be done in 2 or 3 weeks. The route frequently runs close to the Turkish coast.

Rhodes

The starting point of the round-the-island tour is ★★Rhodes town, which with its medieval old town is one of the high spots of the tour. Three nights should be spent here to allow time to see the beauties of the island. From Rhodes town a road runs down the east coast to the popular tourist centre of Faliráki. Beyond the resort of Kolýmbia is Tsambíka, with a beach of fine sand and a little monastery on the cliffs above the village. Then by way of Arkhángelos, the largest village on the island, to the magnificently situated town of ★★Lindos, with a picturesque old town and an imposing acropolis. After a side trip to Asklipío with its beautiful 11th c. church the route turns inland and crosses the island to the west coast. From there the coast road runs north to return to Rhodes town, passing the villages of Monólithos, Kritiná, Kámiros Skála and the beautifully situated ancient city of ★Kameiros.

Sými
Nísyros

The fast boats from Rhodes and Kos call in at Sými and occasionally at Nísyros. The picturesque little town of Sými, with its houses climbing up the slope above a deep inlet, is a popular excursion from Rhodes. The volcanic island of Nísyros is best visited from Kos.

Kos

Arriving in ★Kos town, visitors are at once captivated by the cheerful holiday atmosphere and the charming aspect of the town. Two nights should be spent here, allowing a full day for seeing the island. From Kos town a road runs south-west to Kéfalos, at the other end of the island. Side roads go off to the bathing resorts of Marmári and Mastikhári on the north coast and the mountain villages of Ziá, Pýli and Antimákhia. The archaeological highlight of the island is the ★★Asklepieion, south-west of Kos town, the sanctuary of the god of healing. From the topmost of its three terraces there is a view of the whole coastal plain.

Kálymnos

From Kos town (or from Mastikhári) there is a short crossing to the sponge-divers' island of Kálymnos, still almost untouched by tourism. The whitewashed houses of Kálymnos town climb up the hillside above the little port. In a picturesque bay on the west coast are the bathing resorts of Myrtiés and Massoúri. The next staging posts on the way to Sámos are the little islands of Léros and Lipsí.

Pátmos

A high spot in any tour of the islands in the south-eastern Aegean is ★★Pátmos, where St John the Evangelist is believed to have had his revelation of the Last Judgment. From the busy port of Skála it is a short walk or bus trip to the ★Monastery of the Apocalypse and the ★★Monastery of St John, from which there are views over the whole island.

Sámos

The two ports of arrival on Sámos are the tourist centre of ★Pythagório on the south coast and ★Sámos town at the north-east corner of the island. The best plan is to take the boat to Pythagório, site of the ancient city of Samos, and spend two nights there. Two memorials to the grandiose ambitions of the tyrant Polycrates are the ★Eupalineion, a 1 km (¾ mi.) long water channel tunneling through a hill, and the

★Heraion, 9 km (5½ mi.) west of Pythagório. For bathing enthusiasts there are numerous beaches on the south coast. On the way to the island's capital it is worth while looking in at the interesting natural history museum in Mytilíni. The houses of ★Sámos town cluster picturesquely round the wide inlet containing the harbour. The principal feature of interest is the 5 m (16 ft) high kouros in the Archaeological Museum. From Sámos town there is a pleasant trip along the north coast to the former fishing village of Kokkári and the second largest place on the island, Karlóvasi, with possible side trips to the wine-growing villages of Vourliótes and Manolátes.

3. Ándros to Santoríni

There are good ferry connections between the islands of the eastern Cyclades, but on crossings to the western Cyclades long delays are to be expected. The tour described below will take between one and two weeks, with overnight stops recommended on Ándros, Mýkonos, Náxos and Santoríni. The starting point is Ándros, which can be reached from the port of Rafína on the east coast of Attica. From there the ferry route is by way of Tínos, Mýkonos, Delos, Páros, Náxos and Íos to Santoríni.

Ándros, the second largest of the Cyclades (after Náxos), still preserves the traditional Greek way of life, for tourism has not yet been fully established here. The ferry puts in at the former fishing village of Gávrio on the west coast. From here a road runs past the tourist centre of Batsí and the island's ancient capital of Palaiopolis into the fertile Mesariá valley, with the fortress-like Panakhrándou monastery. To the north-east is the island's present capital, ★ Ándros town, whose neo-classical mansions recall the prosperous shipowners who built their summer villas here. Then back to Gávrio, from which there is a ferry to Tínos. | **Ándros**

The principal sight in ★Tínos town is the great pilgrimage church of the ★Panayía Evangelístria, commandingly situated above the town. Also worth seeing are the lovingly maintained Kekhrovoúni convent, north of Tínos town, and the sculptors' village of Pýrgos. | **Tínos**

Next comes the most visited island in the Aegean, ★★Mýkonos. It has few sights of artistic interest apart from its charming traditional island architecture. It is also the starting point for a visit to the neighbouring island of ★★Delos with its important archaeological sites. | **Mýkonos Delos**

A visit can be paid to Páros on the way to Náxos. The island has been famed since ancient times for its marble, and there are still marble quarries to be seen. The chief town, ★Parikiá, where the ferry puts in, has one of the oldest churches in Greece, the Katapolianí cathedral. | **Páros**

The largest and scenically most attractive island in the Cyclades, Náxos, is worth a stay of some days. There is an unforgettable view of ★Náxos town, picturesquely situated on the slopes of a rocky hill, from its ancient ★marble gateway. From there it is a 50 km (30 mi.) drive to the quiet holiday resort of Apóllonas at the north end of the island. | **Náxos**

The island of Íos, to the south, will appeal to bathing enthusiasts with its beautiful sandy beaches. The beach at Mylopótas, south of ★Íos town, is popular with young visitors. | **Íos**

The end point and high spot of any visit to the Cyclades is the island of | **Santoríni**

Island-hopping

★★Santoríni, whose extraordinary landscape makes it one of the greatest tourist attractions in Greece. The first view of the island from the huge and almost completely enclosed crater of an extinct volcano, with white houses clinging to its rim, is an unforgettable experience. After disembarking in the port of Skála visitors can walk or a donkey ride up a stepped lane, or the cableway, to the chief town, ★Thíra or Firá.

Sights from A to Z

Agathonísi

See Sámos

Aegina   H 6

Island group: Saronic Islands
Area: 83 sq. km (32 sq. mi.)
Altitude: 0–532 m (0–1745 ft)
Population: 12,000
Chief place: Aíyina town

Shipping connections Piraeus–Aíyina–Souvála–Ayía Marína and with
Méthana, Angístri, Náfplio and Póros. Bus services on the island.

Aegina (Greek form Aíyina, Αιγινα), lying in the Saronic Gulf some 19 km
(12 mi.) south-west of Piraeus, is a hilly but fertile island of marly limestones and schists, with a few rounded hills of volcanic origin (Mount
Profítis Ilías, 532 m (1745 ft)). The coasts are mostly fringed by cliffs, with
only a few sheltered coves. The inhabitants live mainly from the tourist
trade – Athens is only a short distance away – and agriculture, producing and exporting excellent pistachio nuts. The locally made *kannatia*
(water-coolers) are wide-necked, two-handled jars of porous fabric that
keep the water cool by evaporation.

History According to legend the progenitor of the Aeginetans was
Aeacus, son of Zeus and Aegina and father of Peleus and Telamon, a
wise and just ruler who became one of the judges of the Underworld
along with Minos and Rhadamanthys.
    The earliest traces of Pelasgian settlement on the island date back to
the 3rd millennium BC. In the 2nd millennium the island carried on a considerable trade in pottery and ointments, evidence of which has been
found in the areas of Helladic, Cycladic and Minoan culture.
    Aegina first appears in history as a colony of the Dorian city of
Epidaurus, ruled in the 7th c. BC by Phaidon of Argos. After breaking away
from Epidaurus in the 6th c. it enjoyed a period of considerable prosperity,
which brought it into competition with Corinth. The Aeginetans had
trading posts in Umbria, on the Black Sea and in Egypt, and their shipowners became the wealthiest in the Greek world. The coins of Aegina, bearing the island's emblem of a turtle, were the earliest in Europe, and were
already circulating widely by 656 BC; and Aeginetan weights and
measures were used throughout the Greek world until Roman times.
    At the beginning of the Persian wars Aegina was at the peak of its
power, contributing 30 ships to the Greek fleet that defeated the Persians
in the battle of Salamis. But Aegina, moved by commercial considerations, was the first Greek city to submit to the Persian king Darius. As a
result, after being called to account on a complaint by Sparta, it came
into conflict with Athens, which saw the powerful island as an obstacle
to the expansion of its naval power. After two Athenian naval victories,
at Kekryphaleia (Angístri) and off Aegina, the island city was forced to
surrender, and in 456 BC. it was compelled to pull down its walls, hand
over its warships and pay tribute to Athens.

The harbour, Aíyina

Finally at the beginning of the Peloponnesian War, in 431, the Aeginetans were driven off their island and their land was distributed to Attic settlers. After the overthrow of Athens in 404 BC many of them were able to return, but the island's prosperity was gone for good. It again came under the control of Athens, whose destinies it henceforth shared.

Aegina was the capital of Greece from January 12th to October 3rd 1828, and the first coinage of the newly liberated state was minted here.

Sights

Aíyina town

Aíyina (pop. 6500), the chief place on the island, lies on a wide bay at the north end of the west coast, roughly on the site of the ancient city. The little harbour with its fishing boats and yachts is lined with tavernas and cafés, and there are others in Odós Pan. Irioti, just off the harbour. From the harbour, which is protected by a breakwater, there are fine views of the little islands of Metópi and Angístri to the south-west and Moní to the south and of the hills round Epidauros.

The Archaeological Museum contains material recovered from the temples of Aphaia and Aphrodite and much else besides, ranging in date from the 3rd millennium BC to Roman times.

On the hill of **Kolóna**, to the north of the town, is an 8 m (26 ft) high Doric column, all that is left of a temple by the harbour (460 BC) – according to Pausanias a temple of Aphrodite but now known to have been dedicated to Apollo. Under the temple were found remains of Mycenaean and pre-Mycenaean settlement (3rd millennium BC); to the west were two smaller temples, probably dedicated to Artemis and Dionysus. The "Aeginetan sphinx" (c. 460 BC) discovered here in 1904 is now in the Archaeological Museum.

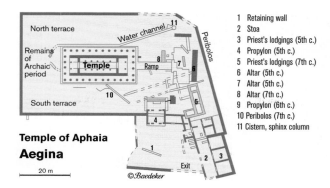

1 Retaining wall
2 Stoa
3 Priest's lodgings (5th c.)
4 Propylon (5th c.)
5 Priest's lodgings (7th c.)
6 Altar (5th c.)
7 Altar (5th c.)
8 Altar (7th c.)
9 Propylon (6th c.)
10 Peribolos (7th c.)
11 Cistern, sphinx column

Temple of Aphaia
Aegina
20 m

©Baedeker

Below the temple of Aphrodite, to the south, was the ancient commercial **harbour**, in which the old quays can be seen under the water. The modern harbour, on the site of the ancient naval harbour, is still protected by the ancient breakwaters. On the long northern breakwater is the early 19th c. chapel of Áyios Nikólaos (St Nicholas).

1.5 km (1 mi.) north of the town is an artificial mound (6th c. BC), traditionally believed to be the tomb of Phocus, half-brother of Peleus and Telamon, who killed him.   **Tomb of Phocus**

From here the road to the temple of Aphaia (see below) runs through hilly country, partly wooded and partly under cultivation, passing the church of the Áyii Theodóri, built in 1289 with stone from ancient temples. It has fine Byzantine frescos.   **Áyii Theodóri**

8 km (5 mi.) from the church of Áyii Theodóri the road comes to Palaiokhóra, chief town of the island until its abandonment around 1800, with the ruins of a medieval castle. In the ruins of the town are more than 20 whitewashed churches of the 13th and 14th c., some of them with frescos; at one time there are said to have been a total of 365 churches. 1 km (¾ mi.) further on is the monastery of Áyios Nektários, named after Archbishop Nektarios (d. 1920, canonised 1961), whose tomb attracts many pilgrims, particularly on November 9th each year.   **Palaiokhóra**

On a terrace above the village of **Mesagró**, which is noted for its pottery and for the harvesting of resin for making retsina, is the Temple of Aphaia (open Mon.–Fri. 8.15am–5pm, Sat., Sun. 8.30am–3pm). The temple (5th c. BC) was dedicated (on the evidence of an inscription and terracottas found here) to a divinity associated with Artemis who was revered as a protectress of women. It is built on the foundations of an earlier 6th c. temple, on the site of a pre-Greek shrine. It is a peripteral temple of 6 by 12 columns, with pronaos and opisthodomos in antis.   **★★Temple of Aphaia**

The roof of the naos was supported on two rows of columns. In the opisthodomos is a stone altar. There survive 23 columns of yellowish limestone, some of them monolithic, mainly on the east end and along the sides; some still preserve remains of the original stucco facing. The roof and sculptural decoration were of Pentelic marble. In the floor can be seen holes left by the railing behind which votive offerings were kept. The sculpture from the pediments is now in the Glyptothek in Munich, and there are some other remains of sculpture in the National Archaeological Museum, Athens, and the Aíyina Museum. Systematic excavations in recent years have brought to light fragments of the earlier

Aegina

The Temple of Aphaia, dedicated to a goddess who was the protrectress of women

temple of around 580 BC, enabling the façade to be partly reconstructed. In the surrounding area were found the remains of dwellings of the late neolithic (4th–3rd millennium BC).

From the temple precinct there are magnificent views over the Saronic Gulf to the mainland, from Athens to Cape Soúnion.

Ayía Marína

Below the temple of Aphaia the road winds its way down through pine forests to the coast. In 3 km (2 mi.) it comes to Ayía Marína (Αγια Μαρινα), situated on a beautiful bay with a sandy beach. This is now the island's tourist centre, with modern hotels and innumerable cafés, tavernas and souvenir shops. There are quieter little bathing beaches below the road to Portes.

Mount Profítis Ilías

The most prominent landmark in the Saronic Gulf is Óros (532 m (1745 ft)), the "Mountain", also known as Mount Profítis Ilías, with a chapel of the Ascension (Analipsis) on the summit. It can be climbed in about 2 hours on a steep and difficult path from the village of Marathón (6 km (4 mi.) south of Aíyina town).

In Mycenaean times (13th c. BC) there was an extensive settlement, surrounded by cyclopean walls, on the terraces round the summit. From here there are tremendous views extending over almost the whole island and across the Saronic Gulf to Salamis, the Methourides (Troupika and Revitousa), the Diaporia, Angístri, the Méthana peninsula and the islands of Póros and Hydra.

Under the north side of the summit, near the chapel of the Taxiarchs (Archangels), was a 5th c. temple of Zeus Panhellenios.

Angístri

5 km (3 mi.) south-west of Aegina is the wooded island of Angístri, whose 1000 inhabitants are the descendants of Albanians who settled on the island in the 16th c. With an area of only 12 sq. km (4½ sq. mi.) it

is the smallest inhabited island in the Saronic Gulf. Many of the inhabitants commute daily to Athens to work. There are good beaches at Skála and Megalokhori.

Áyios Efstrátios

See Lemnos

Alónnisos   H 4

Island group: Northern Sporades
Area: 62 sq. km (24 sq. mi.)
Altitude: 0–476 m (0–1562 ft)
Population: 3000
Chief place: Patitíri

Shipping connections with Salonica, Vólos, Áyios Ioánnis/Platanias (Pelion), Áyios Konstantínos/Kymi (Euboea, Skíathos, Skópelos, Skýros, Trikeri. Boats to bathing beaches and neighbouring islands. Charter flights to Skíathos.

The long rocky island of Alónnisos (Αλοννησος, formerly Khiliondrómia, in antiquity Ikos; held by Venice 1453–1537) lies in the middle of the chain of the Northern Sporades that runs west from Skíathos. Along the whole length of the island extends a ridge of hills that reaches its highest point in Mount Kouvoúli (476 m (1562 ft)). The north-west coast is fringed by cliffs, with little variation; on the gentler south-east coast there are a number of sheltered bays. Here there are traces of settlement going back to Neolithic times. Ancient Ikos is believed to have been situated near Kokkinokástro on the south-east coast, where remains of town walls and tombs have been brought to light.

On Alónnisos are the headquarters of an internationally known Academy of Homoeopathic Therapy. Until a few years ago it was little known to tourists, and it is still one of the more unfrequented of the Greek islands. Most of the population live in the flatter, fertile southern part of the island, where its modest tourist facilities are concentrated. Alónnisos offers good bathing, snorkelling and walking (five waymarked routes).

Until quite recently there were no made roads on Alónnisos, and any exploration of the island still involves a good deal of walking. An easier alternative is to take a boat or caique to the remoter bathing **beaches**. Along the southern half of the east coast, in the southern part of the island and on the west coast as far up as Ormos Megáli Ámmos ("big sandy bay") there are numbers of beaches (accommodation available).

In the Northern Sporades Marine National Park is a colony of some 40 **monk seals,** the largest such colony in the Mediterranean. The European Natural Heritage Foundation has an outstation on Alónnisos that is establishing the National Park (at present existing only on paper) and works in collaboration with the local hotels. The information centre in Patitíri (on the road to Vótsi, on the harbour near the fishermen's cooperative) can provide information about measures for the protection of the natural heritage and offer suggestions about walks on the island.

The little port of Patitíri (Πατιτηρι), now the island's tourist centre, with a number of hotels, has grown up only since the 1950s. It lies in a   **Patitíri** circular bay ringed by steep cliffs. Its only tourist attraction is the little Monk Seal Museum on the harbour front, which tells the story of Alónnisos's monk-seal colony. The exhibits include a 200-year-old skeleton of a monk seal.

Alónnisos town

2 km (1¼ mi.) north-west of Patitíri is the island's old capital Alónnisos (Khorió). It was largely abandoned after an earthquake in 1965 but is now being developed as a tourist centre. Many houses have been bought and restored by wealthy foreigners. From this idyllic little place there are magnificent sea views.

Neighbouring islands

Off the south-east coast of Alónnisos, separated from it by a wide sound, lies the barren island of **Peristéra** (area 14 sq. km (5½ sq. mi.)), also known as Xeró.

The island of **Skántzoura** (area 7 sq. km (2.75 sq. mi.)), which belongs to the monastic republic of Athos and is used for the grazing of goats, lies some 20 km (13 mi.) south-east of Alónnisos. It is occasionally visited for the sake of its sea caves and its underwater fishing.

13 km (8 mi.) north-east of the northern tip of Alónnisos is the wooded island of **Pélagos** (area 25 sq. km (9½ sq. mi.)), known in antiquity as Euthyra. It is also called Kyrá Panayía after the monastery of that name on its east coast. The monastery, which is under the jurisdiction of Athos, has an 11th c. church with historic icons.

The next island to the north-east is the wooded island of Poúra or **Yioúra** (area 10 sq. km (4 sq. mi.)), now a reserve for wild goats (bezoar goats). On the south coast are the Caves of Cyclops that according to legend were the home of Polyphemus. South-east of Yioúra, within the seal reserve, is the little island of **Pipéri** (area 7 sq. km (2½ sq. mi.)).

The little volcanic island of **Psathoúra** (area 6 sq. km (2¼ sq. mi.)) lies at the north-eastern tip of the chain of the Northern Sporades. There are remains of buildings belonging to an ancient city under the sea just off the coast of the island.

Skópelos: see entry.

★Amorgós   K/L 7

Island group: Cyclades
Area: 120 sq. km (46 sq. mi.)
Altitude: 0–826 m (0–2710 ft)
Population: 1600
Chief place: Amorgós town (Khóra)

Shipping connections with Piraeus, Rafína and other Cycladic islands. Bus services on the island.

Amorgós (Αμοργος), the easternmost of the Cyclades, has long been known as a tourist centre, but it also appeals to people who like walking and peace and quiet. It is a bare, rocky island 33 km (21 mi.) long by 2–6.5 km (1¼–4 mi.) across. The cliffs on the south-east coast fall spectacularly down to the sea from a height of up to 800 m (2600 ft); the north-west coast is gentler, with two deeply indented inlets, Katápola Bay to the south, with the island's principal harbour, and Aiyiáli Bay to the north. The islanders – declining in numbers as a result of emigration – live by arable and stock farming, and now increasingly from the tourist trade.

There are attractive **walks** on the numerous donkey paths round Katapola and Amorgós town. The two finest walks on the island are to the Panayía Khozoviótissa monastery on the east coast and by way of Minoa, above Katápola, to the Valsamitis monastery.

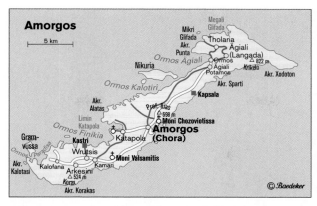

There are a number of bays with sand and shingle beaches on the north and north-west coasts.

History The remains of several ancient towns and extensive cemeteries, finds of coins and rock inscriptions show that in Minoan and Hellenistic times Amorgós was an important port of call on the sea route between Melos and the south-eastern Aegean. In Roman times it was a place of exile, and in later centuries it was repeatedly raided by pirates. The Khozoviótissa monastery, founded in the 9th c., dominated the island, which passed into Venetian hands in 1207 and in 1637 was occupied by the Ottoman general Khaireddin Barbarossa. It has remained into our own day a place of no economic or political importance.

Sights

The pleasant little town of Katápola (Καταπολα) is the island's principal port and the favourite resort of visitors. Here you can stroll along the long seafront promenade, lined with tamarisks, and – at least in the low season – enjoy the island's peaceful atmosphere. The needs of the tourist trade are met by the numerous rooms available for visitors and a number of tavernas. The principal sight is the church of the Panayía Katapoliani, built on the foundations of an Early Christian basilica, incorporating ancient columns. In antiquity the site is believed to have been occupied by a temple of Apollo.

Katápola

From the bay a green valley runs inland. At the south end of the bay, on the hill of Mountiliá, are the remains of the ancient town of Minoa, believed to have been founded by Cretans in the 2nd millennium BC. It is a 30 min. walk from Katápola to the site. From the top of the hill there is a magnificent view extending as far as Náxos.

Minoa

5 km (3 mi.) further on is the chief place on the island, Amorgós town (Khóra; pop. 300). With its typical white Cycladic houses, its more than 40 family chapels (barrel-vaulted; frescos) and the remains of a 13th c. Venetian castle, it huddles round the hilltop. Many fragments of ancient masonry can be seen built into house walls. Many outstanding examples of Cycladic art were found on Amorgós (now in the National Archaeological Museum in Athens and other museums). The island's own Archaeological Museum, with examples of geometric, archaic and classical art, is beside the church of the Zoodokhos Piyí (Life Giving Fountain).

Amorgós town

Amorgós

Monastery of the Panayía Khozoviótissa

Panayía Khozoviótissa

A spectacular sight within easy reach of Amorgós town (30 minutes' walk) is the brilliantly white monastery of the Panayía Khozoviótissa, in a style of architecture quite unusual in the Aegean, dramatically situated 380 m (1250 ft) above the sea, clinging to a sheer brown cliff. Originally founded in the 9th c., it was refounded by the Emperor Alexius Comnenus in 1088. Among its treasures are valuable icons, parchment manuscripts and important historical documents. From the terrace there are fine views of the sea.

Arkesíni

In the south-west of the island, half an hour's walk from Vroutsis, is the old town of Arkesíni (Αρκεσινη Καστρι), now known as Kastrí, strikingly situated on a crag falling steeply down to the sea. It preserves only scanty remains of the classical, Hellenistic and Roman periods.

Aiyiáli

Aiyiáli (Αιγιαλη), the island's second port, is situated in the bay of the same name in north-eastern Amorgós. It is quieter than Katápola, but is now attracting numbers of visitors. Its great attraction is its spacious tamarisk-fringed beach. To the north-west are a number of small and secluded coves with sand and shingle beaches.

★Mount Krikelo

Nearby are the mountain villages of Tholária (church of the Áyii Anárgyri, with a blue dome and two bell towers) and Langáda. From Langáda Mount Krikelo (826 m (2710 ft)) can be climbed. The climb takes 4–5 hours there and back; the best time of year is the spring.

Levíta Islands

North-east of Amorgós is the Levíta group of islands, which belong to the Dodecanese. The main islands are Levíta (area 5 sq. km (2 sq. mi.); alt. 0–167 m (0–548 ft)) and Kínaros (area 9 sq. km (3½ sq. mi.); alt. 0–320 m (0–1050 ft)), and there are a number of small islets, mostly uninhabited. Here it is still possible to find beautiful lonely beaches, since none of these islands has any regular boat services or accommodation for visitors.

Anáfi   K 7

Island group: Cyclades
Area: 36 sq. km (14 sq. mi.)
Altitude: 0–584 m (0–1916 ft)
Population: 300
Chief place: Anáfi town (Khóra)

Shipping connections with Piraeus and with other Cycladic islands via Santoríni.

Anáfi ("the radiant"), the most south-easterly island in the Cyclades, lies 22 km (14 mi.) east of Santoríni. It is 12 km (7½ mi.) long and up to 7 km (4½ mi.) wide. Favoured particularly by backpackers, it offers beautiful hill scenery, peace and quiet, and unfrequented beaches. From the island's chief place, Anáfi, a village of white houses strikingly situated on a high crag, a series of beautiful sandy beaches extend to Cape Kalamos at the east end of the island.
   Anáfi (Αναφη), traversed by a network of donkey paths, must be explored either on foot or on a donkey.

The little port of Áyios Nikólaos (Αγιος Νιλολαος), at the south end of the island, consists of a cluster of houses, occupied only in summer, nestling at the foot of the cliffs. The harbour can be used only by fishing boats and caiques; passengers on larger vessels are landed by boat.

Áyios Nikólaos

From the port a donkey-track runs up to the chief place on the island, Anáfi (Khóra), situated at a height of 256 m (840 ft) under the ruins of a 14th c. Venetian castle.

Anáfi town

North-east of Anáfi (an hour walk from Áyios Nikólaos), on the round-topped hill of Kastélli (304 m (997 ft)), are the fragmentary remains of a **Dorian city** founded in the 8th c. BC.
   From here it is an hour's walk to the Zoodókhos Piyí monastery.

From Áyios Nikólaos there is an attractive walk on a track running east, keeping close to the coast (beautiful beaches) for most of the way, to the monastery of the Zoodókhos Piyí (Life Giving Fountain) or Káto Monastiri, built in 1807 on the foundations of a temple of Apollo and incorporating fragments of ancient masonry.

Zoodókhos Piyí

An hour walk further east, prominently situated on Mount Kálamos (396 m (1299 ft)), a limestone crag falling steeply down to the sea, is the church of the Panayía Kalamiótissa (Pano Monastiri; 1715). From the top of the hill there are extensive views, extending in clear weather as far as Crete. To the south-east are the islands of Ftena, Pakhia and Makra.

Panayía Kalamiótissa

Ándros   I/K 5/6

Island group: Cyclades
Area: 380 sq. km (147 sq. mi.)
Altitude: 0–994 m (0–3261 ft)
Population: 9500
Chief place: Ándros town (Khóra)

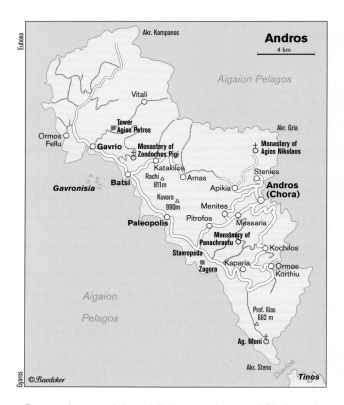

Ferry service several times daily between the port of Gávrio on the north-west coast and Rafína in Attica; local service to the Cycladic island of Tínos. Bus services on the island.

Ándros (Ανδρος), the most northerly and, after Náxos, the largest of the Cyclades (40 km (25 mi.) long by up to 16 km (10 mi.) across), is separated from Euboea by the Pórthmos Kafiréfs, a strait 12 km (7½ mi.) wide, and from the neighbouring island of Tínos to the south-east by the 1200 m (3900 ft) wide Steno Channel. Lying off the main tourist tracks, it is reached not from Piraeus but from the little port of Rafína on the east coast of Attica. Only Batsí and Gávrio on the west coast of Ándros have developed into tourist resorts; otherwise the island has preserved its distinctive Greek character and way of life. Many Athenians visit Ándros at weekends.

Geography At first sight Ándros, with its bare and rugged hills, has a rather uninviting look. The coast is much indented, though it has a number of beautiful beaches. In spite of this misleading first impression, however, this is one of the most fertile islands in the Cyclades. The long valleys reaching inland with their lush green vegetation offer an attractive contrast to the barren hills. In the four ranges of slate and limestone hills that traverse the island from west to east, reaching a height of

994 m (3261 ft) in Mount Petalon, are marble quarries that were already being worked in ancient times. The island's abundance of water has made possible the development of intensive agriculture in the deeply indented valleys on the south side of Mount Petalon as well as the lush growth of natural vegetation.

History In antiquity Andros was dedicated to Dionysus, the god of wine, and its celebrations of his cult were widely famed. Originally colonised by Ionians, the island came under the control of Eretria (Euboea) in the 8th c. BC. In the 8th c. Andros itself sent settlers to Chalcidice in Thrace. After the battle of Salamis Themistocles made war on Andros, which had supported the Persians, but it did not become a dependency of Athens until some time later. In 338 BC it fell into the hands of Macedon and after the defeat of Macedon passed into Roman control. From the early medieval period until the 19th c. the breeding of silkworms – favoured by the abundance of mulberry trees – was an important economic activity. From AD 1207 Ándros was ruled by Venetian dynasts, and the island has many watchtowers dating from the period of Venetian rule. In the early 15th c. many Albanians settled in the north of the island, preserving their own language until the 20th c. Ándros was occupied by the Turks in 1566, and remained under Turkish rule until its incorporation in the new kingdom of Greece in the 19th c.

Since the 19th c. Ándros has been the home of a number of Greece's biggest shipowners, and as result of high tax revenues and their many benefactions is now one of the wealthiest of the Cycladic islands. Like Chíos (see entry), it does not have to depend on the tourist trade for its prosperity.

Ándros town

The island's chief town, Ándros (Khóra; pop. 1800), lies on a ridge between two bays on the east coast. It grew up in the Middle Ages, starting from the islet of Kastélli off the eastern tip of the narrow promontory on which the Venetians (under Doge Dandolo) built a stronghold (Kástro). It is a quiet and prosperous little town of trim streets, patrician houses and churches. The street names commemorate the town's benefactors, the wealthy shipowners who built their summer villas here. To them Ándros owes not only the uniform style of the town's architecture but a variety of cultural and social institutions, including several

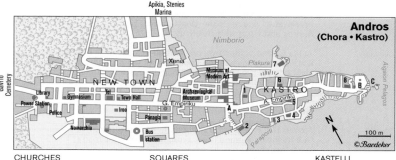

CHURCHES		SQUARES		KASTELLI
1 Palatiani	5 Ay. Yeoryios	A Platia Kairis	B Platia Afani Nafti	C Remains of
2 Theoskepasti	6 Ay. Taxiarches	Marble fountain	Monument to	Venetian walls
3 Ay. Nikolaos	7 Ay. Thalassini	Monument to	Unknown Sailor	and connecting
4 Ay. Athanasios	8 Ay. Varvara	Theopilos Kairis	Seafaring Museum	bridge

museums, a library, various monuments and schools. The town has a marble-paved main street and numbers of vaulted lanes and steep flights of steps.

★Kástro

The tour of the old town starts in Platía Kairis, a small square shaded by tamarisks and plane trees, in the western part of the town. In the square is a marble fountain of 1818. From here stepped lanes run down to the north and south beaches. The taverna in the square serves simple but good meals and has a fine view of the beach.

From the square we go though an arched gateway known as the Kamara into the old town or Kástro (pedestrian zone). Passing a number of handsome neoclassical mansions and St George's Church at the east end of the street, we come to Platía Afani Nafti, in the centre of which is a massive Monument to the Unknown Sailor. This bronze figure by Mikhalis Tombos depicts a sailor, complete with cap and kitbag, gazing out to sea with his right hand raised. Also in the square is a small sea-faring museum (open occasionally) with a number of ship models.

A single-arched bridge leads on to the islet of Kastélli (fortified by Martino Dandolo in the early 13th c.), with remains of the walls of the Venetian castle. Inland from here extends the new town with its bustling streets.

★Archaeological Museum

In Platía Kairis is the interesting Archaeological Museum (open Mon., Wed.–Sat. 8.30am–3pm, Sun. 9.30am–2.30pm). Opened in 1981, it was financed by the shipowner Basil Goulandris. The museum illustrates the history of the island of Ándros, to the accompaniment of classical music. Its major displays are devoted to material from the sites of Zagora (geometric period) and Palaiopolis. Its principal treasure is the "Hermes of Andros", probably an ancient copy (1st c. BC) of a marble statue by the famous 4th c. sculptor Praxiteles.

Museum of Modern Art

From Platía Kairis a stepped lane to the north runs down to the Museum of Modern Art (open Jun.–Sep. daily 10am–2pm; Oct.–May daily 10am–2pm), also established by the Goulandris family. This is the only such collection of international standing in Greece. Housed in a modern building, it displays sculpture, painting and installations by 20th c. Greek artists. The avantgarde sculptor Mikhalis Tombros (1889–1974) is well represented.

Coastline

On both sides of the promontory there are bays: to the south the wide Paraporti Bay (beach), to the north the bay containing the Old Harbour (Plakoúra) and Nimborió Bay (beach), recorded in 1578 as a trading harbour, with the New Harbour (sailing club, landing stage), protected by a breakwater, and a large diesel-fuelled power station that supplies Ándros and Tínos with electricity.

Cemetery

At the far end of the town, on the road to Mesariá, is Ándros's cemetery, laid out in terraces. In the upper part of the cemetery are a number of elaborately designed tombs, often in the form of a temple, belonging to influential shipowning families.

Sights

Steniés

Steniés (Στενιες), 4 km (2½ mi.) north of Ándros town, is surrounded by fruit trees and almond trees. From here there is a road (1 km (¾ mi.)) to Yialia Bay (sandy beach), where a number of holiday houses have been built.

Apikía

6 km (4 mi.) north-west of Ándros, in a beautiful setting with fine views, is Apikía (Αποικια), which produces the well-known Sáriza mineral water; the fountain house can be visited.

Steniés, beautifully situated on a hillside amid luxuriant vegetation

From Apikía there is an attractive walk (3 km (2 mi.)) to the convent of Áyios Nikólaos. It has a domed cruciform church that contains an unusual icon of St Nicholas, woven by a 17th c. nun from gold and silver thread and her own hair and set with pearls.

Áyios Nikólaos

The little fishing village of Ormos Korthíou (Ορμος Κορθιου) lies 10 km (6 mi.) south of Ándros at the mouth of a fertile valley. Sand and shingle beaches.

Ormos Korthíou

From Ándros the wide and fertile Mesariá (Μεσαρια) valley (wine, citrus fruits) cuts across the island. Features of interest are the characteristic local dovecotes and the church of the Taxiarchs (Archangels) of 1158.
   The monastery of the **Panayía Panakhrántou**, founded in 961 by Nicephorus Phocas (later Emperor), lies 4 km (2½ mi.) south of Mesariá at an altitude of 800 m (2625 ft). It is an imposing fortress-like structure with a Byzantine domed cruciform church.

Mesariá

At Zagora, 2 km (1¼ mi.) south of the Stavropeda road junction, are the remains of the only well-preserved settlement of the Geometric period (900–700 BC) in Greece (not open to the public). Finds from the site are in the Archaeological Museum in Ándros.

Zagora

The bay of Gávrio (Γαυριο) on the west coast of Ándros was used in antiquity as a sheltered harbour. The modest little fishing village of Gávrio is now the island's principal port, used by numerous ferries. There are a number of hotels and tavernas and a small beach.

Gávrio

To the east of Gávrio, at an altitude of 300 m (985 ft), is the convent of the **Zoodókhos Piyí** (Life Giving Fountain), founded in 1325. The church has a beautiful marble iconostasis, frescos and valuable icons. A particular treasure is a piece of silk embroidery from Constantinople, 300 years old, with a representation of the Mother of God as the Fount of Life.

Áyios Pétros

2 km (1¼ mi.) north-west, at Áyios Pétros, is a massive Hellenistic watch-tower (3rd–1st c. BC), which has a circumference of 21 m (70 ft) and still stands 20 m (65 ft) high. It probably served also as a place of refuge for the local population and protection for the nearby ore mines. From the tower there are superb views.

Batsí

The former fishing village of Batsí (Μπατσι) is now a busy tourist centre, particularly favoured by British holidaymakers. It is well equipped with accommodation for visitors and with tavernas, and there are several sandy beaches to the south of the village (including a nudist beach). Batsí is a good base from which to climb Mount Kouvára (990 m (3248 ft)) and Mount Rakhi (811 m (2660 ft)); in each case the climb takes 4–5 hours.

Palaiópolis

The ancient capital of the island, which flourished into Byzantine times (500 BC to AD 800), lay on the west coast near the village of Palaiópolis (Παλαιοπολις) (the "old city"), 8 km (5 mi.) south of Batsí. Here, it is said, the god Dionysus turned water from the springs in his shrine into wine. There are scanty remains of the acropolis and the port installations. Most of the material from this site, including the famous "Hermes of Andros", is in the Archaeological Museum in Ándros town.

Astypálaia   L 7

Island group: Dodecanese
Area: 99 sq. km (38 sq. mi.)
Altitude: 0–482 m (0–1581ft)
Population: 1100
Chief place: Astypálaia town (Khóra)

Shipping connections with Piraeus, Kálymnos, Rhodes, Páros, Amorgós, Anáfi, Íos, Kos, Náxos and Santoríni.

The arid karstic island of Astypálaia (Αστυπαλαια), the most westerly of the Dodecanese, lies between Kos (40 km (25 mi.) away) and the Cycladic islands of Amorgós (35 km (22 mi.)) and Anáfi (40 km (25 mi.)). From each of these other islands it is a 3 hour boat trip to this remote and isolated island. Although it has been included in the Dodecanese since 1830 (when the Cyclades became part of the independent kingdom of Greece), in earlier centuries it belonged to the Cyclades, with which it has close affinities in topography and culture: bare hills, barren of vegetation, and white houses.

Two wide bays on the north-west and south-east sides of the island divide it into a higher western half (0–482 m (0–1581 ft)) and a lower eastern half (0–366 m (0–1201 ft)), linked by the isthmus of Áyios Andréas, which is only 110 m (360 ft) wide. Livestock farming (cheese), the growing of fruit and vegetables and fishing bring the inhabitants a modest degree of wellbeing. Facilities for tourists are still limited, but there are enough rooms in private houses and enough discos to cater for visitors.

Astypálaia town

The island's picturesque chief town, Astypálaia (Khóra), is finely situated on a bare rocky hill above the harbour (Skála). Twenty years ago it was a ghost town, but since then the abandoned houses have increasingly been bought up and renovated by foreigners, and as a result many

Astypálaia has all the elements of a Greek island town – windmills, whitewashed houses and a castle

Greeks have also returned. The eight windmills round the village square have also been restored. The Khóra is dominated by a Venetian castle (13th–16th c.), of which only the outer walls remain. The castle is entered through a long passage with Gothic vaulting.

Below the Khóra, to the west, is the green and fertile Livádia valley, the main area of agricultural land on the island. Livádia's tamarisk-shaded shingle beach, with a number of modest tavernas, is the most popular on the island.

Livádia valley

Scattered all over the island are some 200 little churches and chapels, mostly founded by local families and now frequently in a ruinous state.

Round Astypálaia are numerous little islands – Pontikoúsa to the west, Foklonísia to the north and Ligno, Khondro, Áyii Kyriakí, Koutsomiti and Kounoupi to the south-east – and isolated stacks, some of which provide grazing for goats. 12 km (7½ mi.) west of Astypálaia is the islet of Ofidousa. Farther to the south-east (35–45 km (22–28 mi.)) are the lonely little islands of Seírina and Tría Nisía ("Three Islands").

Neighbouring islands

★★Athens H 5/6

Nomos: Attica
Altitude: 40–150 m (130–490 ft)
Population: 1 million (Greater Athens including Piraeus 4 million)

The description of the Greek capital in this guide is confined to the main

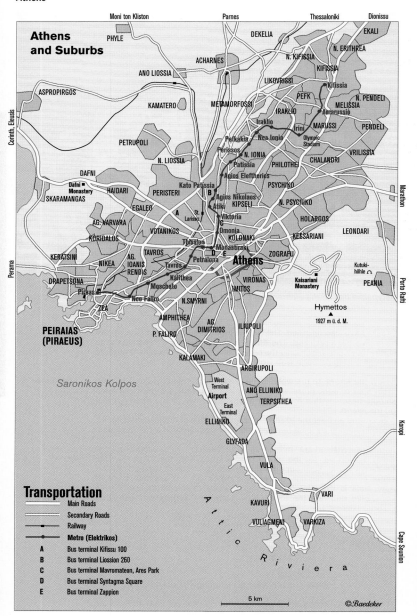

sights. A fuller account of the city is given in the Baedeker guide "Athens".

Greek capital

Elliniko airport lies 15 km (9 mi.) east of the city centre. There is an express bus service between the two terminals and the city centre (Sýntagma Square); the buses run every 15–30 minutes between 5am and 11pm, hourly during the night. A new airport is under construction at Spata, 30 km (19 mi.) south-east of Athens. There are numerous rail and bus connections with all parts of the country. Within the city there are yellow trolleybuses, blue and white buses to the suburbs and green buses to Piraeus.

A fast rail service, the Elektrikos, runs from Piraeus through central Athens to Kifissiá in the north. A new metro system is under construction.

Athens (Αθηνα), with its port Piraeus, lies on the Gulf of Aegina (Saronic Gulf). The endless sea of houses in its nine city wards and 38 surrounding communes occupies the principal plain in Attica; the distance from the northern suburb of Kifissiá to Piraeus in the south is around 20 km (13 mi.) as the crow flies. As in antiquity, Athens is the intellectual and artistic as well as the economic centre of Greece. Since 1834 – when it was an unimportant little town of 6000 inhabitants – it has been capital of Greece. Some 40 per cent of the total population now live in and around the capital. It is the see of the Archbishop of Athens and of Greece. It has an incomparable wealth of historic buildings and archaeological remains and a great range of museums of classical and Byzantine culture, art galleries and natural history collections to fascinate visitors throughout the year. The Athens conurbation is the main centre of Greek commerce and industry, and all the country's banks and most of the large industrial concerns and shipping lines have their headquarters in the city. Of particular importance are the industrial installations in the Bay of Eleusis and the port of Piraeus.

Environment The city's uncontrolled growth, the rapid pace of industrialisation and above all the huge increase in the numbers of motor vehicles in the Athens conurbation (well over half the number of private cars registered in the whole of Greece) have created grave environmental problems. Athens is notorious for its smog (*nefos*), which not only destroys buildings but also is life-threatening for many people. Aggressive substances in the air present conservationists with insoluble problems. Another major problem is the pollution of coastal waters in the Saronic Gulf. Not infrequently there are bans on bathing in the coastal resorts on the Attic Riviera, just to the south of Athens, and it is inadvisable to bathe at all within a wide radius round Piraeus.

Although the territory of Athens extends over more than 400 sq. km (155 sq. mi.), the area of interest to visitors is quite small and most of the sights can easily be reached on foot. The core of **the city** consists of the Acropolis, the buildings on its southern slopes and the Plaka district to the north and east of the Acropolis (Monastiraki Square, Hermes Street, Sýntagma Square and Leofóros Amalias). Round this central area are the National Garden, the Olympieion, the Zappeion and Parliament to the east; the Kolonaki district between Leofóros Vas. Sofias and Likavitos to the north-east; Venizélos (University) Street, with the neoclassical University, Academy of Sciences and National Library, to the north; and Odós Athinas, leading to Omónia Square, with the Market Halls. Farther north is the Archaeological Museum.

The city is dominated by Mount Lycabettus. In the foreground can be seen the Mitrópolis and the Plaka

History

The historical development of Athens begins with the amalgamation (synoecism) of the various settlements in Attica under King Theseus in the 10th c. BC. Social tensions in the 7th c. BC were temporarily resolved by the reforms of the great legislator Solon, but after Solon's death they soon broke out again, leading to the establishment of the tyranny (government by a single ruler) of Peisistratus and his sons (560–510 BC). Under their rule the power of the nobility was weakened – an important precondition for the emergence of democracy in Attica. The Persian wars (500–479 BC), in which Athens supported the Greek cities in Asia Minor, ended in victory for the city under the leadership of Themistocles. The Attic democratic system (from 461 BC) made possible the rise of Athens to become the leading power in Greece in both economic and cultural terms. The city state reached the peak of its achievement under the rule of Pericles (443–419 BC).

Post-classical and medieval Athens

The Peloponnesian War (431–404 BC) was a grave setback for Athens, which now lost the leadership of Greece to Sparta. In 86 BC Athens fell to the Romans under the leadership of Sulla. Other splendid buildings were erected by the Roman Emperors, particularly by Hadrian. This period of renewed prosperity, however, was brought to a sudden end in AD 267, when the city was taken by the Heruli, an East Germanic tribe. During the period of the great migrations Athens was repeatedly plundered (in 395 by Alaric's Goths), and thereafter declined into a provincial town of no consequence in the East Roman (Byzantine) Empire. In the 13th c. it had a further brief period of prosperity under Frankish rule; then, after a short interlude of Venetian rule (1394–1402), it was captured by the Ottomans and remained under Turkish rule until the 19th c.

18th and 19th c.

During the War of Greek Independence (1821–33) Athens was the scene of heavy fighting. After the war, in 1834, King Otto, a prince of Bavarian origin, made it capital of the new kingdom of Greece and enlisted German and Danish architects to provide it with the necessary public buildings. In 1896 the first Olympic Games of modern times were held in Athens. In the 1920s extensive new districts were built up to house the 300,000 refugees from Asia Minor who came to Athens in 1923 after the Greek–Turkish war and whose resettlement was a problem for several decades. Athens and Piraeus have now long joined up to form a single conurbation.

Acropolis and surrounding area

The limestone crag of the Acropolis, rising out of the plain of Attica, was the obvious place for the fortified "upper city" that was originally the stronghold of the kings of Athens and also the seat of the city's oldest shrines and later became exclusively devoted to the city's gods. This religious centre of ancient Athens, which was given its classic form in the time of Pericles, became the supreme monument of western culture. In spite of the destruction wrought by many centuries the buildings on the Acropolis still reflect something of the splendour of the age of Pericles, when Athens was the intellectual, artistic and political centre of the Greek world.

During the 19th and early 20th c. the clearance of post-classical buildings and restoration work revealed the remains of the buildings as they were in the 5th c. BC. The process began in 1836, immediately after the city's liberation from the Turks, with the re-erection of the temple of Athena Nike, which the Turks had converted into a bastion, and culminated in the re-erection of the columns on the north side of the Parthenon in the 1920s.

The 20th c., however, has wrought more destruction in a few decades than all earlier centuries. As a result of the exhaust gases produced by the huge modern city, the disturbance caused by aircraft taking off and landing at the nearby airport (though aircraft are now banned from over-flying the Acropolis) and the 3 million visitors who make their way up to the Acropolis every year the native rock and marble paving have been worn down, the Pentelic marble has degenerated into gypsum and the remaining sculpture has been flaking off. Altogether the destruction has reached alarming proportions. In 1977 UNESCO called for steps to be taken to save the Acropolis. Since then it has been a permanent building site.

An excellent view of the Acropolis – seen at its best in the late after-noon – can be had from the Agora on the north side or the Olympieion on the south-east side. The west end can be seen from the Hill of the Nymphs, on the eastern slope of which is the Pnyx (the meeting place of the popular assembly following Cleisthenes' reform in 507 BC).

Viewpoints

The finest view – indeed the classic view – of the south-west side of the Acropolis is to be had from the ★**Hill of the Muses** or Hill of Philopappos. From the Dionysos restaurant a road runs up through pinewoods, passing cisterns and rock chambers that have been erro-neously identified since the 18th c. as the tomb of Cimon and as Socrates' prison. On the way up there are ever new views of the Acropolis and its buildings, from the Propylaia by way of the Erechtheion to the Parthenon, with Likavitos in the background. On the summit of the hill is an impressive monument of the Imperial period, the tomb of Philopappos, a prince of Commagene (south-eastern Anatolia) who was exiled to Athens by the Romans and died there in AD 116.

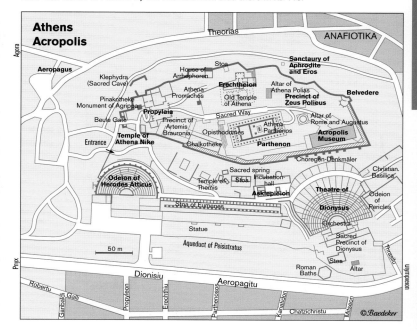

= = = Presumed line of ancient alls

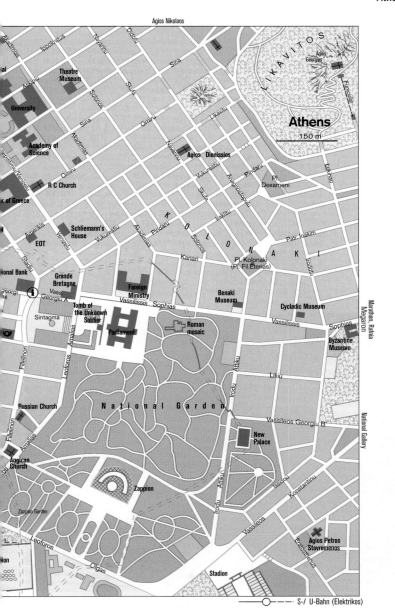

Athens

150 m

L I K A V I T O S

Agios Georgios

Funicular

Agios Nikolaos

Akadimias
Ippokratus
Navarinu
Didou
Sina
Skufa
Solonos
Theatre Museum
University
Asklipiu
Omiru
Likaviu
Academy of Science
Akadimias
Sina
Navarinu
Agios Dionissios
Vukurestiu
Anagnostopulu
Pindaru
Pl. Dexameni
Lukianu
R C Church
Omiru
of Greece
Schliemann's House
Amerikis
Vukurestiu
Akadimias
Pindaru
Irakliu
Patr. Ioakim
Iridou
EOT
Vutsetik, Koumbari/Voukourestiou
Voutsetikis
Kanari
Pl. Kolonaki (Pl. Fil. Eterias)
K O L O N A K I
ional Bank
Grande Bretagne
Vass. Georgiu A
Georgiu
Foreign Ministry
Vassilissis Sophias
Benaki Museum
Cycladic Museum
Marathon, Rafina Megaron
Sintagma
Tomb of the Unknown Soldier
Parliament
Roman mosaic
Vassilissis
Sophias
Byzantine Museum
Stadiu
Amalias
Leoforos
Fillelinon
Attiku
Irodu
Likiu
Russian Church
N a t i o n a l   G a r d e n
Vassileos Georgiu B
National Gallery
Fillelinon
Amalias
New Palace
Irodu
Attiku
Anglican Church
Issodu
Konstantinu
Zappion
Zappeio Garden
Agios Petros Stavromenos
Exostrehous
Leoforos
Olgas
Vassileos
Stadion

○——--- S-/ U-Bahn (Elektrikos)

97

★★Acropolis

Trolleybuses
1, 5, 9 from
Sýntagma to
Makroyiani

Bus
230 to Odeion of
Herodes Atticus

The Acropolis is open Mon.–Fri. 8am–6.30pm, Sat., Sun. 8.30am–2.30pm; museum open only from 11am on Mon., Nov.–Mar. only to 5pm. Admission charge includes Acropolis Museum (free Sun.). Paths are uneven and slippery: good shoes essential. To avoid the crowds, you should visit the Acropolis as early as possible in the day. The steep crag of the Acropolis measures 320 m (1050 ft) from west to east and 156 m (510 ft) from north to south and is 156 m (512 ft) high. The only access is at the west end.

History The cyclopean walls built in Mycenaean times closely followed the contours of the crag. All the buildings of the Archaic period (7th and 6th c. BC) were destroyed by the Persians in 480 BC. The remains of the old temple were razed to the ground in 406 BC after the cult image (xoanon) was transferred to the new temple of Athena in the east end of the Erechtheion. In the rebuilding Themistocles used column drums and fragments of entablature from the old building, still to be seen in the north wall. In 467 BC Cimon altered the line of the defences on the south side, building the straight length of wall that still exists. Within the extended area thus created Pericles carried out his great building programme. The Parthenon, the Propylaia, the temple of Athena Nike and the Erechtheion were all built between 447 and 406 BC. The only later structure to survive is a circular temple dedicated to Rome and Augustus (early Imperial period) of which there are some remains at the east end of the Parthenon.

Beule Gate

The Acropolis is entered by the Beule Gate, named after the French archaeologist Ernest Beule who discovered it in 1853. It was built from the remains of buildings destroyed in the Herulian raid in AD 267.

The Acropolis: the buildings in their present form date from the time of Pericles

The tall and imposing Propylaia were built by Mnesicles between 437 and 432 BC. On the native rock is set a flight of steps, one of which is in grey Eleusinian marble, the others in Pentelic marble. The central feature of the structure is a wall with five doorways that increase in height and width from the sides to the centre. The lintel of the central doorway has an additional metope. On the west side is a deep portico, the centre of which is framed by six Ionic columns. Along the front of the portico are six Doric columns that supported the pediment. Compared with this imposing entrance the portico on the east side, also with Doric columns but shorter and lower, appears small and modest when seen from the higher part of the Acropolis.

★Propylaia

The west portico was flanked by other buildings. On the left was the Pinakotheke, which housed a collection of paintings. In front of it is the tall plinth of a monument in honour of Marcus Agrippa, Augustus' son-in-law, whose quadriga (four-horse chariot) was set up on the plinth in 27 BC.

Monument of Agrippa

This temple, with four Ionic columns on the front and rear ends, was built in 432–431 BC. The form of the columns was old-fashioned for that period, and it is supposed, therefore, that when the temple was built after the end of the Periclean age an older design by Callicrates was used (compare the building history of the Parthenon). In front of this small temple can be seen the altar, and opposite it remains of the Mycenaean walls. The temple platform was originally surrounded by a balustrade, of which there are some fragments in the Acropolis Museum.

★Temple of Athena Nike (at present closed)

The present state of the Propylaia and the temple of Athena Nike is the result of restoration work in the 19th and 20th centuries. Both buildings had suffered from alterations from the 13th c. onwards to serve as the residence of the commander of the stronghold and as part of its defences.

Beyond the Propylaia the ground slopes gently uphill. Passing the shrine of Artemis Brauronia and the Chalkotheke, which houses a collection of bronzes, we come to the Parthenon, the temple of Athena the Virgin (Athena Parthenos), built between 447 and 438 BC. This was the master work of the architect Ictinus and the great sculptor Pheidias, who was entrusted by Pericles with the general direction of the building works on the Acropolis.

★★Parthenon (at present closed)

The Parthenon they built was based on an earlier building on the same site. The new building was longer and broader than the old one, with 8 instead of 6 columns on the ends and 17 instead of 16 along the sides. The Doric columns are 10.43 m (34 ft) high, with a diameter of 1.9 m (6 ft 3 in.) at the foot and 1.48 m (4 ft 10 in.) at the top. Note the entasis (swelling) of the columns and the curvature of the substructure (rising slightly towards the middle): features designed to relieve the rigidity and solidity of the building. The western part of the Parthenon, with a roof borne on four Ionic columns, housed the city's treasury. At the east end was the chryselephantine (gold and ivory) statue of Athena Parthenos, a masterpiece by Pheidias, which was surrounded on three sides by a two-storey colonnade.

No less celebrated than the cult statue was the **sculpture** round the exterior of the Parthenon – on the two pediments, the Doric metopes and the frieze running round the upper part of the cella wall. Parts of this are in the Acropolis Museum, and there are some fragments in the Louvre in Paris, but most of it is in the British Museum in London – the "Elgin marbles", taken to Britain in 1801 by Lord Elgin. There are copies in the Centre for Acropolis Studies. The sculpture in the pediments, which was completed in 432 BC, depicts the birth of Athena from Zeus's head (east end) and the conflict between Athena and Poseidon for the land of Attica (west end). In the east pediment are copies of Dionysus and the heads of the sun god's horses and the moon goddess (in the corners), in the west pediment king Cecrops and one of his daughters. The 92 metopes depict a fight with giants (east), a fight with centaurs (south; the best preserved section), a battle with Persians (or possibly Amazons; west) and the Trojan War (north).

Porch of the Caryatids, Erechtheion

★★Erechtheion (at present closed)

The Erechtheion, on the north side of the Acropolis, was built between 421 and 406 BC. It incorporates a number of very ancient sanctuaries, and its complicated ground plan reflects the need to take account of these earlier structures. The eastern part was occupied by a temple containing a wooden cult figure of Athena Polias, patroness of the city. In the western part of the Erechtheion were the tombs of king Erechtheus, who gave his name to the whole structure, and Cecrops, the mythical founder of the Athenian royal line. The tomb of Cecrops lay under the Porch of the Caryatids that projects on the south side of the Erechtheion, its entablature borne by six figures of maidens (caryatids: originals in Acropolis Museum). Under the north portico is a representation of Poseidon's trident. The east and north porticoes each have six Ionic columns. On the outer side of the cella wall, above elegant palmette ornament, is a frieze of grey Eleusinian marble on which are set white marble figures.

★★Acropolis Museum

The Acropolis Museum was built in 1949–53 at the south-east corner of the Acropolis, lying so low that it does not obtrude. It contains the most valuable collection of Greek art in existence. At the entrance is a large owl, the symbol of Athena (5th c. BC). The rooms to the left contain material of the archaic period (6th c. BC), which was found buried under the "Persian rubble". It includes the pediments of temples and treasuries, among them a pediment of painted poros (No. 1; 600 BC) depicting Heracles fighting the Lernaean hydra. Among the exhibits in the rooms to the right are figures from the marble pediment of the old temple of Athena (Rooms I–V).

Room IV is particularly rich in masterpieces. Among them are several works by the sculptor Phaedimus, including the Rampin Horseman (No. 590), whose head is a plaster cast (original in Louvre); along with another figure of a horseman that is preserved only in fragments, it formed a part of the earliest known equestrian group in Greece. It is believed to represent the sons of Peisistratus, Hippias and Hipparchus, or possibly the Dioscuri (550 BC). A famous mature work by the same sculptor is the Peplos Kore, named after the Dorian garment she wears (No. 679; c. 530 BC).

Central features in the rear part of Room IV are the korai (7th–5th c. BC) – maidens wearing the peplos and later the richer chiton, and usually also a cloak (himation). As a rule they are depicted gathering up their garment with one hand and holding an offering in the other. They were originally painted, and some traces of the painting can still be seen, mainly on their garments.

Rooms VI–IX in the right-hand wing contain mainly sculpture of the classical age (5th c. BC). Among famous pieces of the early classical period are the "Fair-Haired Youth", a figure of unusual melancholy beauty (No. 689: shortly before 480 BC) and a relief of "Mourning Athena" (No. 695: 460–450 BC). Here too are reconstructions of the two pediments of the Parthenon, a number of fragments of the Parthenon frieze (originally 1.05 m (3 ft 5 in.) high, with a total length of 160 m (525 ft)) and parts of the Erechtheion frieze (409–405 BC). In the last room is an idealised portrait of the young Alexander (No. 1331; 335 BC). Also in this room are the originals of the caryatids of the Erechtheion.

Relief, Mourning Athena

Areopagus

In ancient times a path (known from an inscription to have been called the Peripatos) ran round the Acropolis crag, and this can still be followed. Turning left below the exit from the Acropolis, you come, before reaching the path along the northern slope, to the Areopagus (from Areios pagos, the Hill of Ares), to which a flight of steps leads up. (Take care: the rock is extremely slippery as well as steep). This 115 m (377 ft) crag was the meeting place of the supreme court of Athens. Here, too, in Mycenaean times, as Aeschylus relates in his "Eumenides", Orestes stood trial for the murder of his mother Clytaemnestra. The goddess Athena herself secured his acquittal: whereupon the Erinnyes or Furies who had been relentlessly pursuing him turned into the Eumenides or "Kindly Ones".

Chapter 17 of the Acts of the Apostles (verses 22–31) records the address that the Apostle Paul gave to the "men of Athens" on this ancient sacred site, referring to Christ as the "unknown god" whom they worshipped. A modern bronze tablet (to the right of the steps up the hill) is inscribed with this text. On the northern slopes of the Acropolis are the remains of a basilica dedicated to Dionysius, a member of the Areopagus who was the first of Paul's converts in Athens.

From the Areopagus there is a magnificent view of the Propylaia and an excellent general view of the Agora.

South side of the Acropolis

The south side of the Acropolis is rich in important monuments extending from prehistoric times to the 2nd c. AD and indeed into Early Christian times. In the 6th c. BC Peisistratus brought the cult of Dionysus

Trolleybuses 1, 5, 9 from Sýntagma to Makriyiani

from Eleutherai in the Kithairon hills (on the road to Thebes) to Athens, and accordingly Dionysus became known as Dionysus Eleuthereus. A temple was built to house the old cult image from Eleutherai.

★Theatre of Dionysus

Open
8.30am–2.30pm

The Theatre of Dionysus – of which there is a very fine view from the south wall of the Acropolis – was built in a natural hollow on the slopes of the Acropolis and was associated with the cult of Dionysus, the god of drunkenness and ecstasy, of transformation and of masks. It was originally built in the 6th c. BC, but the 67 rows of stone seats (accommodating an audience of 17,000) were installed only around 330 BC. The rows of seats are separated by transverse gangways into three sections. In the first row are the seats of honour, with inscriptions naming the occupants. In the centre is the seat reserved for the priest of Dionysus Eleuthereus, and behind it the seat for the Emperor Hadrian. Round it are holes for posts supporting a canopy. The semicircle of the seating area (the theatron) surrounds the orchestra ("dancing place") on which the actors performed, and round the orchestra is a stone barrier for protection from the wild beasts that took part in shows in Roman times. The stage building to the south was much rebuilt in later times. The striking reliefs with figures of Dionysus date from the Roman period, and, according to recent research were reused in an orator's rostrum of the 5th c. AD.

Greek tragedy The importance of the Theatre of Dionysus lies in the fact that it was built at the time when tragedy was being created in Athens. The first drama was produced by Thespis, who travelled round Greece with his company in a waggon. The early form in which a single actor performed with a chorus was the beginning of a development that led in the 5th c. BC to the brilliant flowering of Greek tragedy. The works of the three great Attic tragedians Aeschylus, Sophocles and Euripides were first performed in the Theatre of Dionysus in celebration of the Dionysiac cult. Thus this theatre became the birthplace and origin of the European theatre. See also Art and Culture, The Greek Theatre.

Stoa of Eumenes

Adjoining the Theatre of Dionysus on the west is the 163 m (535 ft) long Stoa of Eumenes, built by King Eumenes II of Pergamon (197–159 BC), who not only erected magnificent buildings in his own city (the Great Altar of Pergamon) but also sought to do honour to Athens. Unlike the Stoa of Attalus in the Agora (see below) the Stoa of Eumenes was not designed for the purposes of business but was merely a spacious promenade for visitors to the temple and theatre of Dionysus. The stoa was a two-storey structure with Doric columns on the exterior and Ionic columns in the interior, with capitals of Pergamene type on the upper floor. Since the stoa was built against the slope of the hill, it was protected by a retaining wall supported by piers and round arches; the arcades, originally faced with marble, can still be seen.

Asklepieion

On a terrace above the Stoa of Eumenes is the Asklepieion, the sanctuary of the healing god Asclepius, whose cult was brought from Epidaurus to Athens, where it was centred on a spring, in 420 BC. Built against the rock face was a 50 m (164 ft) long two-storey stoa (4th c. BC) to house the sick who came here to seek a cure. Within this was the cave containing the spring, which is still credited with curative qualities.

★Odeion of Herodes Atticus

On the west of the Stoa of Eumenes is the Odeion of Herodes Atticus, built by him after the death of his wife Regilla in AD 161. Herodes Atticus, who was born in Marathon in AD 101 and died there in 177, rose to high office in the reigns of the Emperors Hadrian and Antoninus Pius, and was one of the great art patrons of antiquity. He had a great reputation as a rhetor, but as a writer he was quickly forgotten. The Odeion, which is excellently preserved, was incorporated in the defences of the medieval castle. It is used for dramatic performances and concerts with

leading artists during the Athens Festival (open only during performances). There is a good view of the Odeion from the road up to the
Acropolis.

South-east of the Acropolis, at the Makriyiani bus stop (and the site of a
new metro station), is the old Military Hospital of 1836, which since 1976
has been the headquarters of the Greek Archaeological Service. Here too
is the Centre for Acropolis Studies (open 9am–3pm), which has very
interesting displays illustrating ancient building techniques and the restoration work on the Acropolis, together with copies of the Parthenon
friezes and pediments and models of the planned new Acropolis
Museum.

*Centre for
Acropolis Studies*

*Agorá

To the north-west of the Acropolis are three large open areas – the Greek
Agora, the Roman Agora and the Library of Hadrian. A good general
impression of the Agora, the state market place of ancient Athens, can
be obtained from: the north wall of the Acropolis and the Areopagus.
The layout of the Agora can best be appreciated by entering the site at
the north gate, off Adrianoú Street (opposite the church of St Philip), and
consulting the plan displayed just inside the entrance.

*Metro Thisio and
Monastiraki*

History The Agora, which was excavated by American archaeologists
between 1931 and 1960, is now part of a spacious park. From Mycenaean

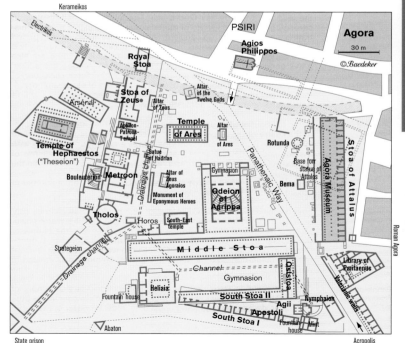

times until the end of the 7th c. BC this was a cemetery area. It began to be used as an agora in 6th c., in the time of Solon. Thereafter it remained for many centuries the centre of the city's public life, each century erecting new buildings, frequently at the expense of earlier ones.

Panathenaic Way

From the north entrance there is a general view of the spacious square area of the Agora, bounded on the east by the Stoa of Attalus and on the west by the Agora Hill, on which is the well preserved Temple of Hephaestus. The Agora is traversed diagonally by the Panathenaic Way, which preserves remains of the ancient paving. On the occasion of the Great Panathenaic Festival the ceremonial procession, coming from the Kerameikos, crossed the Agora on its way up to the Acropolis.

Stoa of Attalus

The 116 m (381 ft) long Stoa of Attalus was built by King Attalus II of Pergamon (159–138 BC), brother and successor of Eumenes II, who built the Stoa of Eumenes on the southern slopes of the Acropolis. It was (and is, following a faithful reconstruction of the original building in 1953–56) two storeyed. The front has Doric columns on the lower floor and Ionic on the upper floor. The stoa proper, behind which are a series of (originally 21) square rooms, is divided into two aisles by Ionic columns. It now houses the Agora Museum.

In front of the Stoa of Attalus, near the north end, are the remains of a small hall and a circular fountain house. Half way along are an orator's rostrum and a base that bore a statue of Attalus.

★Agora Museum

The exhibits in the stoa begin at the south end with a colossal statue of Apollo Patroos (4th c. BC), which Pausanias attributed to the sculptor Euphranor. Opposite the second column are two statues representing the Iliad and the Odyssey (2nd c. AD). The long main hall displays in chronological order a variety of material that is of great interest as illustrating everyday life in ancient Athens. The Mycenaean period (1500–1100 BC) is represented by vases and grave goods, including two ivory caskets with reliefs of a gryphon and a nautilus. There are also grave goods of the early Iron Age (11th–8th c. BC). Among items illustrating life in the 5th c. BC are inscriptions, a machine for the selection of public officials by lot, potsherds used in the process of ostracism (including one inscribed with the name of Themistocles: case 38), a child's pottery chamber pot and domestic equipment.

Odeion of Agrippa

Three tall figures of tritons mark the entrance to the Odeion of Agrippa, in the centre of the Agora to the north of the central stoa. Built around 20 BC by the Roman general Agrippa, it was a rectangular building with a stage and 18 tiers of seats that could accommodate an audience of around 1000 (some remains preserved). A new entrance was built on the north side in the 2nd c. AD.

To the west, beyond a large channel, the Great Drain, are a number of other important buildings.

Metroon, Bouleuterion

First comes a tholos with a diameter of 18.3 m (60 ft), which once contained the sacred hearth and the meeting place of the 50 *prytaneis* (senators) of Athens (c. 465 BC). To the north is the Metroon, the temple of the Mother of the Gods, beyond which is the Bouleuterion (Council Chamber; 5th c. BC), in which the Council of Five Hundred met. In front of the Bouleuterion and the Metroon a row of columns was erected in the 2nd c. BC.

Temple of Apollo Patroos

The next building (also reduced to its foundations) is the Temple of Apollo Patroos (4th c. BC), the cult image from which is now in the Stoa of Attalus. An adjoining building housed the oldest register of the population of Athens.

Stoa of Zeus

Between this point and the Metro (underground) line extended the Stoa

View from the Acropolis of the Agora, with the Temple of Hephaestus

of Zeus Eleutherios (Zeus who maintains the freedom of the city), the
northern part of which was destroyed during the construction of the railway line. It was built around 430 BC, probably by Mnesicles, the architect
of the Propylaia. In front of it, on a circular base, stood a statue of Zeus
Eleutherios. In Roman times an extension was built on the rear of the
stoa, perhaps for the cult of the Emperor. Pausanias tells us that the Stoa
of Zeus contained a number of paintings, including depictions of the
Twelve Gods, Theseus and the battle of Mantinea.

It used to be thought that the Stoa of Zeus was identical with the Royal
Stoa, now known to be a different building.

The Royal Stoa, like the Stoa of Zeus, had projecting wings at each end.   Royal Stoa
It was built soon after 480 BC and was on a considerably smaller scale
than the Stoa of Zeus (18 m (59 ft) by 6.2 m (20 ft)). This was the seat of
the archon basileus, the official on whom some of the religious functions
of the earlier kings had devolved. These included taking part in the trial
of those accused of impiety. It thus seems probable that this was the
scene of the trial of Socrates about 399 BC, when he was condemned to
death by drinking hemlock. Here too Socrates may have spoken in his
defence against the charge of leading the young men of Athens astray,
as recorded in Plato's "Apology".

From the Tholos a footpath runs up the Agora Hill (Kolonos Agoraios),   ★★Hephaisteion
on which stands the Temple of Hephaestus. The erroneous name of
Theseion still persists (and is perpetuated by the name of the nearby
station on the Piraeus railway); but the situation of the real Theseion, in
which the remains of the Attic hero Theseus were deposited after being
brought back by Cimon from the island of Skyros in 475 BC, remains
unknown. The Hephaisteion, lying near the craftsmen's quarter of
Athens, was dedicated to the divinities of the smiths and the arts,

One of the Plaka's many tavernas

Hephaestus and Athena. It is one of the best preserved of surviving Greek temples, thanks to the conversion into a Christian church that saved it from destruction. This Doric temple, with the classical plan of 6 by 13 columns, was built about the same time as the Parthenon but is considerably smaller.

The damaged frieze in the pronaos depicts battle scenes: on the west frieze a battle between Lapiths and centaurs, with the invulnerable Lapith Kaineus being borne to the ground by centaurs in the centre. In the cella, small as it was, there were columns surrounding statues of Hephaestus and Athena by Alcamenes, set up here in 420 BC. During the conversion of the temple into a Christian church dedicated to St George the original wooden roof structure was replaced by the barrel vaulting still to be seen. When King Otto entered the new capital of Greece in 1834 he attended a solemn service in the church. This was the last service held in the church, which thereafter became a museum.

★Plaka

The oldest part of modern Athens, the Plaka (the "flat area"), lies between the northern slopes of the Acropolis, Ermou (Hermes) Street in the north and the Filellinon and Amalias avenues to the east. It is now a busy tourist area that seems to consist of nothing but tavernas and souvenir shops; but the narrow streets and squares with their modest neoclassical houses, a few tiny Byzantine churches and various ancient remains have a very agreeable and attractive atmosphere. The Plaka is now scheduled as a national monument; pedestrian areas have been established and discotheques are banned. It is a relatively small area that can be explored on foot without difficulty and great enjoyment. The following route is suggested as a good way of getting to know the area.

The area round Monastiráki Square is one of the most colourful and chaotic in Athens, with street traders and traditional tavernas contributing to the Oriental atmosphere. It takes its name ("little monastery") from the former convent church of the Pantánassa (17th c.). Two old-world bazaar streets lead out of the square: to the west is Ifestou (Hephaestus) Street, which leads to Avissinias (Abyssinia) Square, to the east Pandrosou Street, which is very much a tourist street; the western part of it (flea market on Sundays) has preserved more of its original character.

Monastiráki Square

Beyond the Tsisdarakis Mosque (now a museum displaying traditional ceramics, the Kyriakopoulos Collection; open daily 9am–2.30pm) can be seen the Corinthian columns of the library founded by the Emperor Hadrian at some time after AD 132 (restored). The entrance is in Eólou (Aeolus) Street, to the east, which opens off Pandrosou Street. The Library was a colonnaded court measuring 122 m (400 ft) by 82 m (270 ft), with exedrae (semicircular recesses) in the external walls. Part of the west side is still standing. The central room in the eastern range of buildings was the actual library, with recesses in which the book rolls were kept. The building as a whole was not designed for business purposes, and the central courtyard was laid out as a garden, with a pool in the centre. The columns in the courtyard belonged to the 5th c. church of the Megáli Panayía.

Library of Hadrian

Eólou Street – from which there is a fine view of the Acropolis and its north wall (into which are built ancient column drums) – leads to the Tower of the Winds. This octagonal tower, 12 m (40 ft) high, was built by a Syrian named Andronicus around 40 BC, and is in an excellent state of preservation. It contained a water clock that showed the time of day by the level of water in a cylinder. The tower takes its name from the reliefs of the eight wind gods. Below the reliefs are sundials.

Tower of the Winds

At the end of Eólou Street is the Roman Market (open Tue.–Sun. 8.30am–2.45pm), a rectangle measuring 112 m (367 ft) by 96 m (315 ft). It has two entrances, a Doric gateway built between 12 BC and AD 2 on the west side and an Ionic propylon, probably dating from the reign of Hadrian (2nd c. AD), on the east side. Colonnades run round the interior, with shops and offices to the rear; on the south side is a fountain. On the north side of the market is the Fethiye Mosque (15th c.), now used as an archaeological store.

Roman Market

Tholou Street leads to the house in which Stamatios Kleanthis, who along with Eduard Schaubert planned the layout of the new town of Athens, lived in 1832–33. It was the first home, from 1837 to 1842, of Athens University, and now houses the University Museum (open Mon., Wed. 2.30–7pm, Tue., Thu., Fri. 9.30am–2.30pm); among the exhibits are historic anatomical drawings and a collection of surgical implements.

Kleanthis House

The Kleanthis House is in the Anafiotika, the district occupied by the building workers from the island of Anáfi, men noted for their craftsmanship, who were brought in by King Otto to build his new capital. The incomers built their own village in the highest part of the Plaka, which still preserves the atmosphere of a little town in the Cyclades.

★Anafiotika

At the end of Lysicrates Street is a park, on the edge of which is the Monument of Lysicrates. The walls of this 6.5 m (21 ft) high rotunda are articulated by Corinthian columns. The frieze that runs round the building under the roof depicts scenes from the life of Dionysus. The stone acanthus flower on the roof originally bore a bronze tripod, a prize won

Monument of Lysicrates

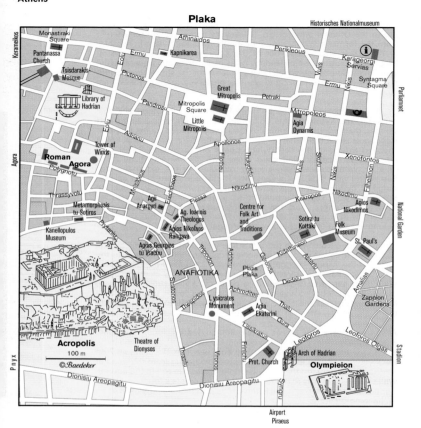

Plaka

by Lysicrates when the choir that he had financed was victorious in the
tragedy competition in 334 BC.

★Little Mitrópolis

In the north of the Plaka is busy Mitrópolis Square, in which are the old and
the new principal churches of Athens. The Little Mitrópolis, which is dedicated to St Eleutherius, is a finely proportioned domed cruciform church
with four columns (12th c.). Built into its outer walls are many fragments
taken from ancient and medieval buildings. Over the entrance are two
parts of a calendar frieze of the 4th c. BC. There are also pilaster capitals,
above which are the arms of the Villehardouin and de la Roche families
(13th c.); below are Byzantine reliefs with Christian symbols (9th–10th c.).

Modern Athens

History Modern Athens dates from the reign of Otto I, a scion of the
Bavarian royal house (1834–62), who converted a backward little village
into the capital of Greece. In 1832–33, when the Greek government was

still based in Nafplia, the German architect Eduard Schaubart and his friend Stamatios Kleanthis drew up a plan for the development of a new town to the north of the old town, which lay for the most part between Omónia, Sýntagma and Monastiráki Squares.

New town From Platía Omónias (Concord Square), on which it was originally intended to site the royal palace, three streets fan out: Odós Athinas (Athens Street) runs south to Monastiráki Square, with views of the Acropolis; Piraeus Street runs south-west; and Stadiou Street and, parallel to it, Venizélos Street (also known as Panepistimiou, or University Street) runs south-east. To these Leo von Klenze added a cross street, Ermou (Hermes) Street, in 1834. In the laying out of this street the Kapnikaréa Church was preserved at the king's express wish, making a Christian monument a central feature of the new town.

At the east end of Ermou and Stadiou Streets is the large square that since the 1843 revolution has been known as Sýntagma (Constitution) Square. In this square was built in 1834–38 the royal palace of Otto I and his queen Amalia, which has been occupied since 1935 by the Greek Parliament (Vouli). Designed by Friedrich von Gärtner, it stands at the highest point in the square, dominating the square and the ministries, hotels and office blocks that surround it. In front of the Parliament building is the Tomb of the Unknown Soldier, guarded by evzones, who perform the picturesque changing of the guard every hour.

Sýntagma Square

The **Grande Bretagne Hotel** on the north side of the square still preserves an air of old-world grandeur. With luxurious rooms and a first-class restaurant, it is one of Europe's legendary Grand Hotels. Built in 1842–43 by Theofil Hansen as the residence of a wealthy Greek exile and converted into a hotel in 1874, it became a centre of European politics, for example as the seat of the first Olympic Committee and, during the Second World War, the headquarters of the German army.

A first impression of modern Athens and the efforts made during the reigns of Otto I and George I to make Athens a worthy national capital can be gained by walking along Venizélos Street (Odós Venizélou), also known as Panepistimiou (University) Street.

Venizélos Street

While enjoying a coffee outside the renowned Café Dionysos (Zonar's) visitors have a view of the mansion in Italian Renaissance style built for Heinrich Schliemann and his Greek wife Sophia by Ernst Ziller in 1879, which Schliemann called Iliou Melathron, the **"Palace of Troy"**. It is planned to establish a Schliemann Museum, which will also display the coin collection of the National Archaeological Museum, in the house.

The showpieces of Venizélos Street are the three elegant but distinctly academic buildings known as the "Athens trilogy": the ★**University** (by the Copenhagen architect Christian Hansen, 1837–52), which is flanked by two imposing buildings designed by his younger brother Theofil, the ★**Academy of Science** (1859–85; to the right) and the **National Library** (1887–1902; to the left). The frescos on the University and the Academy were the work of the Bavarian artist Karl Rahl. In front of the Academy are two columns bearing statues of Athena and Apollo, and the steps leading up to the entrance are flanked by seated figures of Plato and Socrates. Apart from these buildings the pattern of Venizélos Street is set by modern office blocks, between which are squeezed occasional remains of the original two-storey buildings in neoclassical style.

Venizélos Street ends in the hectically busy traffic roundabout of Omónia Square.

The National Archaeological Museum (Patission 44; Metro station Viktoria; open Mon. 12.30–7pm, Tue.–Fri. 8am–7pm, Sat., Sun.

★★National
Archaeological
Museum

8.30am–3pm), built between 1860 and 1889 to the design of Ludwig Lange and Ernst Ziller, houses the world's largest collection of ancient Greek art. Several visits are needed to get anything approaching a complete idea of its riches. The entrance hall is the starting point of a tour of the collections, which are arranged in chronological order, beginning with the Geometric period (9th–8th c. BC) and continuing with the Archaic period (7th–6th c.), the classical period (5th–4th c.), the Hellenistic period (3rd–1st c. BC) and the Roman period.

Zeus hurling his thunderbolt

Straight ahead from the entrance hall (2) is the **Mycenaean Hall (4)**, with Schliemann's finds from Mycenaean sites (1600–1150 BC). In case 3, in the front part of the hall, is the gold mask of a king from Tomb V , the so-called "Mask of Agamemnon" (No. 624; c. 1580 BC). To the left of the Mycenaean Hall is the **Neolithic Hall (5)**, with material from sites in Central Greece, Thessaly, Lemnos and Troy, including Dimini (4th millennium BC), Sesklo (3rd millennium BC) and Orchomenos (3rd–2nd millennium BC). Room 3 contains Mycenaean material from Central Greece, Thessaly and Skópelos (15th–11th c. BC).

Room 6 contains finds from the Cyclades. Characteristic examples of the highly developed art of the Cycladic culture are the "Cycladic idols" with folded arms, the Cycladic "frying pans", the harpist and the musician playing a double flute from Amorgós (2300 BC) and, at the far end of the room, the flying fish frescos from Fylakopí on Melos (16th c. BC).

Kolonáki

Between Leofóros Vas. Sofias and Likavitós is the select district of Kolonáki, with handsome neoclassical villas now occupied by ministries and embassies. Round Platía Filikis Eterias, as Kolonáki Square is officially known, are upmarket shops and cafés. On Leofóros Vas. Sofias are some of the most important museums in Athens.

★Byzantine Museum (partly closed during reconstruction)

The Byzantine Museum (Vas. Sofias 22; open Tue.–Sun. 8.30am–3pm) occupies the palace built for the Duchesse de Plaisance by Kleanthis in 1840, on a site that was then outside the town. It contains a valuable collection of Byzantine art from the 4th to the 19th c. In the forecourt are architectural fragments from Early Christian basilicas and Byzantine churches (5th–15th c.). The wings to left and right contain a large collection of icons. The rooms on the ground floor of the main building illustrate the development of the church interior; the exhibits include a scale model of an Early Christian basilica (5th–6th c.) with a templon (the screen between the sanctuary and the rest of the church), a Byzantine domed cruciform church (10th–11th c.) and a post-Byzantine church with a carved and gilded iconostasis (17th–18th c.). On the upper floor are more icons, including a mosaic icon of the Mother of God Episkepsis (14th c.), as well as Gospels, documents (a gold Bull of the Emperor Andronicus II dated 1301), gold jewellery from Lésbos (Room 2) and liturgical vestments and utensils.

War Museum

Adjoining the Byzantine Museum is the War Museum (Vas. Sofias 24; open Tue.–Sun. 9am–2pm), which displays weapons and equipment from the Stone Age to the Second World War and commemorates wars in which Greece played an important part (e.g. the Persian wars, the battle of Navarino).

★Benaki Museum (at present closed)

The Benaki Museum (Vas. Sofias/Koumbari) developed out of the private collection of Antonios Benakis, the son of a wealthy cotton dealer. The

110

collection, on three floors, includes mementoes of the Greek war of Independence (1821), objects that belonged to kings Otto and George I, Byron and various freedom fighters, letters (including some by Yeóryios Seféris), icons (two attributed to El Greco), beautiful Greek costumes, ancient pottery, Islamic and East Asian material.

The Museum of Cycladic and Ancient Greek Art (Neofitou Douka 4; open Mon., Wed.–Fri. 10am–4pm, Sat. 10am–3pm) is centred on the famous collection assembled by the shipowner Nikolaos P. Goulandris. It displays masterpieces of the Cycladic culture (3200–2000 BC), including the almost abstract figurines of which copies are now sold on an immense scale as souvenirs, and pottery, bronzes and glassware from the Geometric to the post-classical period. In Stathatos House, which was incorporated in the Museum in 1992, is displayed the Academy's collection of ancient Greek art.

★Cycladic Museum

From Dexamíni Square (some 200 metres north of Kolonáki Square) paths run between pines and cypresses to the summit of Likavitós (Lykabettos; 277 m (909 ft)); it can also be reached by road or funicular (from the upper end of Ploutarkhou Street). According to the ancient myth, Athena was carrying a great stone to increase the height of the Acropolis when she heard of the fate of Cecrops's daughters and dropped it here. On the summit are a café, a restaurant and the conspicuous chapel of St George. The site is believed to have been occupied in antiquity by a temple of Zeus Akraios, and in Frankish times the little church of Profítis Ilías was built here. There is also an open-air theatre in which jazz and rock concerts and theatrical performances are held during the Athens Festival. On clear days (which are rare) there is a fantastic view extending as far as the sea.

★★Likavitós

On Leofóros Vas. Sofias, 1.5 km (1 mi.) outside the town, is the Megaron, a concert hall opened in 1991 that is used for opera, ballet and theatrical performances as well as concerts.

Megaron

Parliament to the First Athenian Cemetery

The National Garden was established in 1838 on the initiative of Queen Amalia on a site south and east of the Palace, on what was then wasteland. It was designed by the botanist Karl Froos and laid out and developed until the 1860s by the court gardener Friedrich Schmidt. To the east of the National Garden, in Irodou Attikou (Herodes Atticus) Street, is the Crown Prince's Palace (by Ernst Ziller, 1898), later the residence of the king and now of the President of Greece.

National Garden

On the south side of the National Garden are the **Zappeion Gardens**, with the Zappeion, a neoclassical building (by Theofil Hansen and Ernst Ziller, 1874–88) designed for exhibitions and congresses.

To the west of the Olympieion, confronting the heavy traffic on Leofóros Amalias, is the Arch of Hadrian (AD 131–132), which marks the boundary between ancient Athens and the Roman extension of the city. On one side of the arch is the inscription "This is the city of Theseus" and on the other "This is the city of Hadrian".

Arch of Hadrian

When Odós Syngrou, the road from Athens to Piraeus, was laid out in the 19th c. it was so designed as to lead to two massive columns belonging to the Olympieion, the temple of Olympian Zeus, which still dominates the area to the east of the Acropolis (open Tue.–Sun. 8.30am–3pm). This – the largest temple in Athens – dates from the time of the Peisistratids. The Seleucid ruler Antiochus IV (175–164 BC) resumed work on the building, but it was only completed in AD 130, in

★Olympieion

The mighty columns of the Olympieion, the largest Greek temple

the reign of Hadrian. Its construction thus extended over a period of no less than 700 years.

As an expression of the taste of the tyrants, a Syrian king and a Roman Emperor, the Olympieion ran completely counter to the Attic feeling for measure. In architectural quality it is still overshadowed by the Acropolis. It has lost the cella, which contained a cult image of Zeus and a statue of Hadrian, and most of its 104 columns, which required 15,500 tons of marble; but the surviving group of 13 columns at the south-east corner is of imposing magnificence. On the south side are two columns still standing and another that collapsed in 1852. It is uncertain whether the 13 columns at the south-east corner date from the Hellenistic period and the three on the south side from Roman times or whether they are all from the Roman building.

★Stadion

To the east of the Olympieion, between two hills, is the Stadion. The present structure of Pentelic marble, with seating for 70,000 spectators, is modern, but it is in the same form and on the same site as its ancient predecessor, in which the sporting contests of the Panathenaic Festival were held. It was rebuilt in marble in AD 140–144 by Herodes Atticus, who was buried on the hill to the north. The modern Stadion was built in 1896 for the revived Olympian Games, with financial support from Yeoryios Averof of Metsovo, a private citizen who thus continued the ancient tradition of the *euergetes* (public benefactor).

First Athenian Cemetery

Immediately south of the Olympieion Anapáfseos Street ("Street of Repose") branches off Ardittou Street, a busy traffic artery, and runs up to the entrance hall of the cemetery. Just inside, on the left, are a chapel and the tombs of Archbishops of Athens and of Yeoryios Averof. On the slope beyond this is the tomb of Heinrich Schliemann (by Ernst Ziller, 1891).

Kerameikós

On the north-west side of the Agora, extending west to the Academy, is the potters' quarter of ancient Athens, Kerameikós (named after Keramos, the patron of potters), which has given us the term ceramics. The town wall built by Themistocles in 479 BC, after the Persian wars, divided the area into the districts of inner and outer Kerameikós. Only part of Kerameikós, the area lying along the line of the town walls between Hermes and Piraeus Streets, has been excavated. Here there were two gates. The Sacred Way to Eleusis ran through the Sacred Gate; and from this, within the excavated area, a road (the Street of Tombs) branched off to Piraeus. The larger gateway, the Dipylon, was the starting point of the 38 m (125 ft) wide road to the Academy, 1.5 km (1 mi.) away. The monumental funerary amphoras ("Dipylon vases") from this gate are now in the National Archaeological Museum. The present aspect of Kerameikós is dominated by funerary monuments of the 5th and 4th c. BC. Within the park-like excavated area are numerous individual tombs, family plots and terraces of tombs, partly originals but mostly copies.

Metro Thisio / Bus 025 from Sýntagma

The entrance to the Kerameikós Museum (open Tue.–Sun. 8.30am–3pm) is in Hermes (Ermou) Street. It displays a large collection of pottery ranging from the 10th to the 5th c. BC. The first room contains sculpture from tombs, including a relief of Ampharete with her grandchild (c. 410 BC), an equestrian relief of Dexileos, killed in a skirmish at Corinth in 394 BC, the archaic funerary stele of Eupheros (c. 500 BC), a sphinx as the guardian of a tomb and an equestrian statue.

★Kerameikós Museum

The Dipylon is the more northerly of the two gates and the one of greater architectural consequence. It was the largest of the town gates of ancient Athens. As the name indicates, it is double, with a small court between the two gates. Inside the inner gate are an altar of Zeus, Hermes and Akamas and a fountain house.

Dipylon

Between the Dipylon and the Sacred Gate, on the banks of the river Eridanos, was the Gymnasium (5th c. BC), usually called the Pompeion after the ceremonial procession (*pompe*) to the Acropolis on the occasion of the Panathenaic Festival, which assembled here. The building was destroyed by Sulla in 86 BC and replaced by a triple-aisled hall that in turn was destroyed during the raid by the Heruli in the 2nd c. AD.

Pompeion

From the Dipylon the 38 m (125 ft) wide road led to the Academy. The first academy in the world, this was from 387 BC the meeting-place of Plato and his pupils. Excavations beyond the railway line, between Efklidou (Euclid) and Tripoleos Streets, have brought to light the remains of a square hall and to the north of this a small temple, possibly dedicated to the hero Akademos, as well as a large building of the Roman period laid out round a central courtyard. A structure measuring 8.5 m (28 ft) by 4.5 m (15 ft), now roofed over, is the oldest building so far discovered in Athens (early Bronze Age, 2300–2100 BC).

Academy

From the site of the Academy Tripoleos Street runs north-west to the hill of Kolonos Hippios, which gave its name to the deme (district) of Kolonos, to which the tragedian Sophocles (496–406 BC) belonged. This was the setting of the play, "Oedipus on Kolonos", which he wrote at the age of 90. The hill is surrounded by an impoverished district of Athens.

Kolonos Hippios

Chíos   K/L 5

Islands of the northern and eastern Aegean

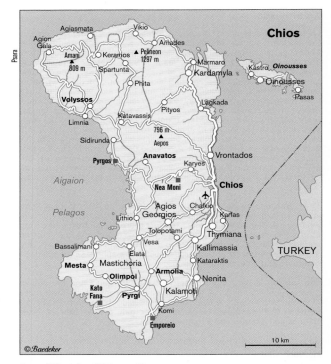

Area: 842 sq. km (325 sq. mi.)
Altitude: 0–1267 m (0–4157 ft)
Population: 54,000
Chief place: Chíos town

Airport 4 km (2½ mi.) south of Chíos (Χιος) town (no airport bus service). Air connections with Athens, Salonica and Mytilíni (Lésbos).
Shipping connections with Piraeus, Salonica and Kavála via Lémnos,
Sámos, Sýros, Lésbos, Inoússai and Çeşme (Turkey). Bus services on
the island.

The island of Chíos, still largely undisturbed by tourism, lies in the eastern Aegean, separated only by the 8 km (5 mi.) wide Strait of Chíos from
the Turkish peninsula of Çeşme, on the south side of the Gulf of Izmir.
Most of the island is occupied by a range of craggy limestone hills tra-
versing it from north to south. This reaches its highest point in Mount
Profítis Ilías (1267 m (4157 ft)), at the north end of the island, and falls
steeply down to the sea, forming impressive cliffs, particularly to the
east. The population is concentrated mainly in the fertile hilly southern
part of the island, where olives, vines, figs and citrus fruits are grown.
The island's major crop, however, is mastic, the aromatic resin of the
mastic or lentisk tree (*Pistacia lentiscus L.*), which was already being
exported in ancient times, making an important contribution to the
island's prosperity. The mastic is also used to make *mastikha*, a bitter-
sweet liqueur, and a rather sickly sweet.

The fortified mastic-growing villages on Chíos such as Olýmpi are reminders of the island's eventful past

Around a third of the Greek merchant fleet is based on Chíos. Many **shipowners** come from the island and the neighbouring island of Inoússai and still own magnificent villas here. The island is also favoured by leading Greek politicians, whose handsome holiday houses can be seen along the coast. Shipping brought the shipowners considerable wealth, but it also brought prosperity to the people of Chíos. Since above-average wages can be earned at sea, many inhabitants have built themselves large new houses. While the main source of income in the past was the production of mastic, this has now been overtaken by seafaring; tourism has played only a small part in the economy of the island. There are malicious suggestions that the shipowners and the politicians want to keep this beautiful island to themselves and have hindered the development of tourism. It is certainly true that facilities for getting to Chíos are poor. There are few charter flights to the island, and Olympic Airways' scheduled flights from Athens and Lésbos are often fully booked. There are only three or four connections a week with the neighbouring islands of Sámos and Lésbos (both 4½ hours sailing time) on the old ships of the Miniotis Line; and the ships either sail in the middle of the night and/or arrive around midnight. Moreover if the wind is force 6 or more they do not sail at all, resulting in a day's delay. Visitors to Chíos from Sámos or Lésbos should arrange for their return flight at least two days in advance.

Nevertheless the people of Chíos are highly skilled at getting subsidies from the **European Union**. New roads of almost motorway standard run through lonely mountain regions, carrying little traffic. Many stretches of road are still under construction. To the north of Chíos town, at Vrontádos, numerous yachting marinas are being constructed with EU subsidies; but not one of them has yet been completed, and only

occasional boats visit them. Visitors may well wonder whom these innumerable moorings are intended for when the flow of tourists is so
restricted. Another EU project is the thorough renovation of the island's
famous monastery, the Néa Moní. But the monastery is do dark that visitors cannot see the mosaics; and if they ask for lights to be switched on
they are asked to pay for the cost of current.

History Excavation has yielded evidence of human settlement reaching
back to the 4th millennium BC. In the 8th c. BC Ionian Greeks settled on
Chios and made it one of the wealthiest members of the Ionian League
of cities that was established around 700 BC. In the 6th c. BC an important school of sculptors was active on the island. From 512 to 479 Chios
was under Persian rule, and thereafter became a member of the Attic
maritime league, but was able to maintain its independence. In 392
Chios broke away from Sparta, and in 377 it became the first member of
the second Attic maritime league, but soon left it. Under the Romans,
with whom it sided in 190 BC, it still maintained its independence. Held
from 1204 to 1304 by the Venetians and later by the Genoese, Chíos
became Turkish in 1566. The popularity in the Sultan's harem of the
mastic that grew on the island and of the sweets made from it gave
Chíos a special status – although no Greeks were allowed to live within
the Turkish citadel. In addition to its mastic, Chíos was famed for its silk
weaving, which also contributed to the island's prosperity.

Throughout their eventful history, the people of Chíos showed themselves to be skilled seamen and shrewd businessmen. In 1822 they
rose against the Turks, who took a bloody revenge. In the notorious
massacres of Chíos, depicted in a famous painting by Eugène
Delacroix, 30,000 Christians were killed or enslaved, giving rise to a
wave of indignation in western Europe. Severe devastation was caused
by an earthquake in 1881 in which 6000 people lost their lives. In
November 1912, during the Balkan War, a Greek squadron appeared off
the island and captured it after a brief resistance by the Turks. After the
catastrophic Greek-Turkish war (1920–2) Chíos lost its economic hinterland in Turkey and had to give asylum to many Greeks expelled from
Asia Minor.

⋆Chíos town

The island's chief town and principal port, Chíos (pop. 30,000), lies
halfway down the east coast, roughly on the site of the ancient city. The
wide arc of the bay is picturesquely lined with street cafés, which are

*The great charm of Chíos town lies in the contrast between the lively
and colourful harbour front and the grey hills that form the backdrop*

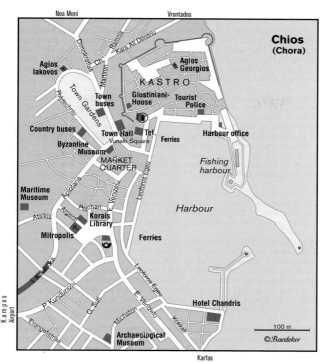

crowded with customers, particularly in the evening. Little is left of the old part of the town, since the houses that survived the 1822 massacre were mostly destroyed in an earthquake in 1881; but the town has preserved an agreeable Oriental air. The background of bare grey cliff-like hills forms a striking contrast with the colourful line of houses along the harbour front.

The heart of the town is Vounaki Square, surrounded by new office buildings, huge plane trees and numerous cafés. Close by are the bus station, the starting point of all local and country buses, and the central taxi rank. Immediately north-east of the square are the Town Gardens. Looking on to the gardens, at the corner of Odós Martyron, is a pretty Turkish fountain of 1768.

Vounaki Square

In Vounaki Square is a former mosque, complete with minaret, which now houses the Byzantine Museum. This displays a variety of objects and architectural fragments illustrating the medieval history of the island, together with a copy of Delacroix's painting, "The Massacres of Chios".

Byzantine Museum

To the east of Vounaki Square is the Porto Maggiore, the main entrance to the medieval fortress, the Kástro. Originally built by the Byzantines in the 10th c., it was strengthened by the Genoese in the 14th c. and was later used by the Turks as the seat of their administration. During the period of Turkish rule only Muslims and Jews were allowed to live

Kástro

within the town walls. The little Turkish cemetery with the marble grave-stones of dignitaries recalls these days. The palace of the former Venetian governor (15th c.) is now occupied by the Giustiniani Museum, with a small collection of Byzantine art and Early Christian pavement mosaics. To the east of the Turkish cemetery is the 10th c. Genoese church of Áyios Yeóryios, which was converted into a mosque in 1566. In front of the church is a Turkish sarcophagus that served as the ablution fountain of the mosque.

Korais Library

From the south-east corner of Vounaki Square the town's main shopping street, Odós Aplotarias, runs south-west. At the far end, on the left, is Odós F. Argentis, which leads to the Korais Library. The nucleus of the library, which now has some 135,000 volumes, was the large collection of books assembled by Adamantios Korais (1748–1833), scion of a Chian scholar who lived for many years in Paris. In the same building is the Argentis family's large collection of paintings and folk art, presented to Chíos by Filippos Argentis (bust in front of the building). The collection also includes some very beautiful embroidery and Chian costumes.

Archaeological Museum

In Odós Mikhalon, which opens off the seafront promenade, is the Archaeological Museum, which contains excavated material from the ancient sites of Emporió and Káto Fána (see below) and a letter of Alexander the Great's engraved on stone (332 BC).

Kámpos

In the plain to the south of the town, the fertile Kámpos, the wealthier Chians had, and still have, their handsome villas. Mostly of two or three storeys, they are surrounded by high walls and cannot be seen from the road. Imposing entrance gates lead into luxuriant gardens. Some of the houses have been restored and converted into attractive traditional inns. The best preserved of these mansions is that of Filippos Argentis, in Odós F. Argentis. Set in a large orange grove, it gives a picture of the way of life of the Genoese and native aristocracy.

Karfás

The road south from Chíos town runs past the airport and comes in 6 km (4 mi.) to Karfás (Καρφας), the island's tourist centre, which was established only in the 1960s. Until a few years ago a sleepy little hotel settlement, much of it covered by sand dunes, it now has all the amenities and facilities of a modern resort. The broad sandy beach slopes gently down to the sea and is particularly suitable for children.

★★Néa Moní

From Chíos town a panoramic road runs north-west by way of the colourful village of Karyés (15 km (9 mi.)) to the Néa Moní, a walled complex of buildings in a beautiful green hill setting now occupied only by a few nuns. The convent was founded by the Emperor Constantine IX Monomachus (1042–55) on the spot where a wonderworking icon of the Mother of God was found in a myrtle bush. It is notable for its magnificent mosaics on a gold ground – undoubtedly the work of artists from Constantinople – which rank with those at Dafní and Ósios Loukás as the finest surviving examples of 11th c. Byzantine religious art. The convent is at present being restored with funding from the European Union.

The dome of the Néa Moní church is borne, as at Dafní, on eight piers and spans the full width of the church. The walls still have their original facing of red marble. Some of the richly coloured mosaics were destroyed in the 1881 earthquake; in particular those on the dome, which collapsed, were lost. In subsequent restoration work the dome was rebuilt and the surviving mosaics made safe. Among the principal scenes depicted are the Baptism of Christ, the Crucifixion, the Descent from the Cross and the Descent into Limbo. In the main apse is the Mother of God, flanked by the Archangels Michael and Gabriel in the lat-

Convent of Néa Moní

eral apses. There are also fine mosaics in the narthex – the Washing of the Feet, the Mother of God surrounded by local saints, the Betrayal. All these mosaics date from the time of the convent's foundation (*c.* 1050) and are thus rather later than those of Ósios Loukás and rather earlier than those at Dafní. The frescos in the exonarthex (among them a Last Judgment) date from the late Byzantine period (14th c.).

The other conventual buildings were damaged during the Turkish punitive expedition of 1822, and many of them are now in a state of dilapidation. By the gateway of the convent is a chapel commemorating those who were killed in 1822; here too is a charnel house. Other notable features are the old refectory (*trápeza*) and a large cistern a few metres to the right of the main gateway. From the terrace of the new refectory (the one used by the nuns) there is a very beautiful view.

A few kilometres above the Néa Moní is the cave monastery of Tríon Patéron (the Three Fathers), which commemorates the three hermits who lived here and founded the Néa Moní. The church is dark and impressive. Women have only recently been allowed to enter it.
Tríon Patéron

A recently upgraded road continues north-west to the village of Anávatos (Ανάβατος), impressively situated under a steep crag crowned by a ruined castle, which has been almost derelict since 1822. Some houses have been restored (for use as holiday homes), as have the two churches in the upper part of the village.
Anávatos

Southern Chíos

The southern part of the island, unlike other Aegean islands, is a lush green landscape. The mountains are covered with dense pine forests

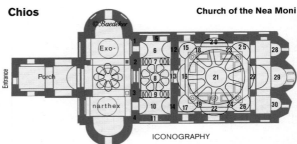

ICONOGRAPHY

1 Simeon the Stylite
2 Isaiah, Jeremiah
3 Daniel, Ezekiel, Simeon the Stylite
4 Daniel the Stylite
5 Washing of the feet
6 Entry into Jerusalem
7 Stephen the Younger, Ephraim, Arsenius, Nicetas,
   Anthony, Maximus, John Calybites
8 Mother of God (in centre);
   round her: Eustratius, Sergius,
   Theodore Stratelates, Bacchus, Orestes
   Mardarius, Eugenius, Auxentius;
   in corners: Joachim, Anne, Stephen
   Panteleimon
9 John of Studion, Theodosius, Euthymius,
   Menas, Pachomios, Sabbas,
   John Climacus
10 Pentecost
11 Prayer in the Garden,
   Betrayal

12 Raising of Lazarus
13 Christ Pantokrator
14 Ascension
15 Descent from the Cross
16 Philip, Crucifixion
17 Transfiguration
18 Mark
19 Luke, Bartholomew
20 Descent into Hades
21 Christ Patokrator with angels
22 Andrew, Baptism of Christ
23 Matthew
24 John the Theologian
25 Annunciation
26 Presentation of Jesus in the Temple
27 Nativity of Christ
28 Archangel Michael
29 Mother of God in prayer
   (Maria Orans)
30 Archangel Gabriel

and in the upland regions mastic, olives and citrus and other fruits are grown.

Pyryí

30 km (19 mi.) south-west of Chíos town is Pyryí (Πυργη; pop. 1300), the largest of the 20 mastic-growing villages in the Mastikhokhoriá, the mastic region. The houses are particularly attractive with their sgraffito decoration in geometric patterns and their strings of bright-red tomatoes hung up on the balconies to dry. Above the village is the tower of a Genoese castle. The church of the Áyii Apóstoli (12th c., with fine frescos of 1665) is modelled, like other churches on the island, on the church of the Néa Moní.

Emporió

8 km (5 mi.) south-west of Pyryí is the archaeological site of Káto Fána, with remains of a temple of Apollo. At the picturesque little port of Emporió (Εμπορειο) on the south coast were found a prehistoric settlement of the 7th c. BC and remains of a temple of Athena. The neighbouring beaches are of black shingle – the result of an eruption of lava by a long extinct volcano.

Olýmpi

From Pyryí a road runs north-west to the port of Ayía Anastasia or Bassalimani (43 km (27 mi.) from Chíos town). On the way there it passes the fortified medieval village of Olýmpi (Ολυμποι), with a little

Tomatoes hanging out to dry on a balcony in Pyryí

square now incongruously furnished with plastic chairs.

Beyond this is Mestá (Μεστα), the finest and most unspoiled fortified village on Chíos. It has an idyllic little square in which you can sit on the wooden seats of the two tavernas under the shade of huge trees. The town walls are formed by the outer ring of fortified houses. The 18th c. church of Palios Taxiarkhis has a fine carved iconostasis. The return to Chíos town is by way of Eláta and the medieval village of Vésa.

★Mestá

Northern Chíos and neighbouring islands

★**Scenery** North of Chíos town is the area known as the Vorlokhóra. In contrast to the fertile southern part of the island the hilly north is arid; but in the valleys of the rivers, which in summer are mostly dry, there are numbers of oasis-like settlements with luxuriant vegetation. Against their backdrop of bare crags these areas seem like a garden of Eden.

On the northern outskirts of the town is the villa suburb of Vrontádos (Βρονταδος), where many seagoing Chians have built houses. In 6 km (4 mi.) the road comes to a large block of dressed stone that is thought to have been a shrine of Cybele. This is popularly known as the Daskalópetra (Teacher's Stone) or Skholí Omírou (School of Homer) – recalling the island's claim to be the birthplace of Homer.

Vrontádos

Langáda (Λαγκαδα) (15 km (9 mi.)) is an attractive village at the end of a bay. Near here is the Delfinion, a site fortified by the Athenians in 412 BC. Beyond Kardámyla (27 km (17 mi.)), which has a pretty village square, is the little port of Mármaro; like the whole of the north coast, it is exposed in summer to the *meltémi* winds. The road continues round the north of the island, passing through Víkio and the picturesque village of Kéramos, to Áyion Gála (50 km (31 mi.)). At the entrance to a stalactitic cave is the 13th c. church of the Panayía Ayiougalosena. From Kéramos a road runs south to Vólyssos, passing a number of wind generators. Another road runs north-west from Chíos town along the northern slopes of Mount Marathovounos to Vólyssos (40 km (25 mi.)) and its harbour at Límnia. From Límnia there are boats to the island of Psará.

Langáda

North-east of the island of Chíos, at the north end of the Strait of Chíos, are the Inoússai Islands (Οινουσσαι), an archipelago extending north-west with a total land area of 14 sq. km (5½ sq. mi.). The only inhabited island is Inoússai (pop. 500). To the east of this are the islets of Pásas, Gaváthion and Váton and numerous isolated rocks. Inoússai is tiny, but

Inoússai Islands

it has beautiful beaches, an attractive village – the chief place on the island – with houses in neoclassical style, and good walking. In spite of these attractions it has very few visitors (there is only one hotel) because – so it is said – the wealthy shipowners want to live in their luxurious mansions undisturbed by strangers. Some 30 per cent of Greek shipowners have houses here.

In the north-west of the island is the convent of Evangelismos, established in the 1960s. A nun who had died young, the daughter of a shipowner, was buried here, and when her body was exhumed it was found to be mummified, which was taken as a sign of holiness. Her mother thereupon founded the convent.

Psará

The bare rocky island of Psará (Ψαρά), ancient Psyra, where Mycenaean tombs were found, lies 18 km (11 mi.) north-west of Chíos, rising to a height of 564 m (1850 ft). The chief place, also called Psará, is on the south coast, below a medieval castle. To the north-east is the monastery of the Dormition (Kímisis). Now impoverished and depopulated, Psará had a period of considerable prosperity in the 18th c., when the descendants of Albanians who had settled on the island in the 16th and 17th c. made it the third naval power in the Aegean, after Hydra and Spétses. The island's dilapidated old mansions and the stumps of windmills on the hills bear witness to this period, when Psará had a population of some 30,000. The former town hall is now a traditional hotel run by the Greek National Tourist Organisation (EOT). The islanders put up such a stubborn resistance to the Turks that a Turkish force invaded the island and completely depopulated it. After Psará became part of the new kingdom of Greece in the 19th c. it was resettled from Chíos.

Corfu   D/E 4

Ionian Islands
Area: 592 sq. km (229 sq. mi.)
Altitude: 0–906 m (0–2973 ft)
Population: 110,000
Chief place: Corfu town (Kérkyra)

Airport 5 km (3 mi.) south of Corfu town. Air connections with Athens and Salonica; many charter flights from Britain. Principal harbour: Corfu town. Direct flights from London and other UK airports. Shipping connections with Italy (Venice, Trieste, Brindisi, Bari, Ancona, Otranto), Igoumenítsa (also from Lefkimmi), Patrás, Paxí/Préveza, the Othonian Islands (from the north coast). Bus connections with Athens and Salonica. Bus services on the island.

Corfu (Kérkyra, Κερκυρα), the most important of the Ionian Islands both historically and from the point of view of the tourist trade, lies between 2.5 and 20 km (1½ and 12 mi.) off the coasts of Albania and the Greek region of Epirus. The beauty of its scenery, with gentle green hills in the south and rugged limestone hills in the north, rising to 906 m (2973 ft) in the bare double peak of Mount Pantokrátor, its mild climate and its luxuriant southern flora have made Corfu a popular holiday area since the period of British rule. In the past it was crowned heads who came here to enjoy the summer coolness: now it is swarms of tourists from far and wide, particularly from Britain. Along the east coast in particular there are strings of hotels; but most of the west coast is not yet built-up, and here visitors can find accommodation that is not mass-produced and many beautiful sandy beaches. The most attractive part of Corfu, however, is the interior, with remote little villages in which time seems to stand still and donkeys are still the regular mode of travel. After tourism agriculture is the islanders' main source of income.

History Corfu (known to the ancient Greeks as Korkyra) is believed to be the Homeric island of Scheria, home of the Phaeacians and their king Alcinous, where Odysseus was found on the beach by the beautiful Nausicaa. Colonised by Corinth in 734 BC, Korkyra developed into a considerable power that threatened Corinth itself. A Corinthian naval victory over Korkyra in 432 BC in the Sybota Islands was a major factor in the outbreak of the Peloponnesian War. In 229 BC it was occupied by the Romans, who called it Corcyra. In the division of the Roman Empire in AD 395 Corfu fell to the Eastern (Byzantine) Empire.

The medieval name of Corfu appears to be derived from the Greek name Koryphoi ("Peaks"). From 1386 to 1797 Corfu was held by the Venetians; then, after a brief period of French occupation, it passed to Britain in 1815 along with the rest of the Ionian Islands. It was returned to Greece in 1864. In the course of its eventful history Corfu suffered frequent devastation, so that most of its ancient and medieval remains have been destroyed.

Horse-drawn carriage in the old town of Corfu

★★Corfu town

The island's chief town is Kérkyra (pop. 30,000), beautifully situated on a promontory on the east coast. The ancient city lay further south on the Kanóni peninsula. Kérkyra is now the see of both a Greek Orthodox and a Roman Catholic archbishop. It has a very beautiful old town (Campiello), now protected as a national monument – the product of periods of Venetian, French and British rule on Greek foundations. Narrow winding lanes spanned by flying buttresses alternate with magnificent palazzos with grand arcading and fine wrought-iron balconies. There is no beach within the town, so that few visitors stay here for any length of time. As a result the town has been able to preserve its own particular charm.

At the north end of the town is the Old Port, now used only by small boats. It is dominated by the massive New Fort (1572–1645; open summer daily 9am–9pm), which since its restoration in 1994 has housed an art gallery and a café. It is worth a visit for the sake of its view of the old town.

New Fortress

From the harbour Odós Nikiforou Theotoki, the town's main shopping street, runs south-east to the Spianada (from Italian *spianata,* esplanade) between the town and the Old Fortress. The northern part of this open space is occupied by a cricket ground, while the southern half is a beautiful park shaded by tall trees. On the east side of the Spianada is a statue of Count Johann Matthias von der Schulenburg (1661–1747), who defended the town against the Turks in 1716.

Spianada

On the north side of the Spianada is the former Governor's Palace, in neoclassical style. It is also known as the Palace of St Michael and St George, since the residence of the British High Commissioner was also the headquarters of the Order of St Michael and St George, created in 1818. Between 1864 and 1913 the palace was the summer residence of the king of Greece. On the main front, facing the Spianada, is a Doric colonnade. On the frieze along the main part of the building are reliefs: in the centre Britannia, an allegorical figure personifying the benefits of

★Governor's Palace

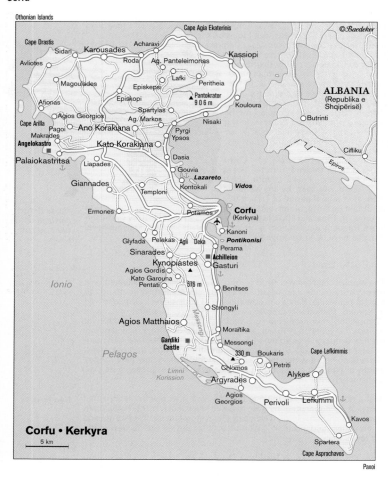

Othonian Islands

Cape Agia Ekaterinis

© *Baedeker*

Cape Drastis
Sidari
Karousades
Acharavi
Kassiopi

Avliotes
Roda
Ag. Panteleimonas

Magoulades
Episkepsi
Lafki
Peritheia

ALBANIA
(Republika e Shqipërisë)

Afionas
Episkopi
Pantokrator
906 m
Kouloura

Agios Georgios
Spartylas
Ag. Markos
Nisaki
Butrinti

Cape Arilla
Ano Korakiana
Pyrgi
Ypsos
Cifliku

Makrades
Pagoi

Angelokastro
Kato Korakiana
Epiros

Palaiokastritsa
Liapades
Dasia

Giannades
Gouvia
Lazareto

Temploni
Kontokali
Vidos

Ermones
Potamos

Corfu
(Kerkyra)

Kanoni

Glyfada
Pelekas
Agli
Deka
Pontikonisi

Sinarades
Perama

Kynopiastes
Achilleion

Agios Gordis
Gasturi

Kato Garouna
Pentati
676 m

Benitses

Strongyli

Agios Matthaios

Moraïtika

Gardiki
Castle
Messongi

Pelagos
330 m
Boukaris
Cape Lefkimmis

Limni Korission
Chlomos
Petriti
Alykes

Ionio

Argyrades

Agios Georgios
Perivoli
Lefkimmi

Kavos

Corfu • Kerkyra

5 km

Spartera
Cape Asprochavos

Paxoi

British rule, peace and prosperity, and to right and left the coats of arms of six of the Ionian Islands.

Museum of Asiatic Art

A visit to the palace is well worth while for the sake of the sumptuous state apartments (throne room, ballroom, dining room) and the interesting Museum of Asiatic Art (open Tue.–Sun. 8.30am–3pm) that is now housed in it. The museum is devoted mainly to Chinese, Japanese and Indian art and crafts. Particularly fine are the screens from Korea.

In a side wing of the palace is the Municipal Picture Gallery, installed here in 1995, with pictures by local artists of the 19th and early 20th c. and works of the 16th–18th c.

Old Fortress

At the Schulenburg monument is the entrance to the Old Fortress

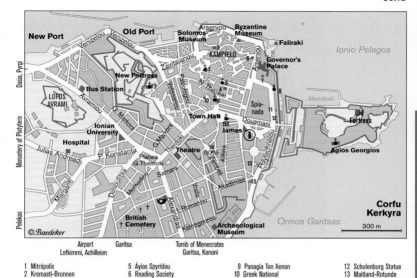

1 Mitrópolis
2 Kremasti-Brunnen
3 Panagia Tenedou
4 Banknote Museum

5 Áyios Spyrídon
6 Reading Society
7 Adam Statue
8 Panagia Mandrakina

9 Panagia Ton Xenon
10 Greek National
   Bank
11 Guilford Statue

12 Schulenburg Statue
13 Maitland-Rotunde
14 Ionisches Parlament
15 Kapodistrias-Denkmal

(open Mon.–Fri. 8am–7pm, Sat., Sun. 8.30am–3pm), reached on a bridge spanning the contra fosse, a channel of sea water. The medieval town grew up within the walls of the fortress, originally built in the 6th c. The fortress was enlarged and strengthened by the Venetians in the late 14th c. and again in the 16th and 17th c. to provide protection against Turkish attacks. The buildings within the fortress mostly date from the period of British rule. St George's Church, in the style of a Doric temple, was built in 1830 as the garrison church. On the open space in front of the church there are concerts and *son et lumière* shows in summer.

To the west of the Governor's Palace is the picturesque old town (Campiello), with Venetian-style houses and a number of beautiful historic churches. Many of the houses date from the 17th and 18th c., with later alterations. Characteristic features are the arcades that provide protection from rain and sun.

★Campiello

In the northern part of the Campiello a flight of steps leads up to the 15th c. Antivouniótissa church, which since 1984 has housed the Byzantine Museum (open Tue.–Sun. 9am–3pm). Restoration work in 1994 restored the nave of the church to its original aspect. The museum, with around 100 icons, occupies the exonarthex.

Byzantine Museum

To the south is the church of Áyios Spyrídon (1589), with a silver sarcophagus containing the mummified remains of the town's patron saint, who was archbishop of Cyprus in the 4th c. Five times during the year (on Palm Sunday, the Saturday before Easter, August 11th, the first

Áyios Spyrídon

Corfu

One of Corfu's landmarks: the Vlakherna Monastery, with the islet of Pontikonísi (Mouse Island) in the background

Sunday in November and December 12th) the relics of the saint are carried in solemn procession through the town.

Panayía Spiliótissa

A little way west is the Orthodox Cathedral of the Panayía Spiliótissa (Mitrópolis), in which is buried Empress Theodora, who restored the veneration of icons in the 9th c. after the Iconoclastic conflict.

Town Hall

To the west of the Spianada is the former Venetian Theatre of 1720 (originally built between 1663 and 1693 as the Loggia of the Nobility), which has been the Town Hall since 1902. On its east side is the 17th c. Catholic Cathedral of St James, with a neoclassical façade.

★Archaeological Museum

Near the south end of the town is the Archaeological Museum (open Tue.–Sun. 8.30am–3pm). Its prime exhibit is the Gorgon Pediment (c. 585 BC) from the sanctuary of Artemis, one of the best preserved examples of archaic sculpture in the whole of Greece. It shows the moment before Perseus strikes the Medusa's head off. Another notable item is a recumbent lion (7th c. BC), which is believed to be from the tomb of Menecrates. The tomb was found in 1843 during the demolition of the Salvator Bastion, a low rotunda of the 7th or 6th c. BC, south-west of the museum in the garden of a police station.

Southern Corfu

★Anemómylos

There are a number of sights on the Analipsi peninsula, 4 km (2½ mi.) south of the town centre. In the southern suburb of Anemómylos is one of the most important churches on the island. It is dedicated to SS Jason and Sosipater, who brought Christianity to Corfu about AD 70. A Byzantine domed cruciform church of the 11th–12th c., incorporating stones from ancient buildings, it was enlarged in the 17th c. Particularly fine are the icons by Emmanuel Tzanes on the iconostasis (Christ Pantokrator and the Mother of God with the Infant Jesus; both *c.* 1650) and the figures of Jason and Sosipater (1649) in the narthex.

Also in Anemómylos, set in a beautiful park, is the villa of **Mon Repos** (1821), birthplace in 1921 of the Duke of Edinburgh. The villa, which was acquired by Corfu town in the mid-1990s, is being extensively restored, and is not at present open to the public. The 280 ha (690 acre) park, however, is open daily. On the north side of the park is the Mon Repos bathing beach.

From the road that runs to the south of the peninsula a narrow street branches off just beyond Ayía Kérkyra, leading to the scanty remains of the Temple of Artemis. The magnificent Gorgon Pediment in the Archaeological Museum was found here in 1911.

Temple of Artemis

The road to Kanóni runs between the sea and Lake Khalikiopoulos (airport). A road on the right leads to the much photographed Vlakherna Monastery on its tiny island, which is reached on a causeway. Since the building is privately owned visitors can see only the inner courtyard of the monastery and the little church of around 1700.

★**Vlakherna Monastery**

From the causeway leading to the monastery there are regular boats to the islet of Pontikonísi (Mouse Island). To the ancient Greeks this was the Phaeacian vessel that took Odysseus to Ithaca, turned to stone.

Pontikonísi

The best view of the Vlakherna Monastery and Mouse Island is from above the Kanóni viewpoint. Because of the proximity of the airport the

★**Kanóni**

The "Dying Achilles", in the grounds of the Achilleion

hotels here are not to be recommended for a long stay, but from the restaurant terraces there is a good view of the islands.

★★Achilleion

The most visited sight on Corfu is the Achilleion (Akhillion), 10 km (6 mi.) south of Corfu town at Gastoúri, 145 m (475 ft) above the sea. This magnificent villa in Italian Renaissance style, set in beautiful gardens, was built in 1890–1 for Empress Elizabeth of Austria, who named it after her favourite hero in the "Iliad", Achilles. She frequently stayed in the villa until her death in 1898. Thereafter it remained empty until 1907, when it was bought by Kaiser Wilhelm II, who spent a few weeks here in spring every year until the outbreak of the First World War. It was acquired by the Greek government in 1928, and was for a time a gaming casino. The ground floor of the villa and the park are open to the public daily 8am–7pm, in low season 9am–4pm).

The villa contains mementoes of its two royal owners. In the park is a statue of the dying Achilles (by Ernst Herter, 1881) commissioned by Empress Elizabeth. The Kaiser preferred to identify himself with the victorious Achilles: a huge bronze statue (5.5 m (18 ft high)) depicts the Greek hero armed and ready for battle.

Benítses

3 km (2 mi.) south of the Achilleion is the charming fishing village of Benítses (Μπενιτσες), now a holiday resort mainly favoured by British visitors, with a tiny shingle beach. A little way inland are the remains of a Roman villa (3rd c. AD).

South-west of Gastoúri is the hill of **Áyii Déka** (the "Ten Saints"; 576 m (1890 ft)), which can be climbed in 2 hours there and back (strong footwear required). From the summit there are magnificent views.

**Moraítika
Messongí**

South of Benítses the coast road continues to the holiday centre of Moraítika-Messongí (Μοραιτικα, Μεσσογγη). The hotels in these two villages, now merged, are mostly off the main road in lush settings. Here too there is only a shingle beach, but it is considerably longer than the one at Benítses. There are numerous bars, tavernas and restaurants.

Lefkímmi

Beyond this is Lefkímmi (Λευκιμμη), the largest place in the south of the island (pop. 5000), where it is well worth making a brief stop. The most picturesque part of the town is the district to the east, on the little river Potami, here enclosed between stone walls.

Kávos

At the south-east tip of the island is Kávos (Καβος), one of the largest tourist centres on Corfu, particularly favoured by British visitors. It has a beautiful long sandy beach.

**★Korission
Lagoon**

Approached from the south, the west coast of Corfu presents itself as a landscape of dunes with long sandy beaches. Particularly beautiful is the country round Korission Lagoon, which offers hours of good walking. More than 120 species of birds, including cormorants and grey herons, have been observed here.

Northern Corfu

The east coast as far up as Pyryí, a not particularly attractive coastal town, is wholly given up to mass tourism. The road passes through the popular holiday centres of Kontókali, Gouviá and Dasiá, which have almost joined up to make a single resort.

**★Mount
Pantokrátor**

Beyond Pyryí a road goes off on the left to Spartylas (alt. 424 m (1391 ft)) and Strinylas and then runs up to Mount Pantokrátor (906 m (2973 ft)), the highest peak on the island. The hill takes its name from the 14th c. monastery of the Pantokrátor on the summit. The present church dates from the 17th c. The climb to the summit of the hill (now disfigured by aerial masts) is well worth while mainly for the magnificent views it offers over the whole island, the Othonian Islands to the north and the mountains of Albania.

Beyond Pyryí the road follows a winding course close to the coast, passing quiet villages and bathing beaches. In a beautiful bay is Kalami, with the White House (now a taverna, with rooms), in which Lawrence Durrell lived for two years and wrote "Black Olives".

Kalami

The road comes to the beautifully situated (but overcrowded) holiday resort of Kassiópi (Κασσιοπη), set against the backdrop of the mountains of Albania. Kassiópi differs from many other resorts on Corfu in its idyllic and unspoiled town centre. After passing innumerable hotels and apartment blocks the road comes to the harbour, above which are the ruins of a 13th c. castle. A short distance from the harbour is the church of the Panayía Kassopitra (1590), built on the site of a temple of Jupiter.

Kassiópi

The whole of the north coast between the popular bathing resorts of Róda (Ροδα) and Sidári (Σιδαρι) has been developed for tourism. Long sandy beaches (good surfing) alternate with picturesque cliffs. On the coast road a signpost points the way to the ★"Canal d'Amour", a deep fjord carved from the local light-coloured sandstone by wind and water. Ladies in search of a husband are recommended to come here in the early morning. They must then swim in the Canal d'Amour while it is still in shadow, thinking of their ideal man. They will then, it is said, find him.

Róda
Sidári

Between Cape Drastis, the north-westerly tip of the island, and Palaiokastrítsa there are other beaches. Particularly beautiful is Áyios Yeóryios Bay at Afionas. Here too the scene is dominated by tourism.

Áyios Yeóryios Bay

The hill road, narrow but asphalted, runs by way of Lakones and Krini to Angelókastro (Αγγελοκαστρο), ending below a picturesquely situated ruined castle. It is a short walk up a steep path to the once mighty stronghold of Angelókastro. Even more impressive than the castle, which is thought to have been built in the 13th c., is the view from the top of the hill. During the Venetian period Angelókastro was repeatedly attacked. On the highest point within the castle walls is a chapel of 1784 dedicated to the Archangels Michael and Gabriel. Round it are the remains of tombs hewn from the rock. One man-made cave was used as a chapel from the 18th c. onwards. With the end of Venetian rule Angelókastro lost its strategic importance, and it was razed to the ground by the British, leaving only the two chapels, the foundations of the castle and remains of the system of cisterns.

★Angelókastro

The road goes over the scenic Troumbeta Pass and comes to Palaiokastrítsa (Παλαιοκαστριτσα), a beautifully situated but also very crowded tourist centre. Its beautiful surroundings and the interesting monastery situated on a peninsula make it a very popular destination for excursions. There are a number of hotels of some size, restaurants and small shingle beaches.
   From the road to the harbour a side road branches off to the monastery of the Panayía Theotókos (open Apr.–Oct. daily 7am–1pm, 3–8pm). The monastery was founded in the 13th c., but the present buildings date from the 18th c. The central feature is the church, which is surrounded by blocks of cells, storerooms and public rooms and by a pretty garden. There is a pergola gay with colour. A staircase leads to the upper floor, on which a collection of 17th–19th c. icons is displayed. There are other icons in the church.

★★Palaiokastrítsa

East of Palaiokastrítsa the road turns south and runs through a relatively level fertile region to Corfu town. 8 km (5 mi.) from Palaiokastrítsa a side

Érmones

road goes off to Érmones (Ερμονες), on the west coast. With a small sandy bay, this is a good place for a restful holiday, though the quality of the water is sometimes poor.

Myrtiótissa

The neighbouring bay to the south, Myrtiótissa (Μυρτιωτισσα), has one of the few beaches on Corfu that have largely been spared by the development of tourism. The sandy bay below steep cliffs is an (unofficial) nudist beach.

Glyfáda

7 km (4½ mi.) south is the pleasant holiday resort of Glyfáda (Γλυφαδα), whose sandy beach (1 km (¾ mi.) long) is framed by picturesque rocks. The sandy beach sloping gently down to the sea is ideal for children.

★Pélekas

The best place on Corfu from which to watch the sun setting is Pélekas (Πελεκας), on a ridge of hill 4 km (2½ mi.) east of Glyfáda. In the centre of the village a signpost "Sunset" points the way to a viewpoint above the village. This was formerly known as the "Kaiser's Throne", since Kaiser Wilhelm II liked to have himself driven up here to watch the sun sinking into the sea. From Pélekas there is a good road back to Corfu town (13 km (8 mi.)).

Othonian Islands

From Sidári, Róda and Kassiópi there are boats to the Othonian Islands, an archipelago north-west of Corfu with the islets of Othóni, Erikoúsa, Mathráki and Diaplo, one or other of which has been thought to be Calypso's island. They have good bathing beaches and fish tavernas.

Crete   H–L 8/9

Area: 8261 sq. km (3190 sq. mi.)
Altitude: 2456 m (8058 ft)
Population: 750,000
Chief place: Iráklion

Airports at Iráklion (5 km (3 mi.) east); Khaniá (12 km (7½ mi.) north-east) and Sitía (5 km (3 mi.) north). Scheduled flights several times daily

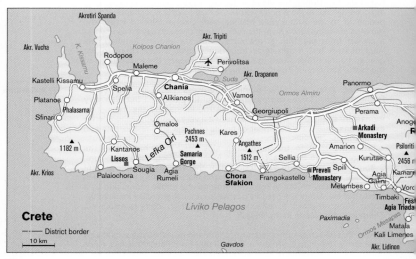

Crete

---- District border

10 km

Athens–Iráklion, Salonica–Iráklion, Athens–Khaniá; also flights Iráklion to Rhodes, Mýkonos and Santorini, Khaniá to Salonica and Sitía via Kárpathos and Kásos to Athens. Direct flights London–Iráklion.

Shipping services: daily ferry connections Piraeus to Iráklion, Khaniá and Réthymon, between Santoríni and Iráklion; slow connections through the Cyclades and the Dodecanese to Áyios Nikólaos and Sitía; ferry from Gythion in the Peloponnese via Kýthira to Kastélli (twice weekly during the season). Dense network of bus services on the island; bus stations (sometimes more than one) in the larger towns.

Crete (Κρητη), the largest of the Greek islands and the fifth largest island in the Mediterranean, lies some 100 km (60 mi.) south-east of the Peloponnese between the Aegean (or Cretan) Sea to the north and the Libyan Sea to the south. The most southerly outpost of Europe, it is an important link in the chain of islands that runs in an arc between southern Greece and Asia Minor.

With its magnificent and varied scenery, its beautiful beaches and its remarkable remains of Minoan civilisation, it has a variety of attractions for visitors. It extends for 260 km (160 mi.) from east to west, varying in width between 12 km (7½ mi.) and 57 km (35 mi.).

Crete is dominated by three karstic mountain massifs almost devoid of vegetation: in the west the Lefká Óri (White Mountains; 2452 m (8045 ft)), which are snow-capped for much of the year; in the centre of the island the Psilorítis range (Ídi Óros, Mount Ida, 2456 m (8058 ft)), which also has a good deal of snow; and in the east the Díkti range (2148 m (7048 ft)). While the south coast for the most part falls steeply down to the sea, the north coast is flatter and more indented. On the north coast are the island's chief towns – Khaniá, the island's capital Iráklion and Réthymnon, its third largest town. Here too are Crete's longest sandy beaches, and as a result most of the tourist resorts.

The **climate** is Mediterranean, with relatively mild and wet winters and completely dry summers of subtropical heat (six or seven summer months). In the Mesará plain and the high Ómalos and Lassíthi plains there is intensive cultivation of vegetables, much of it throughout the year under plastic sheeting. Other important products are citrus fruits,

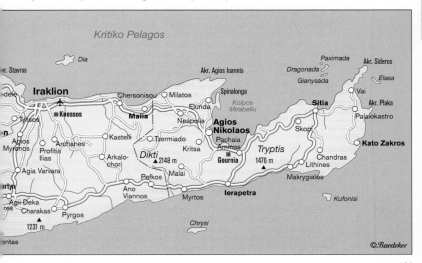

wine and above all olives. Apart from agriculture the most important source of income since the early 1970s has been the tourist trade.

Prehistory The earliest traces of human settlement, by incomers from North Africa, date back to the 7th millennium BC. From the 3rd millennium BC there developed a pre-Greek Bronze Age culture that reached its apogee between 2000 and 1600 BC and is known as the Minoan culture, after the legendary King Minos. The cultural and economic influence of Minoan Crete, and also the political authority of this first maritime power in the Mediterranean, were felt as far afield as the Iberian peninsula. Then, around 1400 BC, for reasons that are not clear, Minoan power collapsed, enabling the Mycenaeans to establish themselves on Crete and gain control of much of the island. With the final destruction of the Minoan palace at Knossos in 1200 BC the Minoan civilisation was extinguished. Around 1000 BC Dorian Greeks conquered most of the island. Between 69 and 67 BC Crete – an important base in the eastern Mediterranean – was occupied by Rome. When the Roman Empire was divided in AD 395 Crete fell to the Eastern (Byzantine) Empire and remained under Byzantine control until 826.

Middle Ages Between 826 and 961 Crete was held by the Saracens (Arabs), but thereafter was recovered by the Empire. From 1204 to 1669 it was ruled by Venice, when the people of Crete fought a long and bitter struggle for independence. Nevertheless the period of Venetian rule saw a considerable cultural flowering on Crete. After the fall of Constantinople to the Turks in 1453 a local school of painting developed on Crete, modifying, under Italian influence, the strict canons of Byzantine art. Among the artists of this period was Domenikos Theotokopoulos, better known as El Greco, who was born in Fódele, near Iráklion, in 1541 and died in Toledo in 1614 (see Famous People).

After many years of war (capture of Khaniá, 1645) the island finally became Turkish with the taking of Iráklion in 1669. The Turks finally left the island in 1898 after a military confrontation with Greece.

20th century After a brief period of independence Crete became part of the kingdom of Greece on May 30th 1913. This was brought about largely by Eleftherios Kyriakos Venizélos (b. Mourniés, near Khaniá, 1864; d. Paris, 1936: see Famous People), a lawyer and liberal politician who later became prime minister of Greece.

In May 1941 German airborne forces occupied Crete, which, lying between southern Europe and Africa, was of great strategic importance, and remained in occupation until October 1944.

From around 1970 Crete developed into a holiday island favoured by package tours. An expressway was built along the north coast and numerous hotels were built in Mália Bay and at Réthymnon, Iráklion and Áyios Nikólaos.

Khaniá

Khaniá (Χανιά; pop. 62,000) lies in the south-east corner of Khaniá Bay on the north coast of Crete. The town was founded by the Venetians in the 13th c. under the name of La Canea, on the site of ancient Cydonia. This lively town (which has a university) is a good base from which to explore the scenic beauties of western Greece.

★Old town

The focal point of the town is the picturesque Venetian harbour, now lined by restaurants and cafés, with colourful boats at their moorings and horse-drawn carriages waiting to take tourists round the sights. From the old lighthouse there is a fine view, particularly in the late afternoon, of the skyline of Khaniá with its minarets, the white dome of the

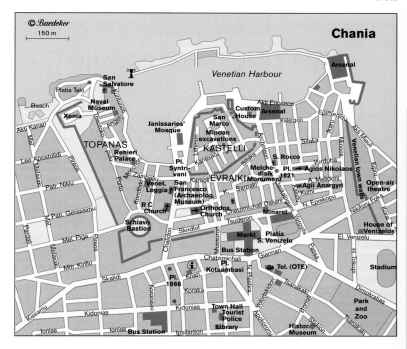

former Janissaries' Mosque (1645) and the karstic hills of the Léfka Orí (White Mountains) as a backdrop.

In the historic **Topanás quarter** at the west end of the harbour are a number of attractive little hotels. At the east end are the Venetian arsenals (1497), now used as boathouses and for exhibitions. On the hill behind the mosque is the **Kastélli quarter**, with Venetian buildings, partly destroyed (doorways of old mansions, remains of the church of San Marco), and Minoan excavations. The area to the south of Kastélli, in the **Evraikí quarter**, was in Venetian and Turkish times the Jewish ghetto. The old town is surrounded by a 3 km (2 mi.) long circuit of 16th c. walls.

In the Gothic church of San Francesco, originally belonging to a Franciscan friary and in Turkish times converted into a mosque, is the ★**Archaeological Museum** (open Mon. 12.30–6pm, Tue.–Fri. 8am–6pm, Sat., Sun. 8.30am–3pm), with an excellent collection of artefacts from neolithic to Roman times.

Round the corner, in Odós Zambeliou, is a Renaissance-style Venetian loggia. At the south-west corner of the harbour, in Odós Moskhon, is the Renieri Palace. At the north-west corner is a Venetian fort guarding the harbour, now occupied by the Naval Museum (open May–Oct. 10am–4pm, Nov.–Apr. 10am–2pm), with ship models and nautical equipment. Higher up is the 16th c. church of San Salvatore. In the eastern part of the old town, in Platía 1821, under the shade of a plane tree, is a monument to a bishop who was hanged by the Turks from this tree

When Zorba Dances the Syrtáki

"**A** stranger of about sixty, very tall and lean, with staring eyes, had pressed his nose against the pane and was looking at me. He was holding a little flattened bundle under his arm. The thing which impressed me most was his eager gaze, his eyes, ironical and full of fire. At any rate, that is how they appeared to me. As soon as our eyes had met – he seemed to be making sure that I was really the person he was looking for – the stranger opened the door with a determined thrust of his arm. He passed between the tables with a rapid, springy step, and stopped in front of me. 'Travelling?' he asked. 'Where to? Trusting to providence?' 'I'm making for Crete. Why do you ask?' 'Taking me with you?'" So begins the encounter between a young English writer and the Cretan, Alexis Zorba – two men who could hardly be more different from one another: one educated, introverted, more at home in his books than in real life, and the other full of vigorous life and impetuous passion in all that he does, a man who lives by his belly and with his heart. It is the story of a friendship between two men, set against the background of everyday Cretan life in all its harshness, but also all its poetry and unspoiled, archaic beauty. The author of the story, Nikos Kazantzákis, came from Crete but, closely bound as he was to his native island, was a thoroughly cosmopolitan spirit and a sharp critic of his fellow countrymen. The publication of "Zorba the Greek" in 1946 made Kazantzákis, already known in Greece as a writer, world-famous at a stroke. Within a few years the novel was translated into English and German.

What is little known, however, is that Alexis Zorba was not a pure invention: there really was such a man. The real Zorba was not called Alexis, but Yeóryios, and was a miner. In 1916 Kazantzákis's and Zorba's ways crossed. In that year the writer spent some months in the Peloponnese with the Macedonian miner, working lignite: the mining project in the novel thus had a basis in real life. After the time they spent together Kazantzákis apparently heard only occasionally from his friend, who died in Skopje in 1942, never having set foot on the island of Crete. No one – and certainly not the man himself – could ever have imagined that Yeóryios Zorba, or rather the Zorba that Kazantzákis had made of him, would feature in literary history as the hero of a novel. The novel's success, however, was merely the prelude to the still greater popularity that the story of these two men was to achieve when the book was turned into a film. The film "Zorba the Greek" (1964), directed by Michael Cacoyannis, drew huge audiences and attracted great critical acclaim. "Zorba the Greek" quickly became a film classic. The film was shot in Crete, particularly in the little fishing village of Stavrós on the Akrotíri peninsula near Khaniá. But much in the film that looks authentically Cretan or authentically Greek is revealed on closer inspection to be a (very skilful) cheat. An example is the *syrtáki* that Anthony Quinn dances so magnificently. Since there was not enough time during the shooting of the film for him to learn the complicated Cretan folk dances, a simpler dance was devised for him to the music of Mikis Theodorákis – who at least was a Greek. As a result most visitors to Crete now think that the syrtáki is a traditional Cretan dance.

The fact that Cacoyannis's film simplifies or schematises the novel will not surprise anyone who has seen other film versions of novels, nor will it diminish the fame of the film. Cacoyannis, of course, created characters who were on the very verge of being over-drawn and almost clichés; but the film's convincing effect was due to the excellent cast. In addition to Anthony Quinn as Zorba, Alan Bates played the young pale-skinned writer, Lila Kedrova the ageing Bouboulina and Irene Papas the beautiful widow.

for viewers of the film: Quinn did not act Zorba, he was Zorba. The additional element in the figure of Zorba in the film as compared with

Anthony Quinn and Alan Bates, in "Zorba the Greek" (still © 20th Century-Fox)

The success of the film, however, was principally due to the fine perform-ance by Anthony Quinn. The charac-ter of Zorba seemed so exactly made to measure for Quinn that the actor and the character became one figure

the character in the novel is the vig-orous, free and boundlessly opti-mistic aura that radiates from this man and sends the audience out into reality with a positive feeling. Who can forget the magnificent scene at the end of the film when Zorba, after the collapse of his cableway, says "Boss, did you ever see anything crashing so beautifully?"

(Quotations from the novel are from the translation by Carl Wildman).

for his opposition to Turkish rule. In the same square are the Venetian churches of Áyios Nikólaos (later converted into a mosque) and San Rocco (1630). To the south, on the edge of the old town, is the large Market Hall, a cast-iron structure erected in 1911 on the model of one in Marseilles.

Historical Museum

In a handsome villa to the south of the old town is the Historical Museum (Odós Sfakion 20; open Mon.–Fri. 9am–1pm), with an outstanding collection of material on the war of Greek independence, the Second World War and the resistance to the German occupation, together with folk costumes and crafts. To the north-east are the Public Gardens, with a small zoo (wild goats).

Khalépa

1.5 km (1 mi.) east of the town centre is the villa suburb of Khalépa, which was developed around the end of the 19th c. as a government quarter. In this area are the Prefecture and various foreign consulates.

Excursions from Khaniá

Soúda Bay

4 km (2½ mi.) south-east of the old town is Soúda Bay, the largest and most sheltered natural harbour on the island, the commercial and ferry port of Khaniá and a NATO base. On the road to the Akrotíri peninsula is a British military cemetery. The fort on the island of Soúda, at the mouth of the bay, was held by the Venetians until 1715.

Mount Profítis Ilías

8 km (5 mi.) east of Khaniá, on Mount Profítis Ilías, is a well-kept memorial garden with the graves of the Cretan-born statesman Eleftherios Venizélos and his son Sofoklís. From here there are magnificent views of the town and the White Mountains.

Ayía Triáda

17 km (10½ mi.) north-east of Khaniá, on the Akrotíri peninsula, is the monastery of Ayía Triáda (1631), one of the largest and most important monasteries on Crete, with a plain façade in Italian Renaissance style and a sumptuous iconostasis in the church. To the left of the entrance to the monastery is a small icon museum. The film "Zorba the Greek" was shot here.

★ Gouvernéto

4 km (2½ mi.) north, in a dramatic setting, is the monastery of Gouvernéto, founded in 1548, with a Renaissance façade (open 7.30am–noon, 3–7pm). This fortified monastery is now occupied only by a few monks. An icon in the porch depicts the legend of St John of Gouvernéto, who, fleeing from the Near East, landed on the shore here and, with 98 companions, lived in a cave until a hunter accidentally shot him. The cave can still be seen.

Bear's Cave

From Gouvernéto a path (to the right) goes down to a spacious cave, called the Bear's Cave from the form of a stalagmite in it. The cave is thought to have been a cult site in Minoan times, and in the classical period was dedicated to the cult of Artemis, to whom the bear was sacred. At the entrance to the cave is the little chapel of the Panayía Arkoudiótissa (Mother of God of the Bear's Cave).

Katholikó

From here a narrow path runs down to the monastery of Katholikó, which was abandoned in the 16th c., with St John of Gouvernéto's cave (to the left, in front of the monastery doorway). The rock-cut church has a Venetian front wall. There is an important procession here on the eve of October 7th.

Áptera

14 km (8½ mi.) east of Khaniá, on a rocky plateau, are the remains of ancient Aptera (Απτερα), which existed from the Dorian period (c. 1000

BC) into Byzantine times. From the Turkish fort of 1868 there is a fine view of Soúda Bay and Akrotíri.

16 km (10 mi.) west of Khaniá, at Máleme (Μαλεμε), is a German military cemetery with 4465 graves, mostly of paratroops killed in the German airborne landings in May and June 1941.

Máleme

8 km (5 mi.) west of Máleme a road goes off on the right to Kolymbári, at the base of the Rhodopos peninsula (Ροδωπος), a grandiose and barren promontory, 6 km (4 mi.) wide, which extends northward, rising to a height of 750 m (2460 ft). To the north of Kolymbári is the fortress-like Venetian monastery of Goniás (1618), with fine 17th c. icons in the church. Beyond this is the Oecumenical Academy of the autocephalous (independent) Cretan Church.

Rhodopos peninsula

At the north-east end of the peninsula, in Meniás Bay, near Cape Skála, is the sanctuary of the nymph Dictynna, which was excavated by German archaeologists during the Second World War. Dictynna was identical with the Cretan cave goddess Britomartis and was later equated with Artemis. She was the patroness of fishermen and their nets (*díktyon,* net). The site is best reached by boat from Khaniá or Kolymbári. From the landing stage (beautiful bathing beach) the route to the site runs up a narrow valley with the ruins of an abandoned village and then up the hill to the left (south) to the excavated area, with the remains of a temple of the 2nd c. AD built on the site of an earlier one of the 7th c. BC, together with an altar, cisterns and other buildings.

20 km (13 mi.) west of Kolymbári is the wine-growing village of Kastélli Kíssamou (Καστελλι Κισσαμου), near which is the little port where the ferry leaves for the Peloponnese. From there there is an attractive boat trip to the island of Gramvoúsa, off the rocky peninsula of that name at the extreme north-western tip of Crete, with a 17th c. Venetian fortress commandingly situated above the steep west coast. 9 km (5½ mi.) west of Kastélli Kíssamou, at the north end of a dune-fringed bay, is the site of the ancient port town of Phalasarna, with remains of buildings and port installations, tombs and sculpture. The town, founded in the 5th/4th c. BC, is believed to have been abandoned in the 6th c. AD, when the coast rose 8 m (26 ft). There is a beautiful view of the Gulf of Kissamos from the remains of the Dorian town of Polyrrhenia (6 km (4 mi.) south of Kastélli; 30 min. walk from the village of Polyrinía).

Kastélli Kíssamou

62 km (39 mi.) south-west of Khaniá is the village of Kántanos (Καντανος), which was destroyed by German forces during the Second World War in reprisal for the activities of the Greek resistance. Memorial tablets in the village tell the story.

Kántanos

18 km (11 mi.) south (77 km (48 mi.) from Khaniá), on a promontory in the Libyan Sea, is the little port town of Palaiokhóra (Παλαιοχωρα), below the ruins of the Venetian fort of Selinou (1282). It is a popular bathing resort with a long sandy beach, fish restaurants and a traffic-free street of tavernas. From here there are ferries to the little island of Gávdos.

Palaiokhóra

The road from Kántanos to Soúyia (Σουγια) runs through Anisaraki, which has four Byzantine chapels of the 14th–15th c. South of the village of Teménia (11 km (7 mi.)) is the church of the Sotír (Saviour; 13th–14th c.), with very fine frescos. 8 km (5 mi.) beyond this is Moní, with the charming 13th c. church of Áyios Nikólaos that, unusually, has a free-standing bell tower. The road ends in 25 km (15 mi.) at the bathing resort of Soúyia, which has very popular shingle beaches (some, unofficially, nudist). The village church has a mosaic pavement, all that remains of an Early Christian basilica of the 6th c.

Soúyia

From Soúyia there is a rewarding walk (1½ hrs) over the hill to the west

Lissós

There are many picturesque spots, like this rocky stretch of coast at Ayía Rouméli, on the south coast of Crete

into the neighbouring bay of Áyios Kyrikos (which can also be reached by boat from Palaiokhóra or Soúyia).This was the site of ancient Lissos (Λισσος), which was famed in Roman times for its healing springs. There are remains of a temple in the sanctuary of Asclepius (cella walls, mosaic floors, the base of the cult image and to the left of this a pit for libations). Water from the sacred spring runs under the floor to a fountain. There are also remains of Roman houses and (on the hillside to the west) Hellenistic and Roman tombs. On the shore are a chapel of Áyios Kyrikos and, to the west of the temple, a chapel of the Panayía, both built on the remains of Early Christian basilicas.

★★Samariá Gorge

42 km (26 mi.) south of Khaniá is the village of Omalós, on the edge of the fertile Omalós plateau (1050 m (3445 ft)). After another 6 km (4 mi.) the road ends at Xylóskalo (1227 m (4026 ft)). This is the starting point of the 6 hour walk through the Samariá Gorge (Farángi Samariás), 18 km (7 mi.) long, up to 600 m (2000 ft) deep and no more than 3–4 m (10–14 ft) wide at its narrowest point, the "Iron Gates" (Síderoportes). The Cretan wild goat (agrimi or kri-kri) still survives in this area, which was declared a National Park in 1965. To undertake the walk through the gorge – which on some days attracts more than 3000 people – you need to be fit, have stout footwear and carry sufficient food; water can be obtained from springs in the gorge. The gorge is open daily 6am–4pm (admission charge); it is closed from November to the beginning of April.

Ayía Rouméli

At the south end of the gorge is the abandoned village of Ayía Rouméli, and on the coast is the new settlement of the same name, which consists almost exclusively of hotels and tavernas. From here there are boats to Khóra Sfakíon, from both of which there are buses to Khaniá.

At Khóra Sfakíon (Χωρα Σφακιων) most of those who have walked **Khóra Sfakíon**
through the gorge make straight for the waiting buses, to the sorrow of
the many tavernas in the little town. 5 km (3 mi.) west of the town is the
little bay of Loutró, which can be reached either on foot or by boat. With
its few blue and white painted houses, Loutró appeals to visitors looking
for a quiet and relaxing holiday. There are attractive walks from here, up
the rocky hill to the villages in the Sfakía plain, where the men still wear
their traditional black costume, or along the coast to the Arádena Gorge
and the church of Áyios Pávlos on the edge of the dunes. From Loutró
visitors can take a boat to various sandy beaches.

To the east of Khóra Sfakíon is the wild Imbros Gorge, which cuts its way **Imbros Gorge**
through the mountains for 7 km (4½ mi.). It is even narrower than the
Samariá Gorge. The walk from the village of Imbros on the Sfakía plain
to Komitádes at the south end of the gorge takes about 3 hours.

17 km (11 mi.) east of Khóra Sfakíon, on the edge of the high ground **Frangokastéllo**
above the sea, is the formidable Venetian fort of Frangokastéllo (1371),
a square structure with massive battlemented walls. Over the main
entrance, on the seaward side, is the lion of St Mark. With its beautiful
sandy beaches, tiny harbour and numerous pensions and holiday
homes, Frangokastéllo (Φραγκοκαστελλο) is now a popular holiday
resort, mainly favoured by young people.

37 km (23 mi.) off the south-west coast of Crete is the flat, wooded island **Gávdos**
of Gávdos (Γαυδος), Europe's most southerly point, which is believed to be
the mythical island of Ogygia in the "Odyssey" (VII, 244), with Calypso's
"vaulted cave", and the island of Clauda in the Acts of the Apostles. With
a population in summer of only 80, Gávdos is a birdwatcher's paradise in
spring. With its beautiful beaches, it attracts many backpacking visitors.
There is a twice-weekly supply boat from Palaiokhóra, and in summer regular excursion boats from Palaiokhóra and Khóra Sfakíon.

Réthymnon

Réthymnon, the third largest town on Crete (Ρεθυμνον; pop. 20,000), lies
half way along the north coast, at the foot of the Psilorítis range (Mount
Ida). The periods of Venetian and Turkish occupation have left their mark
on the town, which presents a charming mingling of cultures. From the
harbour a sandy beach runs east for 12 km (7½ mi.), lined with many
large hotels – making Réthymnon the largest tourist centre on the island.

The old town, situated on a peninsula, is full of atmosphere, with many ★Old town
Venetian mansions, Turkish houses with enclosed wooden balconies
and several small mosques. It is dominated by the Fortezza (1574–82), in
which open-air cultural events are held in summer. The mosque with its
mighty dome was converted in the mid 17th c. from the church of St
Nicholas.

In a former Venetian prison beside the Fortezza is the interesting
★**Archaeological Museum** (open Tue.–Sun. 8.30am–3pm), with a collection of Cretan archaeological finds from the neolithic onwards, including
pottery, vases, bronzes, marble statues and clay figures of various
periods.

At the north-east corner of the old town is the little Venetian harbour,
now lined by one taverna after another. To the south-west, in Odós
Arkadíou, is a 17th c. Venetian loggia. From here Odós Paleologon leads
to the beautiful Arimondi Fountain (1623). On Odós Vernardou, to the
south, are Venetian houses with Turkish additions in wood and the
Nerandzes Mosque. From here Odós Ethnikis Antistaseos continues

south, passing the former church of San Francesco, with a handsome doorway, which is now used for a variety of events, to the Megáli Pórta, a Venetian town gate. Beyond Platía Martiron is the Municipal Garden, in which a large wine festival is held in the second half of July.

★Arkádi Monastery

10 km (6 mi.) east is the largest olive grove in the Mediterranean area, with 1½ million trees. 23 km (14 mi.) south-east, in hilly country, is the fortress-like complex of Arkádi Monastery, a Cretan national shrine and a site of great historical interest. During the 1866 rising against the Turks a thousand Cretans – men, women and children – had sought refuge in the monastery, and after withstanding an attack by 12,000 Turks, realising that further resistance was hopeless, the survivors set light to the powder magazine on November 8th and blew themselves up.

The monastery, now occupied only by a handful of monks, was founded in the 11th c. The present buildings date from the 17th c. but have been much altered. In the inner courtyard is the church (1587), whose façade shows both Italian Renaissance and baroque features.

Préveli Monastery

On the south coast, 38 km (24 mi.) from Réthymnon, is Préveli Monastery, built in the early 1700s, in a lonely, barren and rugged setting. Features of interest are the fountain in the courtyard, the richly decorated iconostasis in the church, and the valuable vestments and bishops' mitres in the museum.

From here a dusty path runs 1 km (¾ mi.) east to a very popular palm-fringed sandy beach at the mouth of the Megálos Potamós ("big river"), which reaches the sea after passing through the grandiose Kourtaliótiko Gorge. The beach can also be reached by boat from Ayía Galíni.

Ayía Galíni

Ayía Galíni (Αγια Γαλινι), 54 km (34 mi.) south-east of Réthymnon, has been transformed from a quiet little fishing village on a rocky coast into a lively holiday resort with a sandy beach that was discovered by hippies from Mátala. From here there are boats to a dune beach at Áyios Pávlos, north-west of Ayía Galíni, and other beaches in the area.

Lake Kournás

Lake Kournás, Crete's only inland lake, beautifully situated amid hills, lies near Yeoryioúpolis, 23 km (14 mi.) east of Réthymnon. It has a number of tavernas.

Iráklion

Iráklion (Herákleion, Ηρακλιον; pop. 110,000), half way along the north coast of Crete, is the island's largest town, its administrative centre and most important commercial port, the hub of its tourist traffic and the see of an Orthodox archbishop. Many of its historic buildings were destroyed during the Second World War, so that the town has lost much of its charm, but it has some attractive corners as well as a number of important sights.

Visitors approaching by sea will see on the right Cape Stavrós and on the left the barren island of Día (265 m (869 ft); wild goat reserve), which offers a safe haven during storms blowing from the north. Straight ahead is Iráklion Bay, bounded on the west by Cape Panayía.

The old town of Iráklion is surrounded by a well preserved circuit of walls. The atmosphere of the busy town centre is best experienced in Platía Venizelou, with the Morosini Fountain and numerous restaurants and cafés. From this square radiate the town's main streets: Leofóros Dikaiosinis, with shops, offices and cafés; Odós 25 Avgoustou, leading to the harbour, with banks and travel agencies; Odós Daidalou, a narrow pedestrianised street; Odós 1866, the market street; and Odós Kalokairinou, the town's main shopping street. Iráklion's other central point is Platía Eleftherias, with the world-famous Archaeological Museum.

Iraklion • Irakleio

History In Minoan times Iráklion (whose name is derived from Heracles) was the port of Knossos, but declined during the Roman period and was given a fresh lease of life from AD 824 onwards by the Saracens, who called the town El Chandak. The Venetians surrounded the town, which they called Candia, with a 5 km (3 mi.) long circuit of massive walls (by Michele Sammicheli, 1538 onwards) and made it the island's capital. In the 16th and 17th c. Iráklion was the centre of an important school of painting. In 1669, after a 21 year siege, it fell to the Turks, who had occupied most of Crete in 1648. Under Turkish rule Khaniá became the administrative centre of the island; but in 1913, when Crete was incorporated in the kingdom of Greece, Iráklion recovered its central role. During the Second World War much of the town was destroyed.

Iráklion's principal tourist attraction, and one of the most important sights in the whole of Crete, is the Archaeological Museum (open Mon. 12.30–7pm, Tue.–Sun. 8am–7pm), which displays the magnificent finds from Knossos, Phaistós, Ayía Triáda and other sites on the island, illustrating the splendid pre-Greek cultures that flourished from the 5th millennium BC onwards. The collection includes material of the Minoan Pre-Palatial period (2600–2100 BC), but the principal treasures of the museum are of the Proto-Palatial period (the period of the Old Palaces; 2050–1800 BC), including the famous Phaistós Disc and the Bull's Head Rhyton (see p. 142). There are also very beautiful frescos from the palaces of Knossos, Phaistós and Káto Zákros dating from the Neo- and Post-Palatial periods (1600–1300 BC). Also of interest are the examples of monumental art of the Archaic period (*c.* 620–480 BC) and sculpture of the Hellenistic and Roman periods (480 BC to AD 337).

★★Archaeo-
logical Museum

Harbour	To the north of the old town is the charming Venetian Harbour, with a fort (Koules) commanding the entrance (1523–40; open Tue.–Sun. 8.30am–3pm) and the former Venetian Arsenals. In Odós 25 Avgoústou, which runs south to the town centre, is the Venetian Loggia, built in 1626–8 by Francesco Morosini, the Venetian governor. The adjoining Armoury (Armería) of the 17th c. is now the Town Hall.

The Bull's Head Rhyton in the Archaeological Museum

Áyios Márkos	Further south, in Platía Venizélou, are the Morosini Fountain (1628), with 14th c. reliefs of lions round the basin, and the former church of Áyios Márkos (1239). The church became a mosque between 1669 and 1915 and now houses a variety of exhibitions and other events. It contains a collection of copies of important Cretan frescos.
Áyios Títos	To the north-west of the square is the church of Áyios Títos, dedicated to Titus, St Paul's companion and the first bishop of Crete. The reliquary containing his skull (in the narthex, on left), which had been carried off to Venice in the 17th c., was returned to Crete in 1966. The church, originally built in the 11th/12th c., was converted into a mosque in 1882, and later became an Orthodox cathedral.
Icon Museum	The best time to walk along Odós 1866 is the morning, when the market is at its liveliest. At its south end is the Bembo Fountain of 1588, which incorporates fragments of ancient architecture and sculpture. Beside it is a Turkish fountain house, now occupied by a café. In Platía Ekaterínis (St Catherine's Square) are the 19th c. Cathedral of Áyios Minás and the little church of Ayía Ekateríni (18th c.). The church now houses an Icon Museum, among whose principal treasures are six icons by Mikhaíl Damaskinós (16th c.).
Historical Museum	The Historical Museum, in the northern part of the old town (open Mon.–Sat. 9am–2pm), illustrates Cretan history from Byzantine times to the present day, and also has a rich ethnographic collection.
Town walls	The circuit of walls built by the Veronese architect Michele Sanmicheli, who came to Crete in 1538, has a total length of 5 km (3 mi.), with five bastions and two demi-bastions. Outside the walls was a dry moat ranging in width from 20 m (65 ft) to 60 m (195 ft). Most of the town's eight gates survive.
	From the Martinengo Bastion, to the south, there is a good view of the town. On this bastion is the grave of the great Cretan writer Nikos Kazantzákis (see Famous People), who was buried here because the church refused to let this freethinker be buried in consecrated ground. The grave is marked by a plain slab of stone with the inscription: "I hope for nothing, I fear nothing: I am free".

Knossos

★★Minoan Palace	5 km (3 mi.) south-east of Iráklion (5 min. by bus), near the village of Makritíkhos, is the site of Knossos, once capital of the island, with a

Wall painting in the Palace of Knossos: the "Prince of the Lilies", wearing a headdress of flowers and peacock feathers ▶

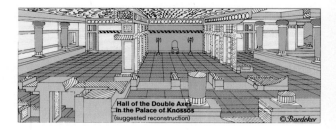

**Hall of the Double Axes
in the Palace of Knossós**
(suggested reconstruction)

© Baedeker

Open daily
8am–5pm
(summer 8pm)

Admission free
Sun.

royal palace that was excavated and partly reconstructed from 1899 onwards by British archaeologists led by Sir Arthur Evans (1851–1941).

The extensive complex, covering over 2 ha (5 acres) on the slopes of Mount Kefála, was partly of three and partly of four storeys. It was several times destroyed, probably by earthquakes, and subsequently rebuilt. Three phases can therefore be distinguished during the 600 years from around 2000 to 1400 BC: the First Palace (c. 2000– 1800 BC), the Second Palace (c. 1800–1700) and the Third Palace (c. 1700–1400). The remains now visible belong mainly to the Third Palace, built after 1700 BC, which was altered and extended in later centuries but is still substantially as it was in the 16th c. BC.

The complicated layout of the palace gave rise to the suggestion that this was the legendary Labyrinth of King Minos, a theory supported by the fact that the double axe (labrys), the symbol of Minoan Crete, featured in the decoration of the palace. More recently a German geologist, H.G. Wunderlich, has interpreted Knossos as a city of the dead, while the French archaeologist P. Faure believes it to have been a sanctuary. Most archaeologists, however, hold to the traditional view of Knossos as a centre of authority and administration.

Round the palace, in the largely unexcavated area of the **town of Knossos** (which may have had a population of anything up to 50,000), are the remains of a number of villas, the Little Palace (200 m (660 ft) north-west), the "Caravanserai" and the Temple Tomb.

The **palace** is entered from the West Court (on the left, remains of the Theatral Area). Continuing along the Processional Corridor (so named from the frescos that decorate it), through the monumental South Propylaia and along a long corridor flanked by numerous storerooms containing large storage jars, we come into the spacious Central Court, in which bull-leaping games (as depicted on various items in the Archaeological Museum in Iráklion) may have been held. On the west side of the court are the Grand Staircase and the Throne Room (with a stone throne; c. 2000 BC), and on the east side are domestic offices, workshops and rooms with baths and lavatories (flushed by water). Adjoining the Hall of the Double Axes (after the double-axe symbols on the pillars) are the King's Megaron and Queen's Megaron. The numerous frescos are copies (originals in the Archaeological Museum in Iráklion).

Excursions from Iráklion

Fódele

29 km (18 mi.) west of Iráklion, easily reached by way of the coastal expressway, is the village of Fódele (Φοδελε), beautifully situated amid olive and orange groves. This is believed to have been the birthplace of the famous painter El Greco. His father's house is near a Byzantine church 1 km (¾ mi.) before the village.

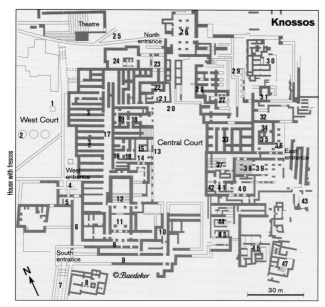

Knossos

©Baedeker

30 m

1 Altar base	17 Storeroom corridor	33 Room with water basin
2 Circular pits	18 Throne room	34 Potter's workshops
3 Storerooms	19 Cult chamber	35 Stone cutter's workshop
4 West Propylaea	20 North ramp	36 East veranda
5 Guard room	21 Prison	37 Staircase
6 Processional corridor	22 Cult chamber	38 Hall of Double Axes
7 Columned staircase	23 North-west Propylaea	39 King's Megaron
8 South House	24 Cult area	40 Queen's Megaron
9 South corridor	25 Royal Road	41 Queen's Bathroom
10 Corridor	26 Custom House	42 Queen's Dressing Room
11 South Propylaea	27 North-east Hall	43 Eastern bastions
12 Staircase	28 North-east storerooms	44 Shrine of Double Axes
13 Shrine	29 Potter's workshops (?)	45 Lustral basin
14 Antechamber	30 Potter's workshops	46 House of the
15 Central shrine	31 Storeroom	Chancel Screen
16 Pillar crypt	32 Light well	47 South-east House

15 km (9 mi.) south-west of Iráklion, at Týlisos (Τυλισος), are the remains of three Minoan villas of the 17th–16th c. BC. The walls, carefully constructed of large blocks of dressed stone, were stabilised by vertical wooden beams. There are remains of another Minoan villa at Sklavókambos, 9 km (5½ mi.) west of Týlisos. **Týlisos**

2 km (1½ mi.) north of Týlisos is the tourist village of Arolithos, established in 1987, where traditional Cretan crafts are preserved.

11 km (7 mi.) west of Sklavókambos is the village of Anóyia (Ανωγεια), which was totally destroyed by German troops in 1944 in retaliation for the capture of General Kreipe by British forces. It is now a popular destination for excursions and a good base for climbs in the Mount Ida range. A Folk Festival is held in the village on August 6th. **Anóyia**

From Anóyia a road (partly made, partly gravel; 22 km (14 mi.)) runs up to the Nida plain (1370 m (4495 ft)). From here it is a 30 min. climb to the **Idaean Cave**

Idaean Cave (Idaío Ándro; 1540 m (5055 ft)), where according to the Greek myth Zeus was brought up by nymphs on goat's milk and honey. The cave was a cult site from Minoan to Roman times.

Mount Ida

The ascent of Mount Ida (Psilorítis), the highest peak in Crete (2456 m (8058 ft)), is rewarding but strenuous, calling for fitness and proper equipment. The climb is usually possible Jun.–Sep. A whole day should be allowed for the ascent and descent. The route, which is part of the E 4 long-distance way, is waymarked with black and yellow signs. The climb can also be done from Kamáres (see p. 147).

Arkhánes

15 km (9 mi.) south of Iráklion is the little town of Arkhánes (Αρχανες), the main wine-growing centre on Crete. The grape mostly grown here is the Rosáki. In the square (several cafés) is the church of the Panayía, which has some fine icons. In the surrounding area there are a number of Minoan sites – the Fourní necropolis, the important site of Anemóspilia (a sanctuary that has been interpreted as the scene of human sacrifices) and at Vathýpetro, 4 km (2½ mi.) a large Minoan villa in a beautiful setting. To the south of Arkhánes is the church of the Archangel Michael (all that is left of the village of Asómatos), with frescos of 1315.

★Mount Yioúkhtas

From Arkhánes a rough track runs up Mount Yioukhtas (811 m (2661 ft)). The climb is rewarded by the wide views, extending as far as Iráklion. On the southern summit is the pilgrimage church of Aféndi Christoú (the Transfiguration), where there is a procession on August 6th.

Myrtiá

In the village of Myrtiá (Μυρτια), 17 km (11 mi.) east of Arkhánes, is a museum (open Mon.–Sat. 9am–4pm) devoted to the great Cretan writer Nikos Kazantzákis (see Famous People), whose father lived in Myrtiá.

From the remains of the palace of Phaistós there is a magnificent view over the fertile Mesará plain to the Mount Ida range

At Amnisós (Αμνισος), 7 km (4½ mi.) east of Iráklion, are the remains of   **Amnisós**
a two-storey Minoan villa with frescos (the "House of the Lilies") and a
harbour building, both dating from around 1800 BC. 4 km (2½ mi.) further
east, near the ancient port of Nírou Kháni, is a Minoan villa with a
sanctuary of the double axe.

Iráklion to Mátala via Górtys, Phaistós and Ayía Triáda

The 75 km (47 mi.) drive from Iráklion to the fertile Mesará plain and
the south coast of Crete is of great scenic beauty and historical
interest. Leaving Iráklion on the road that runs west to Réthymnon,
in 2 km (1¼ mi.) we take a road on the left, signposted to Mires. The
road runs through the main region in Crete for the production of
sultanas, and at Siva begins one of the leading wine-growing areas
on the island, where the famous Malvasia (Malmsey) wine is produced.

A whitewashed rock at Ayía Varvára (Agia Barbara) marks the geo-   **Ayía Varvára**
graphical centre of Crete. 6 km (4 mi.) north of the village are the
remains of ancient Rhizenia. From here there are spectacular views of
the sea and the surrounding area.

The road to Kamáres (29 km (18 mi.) west) runs through very beau-   **Kamáres**
tiful scenery under the Mount Ida range. After passing through
Yeryeri, with a monument commemorating the hostages who were
shot here by German troops in 1944, it comes to Zarós, which is
famed for its trout farm (ponds to the north of the village; fish
restaurant). From the monastery of Áyios Nikólaos, above the village,
there are wide views over the southern foothills of the Mount Ida
range to the Mesará plain. The monastery of Valsamonéro, near
Vorízia (8 km (5 mi.) from Zarós), is magnificently situated. It has
notable frescos of the 14th–15th c. The monastery can be visited only
with the custodian, who lives in Vorízia.
  From Kamáres you can climb to the Kamáres Cave, a Minoan sanctuary in which polychrome vases of the Middle Minoan period were found
(now in the Archaeological Museum in Iráklion). If you want to continue
up to the summit of Mount Psilorítis, the highest peak in the Mount Ida
range (see above), you must spend the night either in the cave, on the
alpine pastures of Kólita or on the summit. The climb takes between 6
and 7 hours.

The main road climbs to the Vourvoulitis Pass (650 m (2133 ft)), from   **Mesará**
which there is a superb view of the Mesará, the largest plain in Crete,
where olives, citrus fruits and even sugar cane flourish. Just before Áyii
Déka the road turns west and comes to the remains of ancient Górtyn
(open daily 8am–5pm).

The town of Górtyn (Górtys), once the rival of Knossos and later chief   **★Górtyn**
town of the Roman province of Creta Cyrenaica, survived until the
coming of the Saracens in AD 826. In an olive grove to the south of the
road can be seen the foundations of a temple of Isis and Serapis (2nd c.
AD), the temple of Apollo Pythios, the palace of the Roman governor,
with a bathhouse (2nd–4th c. AD), a theatre, an amphitheatre and a 374
m (1227 ft) long circus. 500 m further on, to the north of the road (parking), at the foot of the acropolis, are the ruins of the 6th c. church of
Áyios Títos, the remains of an ancient theatre and a tholos that was converted into an odeum (concert hall) in Roman times, on which is
inscribed the Code of Górtyn, a legal code of around 450 BC, the oldest
known European code of laws. The text is written "boustrophedon" (i.e.
as the ox ploughs, with alternate lines running left to right and right to
left).

Crete

Plátanas

At Plátanas (Πλατανας), 6 km (4 mi.) south of Górtyn, are two important Early Minoan tholos tombs. The one to the east is the largest on Crete, with an internal diameter of 13 m (43 ft).

Léntas

At Léntas (Λεντας), on the south coast (17 km (11 mi.) from Górtyn), are the remains of the Greek and Roman town of Lebena, once the port of Górtyn and famed from the 4th c. BC for its healing spring. On a terrace above the present village is a temple of Asclepius (3rd c. BC, rebuilt in 2nd c. AD), with brick walls faced with undressed stone. In the interior are two columns and the base of the cult statue. In a room to the north is a fine mosaic pavement with sea horses and palmette ornament; below this is a chamber in which the temple treasury was kept. From here a stoa and a broad fight of steps led down to the fountain house (still preserved) of the sacred spring. To the east of the temple is an 11th c. chapel dedicated to St John, built on the foundations of a Byzantine basilica of the 5th–6th c., in which ancient masonry was reused. The chapel has frescos of the 14th–15th c.

★Vóri

The road continues west, with constantly changing views of the Mesará plain with its vineyards and olive groves. At Vóri (Βοροι), 2 km (1¼ mi.) off the road to the right, is the finest and most interesting folk museum on Crete (open daily 8am–6pm), with a wealth of material on the fishing, agriculture and forestry and the arts and crafts of the island. To the south of Vóri the road turns off to Phaistós, the most important of the Minoan palaces of Crete after Knossos.

★Phaistós

In the foothills of the Mount Ida range are the remains of Phaistós, a town that according to Greek legend was founded by King Minos (open daily 8am–5pm). At the east end of the hill ridge on which the town is built is the New Palace, laid out on terraces like the palace of Knossos, which was built about 1700 BC on the site of an earlier palace built about 1900 BC and destroyed in an earthquake about 1700. It was itself destroyed by fire about 1450 BC. Of the palace, which was built round a central court, there survive only the remains of the north and west wings, the south and east wings having been destroyed in an earthquake. On the west and north sides of the surviving parts of the later palace can be seen remains of the first palace.

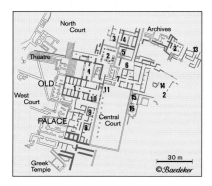

Phaistos
Palace

1 Propylon
2 Peristyle
3 Lustral basin
4 King's Megaron
5 Queen's Megaron
6 Small court
7 Corridor
8 Pillared room
9 Rooms with alabaster benches
10 Hall with columns
11 Altar
12 Storerooms
13 Potter's workshop
14 Foundry
15 Pillared room
16 Luatral basin

Visitors enter the site on the west side. After crossing the North Court they go down a flight of steps, on the right of which are the tiers of seating of a theatre. On the right a monumental staircase 13.75 m (45 ft) wide leading through a propylon into the palace. From the veranda north of the Megaron there is a magnificent view of the Mesará plain.

2 km (1¼ mi.) west of Phaistós are the remains of the Minoan villa of Ayía Triáda (open daily 8.30am–3pm), which was once linked with Phaistós by a paved road. The site is named after the Byzantine chapel of Ayía Triáda on a neighbouring hill; its ancient name is not known. Like Phaistós, the palace dates mainly from the 16th c. BC but was rebuilt after a fire about 1450 and was still occupied in the Dorian period. From the west side of the site there are fine views of the sea and the Mount Ida range. To the south of the villa is the Venetian chapel of St George (14th c.), with frescos and interesting inscriptions. Lower down, to the north-east, can be seen parts of a Late Minoan settlement of the 14th–11th c. BC). At the foot of the hill is a cemetery, with a large tholos tomb.

★**Ayía Triáda**

The road continues south over the Mesará plain, passing the village of Áyios Ioánnis, at the end of which is the interesting church of Áyios Pávlos. Passing through a beautiful olive grove, it comes to the charming village of Pitsidia, with a characteristic old kafeníon in the square. From here a side road goes off to the excavations of Kommos, once the port of Phaistós. The main road ends at Mátala (Ματαλα), in Roman times the port of Górtyn. In the soft sandstone rock face round the harbour are man-made caves used since the neolithic as dwellings and tombs. In the late 1960s they were occupied and damaged by hippies, and are now fenced off. Mátala, now a popular (and overcrowded) holiday resort, has a beautiful beach of sand and shingle, its charm enhanced by the surrounding limestone cliffs.

Mátala

★Áyios Nikólaos

The little town of Áyios Nikólaos (Αγιος Νικολαος; pop. 8500), attractively situated on the beautiful Gulf of Mirabello in eastern Crete, has an agreeably southern air. Thanks to the good beaches in the surrounding area and the other places of interest within easy reach it has long been a very popular holiday resort. The life of the town is centred on the harbour and the beautiful Lake Vouisméni (fresh water, 64 m (210 ft) deep), in which, according to legend, the goddess Athena was accustomed to bathe. Offshore is the island of Áyii Pántes.

Sights Linked with the harbour is the picturesque Lake Vouisméni, surrounded by rock walls. From the harbour Odós Konstantinou Palaeologou leads to the Archaeological Museum (open Tue.–Sun. 8.30am–3pm), which is devoted mainly to archaeological material from eastern Crete, ranging from the neolithic period into Greek and Roman times. In the harbourmaster's office is the Folk Museum (open Sun.–Fri. 10am–1.30pm, 6–9.30pm). The 10th c. church of Áyios Nikólaos, which gave its name to the town, stands below the Minos Palace Hotel (key at reception) on the north-east side of the town; it has frescos of the Iconoclastic period. There is an important procession here at Epiphany.

On a hillside 11 km (7 mi.) south-west of Áyios Nikólaos, amid old olive groves, is the village of Kritsá (Κριτσα), now a crowded tourist centre with numerous souvenir shops selling local arts and crafts and kitsch. It

★**Kritsá**

The harbour of Áyios Nikólaos

became widely known when the film "Greek Passion", based on Kazantzákis's novel, was shot here. 1 km (¾ mi.) before Kritsá on the road from Áyios Nikólaos, surrounded by tall cypresses, is the beautiful church of the Panayía Kera (12th–14th c.), with magnificent frescos of the 14th–15th c. (open Mon.–Sat. 10am–3pm, Sun. to 2pm). Particularly fine are the "Ascension" in the nave and the frescos in the north aisle.

3 km (2 mi.) north of Kritsá, in hilly country, are the remains of the Dorian city of Lato, probably dating from the 7th–4th c. BC. From the acropolis, to the north, there are superb views of the Gulf of Mirabello and the hills. 2 km (1¼ mi.) south of Kritsá, on the road to Kroustás, is the church of Áyios Ioánnis, with a sumptuously decorated iconostasis. 4 km (2½ mi.) south of Kroustás is another church dedicated to St John, with fine frescos of 1347.

★Lassíthi plain

From Áyios Nikólaos a road (40 km (25 mi.)) runs through beautiful scenery to the fertile Lassíthi plain, an almost exactly circular plateau lying at a height of 850 m (2800 ft), surrounded by karstic hills. Almost all of the many thousand windmills that once drew up water for irrigating the intensively cultivated land have been replaced by motor-powered pumps. In the village of Áyios Yeóryios is an interesting Folk Museum (open 10am–4pm). On the south-west edge of the plain, above the village of Psykhró, is the stalactitic Dictaean Cave (Diktaíon Ándron), the legendary birthplace of Zeus, which attracts large numbers of Cretans and visitors. If the climb is too much for you, you can hire a donkey – an expensive luxury. The cave is open 10.30am–5pm (take a pocket torch).

Limín Khersonísou

A short distance beyond Kerá is the 14th c. Kardiótissa Monastery (closed 1–3.30pm). In Krasí a tall cypress in the square provides shade for the tables of the taverna. From here Mália, on the north coast, can be reached either by way of Mokhos, with a lively square, or direct on the new road. This runs through Avdoú, with several Byzantine churches (particularly Áyios Antónios, which has fine 14th c. frescos), and Potamiés, with the abandoned Gouverniótissa Monastery (10th–14th c.), and comes to Limín Khersonísou (Λιμην Χερσονησου), which consists of the old village a little way inland (attractive square) and the bathing resort on the coast, in which are the remains of an Early Christian basilica with floor mosaics. On the coast is the Lykhnostatis open-air museum (open Tue.–Sun. 9.30am–2pm), which contains a reconstruction of a typical Cretan village.

Mália

The bay between Limín Khersonísou and Mália (Μαλια) has a beautiful sandy beach that has made this stretch of coast one of the most popular holiday regions on Crete, with dozens of hotels, discotheques, cafés and tavernas: the old villages have almost been swallowed up. From Mália it is an hour's walk along the beach to a fertile plain in which are the remains (partly roofed) of the Middle Minoan palace of Mália (open Tue.–Sun. 8.30am–3pm). The palace was originally built around 1800 BC and rebuilt after an earthquake about 1700 BC. Round the palace are the remains of the Minoan town and a cemetery area.

Eloúnda

11 km (7 mi.) north of Áyios Nikólaos is the hotel village of Eloúnda (Ελουνδα), at the head of an inlet formed by the Spinalonga peninsula. From the road there is a fine view of the bay. At the near end of the village a road goes off on the right on to the peninsula, on which are some remains (some of them under the water) of the Dorian city of Olous.

Spinalonga

Off the northern tip of the Spinalonga peninsula is the rocky island of the same name (also known as Kalidon). The Venetian fort (1579–85) was occupied from 1903 to 1957 by a leper colony, and is now a rather macabre tourist sight (boats from Eloúnda and Áyios Nikólaos).

Dreros

22 km (14 mi.) north-west of Áyios Nikólaos and 2 km (1¼ mi.) north-east of the village of Neápolis are the remains of the Archaic settlement of Dreros, with an excellently preserved sanctuary of Apollo of the 7th c. BC. A number of bronze cult images found here are now in the Archaeological Museum in Iráklion.

★Gourniá

A good impression of the aspect of a Middle Minoan town of around 1500 BC can be gained from the remains (only partially excavated) of Gourniá, 20 km (13 mi.) south-east of Áyios Nikólaos (open Tue.–Sun. 8.30am–3pm). With its narrow paved streets, its small houses and its palace and temple on higher ground, this is one of the earliest examples of the layout of a European town.

Mókhlos

11 km (7 mi.) north-east of Gourniá is Plátanos, from which there is a magnificent view of the Gulf of Mirabello and the island of Psíra (on which there are remains of a Middle and Late Minoan settlement). 5 km (3 mi.) north-east of this is the charming little fishing village of Mókhlos (Μοχλος) with good tavernas. Offshore is the island of the same name (boat services), with numerous tombs in which objects of the Early Minoan period were found.

Ierápetra

36 km (22 mi.) south of Áyios Nikólaos, on the south coast, is Ierápetra (Ιεραπετρα; pop. 11,000), the most southerly town in Europe, which already has something of a North African air. It lies in a fertile vegetable-growing area with a particularly warm climate (bathing possible even in January). The ancient port of Hierapydna was the see of a bishop in the 4th c. AD, and in 1798 Napoleon is said to have lodged here, in a house north of the harbour known as Spiti tou Napoleon. A former Koranic school in Platía Koupanaki now houses a small archaeological museum

with material of the Roman and Venetian periods (open Tue.–Sun. 8.30am–3pm). South of the square is the old town, centred on a mosque with a beautifully restored minaret and ablution fountain. On the Libyan Sea is a Venetian fort designed to defend the harbour, the starting point of the seafront promenade lined with tavernas and cafés, above a beach of dark sand.

Khrysí

18 km (11 mi.) south of Ierápetra (boat services) is the island of Khrysí (Χρυσί; also known as Galdouronísi), with a magnificent dune beach. Round the landing stage are a number of tavernas that open only in summer.

Sitía

Sitía (Σητεια; ancient Eteia), Crete's most easterly town (pop. 7000), is picturesquely situated on the slopes above the bay of the same name. The town, which was destroyed by an earthquake in 1303 and again in 1508 and was bombarded by a Turkish fleet commanded by Khaireddin Barbarossa in 1538, is mainly modern. It was the home of Vintzentinos Kornaros (d. 1677), author of an epic romance, the "Erotokritos", which is still popular. After destruction by the Turks in 1651 it was not reoccupied until 1970.

Sights Attractive features of the town are the seafront promenade with its restaurants and Platía Iróon Politekhníou with its palm trees and cafés. Above the town stepped lanes lead up to the Kazarma fort (1631), from which there are wide views of the town and surrounding area; in summer there are performances and concerts in the open-air theatre here. To the east of the Custom House (restored) scanty remains of Roman fish tanks can be seen in the sea. On the road to Piskokefalou is the Archaeological Museum (open Tue.–Sun. 8.30am–3pm), with material from eastern Crete ranging from Minoan to Roman times. There is an interesting Folk Museum in Odós Therissou, with a collection of domestic equipment, costumes and implements.

Toploú Monastery

5 km (3 mi.) east of Sitía, at Ayía Fotiá, are the remains of a Minoan cemetery. 16 km (10 mi.) further east is the fortress-like Toploú Monastery (14th–17th c.), a centre of resistance to the Turks and a place of refuge during the German occupation in the Second World War. The monastery has an interesting collection of Bibles and icons (open 9am–1pm and 2–6pm).

★Vái Beach

At the little village of Vái, situated in a beautiful sandy bay 7 km (4½ mi.) north-east of Toploú Monastery, is the largest palm grove on Crete. In summer the beach is overcrowded, and the palm grove, apart from a few trees, is hermetically fenced off.

Itanos

3 km (2 mi.) further north, at Erimoúpolis, are the remains of the ancient port town of Itanos. There are three beautiful beaches of coarse sand, undisturbed by crowds of visitors.

Palaíokastro

On a hill 7 km (4½ mi.) south of Vái, surrounded by olive groves, is the village of Palaíokastro (Παλαιοκαστρο), much enlarged since it has become a holiday resort popular with young independent travellers. Near the beach are the remains of a Minoan town known as Rousolákkos.

★Káto Zákros

17 km (11 mi.) south of Palaíokastro on a magnificent panoramic road, high above the sea, is the village of Zákros, with an abundant supply of water. From there you can drive or walk through the oleander-fringed gorge known as the Valley of the Dead (so called because of the Minoan tombs found here) to the partly excavated remains of Káto

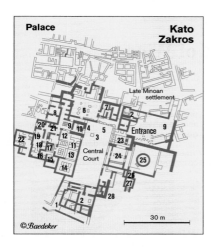

Palace **Kato Zakros**

1 South entrance
2 Workshops
3 Square base (altar?)
4 Entrance to west wing
5 Portico
6 Kitchen and dining room
7 Room with kitchen equipment
8 Storerooms
9 Room with tiled floor
10 Antechamber
11 Large columned hall
12 Light well
13 Square room
14 Banqueting hall
15 Workshop
16 Treasury
17 Lustral basin
18 Shrine
19 Archives
20,21 Talents and elephants' tusks found here
22 Dyer's workshop
23 Queen's Megaron
24 King's Megaron
25 Large circular basin
26 Square fountain
27 Square basin
28 Circular fountain
29 Lustral basin

Zákros (open Tue.–Sun. 8.30am–3pm), in the bay of the same name. The town was occupied from the Early Minoan period. The palace existed between 1600 and 1410 BC and carried on trade with Egypt and the rest of North Africa.

15 km (9 mi.) south of Sitía is Praisós, with a Minoan villa and a Hellenistic cemetery. There are other Minoan sites at Piskokefalou, Zou and Riza. At Akhládia is a Mycenaean tholos tomb.

Praisós

★★Delos   K 6

Island group: Cyclades
Area: 3.6 sq. km (1½ sq. mi.)
Altitude: 0–113 m (0–371 ft)
Population: 15

Boats from Mýkonos, depending on demand and the weather; occasional connections with Tínos, Náxos and Páros. The maximum time available for sightseeing is 3–4 hours. It is advisable to have strong shoes, headgear and (when the *meltémi* is blowing) a warm jacket.
 Delos (Dílos, Δηλος, Δηλος), a rocky island (gneiss, slate and granite) 5 km (3 mi.) long and only 1.3 km (¾ mi.) wide, almost devoid of vegetation, lies 10 km (6 mi.) south-west of Mýkonos. Its highest point is Mount Kynthos (113 m (371 ft)), roughly in the centre of the island.

Location of Delos in the Aegean

Akr. Via
Mýkonos
135 m
Ornos
Rheneia
136 m
Akr. Morti
Mykonos
●Ancient sites
113 m
Prasonisi
Dílos
Delos
Chironisi
Akr. Podio
©Baedeker

Halfway along the west coast is an ancient sacred harbour, sheltered by two small rocks in the strait between Delos and Rinía. From here the main plain on the island extends north-east.

The God of Wine

His head wreathed with vine-leaves and an inebriated smile on his face, Dionysus, the thirteenth of the gods of Olympus, cuts a curious figure among the handsome and imposing divinities of Greek legend. As the god of wine, of wild love, of drunkenness and ecstasy, with a noisy retinue of joyous satyrs and amorous bacchantes, he stood for the enjoyment of all the pleasures of life. As the scene of his activities he chose the island of Naxos, whose inhabitants he taught to grow excellent wine.

Dionysus owed his promotion to Olympus to his father Zeus, who had begotten him on Semele. Zeus's jealous wife Hera, however, had got wind of his affair with Semele and, disguised as a respectable wet-nurse, persuaded Semele to insist that her lover should reveal himself to her in his real form. When, after long hesitation, Zeus agreed to do this Semele was struck dead by his radiance. Then Zeus plucked the unborn Dionysus from her womb and sewed him up in his thigh, from which the child emerged at full term. He then handed him over to the nymphs on Mount Nysa to rear, after which he was educated by Silenus.

Among Dionysus's numerous adventures was his voyage to Naxos, when he fell into the hands of pirates. When they tried to bind him he turned their ropes and their masts into sprays of vine-leaves and vine plants, whereupon the pirates, terrified, dived into the sea and were changed into dolphins. On Naxos he married Ariadne, who had been abandoned on the island by Theseus on his return from Crete after killing the Minotaur and finding his way out of the labyrinth with the help of Ariadne's thread. In the ancient tradition Dionysus is usually depicted in a chariot drawn by panthers or riding on a panther, accompanied by horned silenuses, goat-shanked satyrs and frolicking nymphs. Other attendants such as maenads, thyads and bacchantes crowned with ivy, drunken and ecsta-

The huge phalluses on Delos are symbols of the fertility cult centred on Dionysus

tic, follow him in his progress through the mountain forests.

Dionysus's un-Greek orgiastic rites were not at first generally popular, but gradually won acceptance, and the cult of Dionysus soon became associated with fertility myths and ideas of salvation, the eternal cycle of developing and decaying. There were special festivals on Naxos and Delos in which giant phalluses played a part. The Anthesteria, an ecstatic spring festival, involved offerings of wine and the drinking of wine. The Naxians were particularly fond of their jovial god, and there is still a saying: "Drink wine on Naxos and you will feel like a god."

The northern, lower part of the island was flooded by the sea, creating the sacred lake. Although the island appears so barren, the nature of the ground (sandstone over granite) made it possible to collect the water between the two layers of rock in wells and cisterns.

Although it is one of the smallest of the Cyclades, Delos, as the **birthplace of Apollo**, was a place of such importance in ancient times that the surrounding islands were known as the Cyclades since they lay in a circle (*kyklos*) round the sacred island. As the main centre of the cult of Apollo Delos was also the intellectual, cultural and economic centre of the Aegean.

The extensive area of remains (excavated by French archaeologists from 1873 onwards) is one of the most important archaeological sites in Greece. Delos is thus an island that appeals particularly to those who are interested in Greek antiquity; it has none of the usual tourist facilities.

According to the Greek **myth**, it was on Delos that Leto, the beloved of Zeus, gave birth to Apollo and Artemis. Fleeing from Zeus's jealous wife, Hera, she had travelled through the whole of Greece seeking refuge, but no one would take her in for fear of the angry Hera. Finally Delos emerged from the sea and Poseidon, Zeus's brother, anchored it to the seabed with his trident. Then Leto gave birth under a palm tree to Apollo, the god of light, poetry and beauty, and his sister Artemis.

The **history** of the island was determined by its importance as a pan-Hellenic shrine. The first settlers, in the 3rd millennium BC, were Phoenicians and Carians. In the 1st millennium, after the original inhabitants had been driven out by Ionians, the island became the centre of the cult of Apollo. In 543 BC Peisistratus carried out a "purification" (*katharsis*) of the island, with the removal of all tombs from the vicinity of the temples. In a second purification in 426/425 BC, after an epidemic of plague in Athens, births, deaths and burials were prohibited on Delos, and the existing tombs were transferred to the neighbouring island of Rheneia (Rínia). When the Ionian League was founded after the Persian wars, its treasury was deposited in the temple of Apollo; but in 454 BC the Athenians carried it off to Athens, and thereafter Delos and the other islands remained dependants of Athens until the time of Alexander the Great.

Later Delos developed a flourishing trade that made it the economic centre of the archipelago, and foreign trading corporations like the Hermaists (Romans) and Poseidoniasts (Syrians from Berytos/Beirut) had headquarters on the island. The Romans, who had established a protectorate over the island in 166 BC, handed it back to Athens. As a result – particularly after the destruction of Corinth – Delos enjoyed its greatest period of prosperity, which lasted until the devastation of the island by Mithradates in 88 BC, initiating its decline. Complete destruction followed in 69 BC, when the island was sacked by pirates. Thereafter Delos was practically uninhabited. When Pausanias visited it in the 2nd c. AD he saw only the custodians of the sanctuary. In the Middle Ages and early modern period Delos became a stronghold of the Knights of St John and later a pirates' lair. Thereafter it served as a quarry of building stone.

To the west of Delos is Rínia (also known as Megali Dílos; area 17 sq. km (6½ sq. mi.)), ancient Rheneia. After the second purification it became the burial place for the inhabitants of Delos.

On the west side of the island is the sacred harbour (landing stage just to the south of it), now completely silted up, where delegations attending the annual festival used to land. To the south of this is the old commercial harbour. The coast between the sacred harbour and Foumi Bay was lined in a later period with quays (completed in 111 BC) and warehouses, remains of which can be seen under water.

Sacred harbour

Sacred precinct

Flanking the harbour is the Agora of the Competaliasts, decorated with statues and small shrines, where members of this corporation – Roman slaves and freedmen – gathered for the cult of the Lares Competales, the gods who protected crossroads. From here the Festival Way, 13 m (43 ft) wide, ran north to the sacred precinct. The 87 m (285 ft) long Stoa of Philip V (on left), a columned hall of the Doric order open on its east and west sides, has an inscription on the architrave recording that it was built by Philip V of Macedon about 210 BC. On the south side of the road is a smaller stoa with eight shops along the far side. Beyond this, to the east, is the almost square South Agora (1st c. BC). The area extending north to the Hall of the Bulls was occupied in the Middle Ages by fortifications built by the Knights of St John.

Agora of the Competaliasts

The Festival Way passes through the South Propylaia (2nd c. BC), which have Doric columns on a three-stepped base, and runs north. Immediately on the right is the House of the Naxians (7th c. BC), with a row of columns along its longitudinal axis. At its north end is the base of a 5 m (16 ft) high statue of Apollo, with an inscription (6th c. BC) indicating that the statue and its base were carved from a single block of stone. The dedication on the west side ("The Naxians to Apollo") was a later addition.

House of the Naxians

Opposite the House of the Naxians is its L-shape stoa (c. 550 BC), with Ionic columns. In the angle of the stoa stood the bronze palm presented by the Athenian Nicias in 417 BC, commemorating the palm under which Leto gave birth to Apollo and Artemis.

Further north is the most sacred spot on Delos, the Keraton, a temple dedicated to Apollo. It contained a horned altar, famed as one of the wonders of the world, with rams' horns set round it. In front of the entrance to the Keraton, which faces the harbour, are a number of bases for equestrian statues, the most northerly and smallest of which bore a statue of Sulla (inscription on the ramp to the rear).

Keraton

The Keraton is believed to be older than the smaller shrine of Artemis, the Artemision, on the north side of the precinct. This Ionic prostyle temple (4th–2nd c. BC) on granite foundations was built on the site of an earlier temple of the 7th c. BC. At the north-west corner of the Artemision are the trunk and pelvis of the statue of Apollo in the House of the Naxians. North-west of the Artemision is the Thesmophorion, which was dedicated to the cult of Demeter.

Artemision

To the east of the Artemision, side by side, were three temples of Apollo – the central point of the sanctuary. The most southerly of these (begun in 478 BC, completed in the 3rd c. BC), which resembles the Theseion in Athens in layout, is the largest of the three, covering an area of 29.50 m (97 ft) by 13.55 m (44 ft). The massive foundations, built on a stratum of greyish-blue slate, indicate that the temple was peripteral, with 6 by 13 columns. The pronaos at the east end and opisthodomos at the west end probably had two columns between the antae. The naos measured 11.50 m (38 ft) by 5.60 m (18 ft). Of the temple itself little is left except the Doric columns and some fragments of the frieze of triglyphs, and of the sculptural decoration only the palmette ornament and the lions' heads from the sima remain.

Precinct of Apollo

Immediately north of this temple are the foundations, in poros limestone, of the Temple of the Athenians (417 BC; Doric), which is amphiprostyle, with a naos divided into two parts. In this temple were seven statues on bases of dark marble.

◀ *View from the Temple of Apollo of the excavation site, one of the most important archaeological sites in Greece*

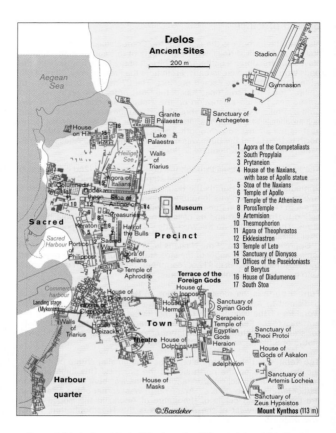

Delos
Ancient Sites
200 m

Aegean
Sea

Stadion

Gymnasion

House
on Hill

Granite
Palaestra

Sanctuary of
Archegetes

Lake
Palaestra

Walls
of
Triarius

*Heilige
See*

Agora of
Italians

Columned
Hall

Dodekatheon

Stoa of
Antigonos

Museum

Treasuries

Sacred

Keraton

Hall of
the Bulls

Precinct

Sacred
Harbour

Portico
of
Philippos

Sacred
Way

Agora of
Delians

Commercial
harbour

Temple of
Aphrodite

Terrace of the
Foreign Gods

House of
Inopos

Landing stage
(Mykonos)

House of
Dionysos

House of
Cleopatra

House of
Dreizack

House of
Hermes

Sanctuary of
Syrian Gods

Serapeion
Temple of
Egyptian
Gods

Sanctuary of
Theoi Protoi

Walls
of
Triarius

Town

Theatre

House of
Dolphins

Heraion

Phil-
adelpheion

House of
Gods of Askalon

Harbour

quarter

House of
Masks

Sanctuary of
Artemis Locheia

Sanctuary of
Zeus Hypsistos

©Baedeker

Mount Kynthos (113 m)

1 Agora of the Competaliasts
2 South Propylaia
3 Prytaneion
4 House of the Naxians,
  with base of Apollo statue
5 Stoa of the Naxians
6 Temple of Apollo
7 Temple of the Athenians
8 PorosTemple
9 Artemision
10 Thesmophorion
11 Agora of Theophrastos
12 Ekklesiastron
13 Temple of Leto
14 Sanctuary of Dionysos
15 Offices of the Poseidoniasts
   of Berytus
16 House of Diadumenos
17 South Stoa

Beyond this is the oldest of the temples (6th c. BC), in which the treasury of the Attic-Delian maritime league was kept. It contained an 8 m (26 ft) high bronze statue of Apollo. In front of this temple is a long statue base on which there were once bronze figures – a monument erected in the 3rd c. BC in honour of Philetaerus, founder of the royal house of Pergamon.

Treasuries

To the north of the temple of Apollo are four small buildings, which on the basis of their similarity to buildings at Olympia and Delphi are believed to have been treasuries. A fifth building to the south, with a pronaos and opisthodomos, was probably a temple.

Prytaneion

To the east of the House of the Naxians are the Prytaneion, the office of the island's chief official, and the Hall of the Bulls or Ship Hall. One of the best preserved buildings on Delos, dated to the Hellenistic period, it measures 67.2 m (220 ft) by 8.86 m (29 ft). The building stood on a granite platform approached by three marble steps (still partly preserved), with walls round the sides and the north end; at the south end was a portico with six Doric columns along the sides and two at each end. The interior was in the form of a long gallery with a cavity in the centre. Of the sculptural decoration only a nereid and a dolphin remain in situ. The core of granite blocks, narrowing towards the north end, may have borne the mast of a ship that Demetrius Poliorcetes, king of Macedon, set up here after a naval victory over Ptolemy I, ruler of Egypt, in 306 BC. At the entrance are pillars preceded by Doric half-columns, with capitals depicting recumbent bulls. The step-like structure south-east of the Hall of the Bulls is part of an altar of Zeus Polieus.

Along the north side of the sacred precinct is the Stoa of Antigonus Gonatas (3rd c. BC), a columned hall measuring 119 m (390 ft) by 20 m (65 ft) with bull's-head triglyphs. Antigonus, son of Demetrius Poliorcetes, was an important king of Greece and Macedonia. To the rear of the columns, only the upper parts of which were fluted, were rooms for housing representatives sent to the annual festival. In front of the stoa, halfway along it, is a semicircular structure – all that is left of the Mycenaean tholos tomb of the Hyperborean Maidens, who attended Leto at the birth of the divine twins.

Stoa of Antigonus Gonatas

To the east of the stoa is the sanctuary of Dionysus, with several marble phalluses. On one of the bases are carvings of scenes from the cult of Dionysus (c. 300 BC).

From here propylaia lead out of the sacred precinct into the commercial quarter. Beyond an archaic temple of Leto (6th c. BC), on the right, is the Agora of the Italians (110 BC), a large rectangular area measuring 48 m (157 ft) by 68 m (223 ft) surrounded by two-storey colonnaded halls containing shops, workshops and recesses for votive offerings (mosaics). These were the business premises of the corporation of Roman merchants who called themselves Hermaists after their patron Hermes.

Commercial quarter

The famous lions of Delos – now no longer to be seen on their original site

Delos

Sacred Lake

The oval Sacred Lake (filled in by the excavators in 1924) marks the end of the sacred precinct. Leto is said to have given birth to Apollo on a small island in the lake. On a terrace to the west of the lake there stood until 1999 a row of five Archaic lions of Naxian marble (7th c. BC). The surface of the marble was being worn away by Aegean storms, and in order to preserve them from further deterioration they were removed to the site museum. North-west of the lake were the offices of the Poseidoniasts of Berytus (Beirut; 110 BC), now represented only by a few re-erected columns. Beyond this is the House of the Diadumenos, in which a Roman copy of the famous statue by Polycleitus (c. 420 BC) was found; it is now in the National Archaeological Museum in Athens. To the north of the lake were the Old and the New Palaestras. Further north-east were the sanctuary of the hero Archegetes, which only Delians might enter, the Gymnasion and the Stadion.

★Museum

To the east of the sacred precinct is the Museum (closed Mon.). Near the entrance is a model of Delos that gives a vivid impression of the one-time splendour of its buildings. In the two central rooms are works of Archaic art, including a marble tripod base with a ram's head and Gorgons (7th c. BC), a sphinx of Naxian marble, several kouroi and korai (6th c. BC), a hand of the Naxian Apollo and three seated figures of women (7th c. BC). The other rooms contain fragments from the Temple of the Athenians, herms, funerary stelae, small sculpture, terracottas and pottery, votive offerings from the temple of Artemis and a variety of small finds that illustrate the life of the inhabitants of Delos and the furnishings of their houses. The finest finds from Delos, however, are now in the National Archaeological Museum and the Museum of Cycladic Art in Athens.

Kynthos precinct

House of Hermes

From the Museum a path runs south-east to Mount Kynthos. Off the path to the right is the House of Hermes, so called after the head of Hermes found here (now in the Museum). The house, originally two storeys, dates from the 2nd c. BC.

Terrace of the Foreign Gods

Higher up is the Terrace of the Foreign Gods, where Egyptian and Syrian gods were worshipped from the 2nd c. BC onwards – an indication of the international importance of the island. Beside the Doric temple of Isis are the foundations of the Heraion (c. 500 BC), a temple of Hera.

★★Mount Kynthos

From here an ancient stepped path runs up Mount Kynthos (113 m (371 ft)), on which are the remains of temples of Zeus Kynthios and Athena Kynthia (3rd c. BC). From the summit of the hill there are fantastic panoramic views – to the south Náxos, to the west Sýros with the residential district of Ermoúpoli, to the north and east Mýkonos with its countless chapels.

Residential area

Between Mount Kynthos and the commercial harbour is the residential area (3rd–2nd c. BC), which gives an excellent impression of housing conditions in the Hellenistic period. The narrow streets are paved with slabs of slate. The houses, many of which stand 4–5 m (13–16 ft) high, had at least one upper storey. There are a number of excellently preserved mosaic pavements.

House of the Dolphins

On the path running down from Mount Kynthos, to the right, is the House of the Dolphins, with a fine dolphin mosaic in the peristyle. Diagonally opposite it is the House of the Masks, with a mosaic depicting actors' masks.

Theatre

Further west is the Theatre (3rd c. BC), which could accommodate an audience of 5000. The orchestra was surrounded by a narrow water channel, the stage building by a colonnade, the east side of which served as a proskenion. Below the stage building is a huge cistern in which rainwater flowing down from the auditorium was collected.

Below the theatre is the House of the Trident, named after a mosaic depicting a trident decorated with a ribbon. Further north is the House of Dionysus, with the finest mosaic on Delos, depicting a winged Dionysus riding on a panther. Opposite it is the House of Cleopatra, with headless figure of the owners, Cleopatra and Dioscurides. From here it is a short distance to the landing stage and the end of the tour.

House of the Trident, House of Dionysus, House of Cleopatra

Erimonísia   K 6/7

Island group: Cyclades

The Erimonísia (Ερημονησια; "Lonely Islands") or Nisídes ("Islets"), officially known as the Little Eastern Cyclades, are a chain of barren but, in spite of their name, by no means lonely islands in the triangular area between Náxos, Amorgós and Íos. The most northerly are the Voidonísi, a group of small islands. To the south of these are Donoúsa and the Makáries, a group of islets between Donoúsa and Náxos. Further south again are the Koufo Islands – Presoúra, Áno Koufonísi (area 8 sq. km (3 sq. mi.)) and Káto Koufonísi (5 sq. km (2 sq. mi.)), and to the east Kéros (14 sq. km (5½ sq. mi.)), on which important Bronze Age remains have been excavated, Antikéros and Dríma. To the south-west is Skhinoússa. The most southerly island in the group is Iráklia. The islands' attractions are peace and quiet, severe beauty and long sandy beaches. There is still only a modest growth of tourism, but since there are only a few rooms in private houses in the tiny villages accommodation can be a problem in the main holiday season.

The centre of activity on Donoúsa (Δονουσα) is the village of that name, also known as Áyios Stávros (pop. 80). There is an attractive walk (about 4 hours) round the little island, passing a number of good beaches.

Donoúsa

The south coast of Iráklia (Ηρακλεια), the largest island in the group (6 km (4 mi.)), falls steeply down to the sea, but elsewhere there are bays and inlets with sandy beaches. The finest beach, at Livádia, is 1 km (¾ mi.) south of the port of Áyios Yeóryios (pop. 80). The chief place on the island is Iráklia (Panayía); from here it is a 1½ hour walk to the stalactitic cave of Áyios Ioánnis.

Iráklia

The two islands of Páno and Káto Koufonísi (Κουφονησι) are separated by a 200 m (660 ft) wide strait. Both islands have beautiful beaches (boat services), but only Páno Koufonísi is inhabited.

Koufonísi

On this relatively flat island (area 10 sq. km (4 sq. mi.); pop. 100) are two tiny villages – Skhinoússa (Σχινουσσα; also known as Panayía after its church, which contains a valuable icon of the Mother of God) and Mesariá, now falling into ruin. There are a number of beautiful unfrequented beaches, the finest of which is Psilí Ámmos.

Skhinoússa

★Euboea   G–I 4–6

Area: 3897 sq. km (1505 sq. mi.)
Altitude: 0–1743 m (0–5719 ft)
Population: 165,000

Chief town: Khalkís

Road connections with the mainland via two bridges at Khalkís. Buses from Athens to Khalkís, Kými and Aidipsós and to the ferry ports of Skála Oropoú and Rafína. Bus services on the island from Khalkís to Kými, Stení and Límni.

Ferry services: Glyfa–Ayiókampos, Arkítsa–Loutrá Aidipsoú, Skála Oropoú–Erétria, Ayía Marína–Néa Stýra, Rafína–Marmári and Rafína–Kárystos.

Shipping services: Vólos–Northern Sporades–Kými and Kými–Lemnos–Kavála and Androúpolis.

Rail service Athens–Khalkís.

Euboea (Ευβοια; Greek Évvia, on maps often Évia), the second largest Greek island (170 km (106 mi.) long, 5.5 km (3½ mi.) across), lies off the north-east coast of Boetia and Attica, from which it is separated by two enclosed arms of the sea, the Northern and Southern Euboean Gulfs. The two gulfs meet in the narrow strait of Evripós (only 35 m (114 ft) wide and 8.5 m (28 ft) deep), roughly at the centre of the island. The principal ports lie on the gentler coast facing the mainland; the rocky north-east coast for the most part falls steeply down to the sea. In terms of topography the island is divided into two parts: the hilly, wooded north and the barren, waterless south, more akin to the islands in the Aegean.

There are four main ranges of hills, some of them heavily wooded: in the north-west the Telétrion range (highest point Xerón, 991 m (3251 ft)), south-east of this the Kandíli range (highest point 1225 m (4019 ft)); to the east the Dírfys range (Delfí, 1743 m (5719 ft)), and at the south-eastern tip of the island the Ókhi range (1398 m (4587 ft)). Below the hills, particularly on the west coast, are small, fertile alluvial plains.

Economy Euboea has minerals (magnesite, lignite) that supply metal-processing industries, particularly round Khalkís. One of island's main sources of income is poultry farming, which accounts for around half of Greece's total production. The attraction of Euboea, which is a popular weekend resort with the people of Athens, lies mainly in its scenic beauty. International tourism has not yet discovered the island, with the exception of Erétria – perhaps because it is not enough of an island. Even at the height of summer few visitors spend their holiday here.

History The earliest inhabitants of Euboea were Ellopians, incomers from Thessaly, in the north-west of the island; Abantes, a Thracian people, in central Euboea; and Dryopians in the south-east. Ionians from Attica mingled with the Abantes, bringing the island a period of great prosperity between the 8th and 6th c. BC. Their two principal cities, Chalcis and Eretria, established numerous colonies in southern Italy, Sicily and the Thracian Chersonese (Chalcidice). In 506 BC Chalcis was conquered by Athens, to which possession of the fertile island soon became a matter of vital importance for its timber, grain and copper. Towards the end of the Peloponnesian War, in 411 BC, Euboea broke away from Athens, but in subsequent wars was usually on the Athenian side. After the Latin conquest of Constantinople in AD 1204 Euboea was held by three Veronese barons, except for the ports, which fell to the Venetians, who after much fighting with the Frankish princes gained control of the whole island, calling it Negroponte (a corruption of Evripos). It became the second most important Venetian stronghold (after Crete) in the eastern Mediterranean, but in 1470 fell to the Turks. It was finally united with Greece under the Second London Protocol of 1830.

Khalkís

Khalkís (or Khalkída; Χαλκις; pop. 80,000), chief town and port of

Euboea, is attractively situated on a number of hills round the strait of Evripós. Its situation at the closest point to the mainland led to the development of a port at a very early stage, and in 411 BC the town was linked with the mainland by a timber bridge at the narrowest point of the Evripós. In the Middle Ages a stone bridge was built, with a central bastion; it was longer than the present bridge, since the narrow channel to the west of the Turkish fort of Karababa (1686) was later filled in. An interesting feature of the modern bridge (1962) is that the two sections of the bridge can be retracted under the access ramps. The Evripós is noted for its alternating currents that change at least six times a day, and sometimes up to 20 times. The phenomenon, which was a puzzle from ancient times, is thought to be due to interaction between the tides and areas of stagnant water. Aristotle was said to have drowned himself in the channel because he could not solve the puzzle: in fact he died a natural death in Chalcis in 322 BC.

The Latin alphabet was based on the script of ancient Chalcis.

From the old Turkish fort of Karababa, which was in use until 1856, there are good views of the town and, to the south, of the Bay of Aulis, from which the Mycenaeans set sail for Troy; there too Agamemnon is said to have sacrificed his daughter Iphigeneia. To the east of the bridge is the main part of the town, with the neoclassical Town Hall, surrounded by hotels, restaurants and cafés. Beyond this is the old Venetian and Turkish town, which still preserves remains of its walls. | Karababa fort

The church of Ayía Paraskeví (second street on the left from the bridge), the town's principal church in Venetian times, was rebuilt by the crusaders in Gothic style (rare in Greece) in the 13th–14th c. Of its 5th–6th c. predecessor there remain some columns of cipollino marble from Kárystos. The palace of the Venetian Governor now houses the municipal prison. | Ayía Paraskeví

Adjoining the old town on the north is the busy Proasteion (suburban district). In Leofóros Venizelou is the Archaeological Museum (open Tue.–Sun. 8.30am–3pm), with interesting material, mainly from Eretria (see below). In Platía Koskou are the Byzantine Museum, housed in a mosque that was converted in 1470 from the church of San Marco di Negroponte, and a beautiful Turkish fountain. | Museums

Khalkís to Límni through north-western Euboea

This route (200 km (125 mi.)) runs north-east from Khalkís, keeping close to the Evripós (some old tombs), and comes in 7 km (4½ mi.) to Néa Artáki (Νέα Αρτακι), an attractive and very popular bathing resort. 23 km (14 mi.) from Néa Artáki is Stení, a pretty mountain village in a green and well watered area. | Néa Artáki

The ascent of the imposing pyramid of Delfí (1743 m (5719 ft)), the principal summit of Mount Dírfys, is strenuous but not difficult (7 hours there and back; too hot in summer). | Mount Dírfys

The gateway to the more rugged and picturesque interior of northern Euboea is Psakhná (Ψαχνα; 7 km (4½ mi.)), 3 km (2 mi.) north of which are the ruins of the Venetian castle of Kástri. 9 km (6 mi.) away, on the coast, is the bathing resort of Politiká (Πολιτικα), with a long shingle beach; the church of the Perivléptos monastery has fine 16th c. frescos. The main route continues to the saddle between Mounts Kandylion (1209 m (3967 ft)) and Pisaria (1352 m (4436 ft)), from which there are magnificent panoramic views. The road continues through beautiful mountain scenery with forests of planes and conifers, passing an ancient fort that was enlarged by the Venetians, to the little monastery | Psakhná

Politiká

of Áyios Yeóryios, and then runs down through the Kyréfs valley, with its abundant growth of arbutus and myrtle.

Prokópi

The prosperous village of Prokópi (Προκοπι) in the green Klisoúra valley was established in 1923 by refugees from the little town of that name in Turkey (now Ürgüp) on the former Turkish estate of Ahmet-Aga. They brought with them a wonderworking icon of St John the Russian (Ioánnis o Rosos), who had served in the Tsarist army, died in 1730 and was canonised in 1962. There is an annual pilgrimage to the church (built in 1930) on March 27th.

4 km (2½ mi.) beyond Prokópi, on the road over the suspension bridge, is a huge plane tree. 4 km beyond this is Mantoúdi, a little industrial town that lives by mining magnesite. From here there is a view northward of the plain of ancient Kerinthos.

Ayía Ánna

8 km (5 mi.) beyond Strofyliá is the prosperous village of Ayía Ánna (Αγια Αννα); at nearby Angali is a long sandy beach. From Agriovótano, south of Cape Artemísio (also known as Cape Amoni), there is a fine view of the islet of Pontikonísi.

Artemísio

Artemísio (Αρτεμισιο) was the scene of first victory of the Greek fleet over the numerically much superior Persians in 480 BC. Near here are the remains of a temple of Athena Proseoa. Off the coast here were found the Jockey and the life-size bronze figure of Zeus that are now in the National Archaeological Museum in Athens. Further west is the fishing village of Pévki, with a long sandy beach.

Istiía

Oreí

Istiía ((Ιστιεια; pop. 6000), the chief place in north-western Euboea, lies in a fertile farming area, described by Homer as "rich in grapes". West of the town is the site of ancient Histiaia, which was conquered by Pericles in 446 BC and bound to Athens by the foundation of a colony at nearby Oreoi. The port of Oreí (Ορεοι) is divided into two by a Venetian fort. To the west of the village is another castle incorporating fragments of Hellenistic masonry. Beside the village church is a massive figure of a bull (4th c. BC) recovered from the sea. From here there is a fine view, across the channel, of the Othrys hills.

Loutrá Aidipsoú

16 km (10 mi.) further on is Loutrá Aidipsoú (Λουτρα Αιδηψου), a popular seaside and thermal resort with hot sulphur springs (32–82°C (90–180°F)) that were already frequented in Roman times. They are used in the treatment of rheumatism, arthritis and gynaecological disorders. Some of the springs are directly on the shore, so that it is possible to have a warm bath in the sea. The town has a modern spa establishment, old hotels and a café built on a pier reaching into the sea. On the seafront promenade are two open-air cinemas. Other features of interest are the remains of ancient baths and the neoclassical pump room.

Roviés

A spectacular road runs along the south coast to the fishing village of Ilia and Roviés (Ροβιες), home of the oracle of Selinuntine Apollo, with a Venetian watchtower and a shingle beach. 10 km (6 mi.) north-east is the 16th c. monastery of St David the Old (Osios David o Gerontas), with 17th c. frescos.

Límni

The road continues to the pretty little port town of Límni (Λιμνη; beach). Here can be seen the remains of an Early Christian church (4th–8th c.), with beautiful mosaics, the church of the Zoodókhos Piyí (Life Giving Fountain) and two buildings designed by the architect Ernst Ziller, the police station and the tax office.

Áyios Nikólaos

A narrow street runs south-east, passing a museum of marine biology, to the convent of Áyios Nikólaos or Galatáki, founded in the 7th/8th c. on the remains of a temple of Poseidon. The present buildings date from the 13th–15th c. The church has fine 16th c. frescos.

Khalkís to Kárystos through south-eastern Euboea

This route (130 km (80 mi.)) also starts in Khalkís. The road runs south-east, passing a number of beaches, and comes in 2.5 km (1½ mi.) to the chapel of Áyios Stéfanos, on the site of ancient Chalcis, with the Fountain of Arethusa that was famed in antiquity. In the fertile Lelantine Plain is the village of Vasilikó. On the road to the medieval castle of Fylla (1.5 km (1 mi.)) are three Venetian watchtowers. Above Fylla is the well preserved 13th c. Venetian stronghold of Lílanto, now known as the Kastélli. At Lefkánti, on the coast (beaches), a sanctuary of the 10th–9th c. BC was excavated in 1981.

Áyios Stéfanos

In 21 km (13 mi.) the road comes to Erétria (Ερετρια; pop. 5000), a ferry port and holiday resort favoured particularly by the British, with the most important ancient site on Euboea, now being excavated by the Swiss Archaeological School.

★Erétria

In ancient times Eretria was the most important town on Euboea after Chalcis, with which it disputed the possession of the fertile Lelantine Plain in the 7th c. BC. A considerable naval power, it was also the seat of a philosophical school. In the 8th c. BC, after the arrival of Ionian settlers from Attica, it enjoyed a period of great prosperity. It supported Miletus in the Ionian rebellion against King Darius of Persia, but in 490 BC was captured and destroyed by Darius and many of its inhabitants were carried off to slavery in Persia. Thereafter it recovered rapidly, and took part in the battle of Salamis in 480 BC. In 411 BC the Eretrians destroyed the Athenian fleet, freeing Euboea from Athenian rule. In 198 BC the town was captured by the Romans, and in AD 87 it was again destroyed by Sulla during the war with Mithradates. This was the end of Eretria's prosperity, and its decline was hastened by the silting up of the harbour and the increasing marshiness of much of the town's area: malaria was rife in the area until the 20th c.

The modern town was established in 1834, when refugees from Psará settled here; for many years it was known as Néa Psará. The German architect Eduard Schaubart then drew up plans for a town of 10,000 inhabitants; but in 1889 Erétria still had a population of no more than 432.

The remains of ancient Erétria are the most important on the island. Here and there between the houses can be seen the foundations of ancient buildings. In the centre of the town are the remains of the Agora and the foundations of a temple of Apollo Daphnephorus, the Laurel-Crowned. The temple, built around 520 BC on the site of several earlier buildings, was peripteral, with 6 by 14 Doric columns, of which there are some remains. The pedimental sculpture, a masterpiece of late Archaic work, can now be seen in the **Archaeological Museum**, established in 1991 on the northern outskirts of the town (open Tue.–Sun. 9am–3pm). Other important items in the museum are a pottery Gorgoneion, prize amphoras won in the Panathenaic festival, and finds from Lefkánti (including a Proto-Geometric centaur of about 900 BC).

Ancient Erétria

Adjoining the museum are most of the excavated remains (usually open to the public): the palace of the archons, a temple of Dionysus, part of the town walls, with the west gate, and the theatre, built into the ground. The oldest part of the theatre is the stone stage building (4th c. BC). Originally it had a wooden proskenion, which was replaced in early Roman times by a marble one. To the east of the theatre were the Gymnasion and a bathhouse. The most important recent discovery is the House of the Mosaics (c. 370 BC; destroyed c. 270 BC), with beautiful and excellently preserved mosaics in the public rooms. To see the fenced-off parts of the site (in particular the House of the Mosaics and the Temple of Apollo) you must obtain a key from the museum staff.

The acropolis was surrounded by polygonal walls. From a tower on the north side there is a fine view. From the east and west sides of the acropolis walls, traceable for only part of the way, run down towards the shore, where there are other remains of walls. The marshland in this area, originally an arm of the sea, was drained in antiquity.

Amárynthos

9 km (5½ mi.) east of Erétria is the little fishing port of Amárynthos (Αμαρυνθος; pop. 3000), 6 km (4 mi.) north-east of which is the monastery of Áyios Nikólaos, with a tiled facade and fine 16th c. frescos. 15 km (9 mi.) beyond this is the industrial town of Alivéri (pop. 6000; coal mining, power station), on the site of ancient Tamynai, with the Panayitsa church (1393) and the castle of Risokastro. 1 km (¾ mi.) away is the port of Karavos, probably ancient Porthmos.

Dystós

Before Lépoura a road goes off on the right, passing a marshy and often flooded depression, out of which rises the acropolis of ancient Dystos (Δυστος), with polygonal walls of the 5th c. BC, beside the village of the same name. The road to Kárystos, the "Eagles' Highway", runs at heights of up to 800 m (2625 ft) above the sea through picturesque bare mountain scenery with a sparse growth of phrygana. From Zarakes there is a view to the west of a long inlet, at the mouth of which is the island of Kavallianí (probably ancient Glauconesus). From Polypotamos there are views over the east coast to Cape Kafiréfs and south-west to the bay of Stýra, with the island of Stýra (ancient Aigleia).

Stýra

On the slopes of the twin-peaked hill of Kilossi is the village of Stýra (Στυρα; pop. 800), with the church of the Nativity of the Mother of God, which has a templon and columns of Kárystos marble. The site of ancient Styra, of which there are only scanty remains, lies 1 km (¾ mi.) away in the direction of the sea. 5 km (3 mi.) from Stýra is the bathing resort of Néa Stýra, with a sandy beach and hotels.

From Stýra a visit can be made to the famous **"dragon houses"** (*drakospita*), three ancient structures of massive stone slabs whose function is unknown (perhaps temples or houses for quarry workers?). It is a stiff 30 min. climb to a saddle above the village, from which it is another 20 min. walk, passing ancient quarries (partly hewn column shafts, dressed blocks, etc.), to the foot of Mount Áyios Nikólaos, with the dragon houses. On the summit of the hill are the handsome Frankish castle of Larména and a chapel dedicated to St Nicholas. From here there are superb views.

There is another dragon house on the road to Marmári.

Marmári

21 km (13 mi.) south-east of Stýra a road goes off to the ferry port of Marmári (Μαρμαρι), which has sandy beaches. Offshore, to the south-west, are the Nisí Petalií, a group of islands (private property), some with country houses on them, others uninhabited.

Kárystos

11 km (7 mi.) further on is Kárystos (Καρυστος; pop. 4500), a pleasant little fishing town and holiday resort and the chief place in southern Euboea, which was founded in the 1840s under the name of Othonoupolis to the design of a Bavarian architect. On the harbour are the ruins of a 14th c. Venetian fort, incorporating masonry from a temple of Apollo. Beyond it is a sandy beach. Ancient Karystos, famed in Roman Imperial times for its greenish marble (cipollino), lay further inland on the slopes of a hill now topped by a 13th c. Venetian castle, Castel Rosso (view).

Mýli

4 km (2½ mi.) north-east of Kárystos, at Mýli, are ancient marble quarries. Above the church of Ayía Triáda is the entrance to a stalactitic cave. From the summit of Mount Ókhi (1398 m (4587 ft)), a 4 hour climb, there are magnificent views.

11 km (7 mi.) beyond Lépoura a road goes off to Avlonári with its tile-roofed houses of undressed stone. Built into the large 12th c. church of Áyios Dimítrios, which has fine frescos, are ancient column drums. Then on to the village of Ayía Thékla with a church (13th–15th c.) containing valuable frescos, and further north-west to Konístres, from which it is a 30 min. climb to the ruined castle of Episkopí, with remains of ancient and medieval walls.

From here it is another 40 km (25 mi.) to Kými (Κυμη; alt. 250 m (820 ft); pop. 2700), a prosperous little town in a fertile hilly area, with many fine old houses and a marvellous view of the island of Skýros. There is an interesting Folk Museum, housed in a neoclassical mansion that belonged the pathologist Yeóryios Papanikolaou, a famous native of the town.

From the town a steep and narrow road (4 km (2½ mi.)) winds its way down to the harbour, the only port on the inhospitable north-eastern coast of Euboea. In the cafés here you can wait for the ferry to Skýros. The ancient city, which founded a colony at Cumae, near Naples in southern Italy, was probably on Cape Kými, to the north, or somewhere near the convent of the Áyios Sotír, near which is a Byzantine and Frankish castle (magnificent views). North-west of Kými are deposits of lignite containing interesting fossils of the Tertiary era.

Farmakonísi

See Léros

Folégandros   I 7

Island group: Cyclades
Area: 32 sq. km (12 sq. mi.)
Altitude: 0–411 m (0–1348 ft)
Population: 600
Chief place: Folégandros town (Khóra)

Shipping connections with Piraeus and other Cycladic islands. Bus service on the island.

The long straggling island of Folégandros (Φολεγανδρος; 13 km (8 mi.) long, 4 km (2½ mi.) across), between Melos and Santoríni, is still barely touched by the tourist trade. The cliff-lined eastern part of the island, with its highest hill (411 m (1348 ft)), is bare and arid; the western half is milder, with water from springs, and supports a modest terraced agriculture (wine, vegetables, corn) and stock farming. Since boats can moor at the little landing stage at Karavostásis only in good weather, travellers may sometimes have to make a longer stay on the island than they intended.

The island was first settled in the 3rd millennium BC. In Roman times it was a place of exile. From the Middle Ages until 1566 it was held by the Gosadini family, and it finally became part of the kingdom of Greece in 1834. Frequent stormy weather may interfere with shipping traffic.

From the landing stage at Karavostásis on the east coast of the island it is 4 km (2½ mi.) to the chief place on the island, Folégandros (Khóra), one of the prettiest little places in the Cyclades. The village (pop. 260) lies at an altitude of 200 m (660 ft) on a crag that falls steeply down to the sea. The old Kástro quarter was founded in 1212 by Duke Marco Sanudo. It is highly picturesque, with its narrow lanes and whitewashed steps leading to the upper floor of the houses, which are frequently decked with flowers. There are two fine churches, the Eleoúsa of 1530 and the

Pantánassa of 1711, with magnificent woodcarving and icons of the Cretan school.

The site of the **ancient Dorian city**, which is believed to have had a temple of Apollo and Artemis, is at the foot of the zigzag path running up the marble hill of **Palaiokástro** (300 m (985 ft)), on which is the white landmark church of the Panayía, crowned by a dome, with a free-standing bell tower. It was built in the 19th c. on the site of an earlier chapel of 1687.

On the summit of the hill, from which there are breathtaking panoramic views, are the remains of the Venetian stronghold of Palaiokástro.

Whitewashed houses in the Khóra – a feature of the Cyclades

Áno Meriá

5 km (3 mi.) north-west of the Khóra is the largest settlement on the island, Áno Meriá (pop. 400), a place of no great interest. On the east coast are the caves of Khrysospiliá and Yeoryítsi (access difficult), with ancient graffiti.

Hydra   H 6

Saronic Islands
Area: 55 sq. km (21 sq. mi.)
Altitude: 0–590 m (0–1936 ft)
Population: 3000
Chief place: Hydra town

Shipping connections with Piraeus–Méthana–Póros, Ermióni–Spétses–Pórto Khéli. In summer boats to beaches. No cars or buses.

The island of Hydra (ancient Hydrea, Ídra, Υδρα) is a bare limestone ridge, 12 km (7½ mi.) long and up to 5 km (3 mi.) wide, lying off the south-east coast of the Argolid. The highest point is Mount Eros (590 m (1936 ft)). Although this long, arid island looks barren and inhospitable, a visitor's arrival in the harbour is an unforgettable experience. Round the harbour with its old cannon and windmills the handsome houses of Hydra town rise in terraces on the slopes of a rocky hill. There are no asphalted roads on the island, so that it must be explored on foot, on a mule or by boat. In summer there is likely to be a shortage of accommodation for visitors; but in fact most visitors spend only a few hours on the island. A tempting local speciality is amygdalotá (almond cake).

History The island was occupied from Mycenaean times. In the 15th c., and again in 1770, after the rising in the Morea, Albanian refugees settled on the island and through shipbuilding, trade, seafaring and piracy made it a wealthy cultural and social centre. The Miaoulis, Koundouriotis, Voulgaris and Tombazis families, who played prominent parts in the shipping industry and during the war of liberation from the Turks, came from Hydra. The island converted the 124 vessels of its merchant fleet into a naval force and also met a considerable proportion of the costs of the war. Thereafter it became increasingly impoverished, until in the 1930s the island was rediscovered by writers and artists. Nowadays tourism is the mainstay of the island's economy.

Sights

The chief place on the island, Hydra town (pop. 2500), climbs picturesquely up the slopes of the hills round its sheltered harbour on the north coast. Its houses resemble those of the Cyclades, but many of them are painted in colours rather than whitewashed. It has a training school for the merchant navy, housed in the former mansion of the Tsamados family, and is a favourite resort of artists, intellectuals and the glitterati, who give the moped-free town its special stamp and atmosphere. Beyond the quay rises the marble campanile of the monastic church of the Dormition of the Mother of God. In the beautiful inner courtyard of the 17th c. Venetian and Genoese monastery are monuments to the freedom fighters of Hydra. The elegant mansions of wealthy shipowning and commercial families of the late 18th and early 19th c. are frequently in the style of Venetian palazzos. The best known of these, the house of the Tombazis family at the west end of the harbour, is now occupied by an outstation of the Athens Academy of Art. Other mansions on the west side of the harbour are those of the Voulgaris and

★Hydra town

Hydra town is picturesquely situated on the hills rising above its small sheltered harbour

Koundouriotis families, while at the east end is the handsome mansion of the Paouris family. Above the town to the west are the ruins of a medieval castle, with fortifications dating from the war of liberation.

Excursions Along the coast to the west (20 min. walk) is the quiet little fishing village of Kamínia, with a shingle beach and tavernas, as well as a number of holiday homes. Further west, at the fishing village of Vlýkhos, are the remains of ancient Chorisa, good tavernas and unfrequented shingle beaches. To the east of the harbour (30 min. walk) is Mandráki, with the most-popular sandy beach on the island. Above the bay is the convent of Ayía Matróna. 1.5 km (1 mi.) south of Hydra town is Kaló Pigádi (fine view), with 18th c. country houses in the surrounding area.

There are pleasant walks to **monasteries** in lonely situations in the mountains. Strong footwear is needed for the walk (3½ hours there and back) to the monasteries of Profítis Ilías (15th c.) and Ayía Efpráxia, from which there are fine views of Hydra town, the Greek mainland and the surrounding islands. At the eastern tip of the island is the 16th c. Zourvas monastery (6–7 hours there and back).

Dokós

North-west of Hydra is the little island of Dokós (ancient Aperopla; Δοκος), now used for grazing sheep, which can be reached by water taxi. Here bathing enthusiasts can still find lonely unfrequented beaches.

★Ikaría   L 6

Southern Sporades
Area: 255 sq. km (98 sq. mi.)
Altitude: 0–1037 m (0–3402 ft)
Population: 7000
Chief place: Áyios Kýrikos

Ports: Áyios Kýrikos, Évdilos. Shipping connections with Piraeus, Sámos, Náxos, Páros, Pátmos and Foúrni. In summer boats to places on the coasts. Air connections with Athens. Bus services are poor; the best plan is to hire a taxi.

Ikaría (Ικαρια), a hilly and largely barren island 40 km (25 mi.) long and up to 8 km (5 mi.) wide, lies in the north-eastern Aegean some 18 km (11 mi.) south-west of Sámos. The whole length of the island is occupied by the bare Athéras range (1037 m (3402 ft)) that divides the island into a green northern half, with many rivers, and a southern half that falls steeply down to the sea. In the south deep gorges slash the massive rock walls, with only a scanty growth of vegetation. The gentler slopes to the north are covered with a macchia of oaks and pines and forests of planes and chestnuts. The narrow gorges in the fertile areas at the mouths of the rivers have a lush and sometimes almost jungle-like abundance of vegetation. The population of the island is concentrated in these well watered valleys. The island's best beaches are on the north coast between Évdilos and Armenistís.
    Ikaría has a number of strongly radioactive springs that have been used for medicinal purposes since ancient times; one of them had to be closed because of possible danger from radiation. The islanders live mainly by agriculture (fruit plantations, particularly apricots) and fishing.

Tourism For long this rugged island was little known except as a place of exile for undesirable communists in the 1940s. Already thinly populated, it lost almost a quarter of its population as a result of a massive wave of emigration between 1981 and 1991. It is alleged by evil tongues that Ikaría was neglected in the distribution of government aid because most of the inhabitants voted for the Communist Party. It is true at any rate that transport connections are poor and the infrastructure inadequate, factors that have hindered the development of tourism. Since the construction of a small airport in 1995, however, there has been a hesitant growth of tourism. Almost all the accommodation for visitors is in Áyios Ky'rikos and Thérma and between Évdilos, Armenistís and Nas.

As a result of these factors Ikaría has preserved much of its original character. Characteristic of the island are its slate-roofed houses, built of undressed large slabs of rock, which are also used to roof churches and cowsheds. The inhabitants still use goatskin rucksacks, elsewhere seen only in museums.

Ikaría, lying off the main tourist routes, has preserved its original character unspoiled

History The name of the island recalls the story of Icarus, son of the Attic and Minoan sculptor and inventor Daedalus. According to legend, Icarus, wearing wings his father had made from feathers bound together with wax, flew too near the sun and plunged to his death in the sea near here. Local legends tell a different tale: that he died when his ship, with great white sails, sank in a storm.

Ikaría was settled from Miletus in the 8th c. BC., when the towns of Oinoë, Histoi, Therma and Drakanon were founded. In Byzantine times Ikaría was used as a place of exile. Later it was held by various Frankish and Genoese barons; in 1481 it passed to the Knights of St John and in 1567 it was taken by the Turks.

On July 17th 1912, after a successful rising against Turkish rule, the inhabitants proclaimed the free state of Ikaría, which soon afterwards joined the kingdom of Greece. During the Greek civil war between 1945 and 1949 left-wing supporters like the composer Mikis Theodorakis were exiled to this lonely island. In the summer of 1993 much of Ikaría was devastated by a great fire.

Sights

The chief place and principal port is Áyios Kýrikos (Αγιος Κυρικος; pop. 2400), which lies near the east end of the south coast. Apart from its traditional cafés and relaxed atmosphere it has little to offer visitors. The much frequented radioactive springs are near he Hotel Akti. There is an interesting archaeological collection in the Gymnasion (irregular opening times)

Áyios Kýrikos

There are a number of small coves with bathing beaches on the rocky coast between Áyios Kýrikos and the little spa of Thérma (Θερμα), 3 km (2 mi.) north-east. Here there are several radioactive and sulphur springs

Thérma

171

at temperatures of up to 52.5°C (126.5°F). The antiquated spa facilities (recommended for the treatment of arthritis, skin conditions and rheumatism) are used only by Greek visitors.

Above the town is an ancient acropolis, which can be reached from Katafíyi (3 km (2 mi.) north-east) on a path lined by tombs of the 6th c. BC. Further inland, 1 km (¾ mi.) north-east of the main road, is the mountain village of Perdiki. Many of its houses still have high walls on the seaward side, designed to prevent pirates from seeing any lights in the village.

Cape Fanári

On Cape Fanári (or Drakanón), which can be reached by boat or on foot, are the remains of the Hellenistic fort of Drakanos, situated at an isolated spot on the inhospitable north-eastern tip of the island.

Évdilos

Until the mid-1990s there was only one asphalted road on the island (though other roads have since been asphalted or are in course of construction) – the 60 km (37 mi.) stretch between Áyios Ky′rikos, Évdilos (Ευδηλος) and Armenistís. This runs through impressive mountain scenery in a wide arc round Mount Fardi, with magnificent panoramic views. The villages have the typical Ikarian slate-roofed houses. Ikaría's second port, Évdilos (pop. 500), is also the second largest place on the island. This picturesque little fishing village is usually only a staging post for holidaymakers.

Oinoë

2.5 km (1½ mi.) west of Évdilos, at the hamlet of Kámpos, are the remains of the ancient city of Oinoë. The name comes from the Greek word for wine, with which the island has been associated since mythic times: the people of Ikaría are credited with being the first winemakers. Also in Kámpos is the church of Ayía Iríni, which belonged to a 12th c. Byzantine palace. The free-standing columns came from an earlier 4th c. church. Beside the church is a small museum containing finds from the site (key from Vasilis Dionysos's general store).

Round the village are a number of beehive tombs (tholaria) and small medieval forts (kastrakia).Below Kámpos is a 400 m (1320 ft) long sand and shingle beach.

Armenistís

15 km (9 mi.) west of Évdilos is the island's tourist centre, Armenistís (Αρμενιστης), with very beautiful and popular sandy beaches. 3 km (2 mi.) west is Nas Bay, with a beautiful little shingle beach (some nude bathing) and the remains of a temple of Artemis of the 5th c. BC. In the unspoiled mountain village of Khristos Rakhes there is a great patronal festival on August 6th and the feast of the Dormition of the Mother of God is celebrated on August 15th.

Foúrni Islands

The Foúrni islands (Φουρνοι) are a group of rocky islets with indented coastlines lying between Sámos, Ikaría and Pátmos. In addition to the main island of Foúrni (area 30 sq. km (12 sq. mi.); alt. 0–486 m (0–1595 ft); pop. 1000), with the village of Foúrni on its west side, the group includes the smaller islands of Thimena (12 sq. km (4½ sq. mi.); 0–483 m (0–1585 ft)) to the west and Áyios Minás (5 sq. km (2 sq. mi.); 0–250 m (0–820 ft)) to the east, together with the isolated rocks of Andro, Makronísi and Diapori. Only Foúrni and Thimena are inhabited, and there is accommodation for visitors only on Foúrni, to which there is a daily boat from Áyios Kýrikos in summer. (also connections with Évdilos, Náxos, Páros and Piraeus). In the Middle Ages the islands were the haunt of pirates, who were able from commanding viewpoints on the hills to keep a lookout for shipping passing between Sámos and Ikaría. The inhabitants now live by farming and fishing. There are beautiful beaches and enough tavernas and rooms for visitors looking for a restful holiday.

Íos   K 7

Island group: Cyclades
Area: 108 sq. km (42 sq. mi.)

Altitude: 0–713 m (0–2339 ft)
Population: 1600
Chief place: Íos town (Khóra)

Port: Yialós. Shipping connections with Piraeus, Rafína and other Cycladic islands. Bus services on the island.

Íos (Ιος), lying between Páros and Santoríni, is a hilly island with a much indented coast alternating between sheer cliffs and beautiful sandy beaches. Until quite recently its only source of income was agriculture on the terraced slopes of the Káto Kámpos valley and its side valleys, but since the 1970s it has been invaded by large numbers of backpackers who have, during the summer months at least, completely altered the character of the island. Its economy now depends exclusively on tourism, and it is to be recommended – at any rate during the main holiday season – only to visitors looking for a holiday with plenty of noise and fun.

History According to an ancient tradition, Homer's mother Clymene was a native of Íos and he himself was buried on the island.

The whitewashed houses of Íos, tightly packed on the slopes of a hill

The Phoenicians who came to the island in the 2nd millennium BC were followed around 1000 BC by Ionians, who founded their city on the site still occupied, after 3000 years, by Íos town, the Khóra. After the battle of Salamis in 480 BC the island became a member of the Attic maritime league. The name Íos may possibly mean "city of the Ionians". Later the island came successively into the hands of Macedon, the Ptolemies and Rome. In later centuries Íos was ruled by the Venetians, the Byzantines and, from 1537, the Turks. In 1821 it played an important part in the war of liberation, and in 1830 became part of the newly established kingdom of Greece.

Sights

★Íos town

From the port of Yialós, situated in a deeply indented inlet on the west coast of the island, with the 17th c. church of Ayía Iríni picturesquely situated on the promontory, a road runs up the fertile valley of Káto Kámpos for 2 km (1¼ mi.) to the chief place on the island, Íos town (Khóra; pop. 1500), finely situated on the slopes of a hill. Occupying the same site as the ancient city (c.1000 BC) and the later Venetian castle (of which there are some remains of walls), it has some 20 churches and chapels in addition to its typically Cycladic whitewashed houses. (There are another 150 churches scattered about the island). Built into the walls of the church of Ayía Ekaterini are fragments of ancient masonry. Above the town are twelve dilapidated windmills, in two rows.

Beaches The beautiful long beach of Mylopótas, 2 km (1¼ mi.) south of the Khóra, is the favourite resort of young people. Much quieter are the beaches at Ayía Theodóti, 8 km (5 mi.) north-east of the Khóra (once-daily bus service), and Koumbára, west of Yialós (with a nudist beach). At the southern tip of the island is the beautiful Manganári Bay (reached by bus or boat).

Other sights Near the monastery of Plakotós, in the far north of the island, are a Hellenistic tower and the remains of a cave sanctuary, probably also Hellenistic, which is said to contain Homer's grave. To the south of the beach at Ayía Theodóti, at a height of over 300 m (985 ft), are the ruins of a castle, probably Venetian.

Ithaca   E 5

Ionian Islands
Area: 96 sq. km (37 sq. mi.)
Altitude: 0–808 m (0–2500 ft)
Population: 4000
Chief place: Vathý (Itháki)

Shipping connections with Patrás, Igoumenítsa–Corfu–Brindisi, Kefaloniá (Fiskárdo, Sámi), Lefkás (Vasiliki). Bus service Vathý–Frikés–Kióni.

Ithaca (**Itháki**; Ιθάκη; popularly called Thiaki) is a largely barren karstic island that is separated from Kefaloniá by a channel 2–4 km (1¼–2½ mi.) wide. In spite of its very mixed landscape pattern – inhospitable hills with some areas of pinewood, olives, cypresses and vines, a steep rocky east coast and a green western half with some agriculture – it is popular with visitors seeking a relaxing holiday. It is generally accepted as being Odysseus's island of Ithaca, as described in the "Odyssey". The island is almost cut into two by the Gulf of Mólos, the two parts being joined only by an isthmus 600 m (1980 ft) wide. In the northern half is the Ani range

(Mount Níritos, 808 m (2651 ft)), in the southern half Mount Stefani (671 m (2202 ft)). There are some beautiful shingle beaches.

History The earliest finds of pottery point to a first settlement of the island in the 3rd millennium BC. A number of Mycenaean sites have been identified, though their poverty is difficult to reconcile with the wealthy Homeric Ithaca, which is dated to the Mycenaean period. During the 1st millennium BC, however, the island seems to have attained a degree of prosperity through an active trade with mainland Greece and Italy. From Roman times Ithaca shared the destinies of the other Ionian Islands. During the Middle Ages the inhabitants were driven out by pirates, who established their base in what is now Vathý. In the 17th c. the island was resettled by peasants from Kefaloniá. After a long history of devastating raids and earthquakes practically all Ithaca's older buildings have been destroyed. In the most recent severe earthquake, in 1953, 80 per cent of the island's buildings were destroyed.

Sights

The chief place on the island is the port of Vathý (Βαθυ; pop. 2000), which was probably founded by the Romans. It is beautifully situated at the head of the long inlet of Dexiá, which is protected by two Venetian forts. It is generally accepted as being the cove of Phorcys, in which the Phaeacians put the returning Odysseus ashore ("Odyssey", XIII, 96 ff.).

    Under a law of 1978 all new buildings are required to conform to traditional architectural styles, so that the little town with its pastel-coloured houses has preserved its attractive original character. The life of the town centres on the seafront with its cafés, restaurants and hotels. Features of interest in Vathý are the neoclassical villa of the Drakoulis family on the harbour, now occupied by a café, and a small archaeolog-

Vathý

Many houses on Ithaca are occupied only in summer, when Ithacans working abroad return on holiday

ical museum (open Tue.–Sun. 8.30am–3pm), with material from excavations on Mount Aetós in the 1930s. The little islet of Lazaretto was a quarantine station in the 19th c., and it is said that both Schliemann (who worked on Ithaca) and Byron swam out to it each morning.

There are a number of beautiful shingle **beaches** round Vathý. From Loútsa Beach (only 50 m (150 ft) long) north-east of Vathý (taverna) there is a charming view of the Lazaretto island. There is a very beautiful beach in Skinós Bay, but part of it is privately owned.

Cave of the Nymphs 2 km (1¼ mi.) west of Vathý, on the slopes of Mount Áyios Nikólaos, is the Marmaróspilia (Marble Cave), a stalactitic cave that has been identified as the Cave of the Nymphs in the "Odyssey" (xiii, 107–8). A marble base found here originally supported a small statue of a divinity. The Cave of the Nymphs was the place where Odysseus, on his return to Ithaca, hid the gifts that he had received from the Phaeacians.

Aetós Soon after this a road goes off on the left to the port of Píso Aetós (Αετος). On this road, on the slopes of Mount Aetós (380 m (1247 ft)), is an excavation site with the remains of a tower of the Hellenistic period. This was part of a circuit of town walls built round the summit of Mount Aetós in the 7th c. BC. Schliemann took this for the site of Odysseus's city and palace, the Kastro tou Odyssea; but it was only after the discovery by American archaeologists of material dating from the 14th–13th c. BC that Schliemann's suggestion received some support. It is more probable, however, that this was the site of the ancient city of Alalkomenai mentioned by Plutarch.

★★Perakhóri 3 km (2 mi.) south of Vathý, clinging to the side of a hill at an altitude of 300 m (985 ft), is the village of Perakhóri (Περαχωρι). It was established in the

16th c. by the inhabitants of the medieval village of Palaiokhóra, higher up the hill, and soon developed into one of the largest settlements on the island. A signposted path leads up in 15 min. to the ruins of the medieval village. Out of fear of pirate raids the houses in Palaiokhóra were built like miniature fortresses, with small windows and large storerooms and cisterns.

The ruined church of St John the Evangelist is a pathetic sight. Its roof has fallen in, leaving the stone iconostasis open to the elements, and the frescos of saints have suffered badly from the weather.

Another stony track runs south from Vathý, coming in 5 km (3 mi.) to a path leading to the Fountain of Arethusa. The legend has it that the fountain came into being when the nymph Arethusa mourned on this spot for her son Corax, shedding so many tears that the fountain was formed. The walk to the fountain (1½ hours from Vathý) is more rewarding than the fountain itself. Still further south is the plateau of Maráthia, with extensive plantations of olive trees, from which there are wide panoramic views. The grazing grounds of the swineherd Eumaeus ("Odyssey", xiv, 6) are supposed to have been in this area.

Fountain of Arethusa

Beyond the isthmus the road climbs steeply to the Katharón Monastery (alt. 550 m (1805 ft)), from which there are magnificent views. The church (1696) has a precious icon of the Mother of God, believed to have been painted by the Apostle Luke himself. There is a great festival here on September 8th, with eating, drinking and dancing.

Katharón Monastery

From here the road continues north by way of Anoy (Ανωγη), an old village, now almost abandoned, in a wild and barren setting. At the entrance to the village are two curiously shaped boulders, one of which is known as Araklis (Heracles). It is well worth looking into the church of the Panayía, which has 16th c. frescos.

Anoyí

An alternative route is the main road along the coast, which runs past beautiful shingle beaches (Áyios Ioánnis, Léfki). On Mount Pilikáta, near Stavrós (Σταυρος), the largest town in the northern part of the island, British archaeologists brought to light a settlement (2200–1500 BC) supporting the suggestion that this is the likeliest site for Odysseus's city and palace. The situation at any rate matches Homer's description. In the district of Pilikáta is an archaeological museum (open 8.30am–3pm) whose most important exhibit is a potsherd, part of a female mask of the Hellenistic period with the Greek inscription "My prayer to Odysseus". The inhabitants of Ithaca in Hellenistic times evidently had no doubt that their island was the Ithaca of the "Odyssey".

Stavrós

1.5 km (1 mi.) below Stavrós is beautiful Pólis (Πολις) Bay, the only harbour of any size on the west coast of Ithaca. On the west side of the bay is a cave that in Mycenaean times was a sanctuary of Athena and Hera. Offshore, near the coast of Kefaloniá, is the tiny islet of Daskalio, identified as the ancient Asteris ("Odyssey", xvi, 365).

Pólis Bay

On the north-east coast of Ithaca are the beautiful bays of Frikés and Kióni (Κιονι). The pleasant little holiday resort of Kióni, which attracts numbers of visitors during the season, is considered the prettiest place on Ithaca. Between Kióni and Frikés, just off the road, are a number of shingle beaches.

Kióni

Kálymnos   L/M 6/7

Southern Sporades
Area: 111 sq. km (43 sq. mi.)
Altitude: 0–678 m (0–2225 ft)

In the Wake of Odysseus

Was it here, on Ithaca, that Odysseus had his kingdom? Was it from here that he set out to fight valiantly in the Trojan War for ten years, as we are told in the "Iliad", and was it to here that he returned, after the adventurous voyage lasting another ten years that is described in the "Odyssey", to embrace his wife Penelope after a twenty-year absence and win back his kingdom?

For John Luce, emeritus professor of classics at Trinity College, Dublin, the mythological island of Ithaca is identical with the island now known by that name and Homer was undoubtedly the author of the "Odyssey", as he sets out in his book "Celebrating Homer's Landscapes" (1998).

Ithaca is smaller and more rugged than Zákynthos or Kefaloniá, but of much greater strategic importance. From here seaborne trade along the coast and traffic between Ithaca, Kefaloniá and Lefkás could be more effectively controlled. In the "Odyssey" Homer describes Odysseus's island as "low-lying",

Dexiá Bay on Ithaca. Is this where the Phaeacians carried the sleeping Odysseus ashore?

"not broad", "surrounded by many islands", "clear-seen" and "rugged and unsuitable for horses" – all of which characteristics apply more aptly to Ithaca than to any other of the Ionian Islands.

Odysseus's last port of call before his return to Ithaca was the island of Scheria (which was already identified in ancient times with Corcyra/Corfu). Here he related to the Phaeacian king Alcinous and his daughter Nausicaa the story of his ten-year voyage and his adventures in the course of his wanderings – his encounters with the one-eyed cyclops Polyphemus, with the death-bringing sirens and with Calypso, who detained him on her island for seven years. With the help of the Phaeacian king he was able finally to return to his own island and, disguised as a beggar, to destroy, with the support of his son Telemachus, the suitors who had been pestering his wife Penelope.

The crew of the Phaeacian ship that took Odysseus back to Ithaca, deposited him, asleep, in the bay of Phorcys, below the Cave of the Nymphs. When he awoke, not knowing where he was, his guardian goddess Athena, in the guise of a shepherd boy, told him that he was on Ithaca. Professor Luce equates the bay of Phorcys with the present-day inlet of Dexiá and the Cave of the Nymphs with a stalactitic cave above the shore of the inlet. The cave, as described in the "Odyssey", had two entrances, one for mortals and one for the gods. The latter could be represented by an opening in the roof of the Dexiá cave. After visiting the cave, in which he prayed and concealed the treasures he had received from the Phaeacians, Odysseus set out, along with Athena, to look for the swineherd Eumaeus. In his search he took "a rough footpath through wooded ground along the heights", which Luce identifies as a path that ran along the eastern flank of Mount Merovigli to the Maráthia plateau – a path that he found still exists. The "Raven's Crag by the Fountain of Arethusa", where Eumaeus's farm lay, is on the north-eastern edge of the plateau.

On this crag, which extends for a length of 650 m (2130 ft) and falls vertically down for 60 m (200 ft), there are still many ravens, and it still bears the name of Raven's Crag (Stefani tou Korakou). Here too is the source of the Fountain of Arethusa; and the swineherd's farm – "on elevated ground, with wide prospects" – could well have been on the plateau above the cliff, at a height of 240 m (790 ft), from which there are wide-ranging views. A nearby cave is now identified on Ithaca with Eumaeus's home. Here Odysseus met his son Telemachus and revealed himself to him. Telemachus then sent the swineherd to his parents' palace to tell Penelope that her husband had returned. The palace may have been at Stavrós, some 24 km (15 mi.) away at the opposite end of the island – and Eumaeus took a whole day to walk there and back.

Professor Luce cites other evidence supporting his belief that Odysseus's palace and the capital of his kingdom were at Stavrós. According to the "Odyssey", there was a view from the forecourt of the palace of "our" harbour and, further away, the harbour of "Reithron under wooded Neion" – which Luce suggests could be Pólis Bay and Frikés Bay, while "Neion" could be Mount Exóyi. Both of these bays can be seen from the hill ridge running north from Stavrós, and Odysseus's palace could have been at present-day Pilikáta, at the intersection of these two sight lines. Although the British excavations there brought to light Mycenaean potsherds and remains of a defensive wall, they found no trace of a palace, as Luce admits. But he maintains that if there ever was a palace of Odysseus it must have been here. And he believes that Homer shows exact knowledge of the topography of Ithaca and must have visited the island.

Not all scholars are convinced. As the German poet Schiller said, "Seven cities fought for the honour of being Homer's birthplace, but now that Wolf has torn him to bits each of them can have a piece!" – an allusion to the classical scholar Friedrich August Wolf's study of a problem that had also exercised the learned world of antiquity: how many different poets are concealed under the name of Homer and when the two great epics, the "Iliad" and the "Odyssey", generally ascribed to a Greek poet called Homer, were composed.

It is now widely believed that the two epics must have had several authors, who based their work on seafarers' tales handed down orally from Mycenaean times (1300 BC), interweaving them with the social circumstances and mythological beliefs of their own time. The "Iliad" is believed to have been composed about 730 BC and the "Odyssey" some 50 years later.

Perhaps the puzzle about the identity of Homer can never be solved, just as it seems likely that it will forever remain uncertain which island was the mythical Ithaca. Perhaps it was Lefkás, as the German scholar Wilhelm Dörpfeld thought, or was it present-day Ithaca after all? Perhaps!

Population: 17,000
Chief place: Kálymnos town (Pothiá)

Shipping connections with Piraeus via the Cyclades. Hydrofoils that ply daily between Kos town and Sámos call in at Pothiá. In summer ferry connections with Mastikhári (40 min.) and Psérimos. Day excursions from Kos and Pátmos. Regular bus services. Boats from Myrtiés to Léros (Xirókampos).

Kálymnos (Κάλυμνος) is a bare hilly limestone island in the Dodecanese, 12 km (7½ mi.) north-west of Kos, separated from Léros to the north-west by the narrow Diapori Channel. Seen from the sea, the island looks rocky and precipitous, with numerous coves and inlets. Most of the beaches are on the west coast, as are most of the settlements on the island.

For centuries the inhabitants, unable to live from the produce of the few fertile valleys and depressions, have turned to the sea for a living; but since the decline of the once important sponge fisheries tourism has played an increasingly important role in the economy.

By the 19th c. the Kalymniots had so far extended their **sponge-diving** grounds that the fleet left in April/May and returned only in September/October – events that then, as now, were celebrated with lively festivities, though over-fishing and the production of synthetic sponges have much reduced the scale of the sponge-divers' activities. Kálymnos is now the only island on which there are still sponge divers. The increasing pollution of the eastern Mediterranean has decimated the sponge population and driven up the price of sponges, which can now cost, depending on size, between £3 and £6. The ecological balance of the sea was severely disturbed by the Chernobyl nuclear catastrophe in 1986, whose effects are still being felt, since it takes several years before a sponge is ready to be harvested.

As a result of the steep decline in the yield of the sponge fisheries and the risks to which sponge fishers are exposed their numbers have fallen to between 40 and 100 (the exact number is not known). The divers go down to a depth of up to 80 m (260 ft) and stay down for about an hour, being supplied with oxygen by garden hoses let down from the boat. It is a hazardous trade: the high pressure at these depths can lead to burst eardrums and the low temperature of the water to pneumonia and rheumatism.

To meet the demand from tourists for natural sponges, cheaper "farmed" sponges are now being imported from Florida and Cuba, which are bleached to produce a lighter colour and last no more than two years. Natural sponges from Greek waters are darker, firmer and rounder and if properly looked after (regularly washed in clean water) will last up to ten years. In various sponge factories in Pothiá (addresses from the tourist information offices) visitors can watch the transformation of the unappealing lumps fished from the sea into bath sponges.

History Finds in various caves round the coasts, particularly at Daskalió, near Vathý, and Ayía Varvára, show that Kálymnos has been continuously inhabited since the neolithic. The island shared the history of the Dodecanese: in 1204 it came under Venetian control and from 1313 was held by the Knights of St John on Rhodes.

★Kálymnos town

A limestone ridge reaching a height of 678 m (2225 ft) separates the north end of the island from the south, where since ancient times most of the population has been concentrated. From the foot of the hills a fertile plain extends south to the island's busy chief town and port, Kálymnos or Pothiá (pop. 12,000). Seen from a boat entering the har-

Kálymnos is one of the most arid and rockiest of the Greek islands, but it has a very picturesque chief town

bour, Kálymnos is a picturesque sight, with its whitewashed houses ranged round the wide bay, reaching up the slope to the foot of the steep, bare hills that form an imposing backdrop to the town.

Tourists are to be seen only on the long seafront promenade with its innumerable street cafés, tavernas and fish restaurants. Street traders offer a wide choice of natural and synthetic sponges, which are popular both as souvenirs and for everyday use. Any visitor who does penetrate into the town's maze of narrow streets will discover that the traditional Greek way of life is still intact, with no trace of the deleterious effects of tourism.

Visitors need not be alarmed if, on a quiet evening at the weekend, they suddenly hear the thunder of cannon resounding from the rock wall behind the town. This is a local custom to celebrate some festive event such as a wedding, a centuries-old tradition designed to intimidate the island's foreign occupying forces.

In Kálymnos itself there are no **beaches**. If you want to bathe you must take a bus to the west coast or a boat to the island of Psérimos to the south.

Handsome 19th c. **neoclassical buildings**, among them the Town Hall at the north-eastern corner of the harbour, bear witness to the prosperity of earlier times. Beside the Town Hall is the Church of Christ (1861), with a templon (screen) by the sculptor Yiannolis Khalepas.

Adjoining the church is the new Seafaring Museum, which offers an excellent survey of the history of Kalymniot seafaring and sponge diving.

Seafaring Museum

From here Odós Venizelou runs through the town, continuing to Khorió.

Vouvális Museum

181

Kálymnos's tourist centre is on the west coast, at Myrtiés and Massoúri. Round the beautiful bay one hotel follows another.

A signpost "Museum" leads to a mansion once owned by Nikólaos Vouvális (1853–1919), a sea captain and businessman, which now houses a small folk and archaeological museum, with 19th c. furnishings and finds from the sanctuary of Delian Apollo.

Opposite the museum is the Villa Themelina, which also belonged to the Vouvális family and is now a hotel (see Practical Information, Hotels).

Other sights

Khorió

North-west of Pothiá, on the left of the busy road to the island's former capital, Khorió (Χωριο; pop. 2600), is the castle of Khrysokhéria, originally built in the 9th c. and later enlarged by the Knights of St John. Khorió, founded in the 17th c., is now joined up with Pothiá. From the highest point in the castle there is a good view of the whole valley, reaching down to Pothiá.

At the west end of Khorió, on the road to the west coast, are the ruins of the Early Christian **basilica of Christ of Jerusalem**, built in the 6th c. on a sanctuary of the Delian Apollo and incorporating ancient masonry in its walls. This is now a quiet, shady spot where you can find shelter from the fierce heat.

Pánormos

★Myrtiés

A tree-lined road leads to Pánormos (Πανορμος; pop. 500), on the west coast, where there are a number of sand and shingle beaches. To the north of the road to Myrtiés (Μυρτιες) and Massoúri is a wonderful view of a beautiful bay enclosed by the little island of Télendos. This stretch of coast, with its modern hotels, travel agencies, bars, tavernas and restaurants, is the island's main tourist centre and a popular destination for package holidays. There are only narrow shingle beaches with imported sand, but this is compensated for by the beautiful view of the bay, the numerous cypress trees and the excellent modern tourist facilities.

Off the west coast is the rocky island of Télendos (Τελενδος; 0–458 m (0–1503 ft)). During the season there are boat trips to the island's little port, where there are a number of tavernas and rooms for visitors. On Mount Áyios Konstantínos is a medieval castle and at the foot of the hill is the ruined monastery of Áyios Vasílios.

Télendos

From Kastélli, the terminus of the bus route, the road continues to Emporiós (Εμπορειος). Round Aryinónta Bay, at Xirókampos and Vriokastro, are remains of ancient fortifications, and high above Emporiós Bay are the ruins of the old (probably Carian) stronghold of Kástri.

Emporiós

The island's other road runs north-east from Pothiá to a deeply indented inlet, not visible from the sea, at the head of which quiet and pretty little settlement of Vathý (Βαθυ). This lies at the mouth of "Mandarine Valley", the only spot on the island that still has some agriculture. Here, artificially irrigated, are thousands of mandarine and orange trees and large numbers of lemon trees. Here too is the Daskalió Cave, where important finds of Middle and Late Minoan material (2000–1400 BC) were made.

Vathý

Kárpathos   M 8

Island group: Dodecanese
Area: 301 sq. km (116 sq. mi.)
Altitude: 0–1220 m (0–4003 ft)
Population: 7000
Chief place: Kárpathos town (Pygádia)

Airport 16 km (10 mi.) south of Kárpathos (no shuttle bus service). Air connections with Athens, Rhodes, Kásos, Crete (Sitía). Charter flights. Shipping connections with Piraeus, Kásos–Crete (Iráklion, Sitía, Áyios Nikólaos), Rhodes, Melos, Páros, Santoríni. In summer boats to Diafáni (in the north of the island), to bathing beaches and to Kásos. Bus services on the island. In the north of the island there are no asphalted roads between Ólympos and Diafáni.

Kárpathos (Καρπαθος) forms, along with the neighbouring island of Kásos to the south-west, a transition between Rhodes and Crete; the sea between Rhodes and Crete is known as the Carpathian Sea. A long narrow island extending for some 48 km (30 mi.) from north to south, it is the second largest island in the Dodecanese. A rugged and infertile range of limestone hills, rising to 1220 m (4003 ft) in Kalí Límni, the highest hill in the Dodecanese, extends along the whole length of the island. The coasts mostly fall steeply down to the sea, with small sandy beaches fringed by numerous caves at the south end of the island, on the west coast round Arkása and on the east coast at Pygádia. Lying so far south, the island has a subtropical climate, with hot, dry summers and rainy winters.

Folk traditions Kárpathos (particularly the north part of the island, which has preserved an old form of Greek dialect) is famed for the traditional costumes worn by women and its folk music. In Ólympos the women still wear costumes that go back to Byzantine times, often richly embroidered. The northern and southern parts of the island were long separated from one another and developed independently.

Economy Until recently the population of Kárpathos lived almost exclusively by agriculture. Since the soil is stony and infertile and could not produce enough food for the population, there was a great wave of emigration after the Second World War. Even today the land is tilled without the aid of modern machinery, and in hilly regions donkeys and mules are frequently the only means of transport. Traditional sources of income are livestock farming, cabinetmaking, woodcarving, weaving and embroidery.

Tourism Since the construction of the airport in 1988 package tourism has taken off. While in 1989 only 6800 tourists came to Kárpathos, by 1997 the number had risen to around 40,000. But Kárpathos is still over-shadowed by its mightier neighbours Crete and Rhodes. With the exception of Pygádia and the beautiful bathing beaches of Ammopí and Lefkós it is still a very quiet island. Thanks to the islanders' increased income from tourism, however, the wave of emigration has been halted.

History The island was originally occupied by settlers from Crete, followed by others from Argos; thereafter it became subject to Rhodes. It had four ancient cities: Arkesia (of which there are scanty traces) at the south end of the west coast, Poseidion at the south end of the east coast, Thoantion on the west coast and Vrykos in the north. In the early Middle Ages the island was part of the Byzantine Empire; in 1282 it was held by Genoa; and from 1306 it was ruled by the Prince of Crete, Andrea Cornaro. In 1537 it was incorporated in the Ottoman Empire and thereafter shared the destinies of the Dodecanese.

Between 1912 and 1948 Kárpathos again came under Italian rule, under the name of Scarpanto. Many inhabitants have emigrated to the United States and Australia, but their continuing attachment to their homeland is reflected in the large sums of money that flow back to the island.

Sights

The young capital of the island, Kárpathos or Pygádia, which is also its principal port, lies in a wide bay at the south end of the east coast, on the site of ancient Poseidion. The little town (pop. 2500) is the island's tourist centre – not a particularly attractive one – with the necessary infrastructure.

Kárpathos town

There is a sandy beach 4 km (2½ mi.) long running round the whole of the bay. It is a short walk along the beach from the little fishing harbour to the remains (columns of light grey marble, parts of the templon, with relief carving) of an Early Christian basilica (6th c.) dedicated to Ayía Fotiní.

Walks From Pygádia it is a 30 min. walk to some caves in the Mili valley that were used in antiquity as tombs. A more strenuous walk (2 hours; take water and provisions) is to the hilltop church of Ayía Kyriakí (6 km (4 mi.) south), from which there are fine views. On the way back to Pygádia is the chapel of the Panayía Larniótissa.

A rewarding walk on an old path leads to the beautiful sandy beaches at Ammopí (8 km (5 mi.) south of Pygádia), which has recently developed into one of the most popular tourist resorts on the island.

Ammopí

The flat and windy southern part of Kárpathos, near the airport, has become increasingly popular with surfers. The bay of Makrýs Yialós, north-east of the airport, where a number of hotels have been built in recent years, is regarded as one of the best surfing areas in Europe, with constant wind. The wind also drives windmills erected here with the help of European Union finance.

Makrýs Yialós

North-west of the airport on a dusty road are the remains of a 3500-year-old Minoan house.

The sleepy little village of Arkása (Αρκασα) on the west coast has also developed into a holiday resort, thanks to the beautiful beach of Áyios Nikólaos, 1 km (¾ mi.) from the village. Here too are the remains of the 4th–6th c. basilica of Ayía Anastasia. Mosaics that were brought to light in 1923 are now displayed in the inner courtyard of the Archaeological Museum in Rhodes. From the church a steep path (partly stepped) runs up (15 min.) to a headland on which are the ruins of the Venetian and Turkish castle of Palaiokástro, with scanty remains of ancient Arkesia. To the south is the beach of Áyios Nikólaos, with a gentle slope that makes it suitable for children. The road along the west coast to Mesokhori, on the lower slopes of Kali Limni, was asphalted some years ago. 3 km (2 mi.) north of Arkása is the remote little fishing village of Finíki. Further north are the quiet and picturesque hill village of Pilés, above the west

Arkása

Kárpathos

coast, and Lefkós, with a sandy beach that attracts many visitors in summer.

Menetés

6 km (4 mi.) west of Pygádia, on a rocky ridge above the town, is the picturesque village of Menetés (Μενετες), with narrow, winding streets lined with brightly coloured neoclassical houses. In the chapel of the Panayía Evangelístria is a small local museum (key from Manolis' taverna), with a collection of old tools and agricultural implements.

Apéri

In the centre of the island, north-west of Pygádia, are the unspoiled hill villages of Apéri (Απερι), Voláda, Óthos and Pilés, with pleasant walks between them. From 1700 to 1892 Apéri was the chief place on the island, and it is still the seat of the bishop of Kárpathos and Kásos. Thanks to the money brought by returning emigrants it is the wealthiest village on the island (followed by Voláda).

Óthos

In Óthos (Οθος), the highest village on the island (510 m (1673 ft)), beside the principal church, is a good folk museum showing the interior of a typical Karpathiot house.

★Ólympos

In the north of the island, on the slopes of the bare hill of Profítis Ilías, is Ólympos (Ολυμπος), one of the prettiest and most old-world hill villages in Greece. The traditional style of its houses and the old customs that are still preserved – the women still wear their beautiful hand-embroidered costumes in everyday life – have made it a popular excursion for package holidaymakers, but it is still a very rewarding place to visit. Thanks to its remote situation centuries-old customs have been maintained, for a gravel road linking it with the outside world was built only in 1980, when electricity also came to the village for the first time. Bread is still baked in wood-fired communal ovens. Under the village's traditional

The hill village of Ólympos in northern Kárpathos has preserved old traditions

inheritance law (no longer observed in all families) the eldest daughter inherited all that her mother had brought to her marriage and the eldest son his father's property. After the Second World War Ólympos had a population of 3000, but massive emigration has since reduced this to 350.

Ólympos is a good base for **walks** in the unspoiled north of the island. An old path runs down in 1½ hours to Diafáni, and there is also a very rewarding walk (4 hours there and back) to the outlying village of Avlona, with magnificent views of Ólympos and Mount Profítis Ilías.

Diafáni (Διαφανι), the harbour of Ólympos, on the east coast, was founded in the late 18th c. The ferry port, opened only in 1995, is used by excursion boats from Pygádia. With its small shingle beach and the attractive little coves in the surrounding area, it is a good place for a quiet bathing holiday.

Diafáni

North of Kárpathos, separated from it by a channel only 100 m (330 ft) wide, is the uninhabited island of Sariá (Σαρια; area 16 sq. km (6 sq. mi.); alt. 0–565 m (0–1854 ft)), the ancient Saros, with the ruins of a Byzantine town (boats from Diafáni).

Sariá

Kásos   not on map

Island group: Dodecanese
Area: 66 sq. km (25 sq. mi.)
Altitude: 0–583 m (0–1913 ft)
Population: 1100
Chief place: Fry

Airport. Air connections via Kárpathos with Athens, Crete (Sitía) and Rhodes. Shipping connections via Kárpathos with Piraeus, Crete (Iráklion, Sitía, Áyios Nikólaos), Rhodes, Santoríni and Khalkí. Bus services on the island.

The little Dodecanese island of Kásos (Κασος), 6 km (4 mi.) south-west of Kárpathos, is a barren rock (numerous caves), offering no shade, with no sheltered inlets and hardly any beaches. The few independent travellers who come here in summer take excursion boats to the offshore islets of Armathiá and Makrá, which have sandy beaches.

The islanders live by small-scale farming and boatbuilding. Throughout its history Kásos has shared the destinies of the neighbouring island of Kárpathos. In the 18th c. Albanians settled on the island and quickly built up a large merchant fleet. In 1824 the Turkish governor of Egypt, Muhammad Ali, occupied the island and slaughtered more than 7000 of the inhabitants, since the ships of Kásos prevented him from attacking the Peloponnese.

Sights

Scattered about on the island are a number of lonely **monasteries**, among them Áyios Yeóryios in the south-west of the island (a 2½ hour walk from Arvanitokhóri) and – high above the south-east coast – the abandoned monastery of Áyios Mamas (a 1½ hour walk from Fry; overnight accommodation, key in Póli). A local legend has it that three cliffs in the bay below the monastery are Turkish warships that attacked the island and were turned to stone by St Mamas.

The best bathing **beach** on Kásos, a shingle beach with no tourist facilities, is near Áyios Yeóryios (in the south-west of the island), in Khelathros Bay.

Fry

Fry (Φρυ; pop. 250), the chief place on the island since 1840, is a partly abandoned and not particularly attractive village on the north coast. The little fishing harbour of Bouka and the brightly coloured domed churches have a certain charm. 1 km (¾ mi.) east is the old port of Emporiós, now used only by fishing boats.

Ayía Marína

The pretty little village of Ayía Marína (Αγια Μαρινα), in which almost half the inhabitants of the island (pop. 500) live, lies 1 km (¾ mi.) south-west of Fry. The name of Arvanitokhóri (2.5 km 1½ mi.) south of Fry) recalls that it was founded by Albanians. To the south-west is the cave of Ellinokamara, in which women and children sought refuge during the 1824 massacres.

Kastellórizo   not on map

Island group: Dodecanese
Area: 9 sq. km (3½ sq. mi.)
Altitude: 0–271 m (0–889 ft)
Population: 250
Chief place: Kastellórizo town (Meyistí)

Shipping connections with Rhodes. Excursion boats to Kaí (Turkey). Air connections with Rhodes (early reservation necessary). The island is almost car free.

Kastellórizo (Καστελλοριζο), a small island only 7 km (4½ mi.) long, also known as Meyistí (the "largest" in a small archipelago), is the most easterly outpost of Greece, lying only some 7 km off the south coast of Asia Minor (the peninsula of Çukurbag). It is 70 sea miles from Rhodes and 325 from Athens (Piraeus). The crossing from Rhodes takes 7 hours. This rocky and arid island now has only some 250 inhabitants, mostly elderly, who live by fishing (including sponge diving), a little livestock farming and a modest tourist trade. In summer many people who have emigrated from the island return for their holidays, and some eventually retire to it.

Due to the island's distance from mainland Greece and its lack of economic resources, life on Kastellórizo for the few surviving inhabitants is hard, in spite of government subsidies. Tourism makes only a small contribution to the economy, since the island is difficult to reach and has no beaches – though the water off its rocky coasts is marvellously clear, making it a paradise for snorkellers.

History Archaeological evidence has shown that the island was already densely populated in the neolithic period. For long under Byzantine sovereignty, it was occupied in 1309, along with Rhodes, by the Knights of St John, who built a mighty castle above the harbour. It became part of the Ottoman Empire in the 16th c. and was under Turkish rule for 400 years. Thereafter it shared the destinies of the Dodecanese. In the course of its history it was frequently raided or attacked, lying as it did on the important sea route linking the Near East by way of Cyprus and Rhodes with the Aegean and the Dardanelles.

At the turn of the 19th c. the island had a population of 15,000, occupying some 4000 houses. Photographs of the 1920s depict busy activity in the harbour, crowded with sailing vessels and boats; some even show seaplanes. In 1943 the island, which had been occupied by Italy since

The picturesque harbour of Kastellórizo (Meyistí)

1920, was heavily bombed by the Royal Air Force. Thereafter many of the inhabitants emigrated, mainly to Australia. The island returned to Greece in 1947.

Sights

The island's only settlement, Kastellórizo or Meyistí, lies on a deeply indented inlet on the north-east coast, its brightly painted balconied houses, many of them abandoned and falling into ruin, climbing up the slopes above the harbour. It is dominated by the castle built by the Spanish Grand Master (1377–96) of the Order of St John, Juan Fernando Heredia, on Byzantine foundations and probably on the site of a fort of the 4th c. BC. The Knights' castle was known as the Castello Rosso: hence the name of Kastellórizo.

Kastellórizo town

At the foot of the hill crowned by the castle is a domed tomb (4th c. BC), of a type common in Lycia, on the nearby coast of Asia Minor. On the east side of the harbour is a former mosque, converted from an earlier church, that was used during the Italian occupation as a warehouse. Above the mosque is the newly built **museum**, whose collection ranges from archaeological finds from the island's past (jewellery, vases, coins) to a sponge-diver's equipment.

Tour

On the northern slopes of Mount Vigla (271 m (889 ft)), which rises above the harbour, is a 100 m (330 ft) long stretch of **cyclopean walls** built of irregularly shaped limestone blocks – probably the remains of a Mycenaean stronghold of the 2nd millennium BC.

Higher up the hill are the **monasteries** of Áyios Yeóryios (to the south) and Ayía Triáda (to the west; abandoned in 1942). On the summit are a military lookout post and the remains of an ancient stronghold, **Palaiokástro** (Hellenistic walls, tower and cistern; churches). On the inhospitable plateau to the east, at Avlonia, are Mycenaean rock tombs, an ancient workshop and other remains.

★Fokalia cave

On the south coast of the island is the sea cave of Fokalia or Parásta, which has been compared with the Blue Grotto on Capri. A visit on an excursion boat is possible only when the sea is calm, since the entrance is only 1 m (39 in.) high.

Neighbouring islands

To the west of Kastellórizo (5 km (3 mi.)) is the islet of Ro (Áyios Yeóryios), now used only for the grazing of stock. Its last inhabitant was an old lady named Despina. who defied the Italian occupying forces by hoisting the Greek flag every day until her death in 1982.

4 km (2½ mi.) south-east of Kastellórizo is the uninhabited islet of Strongylí, an isolated rock 1.6 km (1 mi.) long, 600 m (1969 ft) across and up to 180 m (590 ft) high, with a lighthouse at the south end.

Kéa   I 6

Island group: Cyclades
Area: 130 sq. km (50 sq. mi.)
Altitude: 0–570 m (0–1870 ft)
Population: 1600
Chief place: Kéa town (Khóra)

Port: Korissía. Shipping connections with Rafína, Lávrio and Kýnthos. Bus services on the island.

Kéa (Κεα), the most westerly of the larger Cyclades and the nearest to the Greek mainland, lies some 20 km (13 mi.) south-east of Cape Soúnion. Its tourist trade caters mainly for Athenians, who come here at weekends and on holiday; Kéa has many attractive bathing beaches. The island's traditional stock farming and cultivation of crops on terraces have declined as a result of emigration, and the harvesting of acorns for use in tanning has died out, superseded by chemical products.

History The island was originally settled by Dryopians from Euboea, and later by Ionians, who established a "tetrapolis" of four cities – Ioulis, Karthaia, Koressia and Poiessa. After the battle of Salamis (480 BC), in which Kéa fought on the Athenian side, it joined the Attic maritime league. From AD 395 it belonged to the Byzantine Empire. In 1207 it came under the rule of Venetian dukes, and in subsequent centuries suffered frequent pirate raids. In 1579 it became part of the Ottoman Empire, and finally returned to Greece after the war of liberation.

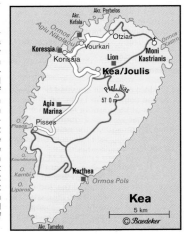

The Lion of Kéa

Sights

At the south end of the bay of Áyios Nikólaos is the little port of Korissía (Κορησσια), known to local people as Livádi, with hotels, pensions and a sandy beach. It occupies the site of ancient Koressia, and there are remains of town walls and a sanctuary of Apollo. The Kouros of Kéa (530 BC), the 1.7 m (5½ ft) high figure of a youth that was found here is now in the National Archaeological Museum in Athens.

Korissía

1.5 km (1 mi.) north is the seaside resort and yachting harbour of Vourkári (Βουρκαρι), with a beautiful sandy beach sloping gently down to the sea.

Vourkári

Beside the chapel of Ayía Iríni, near the north end of the bay of Áyios Nikólaos, is a Bronze Age settlement (2800–1500 BC) excavated by American archaeologists from 1960 onwards, which traded with the Minoan and Mycenaean worlds. Notable features are a large cellared building, the remains of a tumulus tomb and the walls of the oldest temple so far found in Greece (15th c. BC).

★Bronze Age settlement

On Cape Kefála, on the north coast of Kéa, are remains of a neolithic set-tlement (3200–2800 BC). 4 km (2½ mi.) from Vourkári is Otziás (Οτζιας), with a sandy beach fringed by tamarisks. From here a gravel road runs 5 km (3 mi.) south-east to the 18th c. monastery of the Panayía Kastriáni, picturesquely situated on a steep crag, with beautiful views.

Otziás

The chief place on the island is the little town of Kéa (Khóra; pop. 700), situated at the foot of Mount Profítis Ilías (560 m (1837 ft)), 6 km (4 mi.) south-east of Korissía. It occupies the site of ancient Ioulis, of which there are some remains within the Venetian Kástro (1210). Ioulis was the home of two notable poets, Simonides and his nephew Bacchylides

Kéa town

(6th/5th c. BC). The Archaeological Museum in the main street displays ancient remains found locally. Notable exhibits are the headless figures of bare-breasted women, similar to Minoan figures found on Crete. On the hill above the town are scanty remains of the Venetian Kástro, on the site of the ancient acropolis.

★Lion of Kéa

A short walk north-east of Kéa is the famous Lion of Kéa (6th c. BC), a 6 m (20 ft) long figure of a lion carved from the native rock (mica schist) by an Ionian sculptor.

Karthaia

Near the south end of the east coast are the massive terraces of ancient Karthaia (only accessible on foot; stout footwear recommended). On the lowest terrace are the foundations of a Doric temple of Apollo. On a 6 m (20 ft) long block in the polygonal walls of the upper terrace can be seen an ancient inscription; and on this terrace are the foundations of another temple, defensive walls and remains of the upper town.

Písses Bay

The best beach on the island is in Písses Bay, on the west coast 8 km (5 mi.) from Kéa. Above the bay are the remains of ancient Poiessa. The road from Ioulís to here runs past the abandoned monastery of Ayía Marína, which is built against a tower of the 4th c. BC.

Kefaloniá   E 5

Ionian Islands
Area: 781 sq. km (302 sq. mi.)
Altitude: 0–1628 m (0–5341 ft)
Population: 28,000
Chief place: Argostóli

Airport 9 km (5½ mi.) south of Argostóli (shuttle bus service). Air connections with Athens and Zákynthos. Charter flights. Shipping connections: From Sámi: Ithaca–Igoumenítsa–Corfu–Brindisi, Patrás, in summer Fiskárdo. From Póros: Kyllíni (Peloponnese). From Fiskárdo: Vasilikí and Nydrí (Lefkás), Frikés (Ithaca). From Póros: Kyllíni (Peloponnese). From Ayía Evfimía: Vathý (Ithaca), Astakós (mainland). From Pesáda: Skinári (Zákynthos). Ferries: Argostóli–Astakós (mainland). Bus connection with Athens (Póros–Kyllíni). Bus services on the island.

Kefaloniá (Cephalonia, Κεφαλονια), the largest of the Ionian Islands, lies between Lefkás and Zákynthos, roughly in the latitude of Patrás. 45 km (28 mi.) long and up to 30 km (19 mi.) wide, it has a much indented coastline, with two long peninsulas reaching out into the sea, in the north the Erissos peninsula and on the west the Palikí peninsula, bounding the Gulf of Argostóli. The island is traversed from north to south by a range of hills that rises to 1628 m (5341 ft) in the forest-covered Mount Aínos.

Tourism With its magnificent sandy beaches Kefaloniá is a very popular holiday destination, though its tourist trade, which is, along with farming and fishing, its main source of income, is on a much smaller scale than that of Corfu and Zákynthos. The main tourist centres lie southwest of Argostóli (Makrýs Yialós, Platýs Yialós) – though tourism is now gradually extending on to the southern tip of the island (Skála), and new hotels are also being built on the coast south-west of Lixoúri. The very picturesque little town of Fiskárdo at the northern tip of the island is popular with individual travellers for a brief stay. Kefaloniá produces excellent olive oil and white and red Robola wine, and among its other attractions are its interesting flora and fauna and a number of unusual natural phenomena.

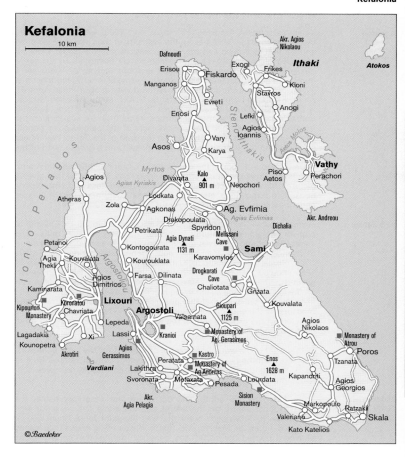

History Kefaloniá is generally accepted as being the Homeric island of Same (but for Wilhelm Dörpfeld's divergent view see Lefkás). In the "Odyssey" the two islands of Same and Doulichion are described as belonging to the kingdom of Ithaca, but Odysseus's subjects are also called Cephallenians. In the 6th and 5th c. BC the island was under the influence of Corinth; then in 456 BC Tolmides compelled it to submit to Athens. At that time there were four city states on the island – Kranioi, Pale, Pronnoi and Same – which Thucydides refers to as a tetrapolis. The cities were members of the Aeolian League, and fought against Philip V of Macedon (220–217 BC) and against the Romans, but eventually the island fell into the power of Rome. From 1483 to 1485 and again from 1500 to 1797 Kefaloniá was held by the Venetians. A devastating earthquake in 1953 destroyed 70 per cent of the island's buildings, and some villages were almost completely wiped out.

Argostóli and the Palikí peninsula

Argostóli

Kefaloniá's capital, Argostóli (Αργοστολι; pop. 8000), which was founded by the Venetians in 1757, lies on the east side of the Lassí peninsula, on an inlet that cuts deep into the south-west coast of the island. Once an attractive old town, it was almost completely destroyed by an earthquake in 1953 and has been rebuilt in traditional style. There are a number of hotels, but few visitors stay in Argostóli for any length of time.

The central feature of the town is the flower-decked Platía Kentrikí, round which are numerous restaurants. To the south, on Rokou Vergóti, is the Archaeological Museum (open Tue.–Sun. 8.30am–1pm, summer until 3pm). Among the most important items from excavations on the island are weapons and everyday objects of the Late Minoan period, which give some impression of life at the time of the Trojan War. Major exhibits from the Roman period are a mosaic and a bronze head of the 3rd c. AD.

On the ground floor of the Koryialenios Library (old books and manuscripts) is a historical museum (open Mon.–Sat. 9am–2pm) that gives a picture of life in Argostóli before the earthquake (lace and embroidery, household furnishings, elaborate traditional costumes, elegant dresses and interesting historical photographs illustrating 19th c. life).

Katavóthres

From Argostóli the coast road runs north, coming in 2.5 km (1½ mi.) to one of Kefaloniá's natural wonders, its famous sea mills. The waterwheel found here was formerly driven by sea water surging along a channel through the rock and then disappearing into clefts (*katavóthres*) in the karstic rock. Investigations by Austrian scientists in 1963 showed that the water flowed right across the island in underground channels, taking in rainwater on the way, to emerge 14 days later on the east side of the island in the Melissáni Cave and in Sámi Bay. The investigators believed that this phenomenon was due to currents and pressures in the underground channels. The 1953 earthquake altered the structure of the ground, so that the waterwheel, formerly used to grind corn, no longer works.

Within sight of the waterwheel, at the northern tip of the Lassí peninsula, is a small **lighthouse** in the form of an ancient circular temple. Built in 1829, the lighthouse was destroyed in the earthquake but was subsequently rebuilt in its original form.

Makrýs Yialós
Platýs Yialós

From Lassí, at the south-west corner of the Lassí peninsula, the largest tourist centre on the island extends along the coast for several miles. It developed round the two beautiful inlets, each 500 m (550 yds) long, of Makrýs and Platýs Yialós. The marvellous sandy beaches, framed by cliffs, are crowded during the main holiday season.

Kranioi

6 km (4 mi.) east of Argostóli, reached on a 2 km (1¼ mi.) track that branches off the road from Argostóli to Sámi, are the remains of ancient Kranioi (or Krane). There are substantial remains of the 5 km (3 mi.) circuit of walls (5th–4th c. BC) that surrounded the city. The trip is worth taking for the sake of the scenery alone.

Lixoúri

On the far side of the Gulf of Argostóli, on the Palikí peninsula, is Kefaloniá's second largest town, Lixoúri (Λιξουρι; pop. 4000). Between Argostóli and the quiet little port of Lixoúri ferries ply almost hourly; the crossing takes about 20 min. On the west side of the town, housed in a late 19th c. neoclassical villa that belonged to the Iakovatos family, is a museum (open Mon.–Fri. 8am–1.30pm, Tue. and Wed. also 4.30–6.30pm, Sat. 9.30am–12.30pm), with a collection that includes valuable icons, manuscripts of the Gospels, priestly vestments and old furniture.

The beautiful beach of Makrýs Yialós is busy both before and after the main holiday season

There are beautiful beaches at Mégas Lákos and Xi (Μεγας Λακος, Ξι), at the south end of the Palikí peninsula. The beaches of fine red sand sloping gently down to the sea, edged by light-coloured limestone cliffs, extend for several miles. There are some tourist facilities, but apart from a number of hotels, this stretch of coast, as far as Xi, is still largely undeveloped.

Mégas Lákos
Xi

There are also beautiful sandy beaches round Kounópetra (Κουνοπετρα), at the southern tip of the Palikí peninsula. There are a few fishing boats in the tiny harbour, and the scenery can be enjoyed from a taverna.

Kounópetra

North-west of Kounópetra the landscape changes. The limestone country with its sparse growth of vegetation gives place to a range of green hills that extend along the whole of the west side of the Palikí peninsula, falling steeply down to the sea. In this beautiful setting, near the coast, is the monastery of Kipouríon, which is still occupied. The first church was built in 1759; it was destroyed in the 1953 earthquake but was soon rebuilt.

Kipouríon

South of the island

In the wine-growing area of Omalós, south-east of Argostóli, is the largest and most important monastery on the island, Áyios Yerásimos. Numbers of pilgrims come here every day to seek help from Kefaloniá's patron saint, St Gerasimus. His remains are preserved in a silver sarcophagus in the old monastery church. To accommodate the hosts of worshippers a magnificent new church was built in the 1980s.

Áyios Yerásimos

The south of the island is dominated by Mount Aínos, which has a road

★Mount Aínos

195

running up to the summit. At higher levels on the hill there are considerable stands of the rare Apollo fir or Cephalonian fir (Abies cephalonica). The summit area was declared a National Park in 1962.

Kástro

At Travilata, on the road from Argostóli to Skála and Póros, a side road goes off to the Kástro (alt. 320 m (1050 ft)), a fortress originally built in the 12th c. and strengthened by the Venetians in the 16th. Round the hill on which the castle was built there grew up Kefaloniá's Venetian capital, San Giorgio, which at one time had a population of more than 15,000. After Argostóli became the capital in 1757 San Giorgio was almost completely abandoned by its inhabitants. Most of the castle's 600 m (1980 ft) circuit of walls still survives.

Áyios Andréas

Below the Kástro is the convent of Áyios Andréas, first recorded in 1264. The church, built about 1600, is now a museum (open daily 9am–1.30pm, 5–8pm), with 13th c. wall paintings. Other frescos of the 16th–17th c. came to light after the 1953 earthquake when the plaster covering them flaked off the walls.

Metaxáta

Metaxáta's (Μεταξατα) fine villas and beautiful gardens declare at once that this is a prosperous little town. In 1823 Byron stayed here for four months before moving on to Mesolóngi on the Greek mainland, where he died of malaria in April 1824. The house in which he lived was destroyed in the 1953 earthquake, and his stay is now commemorated only by a memorial plaque.

Lákithra

Although it is not directly on the sea, the neighbouring village of Lákithra (Λακηθρα) has also developed into a tourist resort. It has a number of very attractive hotels and apartment blocks, some of them with views of the sea (though the Kefaloniá airport now lies between the village and the sea). Near the church were found late Mycenaean tombs (1250–1150 BC) containing rich grave goods.

Skála

At the southern tip of the island is the popular tourist centre of Skála (Σκαλα), with many hotels, rooms in private houses and restaurants. There are very beautiful long beaches of reddish sand, and inland is a charming upland region with pinewoods and cypresses. The neighbouring village of Ratzakli is favoured by independent travellers. Loggerhead turtles (Caretta caretta) come here to lay their eggs, as they do on the beaches of southern Zákynthos (see entry).

Póros

From Skála a recently built road runs north along the east coast to the sleepy little port of Póros (Πορος; 13 km (8 mi.)), still little touched by tourism. 5 km (3 mi.) north is the monastery of Atrou, situated on a hill at an altitude of 535 m (1755 ft), with a magnificent view of Póros. To the north-west, in a beautiful hill setting in the Atros range, is Lake Avythos.

North of the island

★Mýrtos

From the road linking Argostóli with the north of the island there are beautiful views of the Gulf of Argostóli. On this road is one of the most beautiful beaches on Kefaloniá, at Mýrtos (Μυρτος), in a bay framed in high cliffs, with a beach of fine shingle. The best view of the bay is on the return journey, looking north from the main road.

Ásos

Soon Ásos (Ασος), with a castle looming over it, comes into view. A side road zigzags down to the village. Since there are no sandy beaches, most visitors come to Ásos only on a day trip. A path runs up through woodland to a 16th c. Venetian fort, considered in its day to be impregnable.

★Fiskárdo

The prettiest village on Kefaloniá, at the northern tip of the island, is Fiskárdo (Φισκαρδο), named after the Norman leader Robert Guiscard,

The beach at Mýrtos is surrounded by tall crags

who died here in 1085. It survived the 1953 earthquake almost unscathed. Picturesque little houses painted in pastel colours, some of them dating from the 18th c., surround the harbour. In the harbour itself, however, the brightly painted fishing boats are now in a minority. Smart yachts line the quays in summer, for Fiskárdo has long been a meeting place for sailing enthusiasts from all over the world.

1 km (¾ mi.) south of the village is a beautiful shingle beach fringed by trees (taverna). In the channel between the north-east coast of Kefaloniá and Ithaca lives one of the last surviving colonies of **monk seals** in the Mediterranean. This is a much endangered species: worldwide there are estimated to be only just under 500, half of them in Greek waters.

From the road linking Ayía Evfimía with Sámi a side road (signposted) goes off on the right to the Melissáni Cave (open daily 8am–8pm). A short tunnel runs down to the underground lake in the cave. Part of the roof has fallen in, allowing daylight to penetrate and creating a fascinating play of colour. There are boat trips to the lake with its bizarre rock formations.

★**Melissáni Cave**

Kefaloniá's busiest ferry port is Sámi (Σαμη; pop. 1000). The ancient city of Same, which flourished particularly in the time of Alexander the Great's successors, the Diadochoi, lay on the slopes of the twin-peaked hill to the south signposted "Kástro"). There are remains of the town walls, a Roman villa of the 2nd c. AD and a Hellenistic watchtower.

Sámi

3 km (2 mi.) south-west of Sámi is the 100 m (330 ft) long stalactitic cave of Drogaráti, which has very effective floodlighting. It has excellent acoustics , and concerts are occasionally held here in summer.

Drogaráti Cave

The sleepy little town of Kímolos, founded by the Venetians in the 13th c.

Kímolos   I 7

Island group: Cyclades
Area of island: 35 sq. km (14 sq. mi.)
Altitude: 0–398m (0–1306 ft)
Population: 700
Chief place: Kímolos town

Port: Psáthi. Shipping connections with Piraeus and with other islands in the Cyclades. Boats from Melos.

Kímolos (Κιμολος) is a flat and arid island of volcanic origin to the northeast of Melos, usually visited on day trips from there. It can be recommended for visitors who want a quiet and restful holiday and are interested in traditional Greek village life. It also has a number of sand and shingle beaches. It was famed in antiquity for its terra cimolia (cimolith), used both as a detergent and in medicinal baths, which is still worked at Prassa. The inhabitants make a sparse living from agriculture.

Sights

Ships put in at the little port town of Psáthi, in the south-east of the island, which has a beach. 1 km (¾ mi.) from Psáthi is the chief place on the island, Kímolos town (pop. 740), founded by the Venetians in 1207, with a castle built to protect the inhabitants from pirate raids. The windowless outer walls of the houses (now largely ruined) formed a defensive wall. Notable features of Psáthi are the principal church, the Panayía Odiyítria (1873), at the entrance to the town, the church of Áyios Khrysóstomos (17th c.), with paintings by Skordilis, and the Church of Christ in the Kástro (1592). On the highest hill on the island is the ruined medieval castle of Palaiokástro (access difficult).

Off the south-west coast of Kímolos lies the little islet of Áyios Andréas, which in antiquity was connected with the main island by a narrow spit of land. On it was the oldest settlement on Kímolos, Ellinikon (1000 BC), of which there remain only fragments of walls under the sea.

There are good beaches 3 km (2 mi.) west of Kímolos (Alikí Beach; sand and pebbles) and to the north of the town at Prassa (shingle).

Kos   L/M 7

Island group: Dodecanese
Area: 290 sq. km (112 sq. mi.)
Altitude: 0–846 m (0–2776 ft)
Population: 25,000
Chief place: Kos town

Airport at Antimákhia, 26 km (16 mi.) south-west (airport and service bus). Air connections with Athens and Rhodes; many charter flights. Principal port: Kos. Shipping connections with Salonica and Piraeus, Nísyros–Tílos–Sými–Rhodes, Kálymnos–Léros–Lipsí–Pátmos–Arkí–Aga-thonísi–Sámos, Pátmos–Náxos–Páros–Mýkonos and Astypálaia. Hydrofoils to Sámos and Rhodes. Ferry to Bodrum (Turkey). Many boat trips on offer. Bus services on the island.

Kos (Κος) is the third largest island in the Dodecanese and second only to Rhodes in importance and tourist interest. It lies north-west of Rhodes at the mouth of the Gulf of Kos, which cuts deep into the coast of Asia Minor. It was separated from the Bodrum (Halicarnassus) peninsula,

Evidence of Kos's eventful history: view from the Agora of the Khatze-Hassan Mosque

199

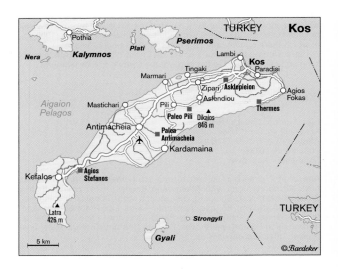

4 km (2½ mi.) north-east, by the collapse of a rift valley in the Pliocene era. The mild, rainy climate gives it an attractive green aspect in spring and early summer, but by September most of the vegetation has withered. There are small areas of woodland only on the slopes of some hills. The island, 45 km (28 mi.) long, is traversed from west to east by a narrow ridge of Cretaceous hills that reach a height of 846 m (2776 ft) in Mount Díkaios. Apart from this Kos is – unlike other Aegean islands – very flat, well suited to cycle touring. It is the only island in the Aegean with a cycle track (a 30 km (19 mi.) circuit round Kos town).

Formerly agriculture was a major element in the island's economy, but nowadays it produces only small quantities of wine, olives, melons, barley and wheat. Since the closure of the tomato factory in Kos town the island has practically no industry. Tourism, with over 450,000 package tourists annually, is now the mainstay of the island's economy.

Tourism With 65,000 beds for visitors, which are fully booked in August, Kos is a stronghold of mass tourism; but it has contrived to avoid the mistakes made by other Mediterranean tourist centres with their gigantic hotel blocks. On Kos there are numerous small guest houses and apartment blocks, widely scattered all over the island. Tourism began in the area round the island's capital, Kos town, where there are only narrow shingle beaches, extending between Paradisi and Áyios Fokás along the busy coast road. Much broader and more beautiful are the sandy beaches on the north coast between Lambi and Mastikhári and in Kéfalos Bay in the south-west.

As a result of the elongated form of the island and the nearness of the coast there are no remote villages in the hills preserving old customs; but Kos has many remains of antiquity, the ruins of Early Christian churches, medieval castles, mosques dating from the Turkish period and handsome buildings left by its Italian rulers.

History Around 700 BC, together with the other five cities of the Hexapolis (Cnidus, Halicarnassus, Lindus, Ialysus and Kameiros), Kos was an outpost of the Dorian League of cities on the Carian coast and the neighbouring islands. The island was celebrated for the oldest cult site of the healing god Asclepius (Aesculapius) and for a medical school of which the most famous representative was Hippocrates (c. 460–357 BC), a native of Kos.

King Ptolemy II of Egypt was born on Kos, and in his reign the island became an important centre of maritime trade. The Romans, Byzantines and Venetians were succeeded as rulers of Kos by the Knights of St John (1309–1523), who called the island Lango, and in the 14th c. established the headquarters of their order in the island's capital, Narangia (now the town of Kos). Kos was taken by the Turks rather earlier than Rhodes. The island was occupied by Italy in 1912, during the Balkan War, but was returned to Greece in 1948.

★Kos town

The island's capital, Kos town (pop. 12,500), lies in a wide bay on the north-east coast, at the east end of the only plain of any size on the island. From here the Turkish coast, with the town of Bodrum, can be seen only a few kilometres away. Some stretches of medieval walls, Venetian-style houses and buildings of the Turkish period that survived an earthquake in 1933 blend happily with the modern town, which with its innumerable street cafés and restaurants, the excavation sites open to the public, the oleander trees lining the streets and the colourful harbour, full of yachts and fishing boats and, in the evening, the excursion ships returning to port, has a cheerful holiday atmosphere.

A palm-shaded promenade runs east along the Mandráki harbour to the formidable castle of the Knights of St John, built between 1450 and 1514 (open Tue.–Sun. 8.30am–3pm). Fragments of ancient sculpture and inscribed stones are built into its walls, and over the entrance is a Hellenistic relief. The castle is reached from the Platía Platánou (Square of the Plane Tree), in which is the Khatze Hassan Mosque (1786), now housing souvenir stalls. The most prominent feature of the square is Hippocrates' Plane Tree, under which the great physician is said to have taught. This mighty tree, however, whose dead main trunk has a girth of 12 m (40 ft), is "only" around 500 years old. It is supported by a Turkish fountain house (with an ancient sarcophagus) belonging to the mosque

Castle of the Knights

The Defterdar Mosque, now housing a restaurant

To the south is the ancient Agora (market square), which – like all the ancient sites in Kos town – is freely open to the public as an archaeological park. There is a

Agora

fine view over the ancient remains and the oleander trees to the minarets and church towers of the town. On the west side of the Agora, in Platía Eleftherías, are the small Market Hall, which dates from the Venetian period, and the charming **Defterdar Mosque** (18th c.), with Hellenistic and Byzantine columns.

Archaeological
Museum

Also in Platía Eleftherías is the interesting Archaeological Museum (open Tue.–Sun. 8.30am–3pm), built in the style of an ancient villa. It contains numbers of Roman marble statues, but its greatest treasure, displayed in the inner courtyard, is a fine mosaic of the 2nd/3rd c. AD depicting the arrival of Asclepius on Kos.

On the south and south-west sides of the town, along Odós Grigoriou, are extensive **excavations**, all permanently open to the public. Going from east to west, there are a temple of Dionysus (3rd c. AD), Roman baths, the reconstructed "Casa Romana" (3rd c. AD; beautiful mosaics), a Roman Odeion, the House of Europa (mosaics), a Gymnasion (2nd c. BC) and the so-called Nymphaion, a public latrine of the 3rd c. BC.

To the west of the town is the densely built-up tourist district of Lambi, with a rather polluted beach (4 km (2½ mi.)) long. To the east the coast road runs past a number of narrow shingle **beaches** to the very busy beach at Psalídi (3 km (2 mi.)), and then on to Áyios Fokás (7 km (4½ mi.)) and Thermes (11 km (7 mi.)), with warm springs on the beach. At about the Hotel Platanista begins what is perhaps the most attractive resort area on the island, with large and handsome hotels and holiday villages like the new Kypriotis Village (see Practical Information, Hotels). Tall eucalyptus trees provide shade here for walkers and cyclists.

From the uppermost terrace of the Asklepieion there is a view of the whole site and of Kos town. The Turkish town of Bodrum is in the distance.

South-west of Kos town is the little village of Platáni (Πλατανι), still ⌐
pied by some Turks, who are distinguished from Greeks only by th
names. The village has a mosque and Turkish and Jewish cemeteries.
From Platáni a pretty lane lined by cypresses and planes leads to the
sanctuary of Asclepius; it can be reached by bus, but it is also a very
pleasant walk.

**Asklepieion

The Asklepieion, the sanctuary of Asclepius (Aesculapius), lies 4 km
(2½ mi.) south-west of Kos town in a commanding situation 100 m (330
ft) above the sea (open Tue.–Sun. 8.30am–3pm, summer until 7pm). The
most important ancient site on the island, it was excavated from 1902
onwards by a German archaeologist, R. Herzog. Reconstruction work
was carried out by Italian archaeologists in the 1940s.

Laid out on three terraces, the Asklepieion was built in the early 3rd c.
BC on the site of an earlier (5th c.) temple of Apollo. The higher you go
on the site the grander is the view of Kos town and, beyond a narrow
channel, the nearby Turkish mainland.

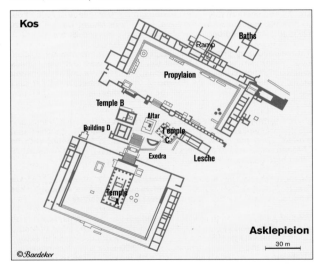

On the **lowest terrace** was the precinct to which patients came for healing, a large area measuring some 90 by 45 m (300 by 150 ft) enclosed by
Doric columns. To the rear of the porticoes were smaller rooms. To the
left of the entrance are three private houses of the Roman or late
Hellenistic period. At the north-east corner of the precinct was a later
bathhouse; and after the destruction of the Asklepieion in an earthquake
in AD 554 its site was occupied by the monastery of the Panayía tou
Alsoús (the Mother of God of the Grove – a reminiscence of the ancient
sacred grove). Adjoining this s a small museum. On the south side of the
precinct is the retaining wall of the second terrace. To the left, between
the second and third buttresses, is the sacred spring. To the right, in
front of a stretch of wall, is a naiskos (small temple) dedicated to Nero,
the "new Asclepius", by C. Stertinius Xenophon, personal physician of
the Emperor Claudius.

From here steps lead up to the **second terrace**, the original cult site. At the top of the steps is an altar, which in its present form is later than the small marble temple of Asclepius (c. 400 BC) to the west; of the earlier temple on this site only scanty traces have survived. To the east of the altar was an Ionic peripteral temple of 6 × 9 columns, possibly dedicated to Apollo; seven of its columns have been re-erected. To the south-west was a semicircular exedra, and facing this, behind the old temple, a Roman building on earlier foundations.

Between these two buildings a monumental staircase 11 m (36 ft) wide leads up to the **third terrace**, with the later (2nd c. BC) temple of Asclepius, a large Doric peripteral temple of 6 × 11 columns. The black-marble sill stone has been preserved. Higher up the hill (45 min. climb) is the Vourinna spring, which supplied the ancient city with water.

Surroundings

Zipári

The road south-west from Kos town runs along the northern slopes of the hills and comes in 10 km (6 mi.) to Zipári (Ζιπάρι), in which is the Early Christian basilica of Áyios Pávlos, with a baptistery and mosaics. 4 km (2½ mi.) south of this is the charming mountain village of Asfendioú, in a fertile vegetable-growing area. From here Mount Díkaios (846 m (2776 ft)) can be climbed (beautiful panoramic views over the island).

Zía

The neighbouring picture-book village of Zía (Ζια) has now been taken over by tourism and is no longer the village it was. Set ion a shady pinewood, it now consists almost exclusively of restaurants and souvenir stalls. Sometimes there are dozens of tourist coaches in the car park below the village. The view over the coastal plain is breathtaking, particularly just before sunset, and the village is worth visiting for that alone.

Mastikhári

On the north coast are the large bathing resorts of Tingáki, Marmári and Mastikhári, which have grown up along the beautiful beaches that extend along the coast. Particularly attractive is Mastikhári, with its Mediterranean air and old town centre, 5 km (3 mi.) north of Antimákhia. From here there are ferries to Psérimos and Kálymnos.

Psérimos

Off the north coast lies the little island of Psérimos (Ψεριμος; area 17 sq. km (6½ sq. mi.); alt. 0–268 m (0–879 ft)), with beautiful beaches. Although it has a population of only 100 there are some rooms for visitors.

Palaío Pýli

West of Asfendioú on the mountain road are the most romantic ruins on the island, in a lonely situation on the wooded northern slopes of Mount Díkaios. The village of Palaío Pýli, strategically situated so as to escape notice from the sea, was abandoned in 1830 after a cholera epidemic. There are ruins of the village church, with Byzantine frescos.

Antimákhia

13 km (8 mi.) further on is Antimákhia (Αντιμαχεια), which has the island's last working windmill. Shortly before the village a track goes off to Palaía Antimákhia, a castle of the Knights of St John that was rebuilt after an earthquake in 1493. The long battlemented walls of the castle, the largest on the island, are visible from a long way off. On the walls are knightly coats of arms.

Kardamaína

6 km (4 mi.) south-east of Antimákhia is the not particularly attractive bathing resort of Kardamaína (Καρδαμαινα), much favoured by British visitors. There are daily excursion boats to Nísyros.

Kéfalos

After passing the airport the road comes in 17 km (11 mi.) to Kéfalos (Κεφαλος), a pretty mountain village of whitewashed single-storey houses that has preserved its original character better than any other

The rocky islet of Kástri in the Gulf of Kéfalos, with the ruined church of Áyios Stéfanos

place on the island. Only a few tourists find their way here. In antiquity it was known as Astypalaia and was the island's first capital. After its destruction in an earthquake in 412 BC the capital was transferred to the site of the present Kos town.

Below Kéfalos is the beach of Kamári. Near the Club Méditerranée (access through the Club site) are the beautifully situated remains of the Early Christian basilica of Áyios Stéfanos. Offshore is the picturesque rocky islet of Kástri, with the chapel of Áyios Nikólaos.

Further north-east are two sandy beaches, Camel Beach and Paradise Beach. To the south of Kéfalos the road climbs steeply (not suitable for mopeds!) and continues through the wild landscape of the southern tip of Kos. There are also possible walks to the monasteries of Áyios Ioánnis (6 km (4 mi.) south) and Áyios Ioánnis Theológos (4 km (2½ mi.) west).

Kýthira   G/H 7

Ionian Islands
Area: 285 sq. km (110 sq. mi.)
Altitude: 0–506 m (0–1660 ft)
Population: 2500
Chief place: Kýthira town (Khóra)

Airport 10 km (6 mi.) north-west of Kýthira town (no airport bus service). Air connections with Athens. Principal port: Ayía Pelayía. Shipping connections with Piraeus, Pórto Káyio, Néapoli, Monemvásia, Elafónisos, Antikýthira and Kastélli Kíssamou (Crete). Hydrofoils to Piraeus via Monemvásia, Kyparissi, Spétses and Hydra. Bus services and many taxis on the island.

Kýthira

Kýthira (ancient Cythera, Κυθηρα) lies 15 km (9 mi.) south of the most south-easterly peninsula in the Peloponnese (Laconia). Surprisingly, it is regarded as one of the Ionian Islands (Eptánisos), though administratively it is part of Attica. It is an island of rugged karstic hills, slashed by numerous gorges, and sheer coastal cliffs. The meagre yields of its agriculture have led many of the younger people to emigrate, particularly to Australia, known to the remaining inhabitants as "Big Kýthira". Until a few years ago it had few tourists, and it can still be recommended to visitors who want a quiet, relaxing holiday.

History Cythera's abundance of murex shellfish (producing a much valued purple dye) led to an early Phoenician settlement on the island. Later it belonged to Sparta, and the Phoenician cult of the goddess Astarte developed into the Greek cult of Aphrodite, to whom a number of temples on the island were dedicated (though none have survived). She was believed to have emerged from the sea spray off the coast of Cythera after Zeus castrated his father Uranus and threw his genitals into the sea.

As a military stronghold off the coast of Lacedaemon the island was of great strategic importance in ancient times. Under Venetian rule (from 1207) Kýthira was known as Cerigo. Thereafter, as a late addition to the Eptánisos, it shared the destinies of the Ionian Islands. It was reunited with Greece in 1864, and on occasion served as a place of exile for opponents of the government.

Sights

Ayía Pelayía

In a wide bay on the north-east coast is the island's principal port, the friendly town of Ayía Pelayía (Αγα Πελαγια), where during the military dictatorship (1967–74) political opponents of the regime lived in exile.

Palaiokhóra

To the south of Ayía Pelayía, magnificently situated above the coast, are the ruins of Palaiokhóra, a medieval stronghold, once the island's capital, that was destroyed by the Turks in 1536. It is reached by way of Logothetianika. The road runs through Potamós, the economic centre of the island, with a lively Sunday market.

Mylopótamos

Half way along the west coast is the pretty little village of Mylopótamos (Μυλοποταμος), with a splendid plane tree, the church of Áyios Kharalambos and a waterfall. From here you can walk down to Káto Khóra, within the walls of a 16th c. Venetian fortress, with well preserved churches, and the stalactitic cave of Ayía Sofía, which contains an underground lake. In the cave is a 12th c. chapel dedicated to Ayía Sofía, with later frescos.

Avlémonas

On the east coast is the bay of Avlémonas (Αβλεμονας; or Áyios Nikólaos), where the yacht "Mentor", carrying some of the Elgin marbles, ran aground in 1802; the marbles were subsequently recovered and sent on to Britain. The village has a small fishing harbour and a shingle beach.

Panayía Myrtidíon

Above the south-west is the 17th c. monastery of the Panayía Myrtidíon, with a wonderworking black icon that is carried in procession on August 15th, the feast of the Dormition of the Mother of God

★Kýthira town

At the southern tip of the island, high above the bay and harbour of Kapsáli, is the charming village of Kýthira (Khóra; pop. 600), the chief place on the island. Over the village looms a massive Venetian castle (16th c.), from the south end of which there are breathtaking views over the island, extending on clear days as far as Crete.

Kýthira town, dominated by a Venetian castle

Antikýthira

South-east of Kýthira, roughly half way to Crete, lies the little karstic island of Antikýthira (Αντικυθηρα; area 22 sq. km (8½ sq. mi.); alt. 0–360 m (0–1180 ft)). There are some remains of ancient Aigila at Palaiokástro, 1.5 km (1 mi.) from the chief place on the island, Potamo. The 700 inhabitants of Antikýthira live mainly by farming and fishing. In the channel between the two islands the wreck of a Roman ship was discovered in 1900; its cargo of bronze and marble statues of the 5th–2nd c. BC, including the famous "Ephebe of Antikýthira", together with pottery, glass and an astronomical clock, is now in the National Archaeological Museum in Athens.

Elafónisos

Kýthira is separated from the neighbouring island of Elafónisos (Ελαφονησος) to the south by a 10 km (6 mi.) wide channel that is a busy shipping route. Elafónisos can be reached only from Athens or Néapoli. Known in antiquity as Onougnathos, it lies just off the south-eastern finger of the Peloponnese (Laconia). The chief place on the island, also called Elafónisos, lies at its northern tip, and it has two sheltered anchorages. This bare and arid island sets out to attract "quiet" visitors (small holiday houses).

Kýthnos   I 6

Island group: Cyclades
Area: 99 sq. km (38 sq. mi.)
Altitude: 0–326 m (0–1070 ft)
Population: 1600
Chief place: Kýthnos town (Khóra)

Port: Mérikhas. Shipping connections with Piraeus and other islands in the Cyclades. Bus services on the island.

Kýthnos

Kýthnos (Κυθνος), a rocky and barren island of karstic limestone, lies south-east of Kéa. The coast is much indented and for the most part falls steeply down to the sea. Like Kéa, it is much favoured by Athenians as a holiday resort. The inhabitants live mainly by agriculture and stock farming.

The first settlers, around 2000 BC, were Dryopians from Euboea, who were later driven out by Ionians. In antiquity iron was mined on the island, which became wealthy and had to make substantial contributions to the treasury of the Attic maritime league. From 1207 to 1537 it was held by Venice; later it was incorporated in the Ottoman Empire; and in 1830 it became part of the new kingdom of Greece.

Sights

Mérikhas

The island's principal port, Mérikhas (Μεριχας), which is dominated by the large Hotel Posidonion, is not a particularly attractive place. 2 km (1¼ mi.) north of the town is the excellent beach of Episkopí. On a 150 m (500 ft) high crag above the beach are the ruins of the island's old capital, Vryokástro. Further north is the finest beach on the island, Stin Kolona ("at the column"), to which visitors are taken from Mérikhas by boat.

Kýthnos town

The chief place on the island, Kýthnos, (officially Mesariá), lies 8 km (5 mi.) north-east of Mérikhas at a height of 160 m (525 ft). The most notable of its many churches are Áyios Sávvas and Áyios Sotír (both 17th c.) and Ayía Triáda, with finely carved iconostases and icons of the Cretan school. Above the village is a battery of wind generators (modern windmills) producing electric power. At the end of the village, on the road to Loutrá, is a solar power plant.

Loutrá

On the north side of the bay of Ayía Iríni (5 km (3 mi.) north) are the hot mineral springs (37–55°C (99–131°F)) of Loutrá (Λουτρα), which were already frequented in the Roman Imperial period. During the period of Venetian rule the island was known, after the springs, as Thermiá (Italian Fermenia). The Hotel Anagennisis was built on the initiative of Queen Amalia, wife of Otto I.

Dryopís

6 km (4 mi.) south of Kýthnos is the picturesque village of Dryopís (Δρυοπις; also called Syllakas), on both sides of a wooded valley. The whitewashed houses are roofed with terracotta tiles.

Kanála

On a promontory in the south-east of the island, 7 km (4½ mi.) from Dryopís, is the village of Kanála (Καναλα), now a holiday resort. In the centre of the village is the church of the Panayía (1906), which has a wonderworking icon. The beaches here are the best on the island.

Lefkás

Ionian Islands
Area: 302 sq. km (117 sq. mi.)
Altitude: 0–1158 m (0–3799 ft)
Population: 23,000
Chief place: Lefkás

Nearest airport: Aktion, on the mainland, opposite Préveza. Air connection with Athens. Bus connections with Aktion, Agrínion, Patrás and Athens. Shipping connections: from Vasilikí to Kefaloniá (Fiskárdo–Sámi) and Ithaca (Vathý); from Nydrí to Meganísi–Zákynthos, Ithaca (Frikés) and Mytikas (mainland). Bus services on the island.

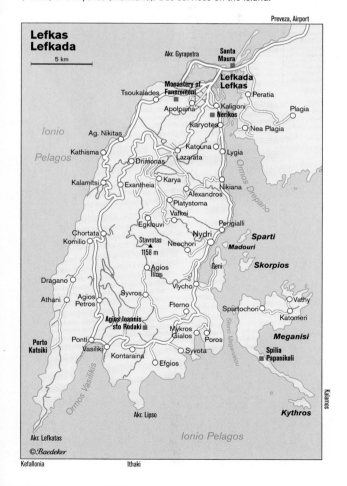

Lefkás or Lefkáda (Λευκας or Λευκαδα, ancient Leukas; Italian Santa Maura) is a hilly island, marked by karstic action, in the Ionian Sea, off the Playiá peninsula in Acarnania, from which it is separated only by a shallow lagoon varying in width between 500 m and 5 km (1650 ft and 3 mi.). It is now linked with the mainland by a causeway and a ferry boat serving as a bridge. Much of the island is occupied by a range of hills, rising to 1158m (3799 ft) in Mount Stavrotás, which runs south–west to end at Cape Doukáto, at the tip of the Lefkáda peninsula. It was from this Leucadian Rock of gleaming white limestone that Sappho was supposed to have thrown herself for love of the handsome Phaon.

Tourism is on a modest scale, and there are no giant hotels – perhaps because of the island's lack of particular attractions. It has no major sights of artistic or historical interest, though it does have varied scenery and largely unspoiled beaches on the west coast. The tourist trade is concentrated on the east coast, with the largest tourist resort on the island, the beautifully situated coastal town of Nydrí.

Apart from tourism the island's main source of income is farming. Vegetables, fruit and vines are grown in small fields, mainly for domestic consumption. Lefkás is famed for its lace and embroidery.

History The earliest evidence of human settlement on the island dates from the neolithic. In 640 BC the town of Leukas was founded by settlers from Corinth, who closed off the south end of the lagoon, opposite the fort of Áyios Yeóryios, by a 600 m (1950 ft) long mole, remains of which are still visible under water. They cut a channel through the spit of shingle at the north end of the lagoon, opposite the fort of Santa Maura (Ayía Mávra) – though by the time of the Peloponnesian War, in which Leukas was allied with Sparta, the channel had silted up. In the time of the Achaean League Leukas was the capital of Acarnania. It supported Philip II of Macedon against Rome, but was conquered in 197 BC by the Romans, who built a bridge linking Leukas with the mainland. The battle of Actium (31 BC) was fought in the waters to the north of the island.

In the Middle Ages the island belonged to various Sicilian and Frankish dynasts. In 1479 it was taken by the Turks – the only one of the Ionian Islands to fall into Turkish hands – but was recovered for Venice by Francesco Morosini in 1684. After a brief interlude of French rule during the Napoleonic wars (1797–1815) it was assigned to Britain, which returned it to Greece, together with the other Ionian Islands, in 1864. As a result of the vicissitudes of its history and a series of earthquakes (most recently in 1953) Lefkás has preserved very few old buildings.

The German archaeologist Wilhelm Dörpfeld (1853–1940), who worked on Lefkás and made his home there, believed that this island, and not the one now called Ithaca, was the Homeric Ithaca, the home of Odysseus. He based his theory mainly on topographical similarities between Lefkás and the Ithaca described in the "Odyssey"; but his excavations failed to produce convincing evidence in support of his theory, which is now generally discounted.

Sights

The chief town, Lefkás (pop. 8000), at the northern tip of the island, is surrounded on three sides by the sea. The lagoon to the north of the town is too shallow for any craft but fishing boats. Excursion boats usually moor along the causeway linking Lefkás with the mainland, yachts to the south and east of the town. Unusually, the hub of the town's social life of the town is not on the harbour but in the centre of the little peninsula. Its principal axis and shopping street is Dörpfeld Street, which runs from the square on the outskirts of the town to Platía

Lefkás town

◀ *The village priest plays a major part in the life of the islanders*

Ayiou Spyridonos and ends in Mela Street. The upper floors of the houses, built of wood, survived the 1953 earthquake, and many of them are now clad in brightly painted sheet or corrugated iron. The stone church towers that collapsed in the earthquake have now been replaced by open bellcotes of lattice steel. A local culinary speciality is soumadia, an almond drink.

Museums and churches

Lefkás has a rather neglected Folk Museum, a Phonographic Museum (signposted), with old gramophones and radios, and an Archaeological Museum (Faneroméni Street; open Tue.–Sun. 9am–3pm), with objects recovered in Dörpfeld's excavations at Nydrí in 1912. Other features of interest are a number of churches dating from the Venetian period and the 18th c. church of Áyios Minás at the end of Mela Street, one of the town's greatest artistic treasures, with a baroque iconostasis made by craftsmen from Zákynthos and fine ceiling paintings.

Surroundings

3 km (2 mi.) north of Lefkás (beyond the bridge), on the shingle spit, stands the Venetian fort of **Santa Maura**, built in the 13th c. by Giovanni Orsini and enlarged in the 17th c. 4 km (2½ mi.) south-west of the town is the beautifully situated **Faneroméni** monastery, founded in 1634 and rebuilt in 1886 after a fire. From here there are magnificent views of the town, the lagoon and the mainland of Greece. 3 km (2 mi.) south, on a hill near Kaligoni, are the remains of ancient **Leukas** (acropolis, aqueduct, town walls, theatre). The nearest beaches are the dunes on the north side of the lagoon, 2 km (1¼ mi.) north.

Áyios Nikítas

The coast on the Ionian Sea is fringed for almost the whole of its length by white cliffs – hence the island's name, from *leukos,* white – up to 500 m (1640 ft) high. Áyios Nikítas (Αγιος Νικητας), once a quiet little fishing village, is situated in a very beautiful bay and is now suffering from the tourist invasion. The picturesque old part of the town is protected as a national monument and closed to motor traffic. To north and south there are quieter beaches, for example at Kathisma.

Karyá

The south coast is almost inaccessible, and the road now runs through the green interior of the island. In the hills is the village of Karyá (Καρυα; pop. 1000), which has preserved its original character. The main event in the year here is a festival on August 11th, with a re-creation of a traditional Lefkás wedding.

★Pórto Katsíki

At Kamíli a road branches off to Cape Doukato. Below Athani is the long sandy beach of Egremni, and 14 km (8½ mi.) further south is the magnificent beach of Pórto Katsíki (Πορτο Κατσικι), under sheer white cliffs. Although this beautiful beach is famed throughout Greece and widely advertised on posters, it is not overcrowded outside the main holiday season.

★Cape Lefkáta

The road (here not asphalted) finally comes to Cape Doukáto or Lefkáta, at the southern tip of the island. The beautiful scenery here, with the sheer cliffs and the lighthouse on a 72 m (236 ft) high crag, is compensation for the difficulties of the road.

Vasilikí

On the way back, at Komíli, the route follows the road to Áyios Pétros (accommodation, tavernas) and Vasilikí (Βασιλικη), the largest tourist resort on the island after Nydrí. This little port on the south coast is particularly popular with surfers, since wind conditions are frequently ideal here. To the west extends a long beach of sand and shingle; even better is the sandy bay of Ayiofýlli to the south of Vasilikí.

Lerikos

The road running south along the east coast from Lefkás comes to the remains of the prehistoric site of Lerikos (2nd millennium BC). At Kariotes begins a stretch of coast with good beaches and the villages of Lygiá (attractive fishing harbour) and Niklána.

One of Greece's dream beaches: Pórto Katsíki

Nydrí

16 km (10 mi.) further on is the beautifully situated little town of Nydrí (Νυδρι), the island's largest tourist centre. From here there is a magnificent view of the densely wooded little offshore islands, to which there are boat excursions from the harbour. There are also ferries to Meganísi, Ithaca and Kefaloniá and excursion boats to or round the little islands of Sparti (sea caves), Mandourí (home of the Greek poet Aristotélis Valaorítis, 1824–79) and Skorpiós, which belongs to the Onassis family. To the west of the town (40 min. walk) is a gorge with a waterfall.

Yéni

To the south of Nydrí the inlet of the same name cuts deep inland. In the village of Vlýkho a road goes off to the Yéni (Γενι) peninsula. From the car park a signpost shows the way to the chapel of Ayía Kyriakí, at the tip of the peninsula. The road to the chapel runs past the villa and the grave of the archaeologist Wilhelm Dörpfeld, who excavated an ancient cemetery on the south side of Nydrí in 1912.

Póros

Returning to Vlýkho, it is another 7 km (4½ mi.) to the attractive mountain village of Póros (Πορος). From here the road winds its way down to the coast at Mikrós Yialós, which has a shingle beach and a number of tavernas. On the south-east coast is Sývota, with beautiful coastal scenery and good fish restaurants.

Meganísi

The largest of the islands off the east coast of Lefkás is Meganísi (Μεγανησι; area 18 sq. km (7 sq. mi.); alt. 0–267 m (0–876 ft); pop. 1500). The ferry crossing takes about 45 min. There are frequent excursion boats to two sea caves on the south-west coast. There are tavernas and accommodation for visitors in the chief place on the island, Vathý. To the west, 1 km (⅝ mi.) inland, is the village of Spartokhóri.

Kálamos

South-east of Lefkás, near the mainland (Acarnania), is the island of Kálamos (Καλαμος). This is a thinly populated hilly island of karstic ter-

213

rain, rising to a height of 785 m (2575 ft), with a cliff coastline. Its 250 inhabitants make a living from stock farming and growing olives, vines and vegetables. The chief place is Kálamos, on the south-east coast. To the south is the island of Kastós, inhabited only by a few fishermen.

★Lemnos   K 3/4

Islands of the northern and eastern Aegean
Area: 476 sq. km (184 sq. mi.)
Altitude: 0–470 m (0–1540 ft)
Population: 20,000
Chief place: Mýrina

Airport 22 km (14 mi.) north-east of Mýrina (airport bus). Air connections with Athens, Salonica, Mytilíni (Lésbos). Shipping connections with Piraeus, Salonica, Rafína, Kavála, Alexandroúpolis, Chíos, Lésbos, Áyios Efstrátios. Bus services on the island, centred on Mýrina.

The island of Lemnos (Λημνος; Límnos) lies in the northern Aegean between Mount Athos and the Dardanelles. It lacks the striking scenery of some other islands, but its fertile and largely treeless upland regions, rising to a height of 470 m (1540 ft), have a charm of their own. Its long coastline is much indented, with two inlets, Pourniás Bay in the north and Moúdros Bay in the south, cutting so deep inland that the eastern and western parts of the island are joined by a strip of land only 4 km (2½ mi.) wide. It does, however, have beautiful beaches – though unfortunately a number of very attractive beaches round Mýrina are shut off by barbed wire, since they lie within a closed military area should on no account be entered (landmines!). Lying off the main tourist tracks, the

On a crag above Mýrina are the ruins of a medieval castle

island has been spared the ravages of tourism. Lemnos is an agricultural island, growing grain, cotton and wine. Its Moskhatos, a sweet muscatel wine, should be drunk with caution.

History The volcanic rock in the east of the island recalls the ancient tradition that, after his fall from Olympus, Hephaestus set up his smithy and married Aphrodite here. The people of Lemnos were notorious for their "wicked actions," as reported by Herodotus, which provided the Athenian general Miltiades with a pretext for his conquest of the island. The walled city of Poliokhni, dated to the beginning of the 3rd millennium BC, belonged to the same pre-Greek culture as Troy and Thermoi (Lesbos). The first Greeks came to Lemnos about 800 BC, but a century later gave way to the Tyrsenoi from Asia Minor, whose language, on the evidence of inscriptions found at Kamínia, was related to Etruscan. This provides some support for the theory, first put forward by Herodotus, that the Etruscans originally came to Italy from the region of Lydia in Asia Minor. The island was resettled by Greeks after the Athenian conquest at the end of the 6th century BC. It was celebrated for the cult of Hephaestus, centred on an "earth fire" near the city of Hephaisteia in the north of the island. In the 4th c. AD Hephaisteia became the see of a bishop, but the bishopric was later transferred to Mýrina on the west coast.

After the Fourth Crusade the island was occupied by the Venetians. A hundred years later it was recovered by the Byzantines, and was then granted to the Gattelusi family of Lésbos as a fief. It was held by the Turks from 1479 to 1912. During the Orlov rising of 1770 it became a Russian naval base. In the First World War Moúdros Bay was the Royal Navy's base during the Gallipoli campaign. Strategically situated at the mouth of the Dardanelles, Lemnos is now a large naval and air base, so that large tracts of the island are closed military areas.

Sights

The chief town and principal port of Lemnos is Mýrina (Μυρινα; pop. 5000), usually called Kástro, which lies on the west coast, on the site of the ancient city of the same name. Above this lively and attractive little town with its neoclassical and half-timbered houses rears a spectacular crag topped by a massive castle, built around 1185 by Andronicus I and enlarged by the Genoese in 1453–57 and by the Venetians in 1477. From the crag there are fine views of the town and surrounding area and a prospect extending on a clear afternoon as far as Mount Athos, some 60 km (40 mi.) away. In the bay to the north of the crag is a long sandy beach. Here too is the Archaeological Museum (open Tue.–Sun. 9am–3pm), with material from Poliókhni, ancient Hephaisteia and the sanctuary of the Cabiri at Khlói.

Mýrina

There are good sandy **beaches** with facilities for bathers at Kaspakas to the north of Mýrina, at Platy (3 km (2 mi.) south) and at Thanos, to the east.

The island's second port, Moúdros (Μουδρος; pop. 1000), lies on the east side of Moúdros Bay, 28 km (17 mi.) east of Mýrina. The town, which is occupied by the Greek army, has a number of hotels, but is not to be recommended as a place to stay. To the east of the town is a British Commonwealth military cemetery.

Moúdros

From Moúdros a road runs via Kamínia, near which were found the Tyrsenian inscriptions (see above), to the excavation site at Poliókhni, where Italian archaeologists found impressive remains of a settlement dating back in four phases to the 3rd and 4th millennia BC (town walls, houses and a town gate approached by a ramp). The

Poliókhni

gold jewellery found here is now in the National Archaeological Museum in Athens. It is worth driving down to the south of the peninsula to see the beautifully situated monastery of Áyios Sozon and the picturesque village of Skandali.

Kontopoúli

In the north-east of the island, at Kontopoúli, is the partly excavated site of ancient Hephaisteia (Ifestía), with a cemetery of the 8th–6th c. BC and a Hellenistic theatre.

Chloe

On the other side of the bay is the ancient port of Chloe (Khlói), where excavations by Italian archaeologists brought to light a sanctuary of the Cabiri (non-Hellenic divinities whose cult was centred on the island of Samothrace) that is earlier than the one on Samothrace. The visible remains include two cult buildings of the 6th and 5th–4th c. BC, and a Hellenistic sanctuary of a mystery cult (46 × 33 m (150 × 110 ft)) with 12 Doric columns.

Áyios Efstrátios

Áyios Efstrátios (Αγιος Ευστρατιος; area 43 sq. km (17 sq. mi.); alt. 0–303 m (0–994 ft)) is a rocky island of volcanic origin some 30 km (20 mi.) south of Lemnos, well suited for anyone who wants absolute seclusion. In ancient times, when it was known as Alonesos, the island protected the sea route between Athens and the islands of Lemnos and Imbros. The little town and port of Áyios Efstrátios lies in the largest bay on the west coast of the island; it was largely destroyed in an earthquake in 1968. Above the town are an old castle and windmills.

There are shipping connections with Chíos, Kavála, Lésbos, Lemnos, Pátmos, Rafína and Sámos.

Léros   L 6

Southern Sporades (Dodecanese)
Area: 53 sq. km (20 sq. mi.)
Altitude: 0–327 m (0–1073 ft)
Population: 8000
Chief place: Ayía Marína

Airport at Parthéni. Air connections with Athens. Principal port: Lakkí. Shipping connections with Pátmos–Piraeus, Kálymnos–Kos–Tílos–Sými–Rhodes, Lipsí–Pátmos–Agathonísi–Sámos, and with the Cyclades. Hydrofoils from Ayía Marína to Pátmos, Sámos, Kos and Rhodes. Bus services on the island, centred on Plátanos.

Léros (Λερος) has problems with its reputation, for it was for many years a leper colony, during the Second World War a German naval base, from 1947 a centre for the re-education of the children of communist partisans and from 1967 to 1974 a concentration camp for opponents of the Colonels' military regime (at Parthéni). Since 1957, moreover, there has been at Lakkí a notorious psychiatric institution, the largest mental hospital in Greece.

This hilly and fertile island, with an abundance of water, has a much indented coast. Its main sources of income apart from tourism are farming and fishing.

In antiquity Leros was dependent on Miletus in Asia Minor. In the 14th c. the Knights of St John established themselves on the island and held it against the Turks until 1523. Under the Turks it retained a considerable degree of autonomy. It was liberated in 1830, but under the London Protocol was assigned to Turkey. From 1923 to 1948 it was under Italian rule.

Arriving in the port of Ayía Marína on Léros

Sights

Excursion boats and hydrofoils put in at the historic port of Ayía Marína (Αγια Μαρινα) on the east coast of the island. Now merged with the port is the chief place on the island, Plátanos (pop. 2500), picturesquely situated on the ridge of hills between Álinda Bay to the north and Plátanos Bay to the south. In Plátanos Bay is the fishing port and yacht harbour of Pentéli. From Ayía Marína you can take either a driveable road or a narrow lane lined by shops up to Plátanos, over which looms a castle of the Knights of St John, built in the 14th c. on the site of the ancient acropolis. In an earlier castle lived St Christodulus (11th c.), who later founded the famous Monastery of St John on Pátmos. From the little village square a flight of 300 steps leads up to the castle.

Ayía Marína

The coast road runs round the wide bay, skirting a narrow sand and shingle beach fringed by tamarisks, to the loosely built-up resorts of Krithóni (where there is a British military cemetery of the Second World War) and Álinda (Αλινδα). Beyond this is the Bellini Tower (with two battlemented towers, one square and the other round), a folly built in 1925 by an inhabitant of Léros who had made his money in Egypt. It now houses a small folk and historical museum (open daily 10am–noon, 6–9pm).

Álinda

3 km (2 mi.) south of Plátanos an inlet cuts deep into the west coast. At its head is the ferry port of Lakkí (Λακκι; pop. 2500), with boulevards and fine buildings laid out on a regular plan by Italian town-planners at a time when Lakkí was important as an Italian naval base in the eastern Mediterranean. During the day the streets and squares are almost empty of life.

Lakkí

South-east of Lakkí, in an inlet of the same name, is the village of Xirókampos (Ξηροκαμπος), with a small beach of sand and shingle. From

Xirókampos

here there are boats to Myrtiés on Kálymnos. Above the village are the remains of ancient Palaiokástro, a stronghold of the 4th c. BC.

Gourna Bay

Gourna Bay, on the west coast, has two beautiful beaches but little in the way of tourist facilities. From here a causeway leads on to a photogenic little islet on which is a chapel dedicated to Ayía Isidóra. At Parthéni, to the north of the airport, are the scanty remains (signposted) of a temple of Artemis. To the east of Parthéni is Plefoudi Bay, with a shady beach of sand and shingle.

Farmakonísi

24 km (15 mi.) north-east of Léros and only 12 km (7½ mi.) south-west of the Turkish cape of Tekagaç Burun (near Didyma) is Farmakonísi (Φαρμακονησι), an almost uninhabited islet (area 4 sq. km (1½ sq. mi.)) of gentle, partly grass-covered hills. Here, in 77 BC, Caesar was captured by pirates and released only on payment of a ransom. There are remains of Roman villas and the ancient harbour, now partly under the sea.

Lésbos   K/L 4/5

Islands of the northern and eastern Aegean
Area: 1630 sq. km (629 sq. mi.)
Altitude: 0–967 m (0–3173 ft)
Population: 100,000
Chief town: Mytilíni

Airport 8 km (5 mi.) south-east of Mytilíni (no airport bus). Air connections with Athens, Salonica, Lemnos, Chíos. Shipping connections with Chíos and Piraeus, Lemnos–Kavála/Salonica, Rafína, Vólos, Pátmos, Sámos, Sýros. Ferry to Ayvalœk (Turkey), near Bergama (Pergamon). Bus services on island, centred on Mytilíni (where it may sometimes be necessary to change buses).

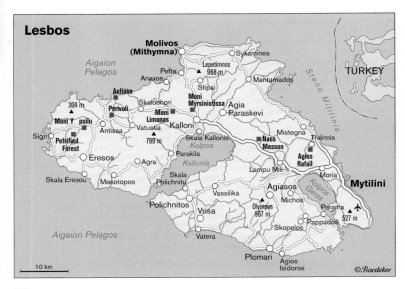

Lésbos (Λεσβος), the third largest of the Greek islands (after Crete and Euboea), lies at the mouth of a large inlet on the coast of Asia Minor, north-west of Izmir; its north coast only 10 km (6 mi.) from the mainland, its east coast only 15 km (9 mi.). An island of great scenic beauty, Lésbos – usually called Mytilíni by Greeks – is also one of the most fertile areas in Greece. It is broken up by the gulfs of Kallóní and Iéra that cut deep inland on its south-west and south-east sides. The east and west sides of the island are very different: the hilly eastern half, with Mount Lepetymnos (968 m (3176 ft)) in the north and Mount Ólympos (967 m (3173 ft)) in the south, is partly forest-covered, while the western half is bare and, round Eresós, desertic. The island's main source of income is the olive oil for which it is famed, produced by an estimated 13 million olive trees. Lésbos is Greece's second largest producer of olive oil (after Crete). It is also noted for its ouzo distilleries.

Tourism on any scale came to Lésbos only in the 1990s, and is concentrated in Mólyvos and Pétra, pretty little places in good walking country. The best beaches, however, are in the south of the island, at Plomári, Áyios Isídoros and Vaterá. There are also beautiful beaches at Skála Eresoú in the west and at Skála Kallóní.

History At Thermí, 12 km (7½ mi.) north of Mytilíni, excavation has brought to light a pre-Greek settlement established about 2700 BC. Around 1000 BC Aeolian Greeks from Thessaly arrived on the island and founded the cities of Mytilene and Methymna, ruled by aristocratic families who were constantly at odds with one another. About 600 BC the tyrant (sole ruler) Pittacus put an end to these quarrels, retired voluntarily after 10 years and thereafter was accounted one of the Seven Sages. From 546 to 479 BC Lesbos was under Persian rule, and after its liberation became a member of the Attic maritime league. Throughout this period, however, and in Hellenistic and Roman times, it was able, like Chios, to maintain its independence.

Ancient Lésbos was a highly productive intellectual and cultural centre. It was the home of the poet Terpander (7th c. BC), who was credited with the invention of the seven-stringed lyre; and around 600 BC the singer Arion was born in Methymna, the poet Alcaeus was born in Mytilene and Sappho, the greatest Greek poetess, was born in Eresos (see Famous People). Aristotle taught in the school of philosophy in Mytilene, and his pupil Theophrastus (322–287 BC), a native of Lesbos, became head of Aristotle's Lykeion (Lyceum) in Athens. Also perhaps a native of Lesbos was Longus, author of the pastoral novel "Daphnis and Chloe", which is set on the island.

Nothing is known of Longus's life, but stylistic considerations suggest that he wrote in the 2nd c. AD. The novel has a clear and simple plot. Daphnis and Chloe are found by shepherds somewhere between Mytilene and Molyvos and brought up by them; they gradually fall in love and marry, and then find their parents. The best of the old Greek novels to survive, "Daphnis and Chloe" still appeals to readers with its charming descriptions of nature and graceful style, and it had considerable influence on the pastoral poetry of the baroque period.

In 1355 a Genoese nobleman named Francesco Gattelusi married Maria Palaeologina, a daughter of the Byzantine Emperor, who received Lésbos as her dowry. Thereafter the Gattelusi family ruled the island as a Byzantine fief until 1462, when Lésbos was captured by the Turks. During the period of Turkish rule, which lasted until 1913, many of the inhabitants moved to the mainland, particularly to the nearby town of Kydonia (now Ayvalœk in Turkey). After the catastrophe of 1922–3 their descendants returned to the island, the economy of which was badly hit by the loss of its Anatolian hinterland.

Island of Poets

He was the greatest singer and musician of all time. With his enchanting singing and cithara playing he moved even wild beasts, plants and stones. He could touch even Hades with his music, but the underworld would still not yield up his beloved Eurydice. In Thrace, where wild women tore him limb from limb, Orpheus himself could not escape his fate. Then the Muses gathered up his scattered limbs and gave them burial. "But his head and his lyre were taken up by the swelling flood of Hebrus and carried downstream. From the strings of the lyre there came sweet sounds of mourning, and the banks of the river gently responded with a melancholy echo. Then the river carried the head and the lyre down to the sea, which bore them to the shores of Lésbos, where the pious inhabitants gathered them in. They buried the head and hung the lyre in a temple. And that is why that island has produced such superb poets and singers (from Gustav Schwab's "Tales of Classical Antiquity").

Orpheus's head was washed ashore at ancient Antissa, on the north coast of Lésbos. And from Antissa came the first considerable figure in the history of music of whom we have any firm knowledge – Terpander, a poet and musician of the 7th century BC who won a prize for music at the 26th Olympiad at Sparta in 675 BC. He ranks as the leading representative of the oldest school of singing to the accompaniment of a cithara, and is believed to have originated the canonical form of composition for the cithara. He is also credited with the invention of the seven-stringed lyre.

Nothing has survived of the works of the poet and singer Arion, who was born in Methymna on Lésbos about 600 BC. According to Herodotus, our chief source on Arion's life and personality, he went to Corinth in the reign of the tyrant Periander (625–585 BC) and performed the first ever dithyramb (choral song in honour of Dionysus), establishing it as a literary art form. According to legend Arion, returning from a trip to Italy, was compelled by the crew of the ship in which he was sailing to jump into the sea, but was granted his one last wish, to sing and play on the lyre. After singing and playing with his usual skill he jumped overboard, whereupon a dolphin, enchanted by the music, rescued him and carried him safely on its back and put him ashore at Cape Tainaron in the Peloponnese. The grateful Arion then set up a votive monument on the cape in the form of a man on a dolphin's back – which Herodotus had seen.

"Eros has shaken my senses, as the wind surging down from the mountains shakes the oaks." In Strabo's eyes Sappho (c. 600 BC) was the greatest poetess of all time, "a thing of wonder"; and an epigram attributed to Plato ranks her as the tenth Muse. The first known female poet in the literature of the world came from a noble family of Mytilene. During a period of political disturbances between 604 and 590 she fled to Sicily, but later returned to Mytilene, where she gathered round her a circle of young girls, whom she instructed until they married in the ways of aristocratic life and in music, poetry and dancing. There has been much learned speculation on the nature of this circle, which was devoted to the cult of Aphrodite as well as to poetry and education; for Sappho, as her expressive songs show, had close passionate relationships with her pupils. The idea of "Lesbian

A statue of Sappho on Lésbos

nine books, but of all she wrote – apart from her poem to Aphrodite – there survive only fragments on papyrus. In 1038 the Roman Church burned all her works along with other "pagan writings".

Sappho had an enduring influence on Greek literature. The Attic comedy featured her as a comic figure, mocking in coarse language relationships between women in the manner of Sappho. There also grew up the legend of her unrequited love for the handsome youth Phaon, which led her to throw herself into the sea from the Leucadian Rock. In many of his odes Horace used the "sapphic metre" which spread from Greece to the literature of the west; and Sappho's influences extended to the minnesingers of the Middle Ages and to the poetry of modern times.

Alcaeus (c. 600 BC), a contemporary of Sappho's, also came from Mytilene and from a noble family. All that is known of his life is that he fought for the rights of the nobility against rule by tyrants, for which he was several times exiled, and that he loved carousing with his friends. The works of Alcaeus, Lésbos's greatest poet after Sappho, fall into three groups: political polemics (including songs mocking the "fat-bellied" Pittacus, tyrant of Lésbos), drinking songs ("Drink with me, Melanippus; drink yourself drunk"), hymns to the gods and mythological tales. His poems, like Sappho's, were collected by the Alexandrines and published in at least ten books, but only fragments have survived. Alcaeus used a variety of metres, particularly favouring the "alcaic verse" named after him, consisting of two lines of eleven syllables, one of nine syllables and one of ten. This form was introduced into Roman poetry by Horace.

love" was already current in antiquity – though there is no evidence to show whether Sappho's affection for her girls found expression in physical homosexual relations.

Love and personal feelings, particularly in her relationships with her companions, music and dancing, flowers and jewellery, are the main themes of Sappho's poems, which, in a language reminiscent of folk songs, express all the nuances of human sensibility – happiness, longing and the anguish of love. Sappho sees Eros as "bitter-sweet", a condition from which there is no escape. She also wrote marriage songs for her pupils when they left her, following the traditional themes of folk poetry. Her poems are written in the Aeolian dialect of Greek, with borrowings from the language of the epics, and in a variety of metres. Her works were published by Alexandrine scholars in

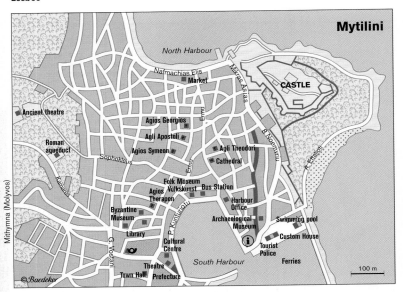

North Harbour

Naïmachias Elis
Market

CASTLE

Ancient theatre

Agios Georgios

Roman
aqueduct

Agli Apostoli

Agios Symeon

Agli Theodori

Sophokleus

Cathedral

Folk Museum
Volkskunst

Bus Station

Agios
Therapon

Harbour
Office

Byzantine
Museum

Archaeological
Museum

Swimming pool

Library

Custom House

Cultural
Centre

South Harbour

Tourist
Police

Theatre

Ferries

Town Hall
Prefecture

©Baedeker

100 m

Mithymna (Molyvos)

Míkras Asías

Ermú

B. Noemvríu

A. Eftaliú

Ermú

Kamaúa

P. Kuntúriu

G. Vóstani

Mytilini

Mytilíni

The island's chief town, Mytilíni (Μυτιλήνη), lies in a bay on the east
coast, on the site of ancient Mytilene. More than a third of the island's
inhabitants (30,000) live in the town, the largest in the eastern Aegean.
The town has – and has always had – two harbours. The north harbour,
in ancient times the more important of the two, is now used only by fishing boats, while the larger south harbour can take large modern ferries.
The busy life of the town is centred round the south harbour, along which
runs the seafront promenade, Odós Koundouriotou, also known as the
Prokymala. The houses are mostly low, and some of them are fronted by
colonnades. Above them rises the church of Áyios Therápon (1883), the
largest on the island, in a style that shows western influence.

Odós Ermoú

The present south harbour and the ancient harbour to the north were
once linked by a canal, on the line of the town's main street, Odós
Ermoú, which has something of an Oriental atmosphere. In a quiet side
street off Odós Ermoú is the 17th c. church of Áyios Athanásios, with an
elaborately carved iconostasis and the bishop's throne. Further up Odós
Ermoú to the north the houses are increasingly dilapidated. This was formerly the Turkish quarter.

Gattelusi castle

To the east of Odós Ermoú is the hill crowned by the massive Gattelusi
Castle (open Tue.–Sun. 8.30am–3pm; various events held here in
summer). The castle, originally built in the time of the Emperor Justinian
(6th c.), was enlarged by the island's Genoese ruler Francesco I
Gattelusi, who ruled from 1355 to 1385, and later by the Turks. A road
runs up to the castle through a pinewood, a popular picnicking spot.
Many remains of ancient masonry show that the extensive castle ward
occupies the site of the ancient acropolis. The Aeolian pottery found
here suggests that there was a sanctuary of Demeter here, dating from

the 7th/6th c. BC. Relics of the Turkish period are a number of mosques and a Koranic school. Over a side gate in the north-west wall are coupled the arms of Francesco I Gattelusi and his Byzantine princess, a horseshoe and a two-headed eagle, with an inscription of 1377. From the north end of the castle there is a fine view of the ancient north harbour and the remains of its breakwater.

To the south-west, above the north harbour, is the ancient theatre (3rd c. BC), which could seat 15,000 spectators. It gave Pompey a model for the first stone theatre in Rome. Although only the orchestra survives, it is worth visiting the site for the sake of the view of the castle, and beyond this the Turkish coast.

Ancient theatre

The old **Archaeological Museum** (open Tue.–Sun. 8.30am–3pm), housed in a neoclassical villa just off the east quay, contains, among other things, a number of capitals of the rare Aeolian type and mosaics of the 3rd/4th c. AD from the Villa of Menander, which was found 500 m east of the ancient theatre. To provide more room for the town's extensive archaeological material the **New Museum** was built on the castle hill (Odós 8 Noemvriou). Beyond the domed cruciform church of Áyios Therápon (1860), the island's largest church, is the **Byzantine Museum** (open Mon.–Sat. 9am–3pm), with an interesting collection of icons. The oldest icon, a figure of St George, dates from the 13th c. On the harbour, beside the monument to Sappho, is the **Folk Museum**, housed in the former harbourmaster's office.

Museums

Mytilíni has a number of handsome old mansions such as the Lesviako Spiti beside the Mitrópolis (open to the public), and neoclassical buildings like the Prefecture and the Lawcourts. To the south, at the foot of the castle hill, are a monument commemorating those who died during the war of liberation (1821–3) and a bathing pool run by the Greek National Tourist Office (EOT; admission charge).

Other sights

Surroundings

5 km (3 mi.) south of Mytilíni is the select suburb of Variá (Βαρεια), with trim old villas and two interesting museums. One of these is devoted to the work of the naïve painter Theofilos, a native of Lésbos. It was established in 1964 by Stratis Eleftheriadis (1897–1983), who was born in Mytilíni and worked in Paris as a publicist, publisher and promoter of art. He also established in 1979 the neighbouring Teriade Museum, with works by modern artists such as Marc Chagall, Fernand Léger and Pablo Picasso. Both museums are open Tue.–Sun. 9am–1pm, 5–8pm.

Variá

From Mytilíni a road runs north along the north-east coast, coming in 4 km (2½ mi.) to a road that goes off to Moriá (Μορια), a handsome and prosperous village with a number of oil-mills. Notable features of the post-Byzantine church of Áyios Vasilios are the carved iconostasis and the bishop's throne.

Moriá

600 m west of Moriá are the imposing remains of a 27 m (90 ft) high Roman aqueduct of the 3rd c. AD, part of a system bringing water to the island's capital.

The terminus of the municipal buses from Mytilíni is the bathing resort of Thermí (Θερμη), a few kilometres north of the town. It has three small beaches and radioactive hot springs. In Pyryi Thermís are a number of partly ruined tower houses of the 16th–19th c., built to provide protection from pirate raids. The village church of the Panayía Troulotis (c. 1100) is one of the few Byzantine churches on Lésbos. Nearby is the site of a prehistoric settlement of about 2700 BC; most of the material recovered from the site can be seen in the Archaeological Museum in Mytilíni.

Thermí

Roman aqueduct near Moriá (p. 223), framed in lush vegetation

3 km (2 mi.) south-west of Thermí is the convent of Áyios Rafaíl, founded in 1963, an important pilgrimage centre. The church has Byzantine-style frescos.

North-eastern Lésbos

Mantamádos

The coast north of Thermí attracts few foreign holidaymakers. One place of interest, however, is the hill village of Mantamádos (Μανταμαδος), with its old stone houses, cheese factories and potters' workshops (open to visitors). 1 km (¾ mi.) north is the church of the Taxiarchs (Archangels), with a wonder-working icon of the Archangel Michael (pilgrimage on November 8th). The icon is said to have been made about 1850 from clay and the blood of monks killed by pirates.

Sykaminéa

Sykaminéa (Συκαμινεα), a hill village of steep lanes and old stone houses, was the birthplace of the contemporary writer Stratis Myrivilis. In his novel "The Virgin with the Fish's Body" the chapel of the Panayía Gorgona (the "Holy Mermaid"), in the fishing village of Skála Sykamineas, 3 km (2 mi.) away, plays a central part. There are several small shingle beaches round the village. A path runs along the coast to Eftalou (thermal springs) and Mólyvos.

★Mólyvos

The tourist centre of the island is Mólyvos (officially Míthymna, the ancient Methymna; pop. 1500), on the north coast, which was equipped with a tourist infrastructure as early as the 1960s. This historic and very picturesque little port (now protected as a national monument) climbs up the slopes of a hill to the massive Gattelusi castle (1373), from which there are fantastic views of the red-tiled roofs and stone houses of the town. The houses facing the sea originally formed a defensive wall. The attraction of Mólyvos lies mainly in its romantic townscape, but there are also an interesting archaeological collection in the neoclassical Town Hall (with historical photographs of the town) and a picture gallery that puts on exhibitions of works by Greek artists.

Of the shingle beaches (mostly small) in the area the best is the long beach of Efalou, 4 km (2½ mi.) east of Mólyvos. At Palaía Míthymna, which also lies east of the town, there was a settlement in the 3rd millennium BC.

The neighbouring village of Pétra (Πετρα; pop. 900), 7 km (4½ mi.) south, which has a small harbour, was discovered by independent travellers only some 15 years ago. It owed its popularity to the cooperative formed by local women, which made headlines with its scheme for letting rooms in private houses. In the centre of the village, on a 27 m (90 ft) high crag (114 steps), is the church of the Panayía Glykofílousa (the "sweetly kissing" Mother of God), built in 1747, which has a fine iconostasis of carved wood. At the foot of the crag is the 15th c. church of Áyios Nikólaos, with beautiful frescos. The Arkhontiko Vareltzidena, a 17th c. mansion with magnificent ceiling paintings, is the finest example of the Macedonian-style houses, with projecting upper floors, which are, surprisingly, to be found on Lésbos.

Pétra

15 km (9 mi.) south of Pétra is the little country town of Kallóní (Καλλονη; pop. 1600), lying 4 km (2½ mi.) north of the Gulf of Kallóní. It has no features of tourist interest, but it is situated at the most important road intersection on the island and is a shopping centre for the surrounding villages.

Kallóní

To the north-west are the convent of the Panayía Myrsiniótissa (1487), with a beautiful inner courtyard, and the monastery of Áyios Ignátios Limónos (1523), dedicated to the Archangel Michael, the largest and

**★Áyios Ignátios
Limónos**

The little port of Mólyvos is the most popular holiday resort on Lésbos

most important monastery on the island. During the Turkish period the monastery ran a clandestine Greek school and thus helped to preserve Greek culture. The monks are still active in education and social work. The principal church of the extensive complex (open to men only: women are confined to the outer monastic buildings) has a richly carved iconostasis and its walls are completely covered with frescos. Housed in new buildings are a library, with ancient and precious books, and a museum displaying icons, liturgical utensils and folk arts and crafts.

Petrified tree, Sígri

Skála Kallonís

Round the little fishing harbour of Skála Kallonís (Σκαλα Καλλονης), 3 km (2 mi.) from Kallóni, are good, gently sloping beaches with hotels and restaurants. A road runs 10 km (6 mi.) east, passing salt pans, to the remains of an Ionic temple of Aphrodite (4th/3rd c. BC) at Mesi. Here too, in an area of wasteland, are the ruins of an Early Christian church.

Western Lésbos

Ántissa

From Kallóni a winding road runs west into an increasingly barren volcanic landscape. After passing through Filia and Skalokhóri it comes to the hill village of Vatoúsa, which has preserved its original character. 5 km (3 mi.) beyond this, on the right, is the abandoned convent of Perivóli, with 17th c. frescos. A path runs down the valley of the river Voulgari (which in summer is almost completely dry) to the scanty remains of ancient Antissa (Αντισσα), and there is also a road, asphalted for part of the way, to the excavation site on the coast (8 km (5 mi.)). The acropolis was originally surrounded by a double circuit of walls.

The present village of Ántissa has an attractive square, with tavernas and cafés shaded by plane trees.

Ypsiloú

Further west, on a steep crag on the road to Sígri, is the monastery of Ypsiloú, founded in the 19th c. It has a museum containing 12th c. manuscripts and Patriarchal vestments. From the monastery there are magnificent views.

Sígri

The remote fishing village and holiday resort of Sígri (Σιγρι; pop. 550), on the west coast, has beautiful beaches and a Genoese and Turkish fort protecting the harbour. The rugged and inhospitable country between Sígri, Ántissa and Eresós is famed for its petrified forest of tree trunks, fossilised after being buried in volcanic ash. The trees are estimated to be between 1 and 10 million years old. Much of the island was once covered by these mammoth trees – sequoias, such as can still be seen in California. Some of the trunks, up to 11.5 m (38 ft) in height and 1.15 m (45 in.) in diameter, are still standing; others lie on the ground. The road to the petrified forest, signposted "Apolithomeno Dasos", goes off 5 km (3 mi.) west of Ypsiloú monastery.

12 km (7½ mi.) south of Ántissa is the village of Eresós (Ερεσος; pop. 1600), and on the coast, in a fertile plain, is the little bathing resort of Skála Eresoú (Σκαλα Ερεσου). Here, on a hill, is the site of ancient Eresos, birthplace of Sappho and Theophrastus. Near the beautiful long sandy beach, immediately beyond the new church of Áyios Andréas, are the ruins of an Early Christian basilica of the 5th c. AD. Beside it is a small museum containing local finds, including coins bearing the head of Sappho.

Eresós

Southern Lésbos

The wooded southern part of the island, between the Gulfs of Iéra and Kallóní, is of great scenic beauty. The chief places in this area are Ayiásos (Αγιασος; pop. 3500), a large hill village with almost the air of a town situated on the northern slopes of Mount Ólympos, and the friendly little coastal town of Plomári. In the centre of Ayiásos is the most important pilgrimage centre on Lésbos, the church of the Dormition of the Mother of God, built in 1170 and rebuilt in 1816. Its icon of the Mother of God, the only one in Greece believed to have been painted by Luke the Evangelist himself, draws thousands of pilgrims on the feast of the Dormition (August 15th). The church museum displays icons – including one painted on a fish's head – liturgical utensils and a collection of folk art. The traditional crafts of pottery and woodcarving and the old folk music are still very much alive in Ayiásos.

Ayiásos

The ascent of Mount Ólympos from Ayiásos is a rewarding climb (5 hours there and back; waymarking in red and blue). The route runs up through shady forests of sweet chestnut and beech to the summit (968 m (3176 ft)), from which there are superb views.

Ólympos

The road runs west, passing the Tsingou springs (mineral water bottling plant), to Polikhnítos (Πολιχνιτος; pop. 3000), which has one of the hottest thermal springs in Europe (91°C (196°F)). The largest spa establishment on the island is now being built with the help of EU funding. 4 km (2½ mi.) north is the harbour of Skála Polikhnítou, with salt pans where large numbers of birds (including occasionally flamingos) can be seen.

Polikhnítos

5 km (3 mi.) south of Polikhnítos is the village of Vrísa (Βρισα), with the church of the Zoodókhos Piyí (Life-Giving Fountain) of 1803, which has a fine iconostasis of carved wood. Beyond this is Vaterá (Βατερα), with the finest beach on the island (sand and shingle, almost 10 km (6 mi.) long). In recent years numerous hotels, pensions and tavernas have sprung up here, mostly patronised by Greek families. On Cape Fokás, to the west of the beach, are the remains of a Doric temple of Dionysus of the 1st c. BC.

★★Vaterá

From Mytilíni a road runs along the Gulf of Iéra to Plomári on the south coast. After passing Káto Tritos, with a Byzantine church dedicated to the Taxiarchs (Archangels), and Mesagros, with the ruins of a mosque, it comes to the little holiday resort of Áyios Isídoros (Αγιος Ισιδωρος), which has almost merged with Plomári, 3 km (2 mi.) west. Both little towns are particularly favoured by Scandinavian visitors.

Áyios Isídoros

Finally the road comes to the busy little town of Plomári (Πλωμαρι; pop. 4000), which has contrived to retain much of its original character. It is famed for its ouzo distilleries. The Barbayiannis distillery (established 1860), on the east side of the town, can be visited. The tile-roofed houses of the town, which was founded in 1845, climb up a narrow valley on an outlier of Mount Ólympos. An old soap factory has been converted into a cultural centre, with displays illustrating local history and the process of soap manufacture.

Plomári

The sleepy little town of Lipsí is a popular holiday place for families

Lipsí L 6

Southern Sporades
Area: 18 sq. km (7 sq. mi.)
Altitude: 0–275 m (0–900 ft)
Population: 600
Chief place: Lipsí

Shipping connections with Piraeus, Agathonísi, Kálymnos, Kos, Léros, Nísyros, Pátmos, Rhodes, Sámos, Sýými and Tílos. To get about the island, which is only 8 km (5 mi.) long, you must either go on foot or hire a vehicle or taxi.

Lipsí (Λειψοι), 12 km (7½ mi.) east of Pátmos, has no features of particular interest apart from the pretty little port of the same name on the south coast. Walking on its low hills is not strenuous, and the remotest bay on the island is no more than an hour walk from Lipsí town. Lipsí is an island for individual travellers looking for a quiet holiday well away from hordes of tourists.

Lipsí was a Greek naval base during the war of liberation from the Turks. The few inhabitants live by farming and fishing, and nowadays by looking after the small numbers of visitors. The island produces good cheese and a strong "black" wine.

Lipsí town

Lipsí town, which has a rather Cycladic air, has two pretty little squares and a local museum (archaeology and folk traditions). The island's best beach is at Platýs Yialós (45 min. walk north-west of Lipsí town), which is sandy and gently sloping. There are other beaches nearer the town.

★Melos | 7

Island group: Cyclades
Area: 151 sq. km (58 sq. mi.)
Altitude: 0–751 m (0–2464 ft)
Population: 4500
Chief place: Mílos (Pláka)

Airport 6 km (4 mi.) south-east of Mílos. Air connections with Athens.
Port: Adámas. Shipping connections with Piraeus, other islands in the
Cyclades and Dodecanese and Crete. Boats from Apollónia to Kímolos
and the Glaronísia. Bus services on the island.

The island of Melos or Mílos (Μῆλος; from the Greek word for "apple"),
in Italian Milo, is the most westerly of the larger Cyclades and the original home of the world-famed Venus de Milo, now in the Louvre in Paris.
It owes its varied and very striking topography and the pattern of its
economy to its origin as the caldera of a volcano of the Pliocene era – an
origin to which its sulphurous thermal springs still bear witness. It has
one of the best harbours in the Mediterranean, formed when the sea
broke into the crater through a gap on its north-west side. The north-
eastern half of the island is flatter and more fertile than the hilly south-
west, which rises to 751 m (2464 ft) in Mount Profítis Ilías. The island's
main economic resources are its rich deposits of minerals, including per-
lite, bentonite, kaolin and barytes. The tourist trade now also makes a
contribution to the economy.

History The island was already populated in the 3rd millennium BC
(Fylakopí), when the inhabitants made implements and weapons from
the local deposits of obsidian and exported them all over the Aegean
and as far afield as Asia Minor and Egypt. About 1200 BC Dorian incomers settled on the island and founded the city of Melos, defended by
walls and towers, on a hill on the north side of Mílos Bay, on the site of
the present-day Kástro, with its harbour at what is now the hamlet of
Klíma. They prospered through the export of sulphur, pumice, clay and
alum, as well as oil, wine and honey. Melos reached the peak of its prosperity and artistic achievement in Roman times, as is evidenced by the
Venus de Milo (2nd c. BC). From 1204 Melos belonged to the Venetian

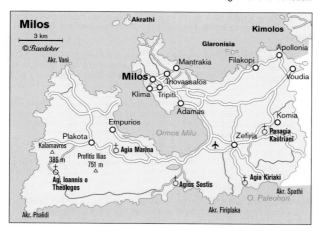

duchy of Náxos; in 1566 it fell to the Turks; and in 1832 it became part of the newly established kingdom of Greece.

Sights

Adámas

The little port of Adámas (Αδαμας; pop. 900), on the north side of the great gulf that was the caldera of the volcano, is the island's tourist centre, where the ferries put in, with numerous hotels, restaurants and travel agencies. The life of the place centres on the harbour with its many tavernas rather than on the village that climbs up a low hill inland. On the highest point in the village is the church, dedicated to the Dormition of the Mother of God and to Áyios Kharalambos, which has fine icons. The forecourt of the church has a beautiful pebble mosaic depicting an eagle flying towards the east. The church of the Ayía Triáda (13th c.; remodelled in 17th c.) also has a fine pebble mosaic depicting allegorical figures by the local artist Iagos Kavroudakis (1937).

★Mílos

7 km (4½ mi.) north-west is the chief place on the island, Mílos (Pláka), a little town of whitewashed houses with a population of 900. The principal church (19th c.), dedicated to the Panayía Korfiátissa, has a gilded iconostasis, Creto-Byzantine paintings and a stone-cut epitaph from Smyrna (c. 1600). There are also a small folk museum and an archaeological museum (open Tue.–Sun. 8.30am–3pm), with obsidian implements, Cycladic idols and a copy of the Venus de Milo.

At a height of 280 m (920 ft) above sea level are the scanty remains of the Venetian Kástro (13th c.). On the way up is the church of the Panayía Thalassitra, and on the summit of the hill is the chapel of the Mésa Panayía, with an icon of the Mother of God.

1 km (¾ mi.) below Mílos, at Tripití (signposted), is a complex of 3rd c. **catacombs** – a feature unique in Greece – with some 2000 burial recesses. In the centre of the principal chamber is the tomb of a saint.

Near the catacombs are the remains of ancient Mílos, a Dorian city of the 1st millennium BC. A sign points to the spot (to the left) where the Venus de Milo was found. There are some remains of the town walls and of a tower, and a short distance away, in a beautiful situation above the gulf, are some rows of the marble seating of the Roman theatre, which was built into the hillside.

From here a path runs down to the shore and the holiday village of Klíma with its two-storey houses, the lower floor serving as a boat-house.

Fylakopí

To the east of Tripití is the ancient settlement of Fylakopí (Φυλακοπη), on top of the cliffs fringing the north coast. Excavations here brought to light various occupation levels of the 3rd and 2nd millennia BC and Mycenaean walls of around 1500 BC.

Apollónia

2 km (1¼ mi.) north-east is the charming little port of Apollónia (Pollónia, Απολλωνια), with a tree-fringed sandy beach. From here there are boat trips to Kímolos and the little "Seagull Islands" (Glaronísia), four bizarrely shaped basalt islets, with the Sykía caves.

Palaiópolis

6 km (4 mi.) south-east of Adámas is Zefýria, with the ruins of the island's former capital, Palaiópolis, founded in the 8th c. AD and abandoned in 1793. A templon and icons from the old Mitrópolis church are now in the church of the Dormition in Adámas.

Beaches 4 km (2½ mi.) further south-east is the beautiful beach in Palaiokhori Bay, with warm sulphur springs (taverna, rooms for visitors). There are also good beaches round Mikos Bay and around the middle of

Beauty in Marble

Yeóryios Kentrotás gazed in amazement at the shimmering white marble body he had come upon on April 8th 1820 while ploughing his stony field below the village of Tripití on the island of Melos. Carefully removing the earth, he brought to light the broken halves of a marble figure, its arms broken off and its left hand holding an apple. It was an over-life-size statue of the goddess of beauty, known to the Greeks as Aphrodite and to the Romans as Venus. Yeóryios naturally told people about his find, and his story aroused the interest of the French forces who were then on the island. Cadet Olivier Voutier, a young officer with an interest in archaeology, drew a sketch of the figure, and his superior officer, Dumont d'Urville, informed the French consul on the island, who reported the spectacular find to his ambassador in Constantinople, the Marquis de Rivière, who decided that the marble Venus must be acquired for France. Agreement was reached with Yeóryios Kentrotás without much difficulty; but when a French embassy official, the Comte de Marcellus, arrived on Melos on May 23rd 1820 to collect the figure he was taken aback to find that in the meantime the Turkish rulers of the island had made a better offer and were in process of loading the statue on to a vessel as a present to a prince in Constantinople. Marcellus at once intervened, insisting on his rights under the agreement with Yeóryios Kentrotás, and finally secured the statue at the higher figure offered by the Turks. It was now without its arms, which had been lost in the course of the dispute and have never been found. The French ambassador decided to present the statue to King Louis XVIII, and the Venus de Milo arrived in Paris in February 1821 to find her final home in the Louvre. With her slender figure, long legs concealed by her garment, naked upper body with full breasts, narrow shoulders and graceful head with parted hair, the Venus de Milo incarnates the ideal beauty of late Hellenistic times, which also appealed to the Romans – for when this 2 m high statue of Parian marble was created around 120 BC the Greek world had long been under Roman rule. From the second half of the 4th century BC the severity of form, unity and delicate lines of classical Greek sculpture, with its balanced positioning of the limbs, increasingly gave place to a spiral turning of the body in which the line of the arms and shoulders contrasted with that of the hips and legs, giving the figure more emotional force. Ancient sculpture was also painted in colour in order to emphasise the human features and increase the impression of life. The Venus de Milo was not carved from a single block of marble, both arms and the left foot being carved separately and added to the figure. There is uncertainty about the position of the arms, but the left arm was probably raised and the right arm held diagonally against the middle of the body. Since the back of the figure is not completely finished, it was probably intended to stand in a niche. The statue now stands by itself in the Louvre, surrounded every day by thousands of visitors paying homage to the goddess of eternal beauty.

the south coast. There is an attractive boat trip to the Kléftiko cliffs at the south-western tip of the island.

Mýkonos   K 6

Island group: Cyclades
Area: 85 sq. km (33 sq. mi.)
Altitude: 0–372 m (0–1221 ft)
Population: 6000
Chief place: Mýkonos town (Khóra)

Airport 3 km (2 mi.) east of Mýkonos town (airport bus). Air connections with Athens, Salonica, Rhodes, Crete (Iráklion) and Santoríni. Charter flights. Shipping connections with Piraeus, Salonica, Rafína, Sámos, Khalkís, Crete, other islands in the Cyclades and Delos. Bus services on the island.

For prospective visitors to Mýkonos (Μυκονος), which lies between the Cycladic islands of Tínos, Páros and Náxos, there are no half-measures: either you want a fun holiday on the beach and in the disco, or you avoid the island altogether. With around 700,000 visitor-nights a year, it is the most-visited island in the Aegean and the most expensive holiday place in Greece. Between June and September you cannot get a room on Mýkonos unless you have booked in advance.
    Apart from its beautiful beaches this bare and infertile rocky island, the last in the chain of islands that also includes Euboea, Ándros and Tínos, has little to offer visitors in the way of scenic beauty. Its most attractive feature is its traditional architecture – whitewashed houses of undressed stone, with windows painted blue or a rusty red.

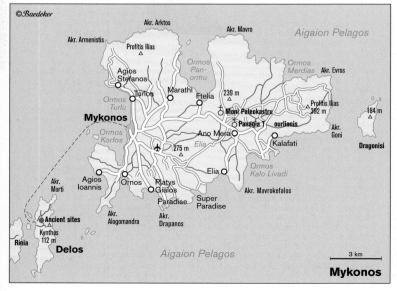

This prototypical Cycladic island has few sights of historical or artistic interest, but it is the usual starting-point for a trip to the neighbouring island of Delos (see entry) with its important archaeological sites.

Information At the landing-stage used by the boats to Delos are offices for booking hotels and rooms in private houses, information about camping facilities and the tourist police. There is no branch of EOT, the Greek National Tourist Organisation.

Beaches The coast of the island is much indented, with numerous bays and inlets, large and small. The beaches nearest to Mýkonos town are Megáli Ámmos (1 km (¾ mi.) south) and Toúrlos (2 km (¾ mi.) north). Further north is the 200 m (660 ft) long sandy beach of Áyios Stéfanos. To the south of Megáli Ámmos is Ornós, and to the west of this Áyios Ioánnis.

On the south coast there are many sheltered sandy beaches. At the west end is Platy's Yialós, a gently sloping beach with excellent facilities (bus services from Mýkonos town). From here the Paranga, Paradise and Eliá beaches can be reached either on foot or by caique (the traditional local fishing boat); Eliá beach also by bus. There is also the 200 m (660 ft) long Super Paradise beach in a deeply indented inlet. All these beaches are well equipped and very busy. Kaló Livádi beach on the south-east coast are quieter.

History There are many legends associated with Mýkonos. It was said to be the rock with which Poseidon slew the giants; and there was also a legend that Heracles had scattered the bodies of the defeated giants over the island. Its name was believed to be derived from Myconus, son of the demigod Anius and grandson of Zeus.

The arid and infertile island was of little importance in antiquity. From 1207 to 1537 it was held by Venice, but was then taken by the pirate and Ottoman admiral Khaireddin Barbarossa. Under Turkish rule it contrived to maintain a considerable degree of autonomy. From 1821 it played a part in the war of liberation, with ships financed by Mantó Mavroyénous, a native of Mýkonos.

Sights

The chief place on the island, Mýkonos (Khóra; pop. 4500), is a charming little town of whitewashed cube-shaped houses, with numerous churches and several windmills, extending round a bay on the west coast. The throngs of people who crowd its maze of winding streets can be most easily avoided in the morning and at siesta time. In the evening the Khóra, wholly devoted to catering for tourists with its innumerable shops, cafés and tavernas, is at its liveliest. The best viewpoints in the town are the Boni windmill, from which the island's magnificent sunsets can be observed, and the crag above the Archaeological Museum.

★★Mýkonos town

The Venetian castle stood on the peninsula to the south of the harbour on the site of the Kástro, the oldest part of the town. Its principal sight is the church of the Panayía Paraportianí ("at the gate"), a name that refers to its situation between the sea and a gate of the former castle. It is a complex of four churches built between 1500 and the 17th c. The play of light and shade on the various planes of the whitewashed walls make it one of the most attractive sights in the town and a popular subject for photographers.

★Kástro

Immediately south of the church is the Alefkándra quarter, known as Little Venice, with its picturesque houses facing out to sea. The houses were built from the mid-18th c. onwards by merchants and sea captains

★Alefkándra

on the rocky shore, with access directly from the sea. The sea-captains, who were probably involved in piracy, could thus readily land and stow away their booty. In Alefkándra are the Orthodox cathedral of the Theotókos Pigadiótissa and a Catholic church with the arms of the Venetian Ghisi family over the doorway.

★Káto Myli

To the south-west is Mýkonos's trademark, the row of disused windmills on Káto Myli, the "lower Windmill Hill".

Archaeological Museum

The Archaeological Museum (open Tue.–Sun. 8.30am–3pm), in a neoclassical house near the ferry landing-stage, displays material from

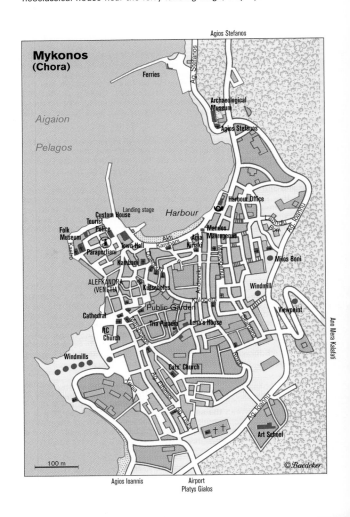

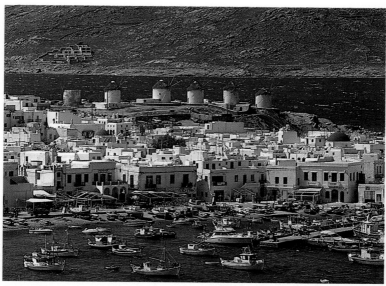

The typically Cycladic town of Mýkonos, with its famous Windmill Hill, is one of the most attractive in the island group

Delos, Rínia and Melos. Its prime exhibit is a 1.34m (4 ft 5 in.) high amphora (c. 670 BC) with the earliest known depiction of the Trojan horse.

The Folk Museum in the Kástro quarter (open Mon.–Sat. 5.30–8.30pm, Sun. 6.30–8.30pm), in an 18th c. sea-captain's house, has a varied collection of everyday objects. At the entrance is the stuffed figure of Pétros I, the pelican who for 30 years was a familiar feature of the harbour.

Folk Museum

The Nautical Museum (open 10.30am–1pm, 6.30–9pm) occupies a former sea-captain's house at Tría Pigádia ("Three Fountains", which supplied the town with water until 1956). It displays ship models, old charts and nautical instruments. In its peaceful green garden is the mechanism of an old lighthouse. Nearby is Lena's House (open Mon.–Sat. 6–9pm, Sun. from 7pm), a 19th c. professional-class house with its original furniture and furnishings.

Nautical Museum

8 km (5 mi.) east of Mýkonos town is the village of Áno Merá (Ανω Μερα). Below the square is the fortress-like monastery of the Panayía Tourlianí, founded in 1542 by monks from the Katapolianí monastery on Páros. In its present form it dates from 1767. Notable features are the marble reliefs on the bell-tower and the magnificently carved bishop's throne in the church. A 20 min. walk north from Áno Merá is the 17th c. monastery of Palaiokástro, which also has the aspect of a fortress.

Áno Merá

Náxos

K 6/7

Island group: Cyclades

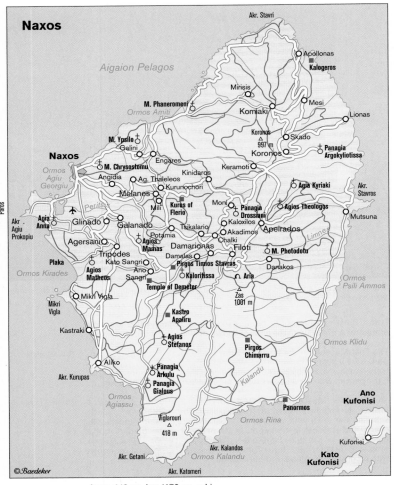

Naxos

Area: 448 sq. km (173 sq. mi.)
Altitude: 0–1001 m (0–3284 ft)
Population: 14,000
Chief place: Náxos town (Khóra)

Airport 3 km (2 mi.) south of Náxos town (reached by bus to Áyios Prokópios). Air connections with Athens. Shipping connections with Piraeus, Ráfina, Sámos, Rhodes, Crete (Iráklion) and all the larger neighbouring islands. Bus services on the island

Náxos (Νάξος), the largest and most beautiful of the Cyclades, is traversed from north to south by a range of hills up to 1001 m (3284 ft) high that fall away steeply on the east but slope down gradually on the west into fertile rolling country and well watered plains. Agriculture is an important element in the island's economy, the principal crops being wine grapes (grown on terraces), citrus fruits, potatoes, vegetables, corn and fruit. Its prosperity has also depended since ancient times on marble-quarrying, emery-mining and the recovery of salt from the sea. Náxos is a popular holiday destination, with good beaches and surfing waters, and less crowded than Mýkonos and Santoríni. As a place of importance in both ancient and medieval times it has also interesting historical monuments and remains.

Myth It was here, according to legend, that Ariadne was abandoned by her lover Theseus after she had enabled him to escape from the labyrinth after killing the Minotaur with the help of her famous thread and had fled from Crete along with him. She allowed herself to be consoled, however, by the young Dionysus, who arrived on Naxos just at the right time. The cult of Dionysus – which was associated with wine, grown here in ancient times – thus became established on the island.

See Baedeker Special p. 154

History There is much archaeological evidence to show that the island was settled by Carians and Cretans and developed a flourishing Cycladic culture in the 3rd and 2nd millennia BC. In the 1st millennium BC these first settlers were followed by Ionian Greeks, who in the 6th c. BC extended their rule over Paros, Andros and other neighbouring islands. During this period there was a celebrated school of sculptors on Naxos, notable for such works as the colossal statue of Apollo in the House of the Naxians on Delos (see entry). A member of the first Attic maritime league, Naxos became subject to Athens after an unsuccessful rising and was compelled to accept Athenian governors. After being held by Macedon it passed under Egyptian rule, was briefly assigned to Rhodes by Mark Antony; in 41 BC it came under Roman rule; and thereafter was part of the Byzantine Empire, becoming the see of a bishop in 1083. After the Fourth Crusade, in 1207, it was occupied by a Venetian noble, Marco Sanudo, who made it capital of the duchy of the Twelve Islands (duchy of Náxos), which existed until 1566. It was taken by the Turks in 1579 and was under Russian rule from 1770 to 1774, but, like the other islands in the Cyclades, retained a measure of independence. In 1830 it joined the newly established kingdom of Greece.

★Náxos town

Visitors entering the harbour of Náxos town (pop. 5000) are struck by a number of features – the little church of the Panayía Myrtidiótissa on its islet, the Venetian Kástro above the town, the town itself climbing up the slopes of a rocky hill, the busy harbour with its tavernas and cafés. On another islet linked to the mainland by a causeway is the famous marble doorway, 6 m (20 ft) high, part of a temple of Apollo built in the 6th c. BC but never completed. A church was built in the 5th c. on the remains of the temple. The square is known as Sto Paláti ("at the palace") because this is supposed to have been the site of Ariadne's palace.

To the north of the Kástro is the oldest part of the town, Grótta, with remains of the ancient city. In this quarter is the Orthodox cathedral of the Zoodókhos Piyí (Life-Giving Fountain"; 1780–90), incorporating ancient granite columns that are believed to have come from the temple of Apollo on Delos. To the rear of the harbour is the picturesque Boúrgos quarter with its narrow winding lanes; particularly charming is the colourful market street. The Boúrgos quarter was occupied by Orthodox Greeks, the neighbouring Evraikí quarter by Jews.

Old town

On the highest point in the town is the Venetian Kástro, built from 1207

★Kástro

Naxos (Chora)

IN KASTRO
1 Tower
2 St Anthony's Church (RC)
3 Sanudo Place
4 Cathedral (RC)
5 Archaeological Museum

©Baedeker

onwards. The Trani Porta leads into a museum-like quarter of handsome mansions sporting coats of arms, many of them derelict, which were once occupied by the Catholic nobility. Notable features of the cathedral, which dates back to the 13th c., are the icon of the Virgin on the high altar and the gravestones decorated with heraldic devices.

Beyond the Cathedral is the Archaeological Museum, housed in a former Jesuit college. It has the most important collection of Cycladic art after that of the National Archaeological Museum in Athens, including numbers of the striking Cycladic idols. On the terrace of the museum is a mosaic of "Europa on the Bull" dating from late antiquity.

Archaeological Museum

Trayéa plain to Apóllonas

The 50 km (30 mi.) drive over the Trayéa plain and along the mountain ridge to Apóllonas, at the north end of the island, gives a good impression of the varied landscape pattern of Náxos, with numerous churches, Venetian castles and fortress-like tower houses. Here we can describe only the main attractions. The return to Náxos town is along the north-west coast (about 35 km (22 mi.)), with breathtaking views and many side roads leading to beautiful bathing beaches.

◄ This 6 m (20 ft) high marble doorway, Náxos's trademark, is one of the most-impressive classical remains on the island

Nísyros

Galanádo

5 km (3 mi.) south-east of Náxos town is Galanádo (Γαλαναδο), beyond which is the Pyrgos Belonis, a tower that belonged to the Catholic bishops of Náxos. Amid the orchards and vineyards of the Potamia (or Trayéa) valley is the 9th c. church of Áyios Mámas (side road in 8 km (5 mi.)).

Khálki

Khálki (Χαλκι; 16 km (10 mi.)) is the market centre of the Trayéa plain. On the main street are the 10th c. church of the Panayía Protóthronis, which has fine frescos, and the fortress-like Pyrgos Grazia that belonged to the Barozzi family (coats of arms). Just off the main road (4 km (2½ mi.) north, at Moní), in its churchyard, is the oldest church on the island, the Panayía Drossianí (6th c.), with frescos, some of them dating from the time when the church was built.

Filóti

The main road soon comes to Filóti (Φιλοτι; 20 km (13 mi.)), on the slopes of Mount Zas (1001 m (3284 ft)). It is worth exploring the village with its whitewashed stepped lanes, the church of the Panayía Filótissa, with its old icons and a fine marble iconostasis, and a Venetian tower house. From the chapel of Ayía Marína it is a 1½ hour climb to the summit of Mount Zas, which takes its name from Zeus, father of the gods. From the summit there are fantastic views.

Apíranthos

On the far side of the mountain ridge is Apíranthos (Απειρανθος), where many Cretans settled in the 17th c. On the marble-paved main street of the village (pop. 900) are a geological, an archaeological and a folk museum, with a variety of material of local interest. From the road to Kóronos there are good views of the east and west sides of the ridge. Kóronos (34 km (21 m.)), prettily situated amid vineyards, is a marble-quarrying and emery-mining centre.

Apóllonas

Finally the road comes to Apóllonas (Απολλωνας; 49 km (30 mi.)), situated in a beautiful bay with a small sand and shingle beach. Above the village are ancient marble quarries (Naxian marble was used in sculpture and architecture and as roofing slabs). In the Ston Apollona quarry is the 10.4 m (34 ft) long figure of a kouros of the 6th c. BC, left unfinished because of flaws in the marble. Above the quarry is the Venetian castle of Kalóyero.

Other sights

3 km (2 mi.) north-east of Náxos town is the dazzlingly white fortress-like monastery of Áyios Ioánnis Khrysóstomos (17th c.; not open), from which there are fine views. 10 km (6 mi.) north-east of Náxos is the Faneroméni monastery, with a church of 1603. In an ancient quarry at Flerio, 2 km (1¼ mi.) east of Kourounokhori – now an orchard, with a kafeníon – is another unfinished kouros of the 6th c. BC. Under the south-east side of Mount Zas is the Hellenistic marble tower of Khimárou.

Nísyros   M 7

Southern Sporades
Area: 41 sq. km (16 sq. mi.)
Altitude: 0–698 m (0–2290 ft)
Population: 1000
Chief place: Mandráki

Shipping connections with Piraeus, Astypálaia, Kálymnos, Kastellórizo, Kos, Rhodes, Sými, Sýros and Tílos. Boats to Yialí. Hydrofoils once weekly to Kos and Rhodes. Bus services on the island.

The island of Nísyros (Νισυρος) lies half way between Kos and Tílos and 18 km (11 mi.) south-west of the Reladiye (Knidos) peninsula in Asia Minor. It was formed by a volcano, Mount Diabates, that was occasion-

The caldera of the volcano that formed Nísyros: a lunar landscape with a number of small craters

ally active in the Middle Ages and last erupted in 1522. The floor of the crater, 3.5 km (2 mi.) long and 1.5 km (1 mi.) across, is surrounded by hills rising out of the sea to a height of 689 m (2260 ft). While the southern half of the island, which is almost circular, is covered with lush vegetation, the northern half is a lunar landscape with a number of small craters. Volcanic activity is now confined emissions of hot sulphurous fumes (solfataras). On the fertile pumice soils in the south, which store up water, wine, citrus fruits, olives and almonds are grown in terraced fields. Pumice is exported from the neighbouring island of Yialí.

Tourism The island's tourist trade is only on a modest scale, partly because of the limited accommodation available for visitors and partly because of the shortage of water. Many visitors, however, come on day trips from the neighbouring island of Kos. There are a few beaches of dark-coloured shingle; the White Beach between Loutrá and Páli has light-coloured sand.

History Nísyros was originally settled by Dorians from Kos and Kameiros. In 1312 it was occupied by the Knights of St John, and later became a fief of the Assanti family. It was taken by the Turks in 1533; in 1912 it was occupied by Italy; and in 1948 it was returned to Greece.

Sights

The capital and principal port of Nísyros is Mandráki (Μανδρακι; pop. 600), which lies on the north coast, extends along the 1 km (¾ mi.) long coast road, which is lined with cafés, tavernas and souvenir shops.

Attractive features of Mandráki are its shady square and brightly

★**Mandráki**

painted wooden balconies. Above the little town, to the west, is the castle of the Knights of St John, now a monastery. Within the precincts of the castle is the late Byzantine cave church of the Panayía Spilianí. To the south is the Palaiokástro, with impressive remains of the Hellenistic city (4th–3rd c. BC). On the way up to the castle is a small local museum.

Loutrá

2 km (1¼ mi.) east of Mandráki is the little thermal resort of Loutrá (Λουτρα), with spa facilities, some of which are rather dilapidated. The sulphurous water, which is recommended for the treatment of rheumatism and arthritis, flows directly from the caldera into baths. There are other hot sulphur springs (with remains of ancient baths) 1 km (¾ mi.) further east in the little fishing port of Páli (Thérma).

From Loutrá it is an hour walk up to the tiny village of Emporió, on the rim of the crater. Most of the houses in the village are empty and falling into ruin.

Nikiá

From Emporió it is another hour along the crater rim, which ranges in height between 410 m (1345 ft) and 570 m (1870 ft), to the beautifully situated village of Nikiá (Νικια). From the cobbled village square there are marvellous views of the sea and the floor of the crater. From here it is an hour walk down into the caldera.

Built against a rock face in Nikiá is the monastery of Áyios Ioánnis Theológos.

From Nikiá you can continue west to the abandoned monastery of Áyios Stavrós (from which there is a path into the caldera) and beyond this to complete the circuit of the crater.

★Lakki

On the floor of the caldera (alt. 139 m (456 ft)), is the little plain of Lakkí, the northern part of which is cultivated, while the southern half is covered with bubbling hot springs and mud pools, brightly coloured concretions and steaming fumaroles. A small crater on the west side is the highest point on the island (698 m (2290 ft)).

Neighbouring islands

Off the north coast of Nísyros in the direction of Kos is the little obsidian island of Yialí (area 6 sq. km (2½ sq. mi.); alt. 0–177 m (0–581 ft)), with a pumice quarry. To the west are the islets of Pasikiá and Peroúsa, both with ancient watch-towers, and Kandelioúsa (area 1 sq. km (¾ sq. mi.); alt. 0–103 m (0–388 ft)), with a lighthouse.

★Páros   K 6/7

Island group: Cyclades
Area: 186 sq. km (72 sq. mi.)
Altitude: 0–771 m (0–2530 ft)
Population: 8000
Chief place: Páros town (Parikiá)

Airport at Alyki. Air connection with Athens. Shipping connections with Piraeus, Rafína, Salonica, Vólos, Crete (Iráklion) and neighbouring islands. Bus services on the island.

Páros (Παρος), lying 8 km (5 mi.) west of Náxos, is the central ferry port of the Cyclades and, after Mýkonos and Santoríni, the most visited island in the group, attracting both package holidaymakers and young backpackers. Most of the visitors make for the coastal resorts with good beaches, and the interior of the island is still unspoiled. Páros has been famed since ancient times for its marble, used in many masterpieces of ancient sculpture.

Economy The island is occupied by a range of gently rounded hills, rising to 771 m (2530 ft) in Mount Profítis Ilías. Three bays cut deep inland: in the west Parikiá Bay, in the north Naoúsa Bay and in the east the shallow Mármara Bay. Much of the island is barren, but in well watered areas of weathered, fertile soil there is quite a substantial amount of agriculture (wine, barley, fruit, vegetables). The fisheries centre on sardines and octopus. In addition there is still some quarrying of marble.

History The island, which has preserved its ancient name, was already well populated in the age of the Cycladic culture (3rd millennium BC). In the 1st millennium BC Ionian Greeks settled on Paros and made it a considerable sea power, supported by the trade in marble. The Parians founded a colony on Thasos, whose deposits of gold made it a place of importance. In the 6th and 5th c. a famous school of sculptors flourished on Paros.

Paros was a member of the first Attic maritime league, and its unusually large contributions to the league are evidence of its wealth in the 5th c. BC. In Hellenistic, Roman and Byzantine times Paros was of little importance. From the 3rd c. BC dates the "Parian Chronicle", an account of Greek history inscribed on marble (now in the Archaeological Museum in Páros town).

In the 9th c. AD the island was plundered and depopulated by Arab pirates. From 1207 to 1389 it belonged to the duchy of Náxos, and thereafter was ruled by various Venetian dynasts. In 1537 it was taken by Khaireddin Barbarossa and incorporated in the Ottoman Empire; between 1771 and 1774 it was occupied by Russia; and finally in 1830 it became part of the new kingdom of Greece.

Páros town

The chief place on the island is Páros town or Parikiá (pop. 3000). It lies on the west coast, on the site of the ancient capital. From the sea it does not look particularly attractive, but its charms are revealed on a stroll through its flower-decked little streets.

The central feature of the town is a 15 m (50 ft) high gneiss crag now occupied by the Kástro, a ruined Frankish castle of about 1260, which has fragments from an Ionic temple of Demeter built into its walls. The tower incorporates a circular building of the 4th c. BC, part of which serves as the apse of the castle chapel. Nearby, on the highest point of the Kástro, are the foundations of an unfinished temple of about 530 BC. A marble wall of the temple was used as one wall of the church of Áyios Konstantínos, which has a fine gilded iconostasis. Built on to the church is a chapel with a three-column portico. From here there are marvellous views, particularly at sunset.

Kástro

In a square at the east end of the harbour is one of the oldest and most beautiful churches in Greece (open 8am–1pm, 4–7pm), built in three

★Cathedral

phases between the 5th and 7th c. AD. This is the Ekatontapyliani ("Hundred-Gated") church – a grand name, but actually a corruption of Katapoliani ("in the lower town"). Much altered over the centuries (notably after an earthquake in 1773), it was restored between 1959 and 1966 and stripped of its coating of whitewash. The church is preceded by a charming inner courtyard, in which are a small Byzantine Museum and the tomb of Mantó Mavroyénous.

The principal church (built in the second phase, about 600) is a two-storey domed cruciform church with a barrel-vaulted gallery for women, in which fragments of ancient architecture were incorporated. The high altar is borne on two Doric column drums and has egg-and-dart moulding of the 6th c. BC. In the apse, which has a cycle of frescos illustrating the Acathist Hymn honouring the Mother of God, are three tiers of stone benches for the clergy, with the bishop's throne in the middle. The oldest part of the building is the chapel of Áyios Nikólaos, originally a 4th c. basilica, with Doric columns of Parian marble and a carved iconostasis. To the right is the baptistery (7th c.), with a cruciform font set into the floor.

Archaeological
Museum

Near the church is the Archaeological Museum (open Tue.–Sun. 8.30am–2.30pm), with material from Páros, Antíparos and Saliagos. The collection includes inscriptions (including one referring to the poet Archilochus, who lived on Paros in the 7th c. BC), funerary reliefs, sculpture and Cycladic idols. Of particular interest is a fragment (336–229 BC) of the "Marmor Parium", a record of events in Greek history that was found here in 1627. The major part of it is in the Ashmolean Museum in Oxford.

Other sights

Delion

On a hill to the north of Parikiá Bay are scanty remains of the Delion, a walled sanctuary of the three Delian divinities Apollo, Leto and Artemis. 1 km (¾ mi.) north-east of Parikiá, on a site once occupied by the Heroon of Archilochus, are the foundations of a three-aisled basilica of the 7th c. AD known as Tris Ekklisíes.

★Páros marble
quarries

The famous Parian marble (known as Lychnites, "candle-lit"), which is purer and more translucent than all other kinds of marble, was highly prized in antiquity. It was used in buildings in Delos, Epidaurus and Delphi, in Imperial Rome and in Jerusalem (Solomon's Temple) as well as in sculpture: celebrated examples are the Hermes of Praxiteles, the Venus de Milo and the pedimental sculpture of the Temple of Zeus at Olympia. The most important marble quarry on Páros, which was worked from the time of the Cycladic culture (3rd–2nd millennium BC) to the 15th c. AD, is 5 km (3 mi.) east of Parikiá in the Maráthi valley (signposted). The ancient shafts can still be seen and entered (pocket torch and non-skid footwear necessary). The entrance (the "Cave of Pan") is on the west bank, at the relief of a nymph in reddish marble.

★Naoúsa

At the north end of the island, in a wide bay with good beaches, is Naoúsa (Ναουσα), the second largest place on Páros (pop. 1400). Its particular attraction is the idyllic little fishing harbour with its tavernas, which ranks as the most appealing in the Cyclades. Used in Roman times for the shipping of marble, it is now in process of changing from a quiet fishing port into a lively holiday resort. On the harbour are a chapel dedicated to Áyios Nikólaos and the ruins of a Venetian fort.

Moní Khristou
Thassou

In the convent of "Christ in the Forest", 7 km (4½ mi.) south of Parikiá, is the tomb of the local saint Áyios Arsenios, canonised in 1967 (large festival on August 18th).

Tiger moths in the Valley of the Butterflies

The road continues to the lush green "Valley of the Butterflies", where there are still some swarms of tiger moths. They should on no account be disturbed by the clapping of hands or other attempts to stimulate them.

Petaloúdes

South-west of Páros, separated from it by a channel varying in width from 1 km (¾ mi.) to 8 km (5 mi.), is the island of Antíparos (Αντιπαρος; area 35 sq. km (14 sq. mi.); pop. 800), the ancient Oliaros, now a popular holiday resort. The population of the island and its tourist facilities are concentrated in the island's capital, also called Antíparos, which clusters round a Venetian castle of 1440. In the village square is the blue and white church of Áyios Nikólaos, which has fine icons and woodcarving. 8 km (5 mi.) south is a beautiful stalactitic cave (reached by bus), in which the French ambassador organised a ceremonial Christmas mass in 1673. It can be reached by boat, then a 30 min. walk.

Antíparos

★★Pátmos

L 8

Southern Sporades
Area: 34 sq. km (13 sq. mi.)
Altitude: 0–269 m (0–883 ft)
Population: 2800
Chief place: Pátmos town (Khóra)

Shipping connections from the port of Skála with Piraeus, Salonica, Léros–Kálymnos–Kos–Rhodes, Sámos–Chíos–Lésbos, Náxos–Páros–Sýros–Tínos. In summer hydrofoils to Sámos, Kos and neighbouring islands. Boats from Skála to beaches on the island. Regular bus services.

The Revelation of St John

"**I** John, who also am your brother, and companion in tribulation, ... was in the isle that is called Patmos, for the word of God, and for the testimony of Jesus Christ. I was in the spirit on the Lord's day, and heard behind me a great voice, as of a trumpet, saying, ... What thou seest, write in a book" (Revelation, 1, 9–11).

According to tradition, John spent many years of his life in a cave on Patmos. In this spot, where no light reached him and he was thus protected from any external sensory perceptions, he heard from the threefold cleft in the roof of the cave the word of God ("I am Alpha and Omega, the beginning and the ending, saith the Lord, which is, and which was, and which is to come, the Almighty"), received the revelation of the future of humanity and had visions of the end of the world in powerful images and words, of the terror and the joys of the last days and of the Last Judgment. John's Revelation, written down by his disciple Prochorus, is the last book of the New Testament, a work of 22 chapters made up of seven letters to Christian communities and visions of three times seven catastrophes that were to afflict the world. The number seven plays a major part in his apocalyptic scenario: the seven Spirits of God, seven stars, seven seals, seven golden candlesticks, seven trumpets, seven plagues, seven golden vials full of the wrath of God, the letters addressed to the seven churches of Asia. In the ancient symbolism of numbers the number seven signified isolation, wholeness and fullness: the seven churches in Asia thus represent the whole of Christendom.

But who was John, the author of the Book of Revelation? It is historically established that around AD 96, in the reign of the Emperor Domitian, he was exiled to the almost uninhabited island of Patmos for his Christian beliefs. It used to be thought that he was the Apostle John, author of the fourth Gospel and three New Testament epistles, who died at a great age in the year 100. On the basis of stylistic and theological differences, however, many scholars now believe that the author of the Apocalypse cannot have been Christ's disciple John. It is thought that the author of the Book of Revelation (now distinguished as John the Divine, in the Orthodox church John the Theologian) may have been an itinerant Christian preacher in Asia Minor, perhaps a Christian of Jewish origin who, like many others, had fled to Asia Minor after the destruction of the Temple in Jerusalem in AD 70.

And was the Book of Revelation actually written on Patmos? In the work itself there is no indication that it was. Perhaps it was a compilation by more than one author in the 2nd century. However that may be, the book was certainly written at a time of ruthless persecution of Christians and in a

Pátmos (Πατμος), the most northerly island in the Dodecanese, lying to the south of Sámos, is one of the most thinly populated of the Greek islands. It is regarded by the Orthodox, Catholic and Protestant churches as a sacred place, the island of St John the Evangelist, who is believed to have lived here in 95 AD and to have written the Book of Revelation.

The Monastery of St John and the Cave of the Apocalypse attract many day-trippers from Rhodes, Sámos and Kos, but large cruise ships also call in at the port of Skála. The island's hotels are concentrated in Skála, Grikoú and Kámpos; in Khóra there are only rooms in private houses. The island is hilly, rugged and barren; it is thought to be the rim

mood of anguish over the future of the faith and radical missionary zeal: the imminent Apocalypse was a source of consolation to those faced with martyrdom. At that time there were many intimations of apocalypse: between the 2nd century BC and the 2nd century AD there were several visions, both Jewish and Christian, of the end of the world. But none of these apocalypses anguished and fascinated men so strongly as John's apocalyptic prophecy, the symbolism of which has never been completely explained.

The Monastery of the Apocalypse on Pátmos

of the crater of an extinct volcano. Nevertheless it is popular with sun-worshippers, though not to the same extent as other islands like Rhodes, since it cannot be reached by air. It has a much indented coast with beautiful little bays and sandy beaches.

History Patmos was originally settled by Dorians and later by Ionians, and had a sanctuary of Artemis. Since it was a place of no political or economic importance, little is known of its early history. Like the barren neighbouring islands, it was used as a place of exile in Roman times. John, author of the Book of Revelation, was exiled to the island

The Monastery of St John, the central landmark of Pátmos

by the Emperor Domitian in AD 95 and remained there until AD 97. While living in a cave on Patmos he had the visions that were included in the New Testament as the Book of Revelation. He has traditionally been identified as St John the Evangelist; but there is no certainty about the identity of either the Evangelist or the author of the Book of Revelation.

During the early Middle Ages Pátmos seems to have been abandoned and desolate. It was given a new lease of life as an intellectual and religious centre when Abbot Christodoulos fled from Asia Minor and transferred his monastery from Mount Latmos, near Miletus, to Pátmos in 1088. The Byzantine Emperor Alexius I Comnenus (1081–8) granted the island to Christodoulos, and Pátmos, receiving rich donations and extensive privileges, grew wealthy and influential. Until the Turkish occupation of the island in 1537 it saw Normans, Turks and Crusaders come and go. Living under its own strict Rule (Typikon), it survived 250 years of Turkish rule unscathed, subject only to the annual payment of tribute. Shipbuilding and seafaring developed into major elements in the island's economy, and also brought it important cultural contacts with the outer world.

From 1912 to 1948 Pátmos was held by Italy. Since 1946 the whole island has been under statutory protection as a national monument. In 1995 the 1900th anniversary of the Revelation of St John was celebrated under the patronage of Oecumenical Patriarch Bartholomew.

Sights

Skála

Pátmos consists of three parts joined by narrow isthmuses. At the head of the longest inlet on the east coast is the busy port of Skála (Σκαλα), the tourist centre of the island. The tourist and post office are in the Italian custom house, an imposing historic building with arcading and a tower. Large cruise ships put into Skála several times a week.

In spite of the large numbers of day-trippers from neighbouring islands Pátmos never seems overcrowded. It has a very agreeable atmosphere, particularly in the evening, when the restaurants and cafés on the harbour and in the street behind the first line of houses are full of life. The Monastery of St John, which is floodlit after dark, forms a harmonious ensemble with the picturesque harbour in which fishing boats rock at anchor and luxury steamers moor at the quay.

To the north of Skála are the beaches of Méloi (2 km (1¼ mi.) and Agriolivádi (4 km (2½ mi.)). In the northern part of the island is beautiful Kámpos Bay, with a gently sloping shingle beach. Passengers from cruise ships are brought here for sunbathing. Gríkou, south-east of the Khóra, is the island's main tourist centre after Skála; it has the best beach on the island, Psilí Ámmos.

Beaches

From Skála harbour it is an hour **walk** (best done in the morning, before it gets too hot; there is also a bus service) to the Monastery of the Apocalypse and from there to Khóra. From Skála you can take either an old paved road or a footpath that for part of the way runs through shady pine woods. On the way up there are marvellous views of Skála and the neighbouring islands.

Halfway up is the Monastery of the Apocalypse, with the cave in which John had his Revelation. (Opening hours are very variable: standard times are roughly 8.30am–1pm, Sun. 10am–noon, Tue., Sat., Sun. 4–6pm). The iconostasis in the right-hand chapel in the cave depicts John's visions. Visitors are shown the spots on the floor and on the wall where he lay and leaned against the wall while listening to the "great voice, as of a trumpet" and writing down his visions and the three clefts in the roof of the cave from which the divine voice came. Many pilgrims come to the cave from all over Greece and from other countries to pray in the chapel.

★Monastery of
the Apocalypse

Immediately above the monastery are the ruins of the influential Patmias School, founded in 1713 by a monk named Makarios, in which both religious and secular subjects were taught. Higher up still is the modern school that continues the tradition.

The chief place on the island, Khóra (pop. 800), is particularly attractive with its handsome whitewashed houses huddled together on stepped lanes and narrow paved streets (which after the departure of the day-trippers return to their normal quietness), in a style reminiscent of the Cyclades. As you stroll about the little town there are frequent glimpses of the battlemented walls of the fortress-like Monastery of St John

★★Khóra

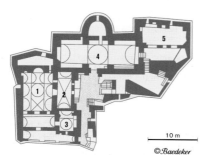

Patmos
**Monastery of
St John**

1 Katholikon

2 Chapel of the
Panayia

3 Chapel of
Christodoulos

4 Refectory

5 Kitchen

10 m

©Baedeker

(Áyios Ioánnis Theológos). Many of the old mansions were built by refugees from other parts of Greece. To the west of the monastery is the "Constantinople" quarter, to the east the "Cretan" quarter, with the houses of the Natalis (1599), Pankostas (1606) and Stefanos (1636) families. The Simandris House (1625) is open to the public. Near it is the monastery of the Zoodókhos Piyí (Life-Giving Fountain) of 1607, with fine frescos.

From Platía Lozia, in which stands the neoclassical Town Hall, there is a good view of the Monastery of the Apocalypse and Skála. The best **views** of the Monastery of St John, the whole island and the surrounding area are to be had from the windmills on the road to Gríkou.

★★Monastery of St John

The present aspect of the Monastery of St John, with its stout walls and battlements, dates from the 17th c. A ramp leads up through the entrance gateway into a beautiful courtyard surrounded by loggias and buttresses. On the left is the principal church (Katholikón), built in 1090, during the founder's lifetime. Unusually, it is free-standing. Its exonarthex (17th c.) contains columns and other marble fragments from a basilica of the 4th c. and some mediocre 17th and 19th century paintings (life of St John). In the narthex (12th c.) are frescos of the 12th and 17th c.; particularly fine is the painting of the parable of the wise and foolish virgins (c. 1600).

Mosaic depicting Christodoulos, founder of the monastery

The **church** itself, the oldest part of the building, has a ground plan in the form of a Greek cross. It was decorated and furnished in the 19th c. at the expense of the Russian Tsars. There is a richly carved iconostasis of 1820. The paintings (17th–19th c.) include many representations of St John and his apocalyptic visions. In the first chapel on the right is the silver-plated sarcophagus of the founder, Ósios (Blessed) Christodoulos. In the second chapel, dedicated to the Panayía, are fine 12th c. wall paintings that were discovered under frescos of 1745 (carefully removed from the wall and now to be seen in the refectory); they include representations of the Mother of God enthroned, Abraham entertaining the three angels, Christ and the woman of Samaria, the healing of the lame man and the blind man, and Mary in the Temple.

Other features of interest are the painted wooden iconostasis (Cretan, 1607) and the ancient architectural fragments (stone step, column).

In the **refectory** (Trápeza) can be seen the marble-faced tables with cavities for cutlery. There are also frescos of the 12th or 13th c. and the wall paintings removed from the chapel of the Panayía.

The **treasury** contains valuable liturgical vestments and utensils, mostly of the 17th c., and icons, mitres, vestments, chalices, crosses, etc., as well as a number of valuable icons. There is a rich library, with 890 manuscript codices and 35 parchment rolls, 2000 early printed books and the monastic archives, containing over 13,000 documents. Of the rich collection of ancient literature once possessed by the monastery there remains a manuscript of the "History" of Diodorus Siculus.

The treasury and the library constitute what is surely the richest collection of its kind outside the monasteries of Athos. They are not open to the public, but some of the finest items are displayed in the **museum**, including the charter of 1088 (1.42 m (5 ft) long, but originally said to have been over 5 m (16 ft) long) granting the island of Patmos to Christodoulos, 33 pages of a 6th c. manuscript of St Mark's Gospel (the Codex Purpureus, most of which is in St Petersburg), an 8th c. manuscript of the Book of Job, with 42 miniatures, and a manuscript of 941 containing a collection of sermons by St Gregory of Nazianzus.

From the roof terraces of the monastery there are magnificent views of Pátmos and the surrounding islands.

Arki

The barren little island of Arkí (area 7 sq. km (2½ sq. mi.)) lies 14 km (8½ mi.) north-east of Pátmos. The island's inhabitants, numbering only about 50, make a poor living, mainly from fishing and stock farming. There are a few rooms in private houses and beaches for refugees from civilisation; the finest beach, with beautiful blue water, is Tiganáki. Arkí is surrounded by numbers of smaller islets and isolated rocks, some of which provide grazing for goats.

Paxí   E 5/6

Area: 19 sq. km (7½ sq. mi.)
Altitude: 0–248 m (0–814 ft)
Population: 2200
Chief place: Paxí town (Gáios)

Shipping connections with Patrás and Corfu. Excursion boats from Corfu and Parga. Boats to beaches. Bus service Gáios–Lóngos–Lákka.

The island of Paxí or Paxos (Παξοι or Παξος), lying to the south of Corfu, is the smallest of the Ionian Islands. Only 10 km (6¼ mi.) long by up to 4 km (2½ mi.) across, it can easily be explored on foot or by moped. Its thousands of olive trees produce olive oil esteemed for its high quality. On the west coast, with its picturesque cliffs up to 185 m (607 ft) high and its numerous sea-caves, there still survive a few examples of the Mediterranean monk-seal, a species in grave danger of extinction. The east coast is very different, sloping gently down to the sea, with a number of shingle beaches. An island of lush vegetation and great scenic beauty, with beautiful bays and inlets for bathing, Paxí has excellent tourist facilities. It is particularly favoured by British and Italian visitors, but also attracts many day trippers from Corfu and Parga on the Greek mainland. The main tourist centres are Gáios and Lákka; Lóngos is a rather quieter resort.

Paxí shared the destinies of the other Ionian Islands, but was more exposed to incursions by conquerors and pirates. From 1814 to 1864 it was under British rule.

Sights

Gáios

From the ferry landing-stage it is a 15 min. walk or bus ride to the chief place on the Island, Gáios (Γαιος) or Paxí (pop. 1000), situated in a sheltered inlet on the south-east coast. There is a wide choice of tavernas on the seafront and in the main square. The Folk Museum, opened in 1996, displays local costumes and domestic equipment. On the uninhabited island of Áyios Nikólaos are the remains of a Venetian fortress of 1423, and on the islet of Panayía beyond it is a church dedicated to the Mother of God. Both of these little islands can be reached from Gáios by water taxi.

Paxi

Lóngos

5 km (3 mi.) north of Gáios is the quiet little fishing village of Lóngos (Λογγος), with old tavernas offering fish dishes. The nearby bay of Glyfáda is one of the most beautiful on the island.

Lákka

Lákka (Λακκα), at the northern tip of Paxí, is the water sports centre of the island, situated in a sheltered bay of crystal-clear water that offers excellent opportunities for surfers and sailing and diving enthusiasts. From the lighthouse a path runs down to the shingle beach of Plátanos (bathing possible only when the sea is calm).

Ypapanti cave

Below the village of Vasiliatika, reached by water taxi, is the Ypapantí sea cave, which during the Second World War was a German U-boat lair.

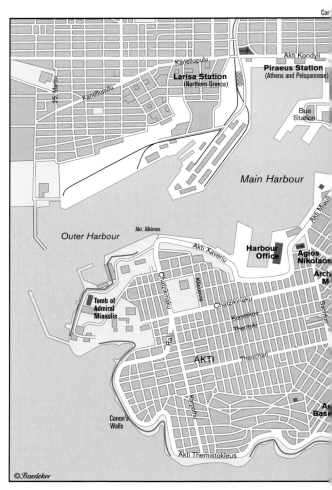

Further south is the Petriti cave, which has been compared with the Blue Grotto on Capri for its remarkable light effects

South-east of Paxí is its rocky little sister island of Antípaxi (area 6 sq. km (2½ sq. mi.); alt. 0–107 m (0–351 ft)). Its 20 or so inhabitants live by sheep farming and produce an excellent wine. It has beautiful, lonely beaches, particularly Voutoumi on the east coast. There are tavernas on the island, but no official accommodation for visitors.

Antípaxi

Piraeus   H 6

Greece's principal port

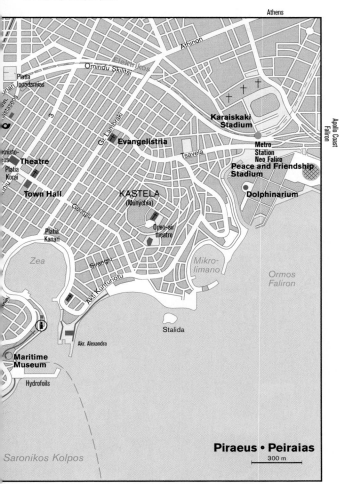

Altitude: 0–15 m (0–50 ft)
Population: 500,000

The port of Piraeus (in Greek Peiraiás or Pireás, Πειραιας) has long formed part of the Athens conurbation. The largest port in Greece and one of the most important in the whole of the Mediterranean, it is a major factor in the country's economy and an important hub of tourist traffic. From here ships sail to ports all over Europe and the Near East, and this is also the starting-point of most domestic shipping routes, including services to the numerous Greek islands. New port installations are being developed in the bay of Fáliron, which was the harbour of ancient Athens before Piraeus existed. The most characteristic parts of the modern town, which combines the atmosphere of a large port with the amenities of a city, are round the principal harbour, the yachting harbour of Zéa and the fishing and yachting harbour of Mikrolímano, in the Kastela district and in Korais Square.

Visitors should not attempt to drive through the centre of Piraeus, a maze of one-way streets and steep and narrow lanes. The best way to get some impression of the town is to take a boat trip from the main harbour round the coast to the Zéa and Mikrolímano harbours with their innumerable yachts and sailing boats. On the seafront promenades are numerous cafés and tavernas. Mikrolímano is famed for its excellent (but highly expensive) fish restaurants.

History Piraeus was developed by Themistocles from 482 BC onwards as a commercial harbour and naval base for Athens. It was connected with Athens by the "Long Walls" and laid out in the time of Pericles on a regular grid of streets, on the pattern evolved by Hippodamus of Miletus. The town was destroyed by Sulla in 86 BC, and thereafter was a place of no importance. In the Middle Ages it was known as Porto Leone, after an ancient marble figure of a lion that stood at the entrance to the harbour but was removed to Venice in 1682 and now stands outside the Arsenal there.

Piraeus recovered its importance after the liberation of Greece in the 19th c., when the modern town was laid out on a regular plan as the ancient one had been.

Piraeus has preserved the remains of boat halls in the ancient harbours of Zéa and Mikrolímano and of a Hellenistic theatre (2nd c. BC) near the Archaeological Museum (Trikoúpi 31; open Tue.–Sun. 8.30am–3pm), which is devoted to the history of ancient Piraeus. Notable exhibits include marble reliefs of the 1st c., the funerary monument of Callithea and four bronze statues recovered from an ancient wreck in the harbour in 1959 – an archaic kouros, two figures of Artemis and a figure of Athena.

★Archaeological Museum

On the south-west side of the bay are some remains of town walls dating from the time of Conon (394–339 BC).

At the south end of Zéa harbour, by the new marina, is the Maritime Museum, which covers the history of Greek seafaring from antiquity to modern times.

★Maritime Museum

Póros   H 6

Saronic Islands
Area: 33 sq. km (13 sq. mi.)
Altitude: 0–390 m (0–1280 ft)

◀ *Piraeus: the Mikrolímano harbour, always crowded with yachts, is famed for its fish restaurants*

Population: 5000
Chief place: Póros town

Ferry connections with Méthana–Aegina–Piraeus, Hydra, Ermióni, Spétses and Pórto Khéli. Hydrofoils to Piraeus (Zéa), Hydra, Spétses, Pórto Khéli and on occasion to Ermióni, Monemvasia and Náfplio. Regular boat services to Galatás on mainland Greece. Bus services on the island.

The island of Póros (Πορος) lies south-west of the Méthana peninsula off the north coast of the Argolid (Peloponnese), separated from the mainland by a strait between 250 and 1000 m (835 and 3300 ft) wide, 1.5 km (1 mi.) long and up to 4 m (13 ft) deep. Most of the island is covered by light woodland and macchia. The inhabitants, many of whom are of Albanian descent, live by farming the fertile coastal areas on the mainland that belong to Póros and by the tourist trade. Most of the hotels and holiday apartments are on the south coast between Neório and Askéli. The best means of transport on the island and in the winding lanes of Póros town are bicycles and mopeds.

History In Mycenaean times there was a settlement on the site later occupied by the sanctuary of Poseidon. The ancient city of Calauria was abandoned after the Roman period, and the modern town was established only in the late Middle Ages. From 1830 to 1877 Póros was the main base of the Greek navy, and it is still the home of a naval training school.

Sights

Póros town   Póros town, the only settlement on the island, is beautifully situated on

Póros, beautifully situated on a small peninsula, is a favourite weekend resort for the people of Athens

a small peninsula of volcanic origin (ancient Sphairia) on the south coast of the island, linked with it by the narrow Bísti isthmus. It is a favourite weekend resort for the people of Athens. From the blue-domed clock-tower there are fine views of the hills of the Argolid and the lemon and orange plantations on the coastal plain. There is a small archaeological museum on the harbour front (Platía Korizi), displaying finds from the temple of Poseidon and classical and Hellenistic statues and vases. To the north-east of the town extends the long Askéli Beach, with a number of hotels; the beach tends to be overcrowded in summer.

5 km (3 mi.) north-east of the town – a pleasant walk – can be seen the scanty remains of the Doric temple of Poseidon (6th c. BC), the centre of the Calaurian amphictyony (religious league) of the maritime cities on the Saronic and Argolic Gulfs. It was here that Demosthenes, fleeing from the henchmen of the Macedonian governor Antipatrer, poisoned himself in 322 BC. From here there are fine views of the Méthana peninsula and the island of Aegina. The numerous remains of buildings in the surrounding area suggest that this was the site of ancient Calauria.

Temple of Poseidon

4 km (2½ mi.) east of Póros town, at Askéli, is the early 18th c. monastery of the Zoodókhos Piyí (Life-Giving Fountain), with a fine gilded iconostasis from Asia Minor. Close by is a pleasant taverna, and in the bay below the site is a beautiful beach.

Zoodókhos Piyí

★★Rhodes   M/N 7

Island group: Dodecanese
Area: 1398 sq. km (540 sq. mi.)
Altitude: 0–1215 m (0–3985 ft)
Population: 110,000
Chief town: Rhodes

Airport 16 km (10 mi.) south-west of Rhodes town (airport buses). Air connections with Athens, Salonica, Crete (Iráklion), Kos, Mýkonos, Santoríni, Kárpathos, Kásos and Kastellórizo. Charter flights. Shipping connections with Piraeus and all the islands in the Dodecanese. Ferries to Marmaris (Turkey). Bus services on the island (timetables available from EOT).

Rhodes (Ροδος), the "Island of Roses", the largest island in the Dodecanese and the fourth largest Greek island (after Crete, Euboea and Lésbos), is one element in the island bridge that extends from the Peloponnese by way of Crete and Kárpathos to Asia Minor, from which it is only 18 km (11 mi.) distant. 78 km (48 mi.) long and up to 30 km (19 mi.) wide, Rhodes is traversed from end to end by a long mountain ridge rising to 1215 m (3986 ft) in Mount Atáviros. The land, well watered and well wooded, falls away gradually towards the coasts, affording good soil for agriculture, particularly near the coast.

Tourism With its beautiful scenery, its excellent beaches and the fine medieval buildings erected by the Knights of St John, now well restored, Rhodes holds a wealth of attraction for visitors and has long been a major tourist centre. In and around Rhodes town and between Rhodes and Lindos is one of the largest concentrations of hotels in Greece, but elsewhere, particularly in the south, the island is still relatively unspoiled.

History The island of Rhodes was occupied as early as the neolithic

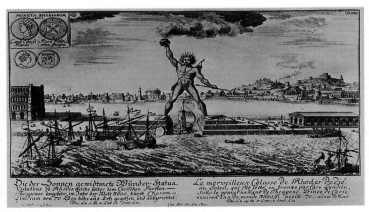

An old representation of the Colossus of Rhodes

period, but its great cultural flowering came only with its settlement by Dorian Greeks. Their three cities of Lindos, Ialysos and Kameiros were members of the Hexapolis, the league of six Dorian cities, which became subject to the Persians around 500 BC. In the 5th c. BC Rhodes was a member of the first Attic maritime league, the Confederacy of Delos. About 408 BC the new capital city of Rhodes was laid out on a regular plan by the famous Greek town-planner Hippodamus of Miletus, and in the 4th c. it overshadowed Athens itself in commercial importance. The great landmark of this wealthy and independent island state was the celebrated Colossus of Rhodes, a 34 m (112 ft) high bronze statue of the sun god Helios standing on a stone base 10 m (35 ft) high that was one of the seven wonders of the ancient world. Cast between 304 and 292 BC by Chares of Lindos, it stood at the entrance to the harbour (probably the present Mandráki Harbour, on the site now occupied by Fort St Nicholas) and served as a lighthouse. It collapsed in an earthquake about 225 BC.

With the extension of Roman control in the East the island's trade declined, but the city of Rhodes remained an important cultural centre, with a well known school of rhetoric that was attended by Cicero and Caesar and a major school of sculptors which in the time of the Emperor Tiberius (AD 14–37) produced the famous Laocoon group (c. 50 BC) now in the Vatican Museums in Rome.

During the Middle Ages possession of Rhodes was contested between Arabs, Greeks (1204–46), Byzantines (1246–83; 1283–1309 Aldinoglou), Venetians and Genoese. In 1309 it was occupied by the Knights of St John, who developed the town into a powerful stronghold and in the 15th c. defended it and the rest of the island against Egyptian and Turkish attacks, but were compelled to surrender it to Suleiman the Magnificent in 1523. After almost 400 years of Turkish rule the island was occupied by Italy in 1912. In 1947, after the Second World War, it was returned to Greece.

★★Rhodes town

The town of Rhodes (pop. 50,000), situated at the northern tip of the island of Rhodes, has been capital of the island since its foundation in 408 BC, and is now the administrative centre of the nomos of the

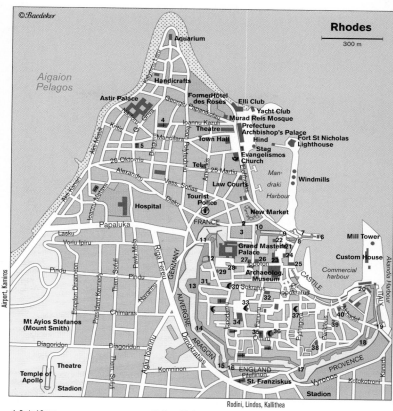

©Baedeker

Rhodes

300 m

Aigaion Pelagos

Airport, Kaminos

Rodini, Lindos, Kallithea

1 Bank of Greece	14 Tower of Spain	27 Inn of France
2 Bus Station	15 St Mary's Tower	28 Turkish School
3 Son et Lumière	16 St Athanasius Gate	(Loggia)
4 St Mary's Church (RC)	17 Koskinou (St John's) Gate	29 Clock tower
5 Church of Dormition	18 Tower of Italy	30 Suleiman Mosque
	19 Gate of Italy	31 Hurmale Medrese
TOWN WALLS	20 St Catherine's Gate	(Ayios Yeoryios)
		32 Aga Mosque
6 Naillac (Arab) Tower		33 Sultan Mustafa Mosque
7 St Paul's Gate	OLD TOWN	34 Baths of Suleiman
8 Arsenal Gate		35 Ayios Fanurios
9 Freedom Gate	21 Temple of Aphrodite	36 Rejab Pasha Mosque
10 St Peter's Tower	22 Art Gallery	37 Ibrahim Pascha Mosque
11 Amboise Gate	23 Old Hospital	38 Ayia Triada
12 Artillery Gate	24 Inn of Auvergne	39 Synagogue
13 St George's Tower	25 Church of the Order (Byz. Museum)	40 Panayia Kastrou
	26 Palace of Villiers de l'Isle-Adam	

Dodecanese. Laid out on a rectangular grid in accordance with the principles of Hippodamus of Miletus, the ancient city extended from the acropolis hill in the west to the east coast of the island. Some of the streets in the considerably smaller medieval town (Street of the Knights,

Homer Street, Hippodamus Street and Pythagoras Street) still follow the ancient grid. The Knights' town, the Collachium, with the Grand Master's Palace, the Hospital and the lodgings of the knights, occupied the northern part of the walled town, with its streets running roughly at right angles. The larger southern part, the Burgus, was occupied by Greeks, while the western part became the Turkish quarter and the smaller eastern part the Jewish quarter, which existed until the Second World War.

The old town, which was included in UNESCO's list of World Heritage Sites in 1988, presents a unique picture of a medieval town, with the imposing series of buildings erected by the Knights of St John and the mosques and other Turkish buildings to give it a distinctive note. In spite of its invasion by mass tourism the town preserves a character of its own with its numerous restaurants, shops and beautiful squares.

The old town of Rhodes, within which no Christian was allowed to live during the Turkish period (1523–1912), is surrounded by a magnificent 4 km (2½ mi.) long circuit of 15th–16th c. walls, with towers, bastions and a moat. Two particularly impressive features are the Amboise Gate, built by Grand Master Emery d'Amboise in 1512, on north-west side of the town, and the Marine Gate of 1468 (with a beautiful relief of the Virgin) on the north-east side, by the Commercial Harbour. Each of the eight "langues" ("tongues") or "nations" (Castile, Provence, etc.) in which the knights were organised was made responsible for the defence of a particular section of the town walls (see town plan). There are good views of the Grand Master's Palace and the old town from the stretch of walls between the Artillery Gate and the Koskinou Gate (access to walls at Grand Master's Palace; open Tue.–Sat. 2.30–3pm). A walk round the town outside the walls (taking a good hour) is also full of interest.

Old town

The busy old town, with its maze of narrow streets and lanes, its domes and minarets, its palms and plane trees, can be entered through the Freedom Gate or the Arsenal Gate. In **Sými Square** are the remains of a temple of Aphrodite of the 3rd c. BC, and on the west side of the square is a gallery displaying work by contemporary Greek artists.

To the south of Sými Square is picturesque **Argyrokastro Square**, with a small fountain constructed from fragments of an Early Christian baptismal font. On the west side of the square is the Old Hospital (mid-14th c.), now occupied by the Archaeological Institute. Facing this is the late 15th c. Auberge (Inn) of the Langue of Auvergne, with a Romanesque inner courtyard. A passage to the south-east leads to the 13th c. St Mary's Church, a church of the Order of St John that now houses an interesting museum of Byzantine art (open 8.30am–3pm). On the south side of the square is the Museum of Folk Art (open Tue.–Sun. 8.30am–3pm), with a collection that includes pottery, woven fabrics and woodcarving of the Turkish period from the Dodecanese.

Diagonally opposite the former church of the Order, in Platía Mousiou, is the massive **Hospital of the Knights**, which dates from 1440. From the inner courtyard a staircase leads up to the large Infirmary ward on the upper floor, which measures 52 × 12 m (171 × 39 ft); in a recess opposite the entrance is a small chapel containing the gravestones of knights. It now houses the Archaeological Museum (open Tue.–Sun. 8.30am–3pm). Among the most important items in the collection are finds from Ialysos, Kameiros and other sites, including two archaic kouroi (6th c. BC) and the funerary stele of Crito and Timariste (end of 5th c. BC), a life-size figure of Aphrodite, an expressive Hellenistic head of Helios (2nd c. BC) and a small crouching figure of Aphrodite known as the Venus of Rhodes (1st c. BC). Also of interest is the rich collection of

◄ *The principal landmark of Rhodes town is the Grand Master's Palace*

vases in Rooms VIII–XXII, round the courtyard, which covers all periods from Mycenaean times onwards

From the north side of the Hospital of the Knights the **Street of the Knights** (Odós Ippotón), one of the principal sights of Rhodes, runs west. In this street, which still preserves the aspect of a 15th–16th c. street, were most of the Auberges (Inns) of the various "nations" in the Order of St John, in which the knights ate in common, discussed the business of the Order and received official visitors. In Turkish times the inns were occupied by well-to-do merchants, who added enclosed wooden balconies so that their womenfolk could look out on the street without being seen. . The most magnificent of the inns is the inn of the French knights, the Auberge de France, built between 1492 and 1503. Above the Gothic-arched doorway are the arms of the Order and of Grand Master Emery d'Amboise.

At the west end of the Street of the Knights, on the highest point in the town, is the **Grand Master's Palace** (open Mon. 12.30–3pm, Tue.–Sun. 8.30am–3pm), originally a massive 14th c. stronghold with a triple circuit of walls. It was restored by Grand Master Pierre d'Aubusson in 1481 after suffering damage in an earthquake. In 1856 it was almost completely destroyed by the explosion of gunpowder in the neighbouring church of St John, which had been used for centuries as a powder magazine, but was rebuilt during the period of Italian occupation (1912–43) on the basis of old plans, but not with absolute fidelity to the original.
   Nor does the internal arrangement follow the original pattern. Notable features of the interior are the many pebble mosaic pavements from the island of Kos, particularly in the Arcaded Hall. In the second hall is a copy of the famous Laocoon group (1st c. AD), one of the finest examples of the Rhodian school of sculpture.
   On the north-east side of the palace are beautiful gardens (entrance in Papagós Street) in which *son et lumière* shows are given in summer. At its south-west corner is the Artillery Gate (St Anthony's Gate), which gives access to the town walls.

To the south of the Grand Master's Palace is a striking 19th c. clock tower. South-east of this is the **Suleiman Mosque** (1523), the largest mosque on the island, with a handsome Renaissance doorway. Facing this, to the south, is the Turkish Library (1794).

To the west of the Suleiman Mosque is **Áyios Yeóryios**, one of the finest churches on Rhodes. Built in the late 14th c. on a four-apsed plan, it was incorporated in a monastery in 1447. A typical Rhodian feature is the series of recesses on the inside and outside of the drum supporting the dome. The Turks converted the church into a Koranic school, known as the Hurmale Medrese ("at the date-palms").

From the Suleiman Mosque Socrates Street (Odós Sokratou), a busy and attractive shopping street, runs east to **Hippocrates Square** (Platía Ippokratou), which is dominated by the twin towers of the Marine Gate. This is the most popular meeting place in the old town, with numerous tavernas and cafés. Here too is the Folk Museum of the Dodecanese, housed in the Kastellania (1503).

To the south-east is the atmospheric **Square of the Jewish Martyrs** (Platía Martyrón Evraión), so called in memory of the Jews deported from Rhodes during the Second World War. In the centre of the square is a modern fountain with three bronze sea-horses. On the north side is the so-called Palace of the Admirality (15th c.), probably in fact the palace of the metropolitan (bishop) of Rhodes.

Hippocrates Square, a popular rendezvous in the old town of Rhodes

To the south of Socrates Street is a picturesque maze of lanes round Fanourios, Homer (both spanned by flying buttresses) and Pythagoras Streets. Numerous mosques give this area a Turkish air, notably the Mosque of Ibrahim Pasha (1531), the oldest in the town, and the Mosque of Sultan Mustafa (1765), in charming Arion Square (Platía Arionos). Opposite the latter are the magnificent Baths of Suleiman. An interesting feature in Fanourios Street is the small Orthodox church of Áyios Fanoúrios, built in Byzantine times (1335; fresco of the founders), partly underground, which was converted into a mosque by the Turks.

Southern old town

The Commercial Harbour (Emborikó Limáni) is the town's principal harbour and ferry port. To the north is the old Mandráki Harbour, which has been in continuous use since 408 BC and is now mainly used by pleasure craft and excursion boats. On the Mandráki breakwater are three disused windmills. On the busy harbour front, which is also the island's transport hub, with a bus station and taxi rank, is the massive New Market Hall (Néa Agorá), with its shops, reasonably priced fish restaurants and cafés. At the northern tip of the breakwater are Fort St Nicholas, built by the Knights about 1400 (round tower 1464–7), and a lighthouse. Flanking the entrance to the harbour are stone columns topped by figures of a stag and hind, the town's heraldic animals. (Red deer are a protected species on Rhodes, and a number of deer are kept in the moat outside the walls). On the east side of the old town is the Akándia Harbour, with a boatyard.

Mandráki Harbour

There are fine views of the town, the island of Sými and the coast of Asia Minor from the hill of Áyios Stéfanos (Mount Smith, named after the British admiral Sydney Smith; 110 m (361 ft)), to the south-west of the old town. This was the acropolis of the ancient city, with the remains of temples, a stadium and a theatre (reconstructed).

Acropolis

Rhodes's old Mandráki Harbour, now used by yachts and excursion boats

Rodíni valley

To the south-west of the town is the beautiful Rodíni valley (reached by way of Odós Stefanou Kazouli; bus from Mandráki), with a park, a small zoo and beautiful walks. Above the valley are several rock-cut tombs, including the so-called Tomb of the Ptolemies.

West coast

★Mount Filérimos

From Rhodes town the route runs along the west coast. The distance to Apolakkiá, excluding side trips, is 82 km (51 mi.). Running south-west from the town, the road comes to the resort of Trianda, with numerous hotels and restaurants. From here a side road runs 5 km (3 mi.) south to Mount Filérimos (267 m (876 ft)), from which there are magnificent views (bus service from Mandráki). This was the acropolis of the ancient city of Ialysos, one of the three city states on the island. There were a series of strongholds on Mount Filérimos from Mycenaean times (c. 1500 BC) onwards. In 1248 it was occupied by the Genoese, in 1306 by the Knights of St John and in 1522 by the Turks. A broad flight of steps led up to the acropolis (open 8.30am–3pm). On the plateau can be seen the foundations of a temple of Athena built in the 3rd c. BC on the site of an older temple. In Early Christian times the site was occupied by a church, which has left its mark in the form of a cruciform baptismal font set into the ground. From the entrance a stepped footpath runs down southward to a Doric fountain-house of the 4th c. BC.

Kremastí

In the little resort of Kremastí (Κρεμαστη) 3 km (2 mi.) west of Trianda, is the church of the Panayía Kremastí, with a fine icon of the Mother of God. There is a great festival here on the feast of the Dormition (August 15th).

★Petaloúdes Valley

At Káto Kalamon (beyond the airport) a road (7 km (4½ mi.)) goes off on the left to Petaloúdes Valley, the Valley of the Butterflies, formerly the haunt in the height of summer of thousands of reddish-brown harlequin moths, a rare species that spent the day settled on tree trunks. Visitors used to clap their hands to make them show their colours in flight, and this eventually drove them away. But even without the "butterflies" this idyllic shady valley is well worth a visit.

From Kalavarda a side trip can be made to Mount Profítis Ilías (798 m (2618 ft)), the second highest hill on the island, returning to the coast road by way of Embonas. Profítis Ilías has a flora unusual in the Greek islands, with pines, spruces and oaks, alpine violets, strawberry trees and orchids. The summit is a closed military area.

Mount Profítis Ilías

On the road from Mount Profítis Ilías to Eleoúsa is one of the most beautiful churches on Rhodes, Áyios Nikólaos Gountoukli ("St Nicholas of the

Áyios Nikólaos Gountoukli

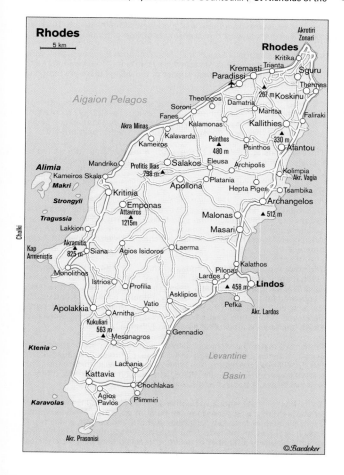

265

Hazelnuts"). Built in the 14th–15th c., it was the church of a monastery of which there are only scanty remains.

★Kameiros

4 km (2½ mi.) west of Kalavarda a road (1.5 km (1 mi.)) goes off to the partly excavated site of the ancient city of Kameiros, which existed from the 6th c. BC to the 6th c. AD. Laid out on terraces on the hillside are the remains of the temple precinct, the agora, cisterns, baths and residential quarters. From the acropolis there are superb views of the extensive and beautifully situated ancient city. Open Tue.–Sun. 8.30am–3pm.

Kamíros Skála

14 km (9 mi.) south of ancient Kameiros is the little fishing village of Kamíros Skála (Καμειρος Σκαλα), from which a caique (large fishing boat) can be taken to the island of Khálki. 2 km (1¼ mi.) south-west of this is the Kastellos, the best preserved castle of the Knights on Rhodes.

Kritinía

Further south, in the hills above the coast, is the pretty little village of Kritinía (Κρητηνια), in a beautiful setting. From Áyios Ioánnis, a church of rather archaic aspect, there is a good view of the Kastellos. The road continues south, against the imposing backdrop of Mount Ataviros.

Émbonas

A rewarding side trip (4 km (2½ mi.)) is to Émbonas (Εμπωνας), the "wine capital" of Rhodes, which attracts visitors with its "folk evenings" and wine-tastings. In the busy main square of the village there are tempting displays of souvenirs.

Monólithos

The road – for part of the way a magnificent highway running high above the coast – continues to the dying hamlet of Monólithos (Μονολιθος). 2 km (1¼ mi.) south-west, magnificently situated at a height of 280 m (919 ft), is an imposing castle of the Knights built in 1476.

Apolakkiá

The road ends at Apolakkiá (Απολακκια), a quiet village little visited by tourists. Beyond this is a stretch of wild and lonely coastal scenery.

East coast

This route runs down the east coast to the southern tip of the island. The distance to Kattaviá, excluding side trips, is 88 km (55 mi.). Along the whole length of the coast, particularly between Rhodes town and Arkhángelos, are beautiful sandy beaches, inevitably lined by large hotels.

Kallithéa

The road runs south from Rhodes town. In 7 km (4½ mi.) a side road (3 km (2 mi.)) goes off on the left to the bathing resort and former spa of Kallithéa, surrounded by palm trees. The springs, which were already frequented for their healing qualities in antiquity, have now dried up, but the spa buildings, built by Italian architects in the 1930s and partly destroyed during the Second World War, are now being renovated. Below the town is a beautiful small sandy beach.

Faliráki

From here the route continues, either on the coast road, lined by large hotels, or by way of the village of Koskinoú, picturesquely situated on a hill, to Faliráki (Φαλιρακι), the island's large new tourist centre. This hotel village developed in the 1980s, with its long sandy beach, offers all that the hearts of bathers and sunbathers can desire.

Afántou

To the east of the unspoiled village of Afántou (Αφαντου) is the Katholiki Afántou church, which incorporates parts of an Early Christian church. From the bathing resort of Kolýmbia, 4 km (2½ mi.) south, a side trip (3 km (2 mi.)) can be made to Eptá Piyés (Seven Springs)an idyllic little green valley with a number of tavernas (reached on a path from the car park on the Kolýmbia–Arkhipolis road).

From Kolýmbia a road goes off on the left to the abandoned Tsambíka convent (2.5 km (1½ mi.)). The last section of the road must be covered on foot, but the effort is rewarded by the spectacular views of the coast and the inland scenery. To the south, below the convent, is Tsambíka beach (fine sand), one of the most beautiful beaches on the island.

Moní Tsambíka

Arkhángelos (Αρχαγγελος), the largest village on the island, is an attractive little place, dominated by the tower, in "wedding-cake" style, of the church of the Archangel Michael. On a hill to the south of the village are the ruins of a castle of the Knights. To the east, round Stégna, are beautiful unfrequented beaches. Outside the village, to the south of the road to Lindos, is a chapel dedicated to St Theodore, with fine frescos of 1377.

Arkhángelos

A little way inland from the coast road, surrounded by orange and lemon groves, is the pretty village of Málonas (Μαλωνας). To the north, outside the village, is the church of Ayía Irini (1728; originally 15th c.). The route continues by way of Mássari, passing the 14th c. church of Áyios Yeóryios Lorima (with frescos in popular style), to Lindos (see below). Shortly before the road reaches Lindos there is a magnificent view of the town. Beyond Lindos the route continues through beautiful country to Lardos, then south-west to Yennadion.

Málonas

From Klotari a road runs north-west to Asklipío (Ασκληπειο), with the fine church of the Dormition (13th–14th c.), on a Latin-cross ground-plan. Commandingly situated above the village is a ruined castle, probably dating from the 15th c.

Asklipío

3 km (2 mi.) beyond Yennadion a road goes off on the right to Lakhaniá (Λαχανια), a village discovered in the 1980s by foreign dropouts. It has an attractive little square. On the south side of the village is the church of St Irene, with a baroque tower and an Early Christian (6th c.) font. 6 km (4 mi.) south of Lakhaniá, in a wide bay, is Plimmiri, which has a beach of dark sand.

Lakhaniá

The road continues, passing the abandoned monastery of Áyios Pávlos, to Kattaviá (Κατταβια), the most southerly village on the island. Its most notable feature is the church of the Dormition, the oldest part of which, the domed cruciform structure, is believed to date from the 14th c.

Kattaviá

The southern tip of Rhodes, the Prasonísi (Πρασονησι) peninsula, which is joined to the main island only by a narrow isthmus, can be reached only by all-terrain vehicles or on foot (9 km (6 mi.)). On its lonely beach, fringed by white dunes, are a number of simple tavernas. The strong winds offer good wind-surfing.

Prasonísi

★★Lindos

With its magnificent situation between two bays and its attractive townscape of low whitewashed houses under a medieval castle and an ancient acropolis, Lindos is, after Rhodes town, the island's principal tourist attraction.

History Remains of the neolithic period and finds in Mycenaean cemeteries bear witness to the occupation of this site, on the island's only natural harbour, from the 3rd millennium BC onwards. During the Dorian period Lindos – a city mentioned in Homer – was the most powerful city state on the island (ahead of Ialysos and Kameiros), owning more than half its total area. About 700 BC it founded a colony at Gela in Sicily.

The city's heyday was in the 7th and 6th c. under the tyrant (sole ruler) Cleobulus, one of the Seven Sages, who built a temple to the goddess of Lindos on the acropolis. Important historical sources found here were

The town of Lindos is beautifully situated between its popular beach and the medieval castle crowning the hill

the Temple Chronicle of Lindos and a list of priests for the years 375–327 BC.

The city continued to develop during the Hellenistic period and into late Roman times. In the 6th c. AD a Byzantine castle was built on the acropolis, and in the 15th c. the Knights of St John built this up into a mighty stronghold. During the 15th, 16th and 17th c. the shipowners and sea-captains of Lindos grew wealthy, leaving handsome mansions to bear witness to their prosperity. The economy of the town is now centred on the tourist trade.

Lindos has good bathing **beaches**. Below the town is beautiful Pallas Bay, and on the other side of the acropolis is the almost completely enclosed and very beautiful St Paul's Bay. The Apostle Paul is said to have sought shelter from a storm here during his voyage from Ephesus to Syria in AD 51. There is a small chapel dedicated to St Paul.

Town Just before Lindos the road from Rhodes town goes over a low pass, beyond which there is a fascinating view of the bay, the town and the acropolis. Cars must park in Platía Eleftherias, at the entrance to the town, which is closed to all but pedestrian and donkey-borne traffic. Acropolis Street (Odós Akropoleos), lined by cafés, souvenir shops and travel agencies, leads into the town. The houses in the picturesque little lanes of the town date from the 17th and 18th c., apart from one Turkish house of 1599. Particularly notable is the Sea-Captain's House in the southern part of the town, whose façade of undressed stone has characteristic relief decoration.

On the way up the hill, to the left, there is a fine view of the harbour and a circular tomb on a hill to the north of it known as the Tomb of

Cleobulus, though in fact it probably dates from the Hellenistic period. There is a rewarding walk to the tomb (45 min.).

To the left of the road up to the acropolis is the beautiful church of the Panayía, built in the 14th c. and restored and enlarged in 1489–90 by Pierre d'Aubusson, Grand Master of the Order of St John from 1476 to 1503. It has a richly decorated and gilded iconostasis and a fine pebble mosaic pavement. On the barrel-vaulted roof and the dome are ceiling paintings of 1779.

Church of the Panayía

A short distance to the north-east is the oldest church on Rhodes, Áyios Yeóryios Khostos (8th–9th c.), with frescos dating from the Iconoclastic period, which are very rare. To the south of the square is an impressive rock-cut tomb of about 200 BC, known as the Tomb of Archocrates, which originally had an imposing façade with blind arcading.

Áyios Yeóryios Khostos

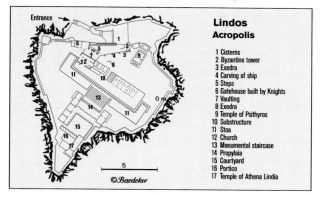

Lindos

Acropolis

Entrance

1 Cisterns
2 Byzantine tower
3 Exedra
4 Carving of ship
5 Steps
6 Gatehouse built by Knights
7 Vaulting
8 Exedra
9 Temple of Psithyros
10 Substructure
11 Stoa
12 Church
13 Monumental staircase
14 Propylaia
15 Courtyard
16 Portico
17 Temple of Athena Lindia

© Baedeker

From the entrance to the acropolis a stepped path leads up to a small square with three cisterns and a Byzantine tower on its south side. Beside it is an exedra with a base on which there were probably votive statues. An inscription of the 3rd/4th c. on the rear of the exedra records that a priest named Agiochartos had planted olive trees on the acropolis. To the right of this, on a sheer rock face, is a carving of a ship, commemorating a victory by Admiral Hegesandros of Miklon in the 2nd c. BC. To the left of the modern steps leading up to the acropolis can be seen remains of the ancient steps and, higher up, steps dating from the period of occupation by the Knights. A vaulted gateway leads into the ground floor of the buildings erected by the Knights. Under the vaulting to the south are ancient steps hewn from the rock.

★★Acropolis

Open Mon. 12.30–3pm, Tue.–Sun. 8.30am–3pm

Beyond this is an exedra of the 3rd c. BC, with an inscription recording that a priest named Pamphillidas commissioned the famous sculptor Phyles to create a statue of him. To the rear is a temple of the 3rd c. AD dedicated to the daemon Psithyros, a seer. The 87 m (285 ft) long stoa, dating from the end of the 3rd c. BC, is one of the finest examples of Hellenistic architecture in Greece. To the right of the stoa is the Byzantine church of St John (13th c.).

A monumental staircase 21 m (70 ft) wide leads up to propylaia of the early 3rd c. BC, in the rear wall of which – as in the Propylaia on the Acropolis in Athens – are five doorways leading into the sacred precinct. This consists of a courtyard surrounded by columns, on the south side of which an Ionic stoa was added in the 2nd c. AD, and a comparatively modest but artistically impressive temple of Athena Lindia, rebuilt in 342

BC after a fire as an amphiprostyle temple, occupying the site of an earlier shrine of the 7th c. BC. From here there is a fantastic view of St Paul's Bay (see below).

Boukopion

From the north end of the town, on the Vigli peninsula, there are good views of the acropolis, the temple of Athena Lindia and the cave below the temple in which the goddess was originally worshipped. Scattered about the area are the scanty remains of the Boukopion, in which bulls were sacrificed.

Neighbouring islands

Some 6.5 km (4 mi.) west of Rhodes, are the islands of **Alimniá** (Αλιμνια) and **Khálki** (Χαλκη). Alimniá is uninhabited, but has beaches that can be reached from Khálki by fishing-boat. Khálki itself can be reached by hydrofoil from Rhodes town or fishing-boat from Kameíros Skála (arrangements must be made for overnight accommodation, since the boat sails back only on the following day).

Khálki is a small rocky island with an area of only 28 sq. km (11 sq. mi.); the chief place, Emborió or Nimborió, has a population of around 300. Near Emborió, in Pótamos Bay, is a popular sandy beach. 3 km (2 mi.) west of the village is the island's former capital, Khorió, where apart from two old churches there are only ruins. On a hill to the south of Khorió is a castle built by the Knights of John; the ascent of the hill is rewarded by magnificent views from the top.

Salamis   H 6

Saronic Islands
Area: 93 sq. km (36 sq. mi.)
Altitude: 0–365 m (0–1200 ft)
Population: 20,500
Chief place: Salamína (Kouloúri)

Ferries between Pérama (5 km (3 mi.) west of Piraeus) and Paloúkia, between Piraeus and Paloúkia/Kamatero/Selinia and between Néo Pérama and Faneroméni. Bus services on the island.

Salamis (modern Greek Salamína, Σαλαμινα), the largest of the Saronic Islands, lies immediately west of Piraeus, closing off the Bay of Eleusis (Ormos Elefsina) on the south. Its limestone hills, much eroded by karstic action, bear a scanty growth of trees. The island's agriculture is only on a modest scale, and many of the inhabitants work in Athens and in the industrial installations (refineries, shipyards) that have been established round the naval base in the north-east of the island and at the east end of the Bay of Eleusis. At weekends the island attracts crowds of visitors from Athens and round about, but it is not a place to spend your holiday – though there are bathing beaches on the south coast (Paralia, Perani, Peristeria, Karakiani). In 1997 archaeologists discovered a cave at the southern tip of the island in which Euripides is believed to have written some of his plays.

History The island owes its name (from *shalam*, "rest, peace") to Phoenician settlers from Cyprus. For long a bone of contention between Athens and Megara, it was finally won for Athens by Solon and Peisistratus in 598 BC. The ancient capital lay on a tongue of land between the bays of Kamateró and Ambeláki on the east coast; then in the 6th c. BC it was moved south-west to Ambeláki, where there are remains of the acropolis and, visible under water, port installations.

Salamis is celebrated as the scene of the **great naval battle** on September 27th–28th 480 BC in which the Athenians under Themistocles, their resources depleted by war, inflicted a devastating defeat with their force of 378 triremes on a much larger Persian fleet of over 1200 vessels and thus finally frustrated Xerxes' plans to expand westward into Europe. The battle – which Aeschylus, an eyewitness, took as the theme of

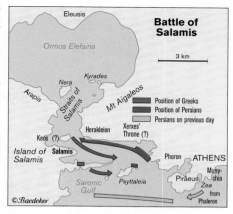

his tragedy "The Persians" – was fought in the waters to the east of Salamis, between the island of Áyios Yeóryios to the north and the island of Psyttaleia and the Kynosoura ("Dog's Tail") peninsula to the south. The decisive factors in the Greek victory were the manoeuvrability of their triremes and their familiarity with the area. Xerxes is said to have watched the battle from Mount Aigaleos, above Pérama.

Sights

The chief place on the island is Salamína or Kouloúri (pop. 20,000), a not particularly attractive town at the north end of a long inlet on the west coast. The only feature of tourist interest is a small archaeological museum. 3 km (2 mi.) east is the island's principal port, Paloúki, the home port of the Greek navy.

Salamína

6 km (4 mi.) west of Salamína on a scenically beautiful road is the Faneroméni convent, with a much revered icon of the Mother of the God and a large fresco of the Last Judgment with over 3000 figures. The convent was founded in 1661 on the site of an ancient sanctuary, reusing architectural elements from the older buildings. To the south are the remains of the little fort of Boudorón (6th c. BC). At the foot of the hill on which the convent stands is the landing-stage used by the ferry to Néo Pérama.

Faneroméni convent

6 km (4 mi.) south of Salamína is the village of Enántio, with two churches of the 12th and 13th c. Further south-west is the 18th c. monastery of Áyios Nikólaos, in the construction of which stonework from an earlier 12th c. building was incorporated.

There are scanty remains of Mycenaean settlements at many places on the island.

Sámos

L/M 6

Islands of the northern and eastern Aegean
Area: 476 sq. km (184 sq. mi.)
Altitude: 0–1433 m (0–4702 ft)
Population: 33,000.
Chief place: Sámos town

The harbour, Sámos town

Airport 3 km (2 mi.) west of Pythagório. Air connections with Athens and Salonica. Charter flights. Principal port: Sámos town. Other ports: Pythagório (hydrofoils in direction of Kos) and Karlóvasi (ferries to Chios, etc.). Shipping connections with Piraeus, Salonica, Rhodes, Ikaría, Chios, Agathonísi, Foúrni, Kálymnos, Kos, Léros, Lésbos, Lemnos, Náxos, Páros, Pátmos, Sýros. Ferries between Sámos and Kuĺadasœ (Turkey). In the holiday season excursion boats from Pythagório to Kuĺadasœ.

The island of Sámos (Σαμος) in the eastern Aegean has other attractions as well as the sweet wine for which it is famed. This hilly, green and well wooded island offers good bathing and excellent walking, and it also has the site of one of the most important sanctuaries and cultural centres of the ancient world, the Heraion.

Geographically an outpost of Asia Minor, it is separated from the Turkish coast (Dilek peninsula) by a strait only 1.9 km (1¼ mi.) wide. It rises in the centre to a height of 1163 m (3816 ft) in Mount Karvouni and in the west to 1433 m (4702 ft). Of the Greek islands only Crete, Euboea and Samothrace have higher hills.

The island's main sources of income are agriculture (wine, olives, oranges, figs, tobacco, grain, fruit, vegetables, etc.), shipbuilding and fishing. In the last twenty years tourism (including "agro-tourism" – country holidays) has developed on a considerable scale and now accounts for over half the island's income.

The **wine** of Sámos, which has been produced since ancient times, was the first Greek wine to be recognised as of high quality. In the past it was mainly prized as a sweet aperitif and as communion wine for the Catholic church. Nowadays the island's wine-growing area of some 1800 hectares (4500 acres) is still mainly devoted to the production of white muscatel grapes, but the dry wines that are now more popular are also being produced on an increasing scale.

Along Sámos's much indented coast there are numerous small coves and inlets with shingle **beaches**, many of them accessible only on foot or by boat. Long beaches fringing lowland plains are to be found only in the south-east between Iraíon and Mykáli (near Pythagório) and in the south-west between Votsolákia, Órmos Marathókampos and Baios. There are beaches of fine sand only on the south coast. To the east of Pythagório, opposite Cape Mykáli in Turkey, is the gently sloping beach of Psilí Ámmos, the most suitable beach for small children on the island. There is a sandy beach of the same name to the west of Votsalákia.

History The first inhabitants of Samos, probably Carians, were displaced at an early stage by Ionians, who used the island as a base for the conquest and settlement of the nearby coast of Asia Minor. In the second half of the 6th c. BC, under the tyrant (sole ruler) Polycrates, the island grew wealthy and powerful. Like other tyrants of the period, Polycrates erected magnificent buildings and fostered the arts; among the beneficiaries of his patronage was the poet Anacreon. Although allied with Persia, he was crucified by the Persian satrap Oroetes about 522 BC and succeeded by his brother Syloson, ruling subject to Persian overlordship. Samos fought on the Persian side in the battle of Salamis, but in 479 it destroyed Xerxes' fleet. A rising in 440 BC against Athenian rule was repressed by Pericles, and thereafter, until the end of the Peloponnesian War, Samos became a base for the Athenian fleet. In the 3rd c. BC it seems to have belonged to the empire of the Ptolemies, and from 190 to 143 BC it was part of the Roman Empire.

Samos was the home of the mathematician and philosopher Pythagoras (c. 570 to c. 496/497 BC), the philosopher Epicurus (341–271 BC) and the astronomer Aristarchus (c. 310 to c. 230 BC), who anticipated the Copernican conception of the world and tried to measure the distance between the earth and the moon.

In subsequent centuries Sámos was held by Byzantines, Arabs (from AD 824), Venetians and Genoese. After the island was plundered by the Turks in 1475 the population emigrated to Chíos and Lésbos; then in 1562 it was resettled, and thereafter was granted considerable privileges. During the war of Greek independence the islanders held out against the Turks, and in 1824 the Turkish fleet was destroyed off Pythagório. Under the London Protocol of 1832 Sámos was declared a principality tributary to the Ottoman Empire, ruled by a prince who was to be appointed by the Sultan but who must be a Christian. Its flag was to bear a Greek cross.

Monument to Pythagoras in Pythagório

During the Tripolitanian war of 1912 Italian troops drove out the Turkish occupying forces, and after further military action the island was reunited with Greece in 1913.

In spite of repeated forest fires Sámos's tree cover has regenerated, and it is still one of the greenest islands in the Aegean.

Sámos town

Since 1832 the island's capital has been the little town of Sámos (Vathý; pop. 8000), which was founded in that year. It lies in a semicircle round its harbour in the sheltered inlet of Vathý, an arm of the sea 5 km (3 mi.)

long and up to 1.5 km (1 mi.) across. To the south of the ferry port extends a string of cafés. Near the Aeolis Hotel is the Roman Catholic church, part of a former warehouse where communion wine was stored for export.

500 m beyond this is the real centre of the town, Pythagoras Square. Under four tall palms is a large marble lion, erected in 1930 to commemorate 100 years of liberation from Turkish rule.

The houses of the town climb up the slopes of the hill with its vineyards and olive groves to the upper town of Áno Vathý. The oldest part of the town, it has preserved its village-like character with its picturesque little streets and old houses with narrow windows and wooden balconies. Innumerable stepped lanes run up the hill: here, thankfully, there are no mopeds to shatter the quiet of the town.

★Archaeological Museum

Vathý's main street runs parallel to the harbour front, leading to the town's small public garden. Adjoining this is the Archaeological Museum (open Tue.–Sun. 8.30am–3pm), housed in the former residence of the Prince of Sámos and a new building financed by the Volkswagen Foundation and opened in 1987. It displays material recovered in the German excavations of the Heraion from 1910 onwards (see below).

The main hall of the museum had to be specially enlarged to accommodate the most sensational find made in the Heraion, the colossal marble figure, 4.8 m (16 ft) high, of an Archaic kouros (c. 580–570 BC), a votive statue from the Sacred Way. Also displayed in the hall is an Archaic over-lifesize female figure (c. 570 BC), a counterpart to the famous Hera of Cheramyes, found in the Heraion in 1879, that is now in the Pergamon Museum in Berlin.

In the room to the left are the base and three of the original six figures in a group by Geneleos, a sculptor of the archaic period (c. 560 BC). The room to the right contains Hellenistic and Roman sculpture. On the upper floor is prehistoric material (pottery, ivories, bronzes). Particularly notable is the large collection of bronze griffins' heads, decorative features from large metal cauldrons.

Byzantine Museum

The Byzantine Museum was opened in 1998 in the new episcopal palace. The collection includes fine icons of the last six centuries, liturgical utensils and vestments.

Other sights

Mytilíni

12 km (7½ mi.) south-west of Sámos town is the little agricultural town of Mytilíni (Μυτιλήνη; pop. 2500), one of the few settlements on the island without a view of the sea. It was founded in 1700 by settlers

The focal point of Vathý is Pythagoras Square, with a large marble lion commemorating the liberation of Greece from the Turks

from the island of Lésbos, then known as Mytilíni. It has a very interesting **Palaeontological Museum**.

The museum displays finds from the palaeontological excavations carried out between 1887 and 1963 in valleys and river beds round the town. Among them are fossils of various species of mammals from Asia, which 10 million years ago was linked with Sámos, including rhinoceroses, mammoths up to 3 m (10 ft) high, primeval dwarf horses, short-necked giraffes, antelopes and hyenas. Later tectonic movements separated the island from Asia, and these animals, confined to this small island, became extinct.

From Sámos town a road runs 15 km (9 mi.) south to the friendly little port of Pythagório (Πυθαγορειο) or Tigáni on the south coast, occupying the site of the ancient city of Samos. This little town of 1500 inhabitants, with a well-preserved old town and a beautiful seafront promenade, has developed into a popular tourist centre, with the island's largest number of beds for visitors (5000).

★**Pythagório**

The original name of the town was Tigáni, but it was renamed Pythagório in 1955 in honour of the Samian philosopher Pythagoras, who is commemorated by a modern bronze sculpture on the eastern breakwater protecting the harbour, now used mainly by fishing-boats. Larger vessels, ferries and hydrofoils (from Pátmos and Kos) moor on the longer western breakwater, constructed in the 19th c. This was the site of the first man-made harbour in the Mediterranean, constructed in the 6th c. BC in the time of the tyrant Polycrates. There are also remains of the 6.5 km (4 mi.) long circuit of walls that surrounded the town in the 4th c. BC and are said to have had 35 towers and 12 gates.

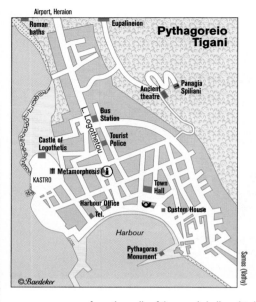

On the **Kástro Hill** are the modern church of the Transfiguration (Metamórfosis; 1932) and a castle built by the Greek freedom fighter Lykourgos Logothetis in 1822–4, incorporating fragments of ancient stonework. From here there is a good view of Cape Mykali on the Turkish mainland. Close by is the site of a Hellenistic villa, on which a Christian basilica was built in the 5th c.

In the Town Hall, behind the harbour front, is a small **archaeological museum** (open Tue.–Thu. 9am–2pm, Sun. 9am–2pm, Fri., Sat. noon–2pm), with archaic and Hellenistic funerary stelae, portraits of Roman Emperors and a seated figure of Aiacus, father of Polycrates.

In the eastern part of the site of the ancient city is the monastery of the **Panayía Spilianí**. Here too is a cave containing a small chapel. The water dripping from the walls of the cave is believed to be holy and wonder-working. In a depression below the monastery are the remains of an ancient theatre.

Further north is the entrance to the ★**Tunnel of Eupalinus** or Eupalineion, an underground aqueduct 1036 m (3399 ft) long constructed by Eupalinus of Megara in the 6th c. BC. Between 1.6 and 1.8 m (5 ft 3 in. and 5 ft 11 in.) high and wide, it has been made passable for visitors (open Tue.–Sun. 9am–2pm). The water flowed in clay pipes at an average gradient of 0.5° from the far side of the hill into the city. About 425 m (1395 ft) from the south entrance can be seen the point where the two shafts, one driven from each end, met one another, making an almost perfect join. This water supply system remained in use for around a thousand years.

On the northern outskirts of Pythagório, near the shore, are the well preserved remains of a large **Roman bath-house** of the 2nd c. AD.

Doryssa Bay

On the road from Pythagório to the airport is the extensive holiday complex of Doryssa Bay, modelled on a traditional Samian village. The rates for accommodation here are very high.

The complex includes villas in neoclassical style, houses with

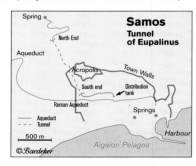

Samian Heraion

wooden balconies, fishermen's cottages and a village square with a church and a coffee-house. The **Folk Museum** displays the equipment and implements used by peasant farmers, basket-makers, fishermen and beekeepers. Potters, blacksmiths, barbers and bakers can sometimes be seen at work in their traditional work-places.

9 km (5½ mi.) west of Pythagório is the Heraion, the sanctuary of the goddess Hera, which was linked with the ancient city of Samos by the Sacred Way. The Sacred Way was lined with huge figures of kouroi and other votive statues, among them the large kouros and the group by Geneleos now to be seen in the Archaeological Museum in Sámos town; there is a copy of the Geneleos group on its original site.   ★Heraion

According to an ancient legend Ionian settlers led by Procles found a wooden image caught in the branches of a willow tree at the mouth of the river Imbrasos. Recognising it as a cult image of Hera, they set up an altar beside the tree, and this altar was followed by others. The seventh was an altar by the sculptor **Rhoicus** (*c.* 550 BC; partly rebuilt), which in size and magnificence was surpassed only by the great altar of Zeus at Pergamon.

To the west of the altar is the **Temple of Hera**. The modest wooden Temple I (first half of 8th c. BC) and Temple II (after 670 BC) were succeeded by a colossal stone structure, Temple III, built by Rhoicus and Theodorus in 570–550 BC. This covered an area 105 × 52.5 m (345 × 172 ft) and had a double peristyle of 104 Ionic columns 18 m (60 ft) high. Soon afterwards this temple was destroyed, and Polycrates thereupon built a new one, Temple IV. Covering an area 112.2 m (368 ft) by 55.16 m (181 ft), this was the largest temple ever designed by Greek architects, but – like other gigantic Ionic temples – it remained unfinished. Nothing of this temple now survives except its massive foundations and a single

A Despot with a Philosophical Turn

Polycrates was tyrant of Sámos from 538 to 522 BC. The Greek word *tyrannos* meant an absolute ruler, one who gained or usurped power by his personal authority rather than by election: it did not necessarily have the modern meaning of tyrant. Polycrates could be regarded, more charitably, as an enlightened despot in the 18th c. sense; but he did have some characteristics of a tyrant in the modern meaning of the word.

His brief reign was a period of military successes and a brilliant court. "Wherever he turned his arms, " wrote the Greek historian Herodotus in the 5th c. BC, "success waited on him. He had a fleet of a hundred pentaconters [ships driven by fifty oars] and bowmen to the number of a thousand. Herewith he plundered all, without distinction of friend or foe" (Rawlinson's translation). As with many tyrants of his time, the wealth accumulated by Polycrates served not only to support a life of luxury and splendour but also to promote art and learning. He summoned to his court the leading writers and scholars of the day. It has been said that everything he did went the way he wished except his death – and even that was in keeping with his life.

Polycrates, a scion of an old Samian noble family, was a prosperous and influential merchant on Sámos who in the course of a conflict between the ruling aristocracy of Sámos and the rising middle classes seized power during a festival in honour of Hera in 538 BC with the help of his two brothers Pantagnostus and Syloson and the tyrant of Naxos, Lygdamis. For some years he shared power with his brothers, but then had one murdered and the other driven off the island, and from 532

BC was sole ruler of Sámos. In his external policies he showed the same absence of scruple. He was the first Greek to practise the traditional trade of piracy on a large scale: in the words of Herodotus, "Polycrates entertained a design which no other Greek, so far as we know, ever formed before him, unless it were Minos the Cnossian ... the design of gaining the empire of the sea." With a war fleet of a size never before seen in the Aegean he spread terror throughout the eastern Mediterranean with his piratical raids. His opponents and his victims had nothing to match his ships – oared galleys of a new and particularly seaworthy type, and especially his fast and manoeuvrable triremes with their three banks of oars. Within a short time innumerable islands and coastal cities in Asia Minor were paying tribute to the ruler of Sámos. Polycrates himself liked to say that a friend to whom he gave back something he had taken from him was more grateful than one from whom he had taken nothing.

But it was not only piracy that contributed to Polycrates' wealth. He carried on trade with the entire Greek world, but here too he was hampered by no scruples. On one occasion he called in all silver coins in circulation, replaced part of the silver by lead and returned the debased coins to circulation.

Polycrates was a contradictory character: as one scholar has said, on the one hand he resembled a Persian despot, on the other a Greek philosopher. To satisfy his lust for power and his greed for money he was prepared to resort to any means – deceit, treachery, cruelty gambling. Only those who were devoted to his service could hope to benefit from his munificence – in particular the soldiers who fought for him, for whose dependants he provided pensions. But he also brought his island great prosperity and a unique cultural flowering. During his reign Sámos was – again in Herodotus's words – the most famous city in the world. His court was as sumptuous as that of any Asian ruler and was entirely given up to the pursuit of pleasure and luxury. Adjoining his palace was another one in which he housed hetaeras from Lesbos so

Only a single column in the Heraion is left to commemorate the Samian tyrant Polycrates

that they might initiate the young men of the island, to the accompaniment of music, dancing and wine, into the most refined arts of love.

But Polycrates was also greatly interested in art and learning, inviting to his island the leading artists and scholars of the day, including the poet Anacreon, from the Ionian island of Teos, the engineer Eupalinus of Megara and the mathematician and philosopher Pythagoras (c. 580–496 BC). But Pythagoras was so disgusted by the hedonism of the court and Polycrates' ruthless tyranny that he left Sámos and moved to Croton in southern Italy, where he founded the religious and philosophical community of the Pythagoreans.

Polycrates was also famed for carrying out "three of the greatest works in all Greece" (Herodotus again): the breakwater protecting the harbour of Pythagoreion, the tunnel of Eupalinus and the sanctuary of Hera ("the largest of all the temples known to us"), though the Heraion was never actually completed. These three monuments were all designed to provide work for the population but also to keep them poor – as Aristotle noted in his "Politics" in discussing the nature of tyrants.

Polycrates' legendary good fortune, many thought, could not last for ever. Herodotus tells the story of the emerald ring that he threw into the sea in order to avoid making the gods envious of his luck; but soon the ring was found in the belly of a fish caught by a Samian fisherman and returned to the tyrant – a sure sign, in Herodotus's views, that he would come to a miserable end.

For the Persian empire, then expanding westwards, Polycrates was an obstacle which had to be removed. The Persian satrap Oroetes, knowing his greed for gold, lured him to the mainland of Asia Minor with the promise of riches; and there Polycrates did indeed come to a miserable end – crucified on Mount Mykale, which looks out on to Sámos.

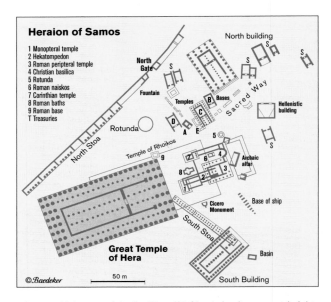

Heraion of Samos

1 Monopteral temple
2 Hekatompedon
3 Roman peripteral temple
4 Christian basilica
5 Rotunda
6 Roman naiskos
7 Corinthian temple
8 Roman baths
9 Roman base
T Treasuries

column, which was originally 20 m (65 ft) – twice its present height. Finally a small peripteral temple of 4 × 6 columns (Temple V) was built close to the altar to house the cult image.

In 1963 the excavators claimed to have found the remains of the willow branch near the altar, though this claim is disputed. 40 m (130 ft) east of the surviving column is a Roman exedra built in honour of the two Ciceros, Quintus Tullius and Marcus Tullius. Nearby is the apse of an Early Christian basilica (5th or 6th c.).

The high water-table made excavation of the site difficult, but the excavators were able to identify further remains, including the basin in which the image of Hera was annually bathed.

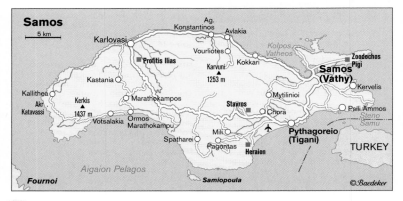

Tour of the island

The scenery along the north coast of Sámos, which for most of its length falls steeply down to the sea, is particularly attractive, with narrow valleys, terraced hillsides and secluded coves.

11 km (7 mi.) west of Sámos town is the former fishing village of Kokkári (Κοκκαρς; pop. 1200), which has developed in recent years into the largest holiday resort on the north coast, particularly popular with young visitors. It has preserved the old town and has so far been spared the intrusion of large new hotels that would destroy the village-like atmosphere.

Kokkári

Beyond Avlákia (20 km (13 mi.)) a road goes off on the left to the wine-growing village of Vourliótes (Βουρλιωτες; 3 km (2 mi.)), whose once pretty village square has been spoiled by tasteless modernisation. From here you can either walk to the picturesque wine-growing village of Manolátes (Μανολατες; 1 hour) or drive to the remote Vronda monastery, founded in 1566 (2 km (1¼ mi.)). From the monastery there is an attractive path to Kokkári (1½ hours).

Vourliótes

Back on the coast road, the route continues to Áyios Konstantínos (26 km (16 mi.)) and the second largest town on the island, Karlovási (Καρλοβασι; 32 km (20 mi.); pop. 5500). This little port town, extending for several kilometres along the coast and also reaching inland, is the economic centre of western Sámos (export of wine). Most of the hotels are round the harbour. The steep hill above the harbour, along whose slopes extends the old part of the town, is topped by a little church dedicated to the Holy Trinity. On the eastern outskirts of the town are disused tanneries, soap factories and warehouses – relics of the town's once prosperous 19th c. industries.

Karlovási

The road ends a few kilometres beyond Karlovási, and the remote and beautiful west coast of the island can be reached only on all-terrain vehicles or on foot, following steep paths. The return to Sámos town can be through the hilly interior by way of Marathókampos, Koumaradéi and Khóra. Marathókampos, the largest inland village on the island, clings to the hillside above the coastal plain, with magnificent sea views.

Western Sámos

The ascent of Mount Kérkis (1437 m (4715 ft)), at the west end of the island, is strenuous but very rewarding. From the little bathing resort of Votsolákia the route (well waymarked) runs by way of the still-occupied monastery of the Evangelístria (675 m (2215 ft)) and the chapel of Profítis Ilías (1150 m (3773 ft)) to the summit, from where there are views of the Aegean and the hills of Asia Minor. The ascent takes 4 hours, the return 3 hours. The best route back is by way of Marathókampos, which takes an hour longer but is not so steep.

Mount Kérkis

Half way between Sámos and Léros, off the west coast of Asia Minor, is the little island of Agathonísi (Αγαθονησι; area 13 sq. km (5 sq. mi.)), which has local shipping connections with Sámos, Pátmos, Lipsí and Arkí. Formerly called Gaidouronísi, it is the most northerly island in the Dodecanese. It was ancient Tragia, where in 76 BC the young Julius Caesar was captured by pirates.

The whole coastline of this karstic island, 7 km (4¼ mi.) long by up to 3 km (2 mi.) across, is ringed by sheer cliffs, with few sheltered anchorages in which occasionally a few yachts are to be seen. Off the north, east and south coasts of the island are seven uninhabited islets, some land on which is farmed from Agathonísi. The remaining 130 inhabitants live modestly by farming and fishing. With no sandy beaches and no ancient monuments, Agathonísi has remained completely untouched by tourism – an example, now difficult to find, of a totally unspoiled Aegean island.

Agathonísi

Samothrace   K 3

Island of the north-east Aegean
Area: 178 sq. km (69 sq. mi.)
Altitude: 0–1611 m (0–5286 ft).
Population: 2900
Chief place: Samothráki (Khóra)

Port: Kamariótissa. Ferry connections with Alexandroúpolis, Kavála and
Lemnos. Bus services on the island. Boats to beaches.

Samothrace (Samothráki, Σαμοθρακη), lying 40 km (25 mi.) off the coast
of Thrace, is the most north-easterly of the Greek islands. It is an island
of great scenic beauty with a regular coastline, rising to a height of 1611
m (5286 ft) in Mount Fengári, from which, according to Homer, Poseidon
watched the fighting round Troy. Above the green, well watered coastal
plain rises a wild and rugged mountain region with an interesting variety of fauna. The sanctuary of the Cabiri is one of the most impressive
ancient sites in Greece.
    The inhabitants live by arable farming (particularly corn, fruit and veg-
etables). There is no package tourism on the island: there are only a few
hotels of limited capacity, which in July and August are almost fully
booked by Greek holidaymakers; advance reservation is therefore advisable. On the north coast and in the larger villages accommodation can
be found in private houses. Apart from the sand and shingle beach at
Pakhía Ámmos, south-east of Lákoma, the beaches (for example at
Vátos and Kípos) are mostly shingle.

History As its name ("Thracian Samos") indicates, Samothrace was originally populated (around 1000 BC) by Thracians, who founded the sanctuary of the Great Gods (Cabiri). About 700 BC the first Greeks arrived on the
island, and thereafter the sanctuary grew and developed, the cult of the
Great Gods being now combined with that of the Greeks' Olympian gods
– though Thracian remained the cult language until the 1st c. BC. In the 4th
c. BC Philip II of Macedon was initiated into the mysteries, and it is said that
he met his wife Olympias here. From the early 3rd c., when Ptolemy II and
his sister Arsinoe erected splendid new buildings in the sanctuary, the cult
– and the fame of Samothrace – spread widely through the Hellenistic
world. Under the Romans (from 168 BC) the cult of Cybele, which had originated in Asia Minor, became associated with that of the Great Gods.
Aristarchus of Samothrace (c. 217–145 BC) was the best known text critic
of antiquity, the author of important commentaries on Homer. The Apostle
Paul landed on the island in the course of his voyage to Philippi. In spite of
repeated destruction by pirates, wars and earthquakes the sanctuary continued to exist until the 4th c. AD. Only the spread of Christianity put an end
to the cult around AD 400; but the town of Palaiopolis, immediately east of
the sanctuary, was still inhabited in the 15th c. During the Middle Ages the
ruined ancient buildings provided dressed stone for the construction of
fortifications. After the fall of the Roman Empire Samothrace alternated
between Byzantine, Venetian and Genoese rule, and finally fell to the Turks
in 1457. It became Greek in 1812, during the Balkan wars. In the Second
World War the island was occupied by Bulgarian forces.

Sights

★Samothráki

The port of Kamariótissa has little to offer but a few hotels and a ruined
castle. 5 km (3 mi.) east , on a steeply sloping hillside amid a bizarre
rocky landscape, is the chief place on the island, Samothráki (Khóra;
pop. 1600). There is accommodation for visitors in pensions and rooms
in private houses. From the ruined castle there are views extending
down to the coast.

The Sanctuary of the Cabiri, home of a mystery cult

5 km (3 mi.) north of Samothráki, above the island's ancient capital Palaiopolis, are the remains of the Sanctuary of the Cabiri (Kabeiroi) or Great Gods, impressively situated in a narrow, steep-sided valley. From the highest point there are good views of the sanctuary and the sea. Site and museum open Tue.–Sun. 8.30am–3pm. ★**Sanctuary of the Cabiri**

There is a very rewarding walk (about an hour) from the Khóra along the slopes of Mount Fengári, with superb views of the sea. The chapel of Ayía Paraskeví and the ruins of a Gattelusi castle mark the site of the ancient harbour (shingle beach).

The first excavations of the site were carried out in 1863–6 by the French consul in Adrianople (Edirne), Champsoiseau, who was followed by the Austrian archaeologist A. Conze in 1873–5. More recent American investigations (Karl and Phyllis Lehmann, 1939 and 1948 onwards) have thoroughly explored the site and thrown some light on the mysteries practised there, but our knowledge of the cult remains imperfect, partly because the adepts were sworn to secrecy and partly because the remains have been overlaid in the course of the centuries by other cultures and cults.

The cult of the **Cabiri** (Great Gods) originated in Phrygia (Asia Minor) in pre-Greek times. The Greeks themselves were ignorant of the meaning of the name, and there was uncertainty about who the Great Gods were. It is known at any rate that a central figure was Cybele, the "Great Mother" of all life, a primal fertility goddess. Inscriptions give the names of other divinities: the Thracian mother goddess Axieros as mistress of nature; Axiersos and Axiersa, two divinities of the underworld who were identified by the Greeks with Pluto and Persephone; and the youthful vegetation and phallic god Cadmilus. They were revered as the protectors of nature, and later increasingly as the patrons of seafarers and rescuers of those in peril on the sea. Initiation into the mysteries, which

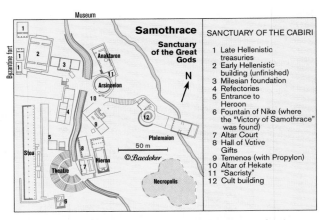

Samothrace
Sanctuary
of the Great
Gods

Museum

Byzantine fort

Anaktoron

Arsinoeion

Ptolemaion

50 m

©Baedeker

Stoa

Hieron

Theatre

Necropolis

N

SANCTUARY OF THE CABIRI

1 Late Hellenistic
   treasuries
2 Early Hellenistic
   building (unfinished)
3 Milesian foundation
4 Refectories
5 Entrance to
   Heroon
6 Fountain of Nike (where
   the "Victory of Samothrace"
   was found)
7 Altar Court
8 Hall of Votive
   Gifts
9 Temenos (with Propylon)
10 Altar of Hekate
11 "Sacristy"
12 Cult building

took place in two stages, was open to both Greeks and non-Greeks, men and women, free men and slaves – a feature that no doubt promoted the later spread of the cult.

A signposted route round the site, with names in English as well as Greek, starts from the museum, running south-east by way of a view-point to the **Anaktoron** (House of the Masters or House of the Gods; c. 550 BC), in which the worshippers underwent the first degree of initiation (*myesis*). The northern part of the building, the holy of holies, was closed off. At the south-east corner is an offering table. To the south, on a higher level, is the "Sacristy", in which registers of the initiates were maintained.

The **Arsinoeion**, a place of public sacrifice, was built in 289–281 BC by Arsinoe (later Queen Arsinoe II of Egypt). With a diameter of over 20 m (65 ft), it was the largest roofed rotunda of Greek antiquity. It occupied the site of an earlier cult building, now represented by walls and a rock-cut altar brought to light by the excavators. On the hillside above the Arsinoeion are remains of an ancient road and a circular building.

There are a number of other altars dating from the early period of the cult between the Arsinoeion and the next building to the south, the **Temenos**. Built between 350 and 340 BC at the expense of Philip II of Macedon, this was the first marble structure on the site. It had an Ionic propylon with a frieze of female dancers in archaicising style, parts of which can be seen in the museum.

On the middle terrace is the **Hieron**, 28.30 m (93 ft) long, with its re-erected colonnaded façade. This Doric structure dates from about 325 BC; its portico was added in the 2nd c. BC. At the south end is an apse (under which a crypt was built in Roman times), giving the building a plan reminiscent of a Christian church. Here the adepts were admitted to the second degree of initiation (*epopteia*), probably after confessing their sins at two marble blocks outside the east side of the building.
   Parallel to the Hieron are the Hall of Votive Gifts (6th c. BC) and the Altar Court (340–330 BC), the colonnade of which probably served as the stage wall of the (badly ruined) theatre built about 200 BC.

To the south of the theatre is the Fountain of Nike (goddess of victory), where Champsoiseau found the broken parts of the famous **Victory of**

Samothrace, now in the Louvre in Paris, in 1863. This 2.45 m (8 ft) high figure of Parian marble, dating from about 190 BC, may be a work by the Rhodian sculptor Pythecritus commemorating a Rhodian victory over Antiochus III of Syria.

At the south-east corner of the site, to the south of the Ptolemaion, a propylon built at the expense of King Ptolemy II of Egypt about 270 BC, are an ancient cemetery (7th–2nd c. BC) and the **museum**. This contains a variety of finds from the site, but its most interesting exhibit is a copy of the Victory of Samothrace.

Above the sacred precinct, to the north-east, is the site of ancient **Palaiopolis**, founded by Aeolian Greeks in the 7th c. BC, whose colossal walls of the 6th c. BC extend up to the crest of the hill. Little is left within the walls. On the site of the ancient acropolis are the ruins of a castle (1431–44) of the Genoese Gattelusi family.

13 km (8 mi.) east of Palaiopolis a hot spring (55°C (131°F)) emerges from a 10 m (35 ft) high cone of silica deposits. The resort of Thérma (Θερμα) that has grown up here is beautifully situated amid forests of chestnuts and planes. It is a good base for the ascent of the island's highest peak, Mount Fengári (1611 m (5286 ft)), and the starting point of a pleasant walk under tall trees to the waterfalls on the river Tsivdoyiani.

Thérma

★★Santoríni   K 7

Island group: Cyclades
Area: 76 sq. km (29 sq. mi.)

Santoríni – the Legendary Atlantis?

In 1628 BC a violent volcanic eruption shook the island world of the Cyclades, engulfing much of the island of Thera (Santoríni) in the sea. The explosion destroyed a highly developed civilisation, which has been brought to light in fragments only since the 1960s thanks to the sensational finds made by the Greek archaeologist Spyridon Marinatos (1901–74) in his excavations at Akrotíri. Marinatos was convinced that Santoríni was the legendary island state swallowed up by the sea of which the Greek philosopher Plato (427–347 BC) gives a detailed but incomplete account in his dialogues "Critias" and "Timaeus". A variety of theories about the geographical location of the lost island world of Atlantis have been put forward in the past, ranging from Tartessus in southern Spain to the mouth of the River Niger, Lake Triton in Tunisia, America and even the North Sea island of Heligoland, but all of them are now regarded as having no more validity than the legends of islands lost in the Atlantic. Few scholars, indeed, believe that there ever was an island state called Atlantis. Were Plato's accounts of Atlantic, therefore, merely a poetic fiction, or was there some element of truth in the fable? In his quest for Atlantis Marinatos, at any rate, was guided by the ancient accounts, as Heinrich Schiemann was guided by the "Iliad" in his search for ancient Troy. Let us, then, consider what Plato has to say about Atlantis: "For outside the passage which you in your language call the Pillars of Hercules [the Strait of Gibraltar] there once lay an island, and this island was larger that Libya and Asia Minor together. From this island there was access to the other islands, and from these to the whole of the continent opposite, round that ocean so rightly named the Atlantic.

For all that lies within the said passage is like a natural harbour with a narrow entrance. It can justly be called a sea, and the land lying round it is in the fullest sense of the word a continent."

Plato did not know Atlantis from his own experience, but was merely relating what Egyptian priests had told the great Athenian legislator Solon during his visit to Egypt in 690 BC. According to this account the layout of the island continent in the form of concentric rings was the work of the sea god Poseidon himself: "He laid one round the other ... in rings of water ... as if, starting from the centre of the island, he had turned a potter's wheel." Plato also refers frequently to the volcanic character of the island world, speaking of hot and cold springs and rocks of many colours.

According to the ancient legend the inhabitants of Atlantis had developed a remarkably advanced culture, with a system of government in the form of a parliamentary oligarchy, with an "assembly of ten kings who deliberated on the affairs of the community ... and dispensed judgment."

Plato then goes on to relate how the people of Atlantis, originally virtuous and enjoying great prosperity, military strength and good and just laws, became enamoured of power and waged wars of conquest against their neighbours, in particular against Athens, while their manners and morals declined. The judgment of the gods was inescapable, leading to the inevitable catastrophe: "Then there occurred violent earthquakes and disturbances, and within the space of a single day and night all the warriors and the whole people were swallowed up in the earth and the island of Atlantis was engulfed by the sea."

At first sight, if we compare the present form of Santoríni with Plato's description of Atlantis there do indeed appear to be numerous resemblances between the two, with the exception of the geographical location and the size of the island state. But there may have been some poetic licence at work here, given the fact that in the 4th century BC the whole Mediterranean world was dominated by the Greeks and the legendary Atlantis was deliberately located outwith the known world. The great size of Atlantis as described by Plato may reflect his belief that only an enemy of enormous power could defeat Athens. In the unusual circular shape of the island, the small island in the centre, the colouring of the rock, the cliffs and high mountains and the evidence of volcanic activity there are clear parallels between the geography of Santoríni and Plato's tradition of Atlantis. Spyridon Marinatos was sure, therefore, that he had at last found Atlantis. But per-haps Plato had visited Santoríni, only three days' sail from Athens, to seek inspiration from the island's unique situation for the fable with which he sought to convey his wisdom? In his "Critias" and "Timaeus" he sought to depict an ideal state, for which Santoríni would provide an impressive setting. As so often, poetry and reality are mingled in his work. Only one thing is certain: the search for Atlantis still continues.

Recent investigations have shown that the Santoríni caldera had collapsed long before the fall of Atlantis, and the island cannot therefore have been the site of the legendary island state. Since the mid-1990s some German scholars have been propounding the theory that Atlantis was in fact Troy, on the coast of Asia Minor, and the quest for Atlantis is now being pursued with the aid of magnetometers and electronic detectors.

Volcanic activity in the caldera of Santoríni in the 19th c. (from the "Illustrated London News", 1866)

Altitude: 0–566 m (0–1857 ft)
Population: 7000
Chief place: Thíra (Firá)

Airport: 7 km (4½ mi.) east of Thíra. Air connections with Athens, Salonica, Iráklion (Crete), Mýkonos, Rhodes. Charter flights. Shipping connections with Piraeus, other islands in the Cyclades, the principal islands in the Dodecanese and Iráklion (Crete). Cruise ships call in at Athiniós, 10 km (6 mi.) south of Thíra. Bus services on the island.

With its extraordinary landscape, the result of volcanic activity, Santoríni or Thíra (Σαντορινη or Θηρα); Thera, the "Wild Island"; Italian Santorino, after the island's patron saint, St Irene), the most southerly of the larger Cyclades, is one of Greece's greatest tourist attractions, annually attracting something like half a million visitors, including many from cruise ships. This inevitably creates problems for the island's infrastructure (water supply, waste disposal). For visitors arriving by sea the entry into the huge and almost completely enclosed volcanic crater, with the island's whitewashed houses clinging to its rim, is an unforgettable experience. Santoríni is not for those who want a holiday entirely devoted to bathing and sunbathing; but its ancient sites are among the most important in Greece.

Geography Santoríni and the smaller islands of Thirasía and Aspronísi are remnants of a volcanic crater that has been engulfed by the sea. The rim of the caldera emerges from the sea with a diameter from 12 to 18 km (7½ to 11 mi.), open to the north-west and south-west, enclosing a basin up to 400 m (1300 ft) deep, in the centre of which are the two Kaiméni islands, the peaks of a later volcano that came into being in historical times. Hot springs and emissions of gas bear witness to continuing volcanic activity. The dense volcanic deposits of ash, pumice and lava lie on top of a massif of argillaceous schists and greywacke overlaid by limestone. The highest point on the island is Mount Profítis Ilías (566 m (1857 ft)), in the south-east; at the northern tip is Megálo Voúno, on the east side Mount Monólithos. The inner wall of the crater falls down to the sea in sheer cliffs, ranging in height from 200 to 400 m (650 and 1300 ft), of grey-black lava with bands of white pumice and reddish tufa. On the outer side the land slopes gradually down to the sea in fertile slopes of pumice soil covered with vines and market gardens. Owing to lack of water Santoríni is treeless. In addition to tourism the island's main sources of income are the export of wine, tomatoes and vegetables, and also of Santorin earth (pozzolana).

This volcanic island has few good **beaches**. Perhaps the best are the beaches at the popular and well-equipped resorts of Kamári and Boríssa on the east coast. The beaches at Monólithos and further north are considerably quieter. Bathers will find that the dark-coloured sand becomes very hot in the sun. The most beautiful beach on the island is perhaps the Red Beach below Akrotíri, with grey sand and shingle enclosed by imposing red cliffs.

History Thera was inhabited, probably by Carians, in the 3rd millennium BC (the Cycladic culture). They were followed around 1900 BC by Achaean Greeks. The excavations at Akrotíri have shown that in the first half of the 2nd millennium BC Thera was a flourishing and prosperous island that was in contact with Minoan Crete but had developed a distinctive culture of its own. It seems likely that Akrotíri was ruled not by some central authority but by a plutocracy of merchants and shipowners who had trading links reaching as far afield as Libya. This can be deduced from the wall paintings of astonishingly high quality that are now in the National Archaeological Museum in Athens.
  The golden age ended with the eruption of the volcano about 1628 BC.

Spyridon Marinatos, who carried out the excavations at Akrotíri, believed that this catastrophe was identical with the fall of the legendary Atlantis and that it also brought about the end of the Minoan cities on Crete.

After the eruption the island remained uninhabited for 500 years, until the beginning of the 1st millennium BC, when it was resettled by Dorian (Minoan) incomers from Crete. About 630 their king, Grinos, founded a colony at Cyrene – the largest Greek colony in North Africa. In Greek times Thera was known as Kalliste (the "fairest" island) or Strongyle (the "round" island). It enjoyed a measure of prosperity under the Ptolemies, who maintained a base on the island. Thereafter it came under Roman rule. In the 4th c. AD it was the see of a bishop, but from the 6th c. belonged to the diocese of Rhodes. In 1207, after the Fourth Crusade, the island was conquered by the Venetian Marco Sanudo, later duke of Náxos, and was given its present name. In 1537 it was occupied by Khaireddin Barbarossa, but did not become part of the Ottoman Empire until 1579. It was reunited with Greece in 1834.

Throughout the island's history volcanic forces have continued to be a danger. There were major eruptions in 197 BC and in AD 1650, 1707, 1712, 1870, 1925 and 1950. The most recent major outbreak of volcanic activity was in 1956, when Thíra and Oía were destroyed.

Sights

From the quay in the little port of Skála, where passengers are landed in small boats, the island's chief town, Thíra or Firá (pop. 2000), is reached either by walking or riding (on mule- or donkey-back) up the steep and winding stepped path (587 steps) or by cableway. Large passenger ships now regularly put in at the new port of Athiniós, 17 km (11 mi.) south. The cableway was constructed in the early 1980s at the expense of a wealthy shipowner; part of the proceeds from fares goes to the owners of the donkeys and mules.

★Thíra

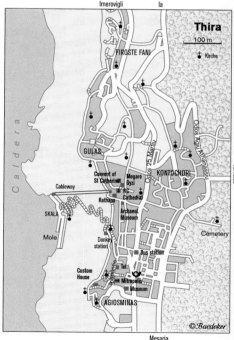

With its whitewashed houses, many of them built into the rim of the crater, its winding lanes and little squares, which continually open up new and spectacular views, and the turquoise-blue domes of its churches and chapels, Thíra is a charming little town that even mass tourism and its associated commercialisation have not been able to spoil. A must for every visitor is a walk (preferably at sunset) along the rim of the crater to the villages of Firostefáni and Imerovígli. There are also magnificent views from the restaurants on the crater rim.

At the south end of the little town is the fine modern Mitrópolis church (1856). The Archaeological Museum (open Tue.–Sun. 8.30am–3pm) displays a representative collection of material, ranging in

date from Cycladic to Roman times, from the Thera and Akrotíri excavations. A little way north of this is the former Catholic quarter of the town, with the cathedral and a convent of Dominican nuns. Here too, housed in a Venetian mansion, is the Mégaron Gýzi Museum (open Mon.–Sat. 10.30am–1.30pm, 5–8pm), with an interesting collection of material on the history of the island.

At the northern tip of the main island of Santoríni, clinging to the rim of the crater, is Ía (Oía, Οια; pop. 600), a trim little town that was rebuilt after the 1956 earthquake. With the innumerable blue domes of its churches, its maze of whitewashed stepped lanes and its white flat-roofed houses, it is the very image of an idyllic little Cycladic town. Housed in an old mansion adjoining the Town Hall is the Nautical Museum (open Mon.–Sat. 10.30am–1.30pm, 5–8pm), with a collection of nautical instruments, ship models and ships' figureheads. Steep footpaths zigzag their way up the crater wall to Oía from Ammoudi Bay to the west and Áyios Nikólaos Bay to the south. The finest view is to be had from the west end of the main street. ★Oía

4 km (2½ mi.) south-east of Thíra is the village of Mesariá (Μεσαρια). The main feature of interest is a neoclassical mansion (arkhontiko) of 1888, the sumptuously appointed villa (restored) of the wine merchant Yeóryios Argyros (open Apr.–Oct.; conducted tours every hour 11am–1pm and 4–7pm). Mesariá

Wine tasting 2 km (1¼ mi.) east of Pýrgos is Mesa Goria, the island's wine-producing centre. Here and in Exo Goria, higher up, the wine producers offer samples of their wares. Here too is the Canava Russo establishment of 1836. In Megalokhori, 10 km (6¼ mi.) south of Thíra, is the visitor centre of the Boutari firm. In September visitors can take part in the traditional vintage festival.

From Thíra a road runs south for 12 km (7½ mi.), offering magnificent panoramic views, to the summit of Mount Profítis Ilías (566 m (1857 ft)), the highest point on the island, now disfigured by aerial masts. During the Turkish occupation the monastery of Profítis Ilías (not open to the public) ran a clandestine school, as did many other monasteries. The church has a fine carved iconostasis and contains a Cretan "crown of Elijah" (15th c.), and in the monastery's museum can be seen the mitre and pastoral staff of Patriarch Gregory V, who was hanged by the Turks in Constantinople in 1821. From Profítis Ilías a road runs down eastward to the Selláda (a saddle between two hills), on either side of which are the cemeteries of ancient Thera. From here a road on the left runs down to Kamári on the east coast, on the site of ancient Oia, and a road on the right leads south to Períssa. Straight ahead the road winds its way up to Mount Mésa Vounó, passing the church of Áyios Stéfanos, built on the site of an Early Christian basilica and incorporating ancient masonry, continuing to the Evangelismós chapel (alt. 297 m (974 ft)), adjoining which is a heroon of the 2nd c. BC. Mount Profítis Ilías

The remains of Thera, the ancient capital of the island (site open Tue.–Sat. 8.45am–2.30pm), 3 km (2 mi.) south-west of Kamári, extend from the Selláda over the rocky ridge of Mésa Vounó, which falls steeply on three sides. The town was founded about 1000 BC, enjoyed a period of prosperity under the Ptolemies (300–150 BC), when it had a population of 5000, and was still inhabited in the 13th c. Thera
  The signposted route round the site comes first to a temple built in the 3rd c. BC by Artemidorus, an admiral in the service of the Ptolemies. Carved from the rock are reliefs depicting Artemidorus and other figures. From here a stepped path leads to the barracks and gymnasion of

◀ Santoríni: at its most impressive in the twilight

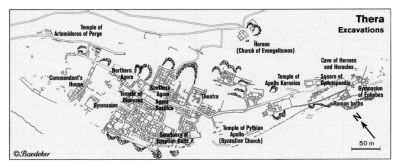

the Ptolemaic garrison on the summit of Mésa Vounó. The Agora (market) is surrounded by houses and workshops. On its south-east side is the Stoa Basilike (1st c. BC), the Royal Hall, the interior of which is divided into two aisles by a row of Doric columns. On a terrace above the north-west corner of the Stoa can be seen the Temple of Dionysus, rededicated in the 2nd c. BC to the cult of the Ptolemies and later to the cult of the Roman emperors.

Flanking the main street are the foundations of a number of Hellenistic houses with ground-plans of Delian type and the Theatre, with a Roman stage building, under which are traces of the Ptolemaic proskenion. At the entrance to the theatre a side street branches off and runs up to the rock sanctuary of the Egyptian deities Isis, Serapis and Anubis.

At the south-east end of the city is an artificially enlarged terrace of the 6th c. BC, with the Square of the Gymnopaedia, where cult ceremonies in honour of Apollo Kameiros were held. Evidence of this is given in archaic inscriptions, some of them of erotic content, carved from the rock. The Temple of Apollo Kameiros, to the north-west, consists of a pronaos, naos and two other chambers (possibly treasuries). At the south-east end of the ridge are the Gymnasion of the Ephebes (2nd c. BC), the Caves of Hermes and Heracles and Roman baths.

★ Akrotíri

At Akrotíri, 12 km (7½ mi.) south-west of Thíra, the Greek archaeologist Spyridon Marinatos brought to light between 1967 and his death in 1974 considerable areas of a major city destroyed in a great volcanic eruption. The civilisation revealed by his excavations seems to have combined the old Cycladic culture with the innovations of Minoan culture. The inhabitants must have fled to safety in time, for no human remains were found on the site. The surviving buildings date from the 7th c. BC and show signs of damage from the earthquakes preceding the catastrophe of 1628 BC – for example walls that were out of true but were held in position by the pumice sand that covered the entire site.

The massive sand cover and the height of the buildings, which had several storeys, created problems for the excavators, and Marinatos himself was killed in an accident on the site and is buried opposite the spot where he died. His work is being carried on by his daughter Nanno.

A tour of the site (open Tue.–Sun. 8.30am–3pm) – hailed as a "second Pompeii" but 1700 years older than the Italian town – may prove disappointing, since the marvellous frescos found here are now in the National Archaeological Museum in Athens and the effect is spoiled by the protective roof erected over the remains. On the most important buildings ground-plans and explanations are displayed. Similar remains were found on the south coast of Thirasía.

Kamári

The island's principal resort for package tourists, Kamári (Καμαρι), lies on the east coast, to the north of the imposing cliff-fringed promontory of Mésa Vounó. It has a beautiful and very long beach of dark-coloured shingle. On the tamarisk-shaded seafront promenade are numerous hotels, bars and tavernas.

The second large resort on the east coast, Aeríssa (Περισσα), which is favoured by young backpackers, has an excellent tourist infrastructure, still in process of development.

Períssa

From Thíra Skála a boat can be taken to the little island of Thirasía (Θηρασια; area 9 sq. km (3½ sq. mi.)), another part of the crater, from which there is a good view of Santoríni. A stepped path leads up to the chief place on the island, also called Thirasía, situated high above the east coast.

Thirasía

Sérifos   I 6

Island group: Cyclades
Area: 73 sq. km (28 sq. mi.)
Altitude: 0–587 m (0–1926 ft)
Population: 1200
Chief place: Sérifos town (Khóra)

Port: Livádi (bus service to Sérifos town). Shipping connections with Piraeus, Rafína, Kárystos (Euboea) and the other islands in the Cyclades.

At first sight Sérifos (Σεριφος), the middle island in the western Cyclades, is a bare and rocky island, its hills slashed by gorges; but in fact it is relatively well watered and has many green spots. In spite of the beauty of the island it has only a modest tourist trade, mainly concentrated in the little port of Livádi, which is the only place with any accommodation for visitors. The view from boats approaching the harbour is impressive: a deep inlet with a beautiful beach, with the little town of Sérifos (Khóra) on a steep-sided crag above the harbour.

History In Greek mythology Seriphos was the place where Danae and her son Perseus (begotten by Zeus in the form of a shower of gold), who had been cast into the sea by her father, were washed ashore. Perseus later returned to Seriphos with the head of the Medusa, with which he turned King Polydectes, who had been threatening his mother, to stone.

Originally settled by Ionian Greeks, the island thereafter shared the fortunes of the other Cyclades. It was a Venetian possession from 1207, became part of the Ottoman Empire in 1537 and was reunited with Greece in 1830.

Sights

The little port of Livádi (Λιβαδι) is the island's tourist centre. Most of the tourist facilities are round the harbour and on the neighbouring sandy beach of Livadákia. There are other beautiful beaches in the surrounding

Livádi

From the upper town of Sérifos there is a fine view of Livádi harbour

area, for example the little sandy bay of Karávi and the magnificent dune beach of fine white sand at Psilí Ámmos, on the north side of the peninsula.

★Sérifos town

Sérifos town can be reached from Livádi by road (5 km (3 mi.)) or on a shorter but steeper footpath up the hill. Its great attraction lies in its beautiful situation on a crag above the coastal plain and the harbour inlet. Many of the houses in the town cannot be seen from the harbour. It consists of a lower town (Káto Khóra), with the beautiful Evangelístria church, and an upper town (Áno Khóra), on the site of a Venetian castle. From here there are magnificent views of the harbour inlet and the island – one of the most beautiful places in the Cyclades.

Panayía

There is a rewarding walk of 20 km (13 mi.) from the Khóra by way of the village of Panayía (Παναγια; 5 km (3 mi.) north) to the monastery of the Taxiarchs and back (about 6 hours). The pretty little hill village of Panayía has the oldest church on the island, founded about 950. It contains two antique columns, frescos of the 13th–14th c. and icons of the 18th and 19th c.

Monastery of the Taxiarchs

4 km (2½ mi.) further north is the most important sight on the island, the fortress-like 17th c. Monastery of the Taxiarchs (Archangels), with a richly furnished church of 1447 (the Katholikon) and frescos by Emanuel Skordilis (c. 1700), with representations of the torments of Hell that show a delight in detail. After resting in Kentárkhos (Kalítsos) the return route is by way of the beaches of Áyios Ioánnis and Psilí Ámmos.

Island group: Cyclades
Area: 73 sq. km (28 sq. mi.)
Altitude: 0–680 m (0–2230 ft)
Population: 1800
Chief place: Apollonía

Port: Kamáres. Shipping connections with Piraeus, Rafína and other
islands in the Cyclades. Bus services on the island.

Sífnos (Σιφνος) lies roughly in
the centre of the triangle
formed by Melos, Sérifos and
Páros. In recent years this
scenically attractive island
has been the most visited of
the western Cyclades. The
north and north-west of the
island are occupied by barren
ranges of hills, the east and
south by gentler uplands, in
which olives and almonds are
grown in terraced fields. The
landscape is punctuated by
dovecotes and white monasteries and churches. On the
coast, which is much
indented and lined by cliffs
for much of its length, there
are numbers of Hellenistic,
Roman and medieval
watchtowers.

Agriculture is favoured by the island's fertile soil. The island is
renowned for its excellent (and expensive) olive oil. Thanks to its
deposits of good clay it has a long-established pottery industry.

History Already populated in the period of the Cycladic culture (3rd and
2nd millennia BC), the island grew so wealthy in classical times from the
mining of lead, silver and copper that the Siphnians had a treasury at
Delphi. When the mines were flooded by the sea the island declined into
insignificance. (Entrances to the workings can be seen in the sea at
Áyios Sóstis and Áyios Minás). Thereafter Sífnos shared the fortunes of
the other Cycladic islands.

Sights

The little port of Kamáres (Καμαρες; pop. 200), where the ferries and   **Kamáres**
excursion boats put in, is not a particularly attractive place, but in
summer becomes a lively tourist centre. It has a beautiful beach, and
boats take visitors to other beaches on the island.

6 km (4 mi.) east of Kamáres, on a fertile plateau, is Apollonía   **Apollonía**
(Απολλωνια), the chief place on the island. In the village square is the
Folk Museum (open daily 9.30am–1.30pm, 6.30–10.30pm), with a collection that includes embroidery, old costumes, weapons and traditional
pottery. The narrow main street is lined by souvenir shops, tavernas and
coffee houses. There are fine wall paintings in the churches of Áyios
Sózon, the Panayía Gourniá in the neighbouring village of Artemónas, to
the north, and the Panayía in Katavatí, to the south.

Síkinos

Monasteries

3 km (2 mi.) south of Apollonía is the **Vrissis monastery** (1654), which is still occupied. On the stretch of coast between the fishing village of Faros and the popular holiday resort of Platýs Yialós, which has a 2 km (1¼ mi.) long sandy beach, is the **Khrysopiyí monastery** (founded 1650), situated on a projecting spur of rock.

★**Kástro**

From Apollonía there is a pleasant walk (5 km (3 mi.) east) to the picturesque little town of Kástro (Κάστρο), situated above a bay on the east coast of the island. This well-preserved medieval village was the chief place on the island from ancient times (according to Herodotus) until 1834.

There are remains of the ancient walls (4th c. BC). The outer ring of walls was formed by the

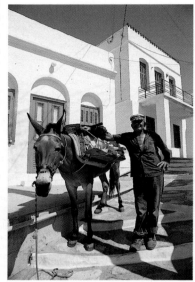

Perhaps a donkey ride through the narrow streets of Apollonía?

outer walls of the houses, which have outside staircases, verandas and balconies and are decorated with coats of arms. Features of interest are a small archaeological museum, the Theoskepasti church (1631), and the chapel of the Efta Martyres (Seven Martyrs), situated on a rock pinnacle.

Mount Profítis Ilías

On the island's highest hill, Mount Profítis Ilías (see p. 291), which can be climbed from Apollonía in just under 2 hours, is the unoccupied monastery of Profítis Ilías, which dates back to the 9th c. From here there are panoramic views of the island and the sea.

Síkinos   K 7

Island group: Cyclades
Area: 41 sq. km (16 sq. mi.)
Altitude: 0–553 m (0–1814 ft)
Population: 300
Chief place: Síkinos town (Khóra)

Port: Aloprónia (buses to Síkinos town). Shipping connections with Piraeus and other Cycladic islands. Boats to Folégandros.

Síkinos (Σίκινος), 6 km (4 mi.) south-west of Íos, is one of the smaller of the southern Cyclades, 15 km (9 mi.) long by 5 km (3 mi.) across. The neighbouring island of Folégandros has better tourist facilities, but Síkinos offers a much quieter holiday and a largely unspoiled landscape. The only road on the island (a very narrow one) is between the port and the Khóra. Síkinos is a bare and rocky island; the north and north-west are hilly, while in the gentler terrain of the south-east vegetables, vines and corn are grown in terraced fields. With its inhospitable soil and lack of sheltered anchorages, Síkinos was never a place of any importance in antiquity. Its history was closely linked with that of Náxos. In Roman times it was used as a place of exile. After the Second World War many of the inhabitants emigrated to Australia and the United States.

Sights

The little port of Aloprónia (Αλοπρονοια) in the south-east of the island operates only during the season. The tavernas too are open only in summer. There is accommodation for visitors in private houses. There is a small sand and shingle beach.

Aloprónia

A concrete track 4 km (2½ mi.) long runs from Aloprónia to Síkinos town, the chief place on the island, which consists of the Khóra ("town") and the Khorió ("village"). Alternatively, it is an hour climb (2.5 km (1½ mi.)) up a wooded gorge. The Khóra of this typical Cycladic village occupies the site of a Venetian castle that was pulled down by the Italians in the 1940s. In the square are two 18th c. mansions and the church of the Tímios Stavrós (Holy Cross; 1787), which has a carved iconostasis and post-Byzantine frescos of the Cretan school. Above the Khóra are three windmills and the ruins of the convent of the Zoodókhos Piyí (Life Giving Fountain), which was abandoned in 1834. From here it is 300 m to the main village, the Khorió, where some of the houses are falling into ruin.

Síkinos town

From the Khóra it is an hour walk south-west to the **Heroon**, a tomb built in the 3rd c. BC in the style of an ancient Greek temple. In Byzantine times it was converted into a church, and in the 17th c. it was incorporated in the **Episkopí monastery**. On a hill to the north, round the little church of Ayía Marína, are scanty remains of the ancient city.

★★Skíathos   H 4

Northern Sporades
Area: 48 sq. km (19 sq. mi.)
Altitude: 0–438 m (0–1437 ft)
Population: 5100
Chief place: Skíathos town

Airport 4 km (2½ mi.) north-east of Skíathos town. Air connections with Athens. Charter flights. Shipping connections (ferries and hydrofoils) with Vólos, Áyios Konstantínos, Kými (Euboea), Skópelos and Alónissos, and with Salonica. Bus services on the island.

Skíathos (Σκιαθος) is a gently rolling wooded island in the Northern Sporades, 4 km (2½ mi.) east of the Magnesia peninsula (Mount Pelion) on the Greek mainland. With its many sandy beaches, which rank as the most beautiful in Greece, it has become a very popular holiday island and been taken over by mass tourism; as a result it has become expensive as well as overcrowded. This is a resort for those who seek the high life, who want to see and be seen. Its main source of income apart from the tourist trade is its 600,000 olive trees.

Skíathos has more than 60 **beaches**; round Skíathos town they tend to be busy, but the further away and the more difficult of access they are the less crowded they are. They are all beautiful, but the most attractive are the 600 m (1980 ft) long sandy beach of Koukounariés, fringed by umbrella pines (9 km (5½ mi.) west of Skíathos town), and Lalária, a beach of light-grey shingle 8 km (5 mi.) north of the town, which is accessible only by boat. Off Lalária beach is a rock with a large natural arch through which bathers can swim. Close by are two sea caves that can be entered by swimmers. Banana (or Krasa) beach, in a wild and romantic bay shaded by tall trees, is particularly favoured by nudist bathers.

History Skíathos was never a place of any importance in ancient times. Herodotus mentions the island in connection with the naval battle off Cape Artemision in 480 BC, recording that the men of Skíathos conveyed information about Persian naval movements by means of fire signals.

Sights

Skíathos town

The chief place on the island, and indeed its only town, is Skíathos, on the south-east coast. Founded in 1830, it occupies the site of the ancient city, on two low hill ridges flanking a small sheltered harbour that is divided into two by the wooded Boúrtzi peninsula. On this promontory between the old and the new harbours are the ruins of a Venetian fort. From the church of Áyios Fanoúrios, north-west of the town, there is a fine view. Skíathos was the home of the writer Alexandros Papadiamantis (1851–1911), author of 200 short stories, whose house is now a museum. There is a monument to him on the harbour front.

Kástro

On the north coast of the island, spectacularly situated on a high crag from which there are magnificent views, are the ruins of the medieval town of Kástro, which was capital of the island from 1538 to 1829. It can be reached only on foot (2½ hours) or by boat. There are remains of the town walls, with a drawbridge, Turkish baths and three of the 22 churches the town once possessed, including the church of Christós sto Kástro, which has a templon of 1695 and fine frescos.

Half way between Skíathos town and Kástro is the **Evangelístria monastery**, finely situated above a gorge. This cave monastery, founded in 1797, was a refuge for Greek rebels during the struggle for liberation. The Greek flag is said to have been hoisted here as early as 1807. The frescos in the church date from 1822.

Skíathos town, capital of this popular holiday island

There are pleasant walks from Skíathos town to a number of abandoned
monasteries. 8 km (5 mi.) from the town, to the north of the
Evangelístria, is the 17th c. monastery of Áyios Kharalámbos; 8 km
north-west is the Kekhriá monastery (1540), which has fine frescos of
1745; 9 km (5½ mi.) west is the 17th c. monastery of the Panayía
Kounistrá; and at Troúlos, south-west of the town, is the monastery of
Ayía Sofía.

South-east of Skíathos are nine smaller islands. The only one with any   **Tsoungriá**
land under cultivation is the largest of these, Tsoúngria (Τσουγκρια; area
6 sq. km (2½ sq. mi.)). The smaller islets of Tsoungriáki, Daskalonísi
(lighthouse), Myrmingonísi ("Ant Island") and Marangós lie off the harbour. Further north, off the east coast, are the isolated rocks of Répi, Arkí
and Aspronísi; to the south is Prasonísi.

★★Skópelos   H 4

Northern Sporades
Area: 96 sq. km (37 sq. mi.)
Altitude: 0–680 m (0–2230 ft)
Population: 3000
Chief place: Skópelos town

Ports: Skópelos (Σκοπελος) and Loutráki. Ferry connections with Áyios
Konstantínos, Vólos, Kými (Euboea), Salonica, Skíathos and Alónissos.
Hydrofoils to Skíathos, Alónissos and Euboea. Bus services on the
island. Only the main road between Skópelos and Loutráki is
asphalted.

Skópelos is a hilly and well wooded island in the Northern Sporades. Like the neighbouring island of Skíathos, it has many excellent (shingle) beaches and is seeking to vie with Skíathos in the development of tourism, though so far on a more acceptable scale. The steep north-east coast is unwelcoming, and, apart from the wide bay of Skópelos, without any considerable inlets or irregularities. The gentler south-east coast is also relatively featureless. The fertile areas on the island are mainly devoted to the growing of almonds and fruit (particularly plums; dried fruit packing station in Skópelos town). There are many convents in which the nuns make woven goods and other craft products for sale.

Tourism The tourist trade is now an increasingly important element in the island's economy. It is no longer confined to its picturesque chief town but centres on the development of Skópelos's many good beaches. Almost all the beaches (with hotels, tavernas and other facilities) lie between the bays of Stáfylos, on the south-east coast, and Loutráki, on the north-west coast, to which there are buses from Skópelos town. The island's best bathing beach is at Miliá, north-west of Pánormos beach. There are pleasant walks to numerous monasteries and churches in the beautiful interior of the island.

History The oldest traces of human settlement date from the neolithic period. The ancient city of Peparethos was said to have been founded by the Cretan hero Staphylus, son of Dionysus and Ariadne. Staphylus – the name means "bunch of grapes" – was credited with bringing the making of wine to Skópelos from Crete. In the so-called Tomb of Staphylos were found gold jewellery, idols, a variety of implements and utensils and Minoan double axes; they are now in the museum in Vólos. The archaeological evidence indicates, however, that from an early stage the inhabitants of the island were influenced by Mycenaean rather than Minoan culture.

From the 7th c. Skópelos enjoyed a brief period of prosperity, and the tribute it paid as a member of the first Attic maritime league was substantial. The Peloponnesian War, however, quickly and finally put an end to its prosperity. Thereafter it had a succession of different masters – Macedonians, Romans, Byzantines, Venetians and finally Turks – who allowed this remote and economically unimportant community a considerable measure of autonomy. In 1830 it was reunited with Greece.

Sights

★Skópelos town

The chief place on the island, Skópelos town (pop. 3000), is attractively situated in a wide bay, on the site of the ancient and the Byzantine capital. Its narrow lanes and whitewashed houses (originally slate roofed) extend in a semicircle on the slopes of the hill above the harbour, on which are the ruins of a castle, originally established by Philip II of Macedon and enlarged by the Venetian Ghisi family in the 13th c., and the foundations of a temple of Asclepius of the 5th/4th c. BC. The flanks of the hill are covered with beautiful olive groves.

The town has a folk museum (open 7pm–10pm) and some 120 churches and chapels, some of them dating from Byzantine times. The most notable is the oldest of the churches, Áyios Athanásios, which was built in the 9th c. on the foundations of an ancient temple and has fine 17th c. frescos. Also worth visiting is the church of the Archangel Michael, with fine carved woodwork, icons, Roman sarcophagi built into its walls and an ancient gravestone of the 2nd c. AD.

There are around 360 churches, chapels and **monasteries** on the island. A number of monasteries lying within a few kilometres east of Skópelos town can be seen in the course of a pleasant walk of about 3 hours. 4 km

Chapel above the harbour of Skópelos

(2½ mi.) from the town is the Evangelístria monastery (1712), which has an ornate carved iconostasis and a 10th c. icon of the Mother of God framed in silver. From here there is a marvellous view of the town. Further east is the oldest monastery on the island, the 16th c. monastery of the Metamorfósis (Transfiguration), which is occupied only by a single monk. Beyond this is the convent of the Tímios Pródromos (St John the Baptist) of 1721, with an inner courtyard gay with flowers; and facing this is the abandoned monastery of Ayía Barbára (1648).

Glóssa (Γλώσσα), near the north-western tip of the island, is beautifully situated in a green landscape on the slopes of a hill above the harbour of Loutráki. It is much quieter than Skópelos town and has preserved much of its original character. Round the village are many remains of ancient Selinus, whose site it occupies.

Glóssa

At the north-western tip of the island are four historic watchtowers. In Agnóndas Bay, on the south coast, is the Tripití sea cave. At Pánormos are remains of an ancient settlement.

Other sights

★Skýros   I 4/5

Northern Sporades
Area: 209 sq. km (81 sq. mi.)
Altitude: 0–814 m (0–2671 ft)
Population: 2800
Chief place: Skýros town (Khóra)

Airport 10 km (6¼ mi.) north-west of Skýros (Σκυρος) town. Air connec-

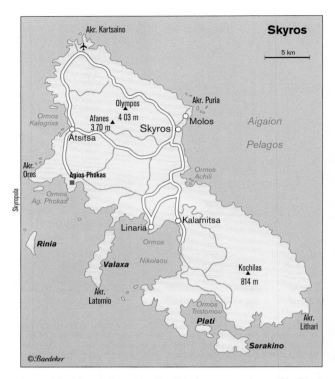

tions with Athens. Port: Linariá. Shipping connections with Kými (Euboea), Vólos and other islands in the Sporades. Buses between Skýros and the airport, Linariá and Mólos; otherwise few services.

Skýros, the largest of the Northern Sporades, lying considerably further east than the other islands in the group, is divided into two distinct parts by a strip of sandy low-lying land between Áyios Nikólaos or Kalamítsa Bay, which cuts deep into the west coast, and Akhílli Bay on the east coast. The south-eastern half of the island (Vounó, the "Mountain") is occupied by the rugged and arid massif of Mount Kókhilas (814 m (2671 ft)). In this area are the quarries of the coarse-grained variegated marble that was much prized in Roman times. The north-western half (Meri), rising to 403 m (1322 ft) in Mount Ólympos, is a region of gentler contours, with more water, a more fertile soil and forests of pine trees. Here too are marble quarries that have been worked from antiquity down to modern times.

The coasts of the island are steep and inhospitable, but there are beautiful sandy beaches at the foot of the cliffs that are particularly popular with young holidaymakers. Although Skýros lies off the main tourist tracks its charming little capital on the east coast, Skýýros town, attracts many visitors in summer.

The small semi-wild horses, no bigger than Shetland ponies, that live in the barren south-eastern part of the island are now on the way to extinction. The island's main sources of revenue are farming, the tourist trade and the sale of its high-quality craft products (embroidery, hand-woven fabrics, carved furniture, pottery, copperware). Old men can still be seen wearing their traditional costume of baggy black trousers, black or white shirts of thick cloth and the flat leather sandals with many straps that are characteristic of Skýros.

Skýros is famed for its **carnival**, a celebration of obviously pagan origin. On the last two Sundays before the Great Fast (Lent) some men disguise themselves as goats, wearing masks, skins and bells, while others, also wearing goat masks, are disguised as women. Women and children also wear disguises, and there is much singing and dancing in the streets, as well as much eating and drinking.

History According to the ancient legend Thetis brought up her son Achilles on Skyros disguised as a girl in an attempt to prevent him from fighting in the Trojan War. Traces of neolithic occupation (5th millennium BC) have been found in the north-eastern part of the Kástro. In the 2nd millennium BC Carian and Pelasgian farmers and seafarers settled on the island, which then became known as Pelasgia. In the 1st millennium BC they were displaced by Dolopians, a Dorian people, who made the island, now called Dolopia, a base for plundering raids in the Aegean. In 469 BC Athens drove out the pirates and settled farmers from Attica on the land. In Roman times the islanders achieved a modest degree of prosperity through the export of their much prized marble, but their remote island remained of no political importance.

In AD 1207 Skýros passed into the hands of the Venetian Ghisi family; from 1453 to 1537 it was under direct Venetian control; in 1566 it became part of the Ottoman Empire; and in 1829 it was reunited with Greece.

Sights

The chief place on the island, Skýros town or Khóra (pop. 2400), lies on the east coast. With its white-washed houses it has all the air of a town in the Cyclades. From the beach it is a short walk up to the busy main street with its souvenir shops, cafés and tavernas. The houses of the town, finely decorated and furnished, nestle in a semicircle round a hill once crowned by the ancient acropolis of the 4th c. BC (remains of walls) and later by a Byzantine and Venetian castle, the Kástro, from which there are fine views. From this crag, it is said, Theseus was cast down to his death; according to the legend his remains were later found here and deposited in the Theseion (actually the Hephaisteion) in Athens.

★**Skýros town**

Below the Kástro is the church of **Áyios Yeóryios** (St George), which originally belonged to the monastery of that name that was founded by Nicephorus Phocas in 962. It has an 18th c. iconostasis.

In Brooke Square is a nude bronze statue, erected in 1931, commemorating the poet **Rupert Brooke**, who died of blood poisoning on Skýros on his way to the Dardanelles in 1915 and is buried in the bay of Tristomou or Tris Boukés (see below).

Museums Just below Brooke Square is Faitaits Museum (open 10am–1pm, 5.30–8pm), including Skyriot arts and crafts, traditional costumes, furniture, ceramics and photographs. Close by is the Archaeological Museum (open Tue.–Sun. 8.30am–3pm), with pottery, sculpture and inscriptions from Mycenaean to Byzantine times and a traditionally furnished Skyriot home. To the left of the road is the Yiaouri House, a traditional Skyriot house.

The nearest (and very popular) **beach**, Khorió, lies to the north of Skýros town. Altogether 4 km (2½ mi.) long, it consists of four separate sections (Magaziá, Mólos, Pourio and Gyrismata). The finest stretch is the sandy beach of Mólos, which can be reached by bus.

Linariá

10 km (6¼ mi.) south of Skyros town, in Linariá (Λιναρια) Bay, which is sheltered on the north-west by the island of Valáxa, is the port of Linariá. To the east is Áyios Nikólaos or Kalamítsa Bay, with the best beach on the island (shingle). North-west of Linariá are other good beaches (Péfkos, Áyios Fokás, Atsítsa, Kyra Panayía).

Tris Boukés Bay

Tris Boukés (Tristomou) Bay, at the south end of the island, is almost completely cut off from the sea by the islands of Platy and Sarakino. In an olive grove on the east side of the bay is the grave of **Rupert Brooke**.

Spétses   H 6

Argolic Islands
Area: 22 sq. km (8½ sq. mi.)
Altitude: 0–244m (0–801 ft)
Population: 3800
Chief place: Spétses town

Shipping connections with Hydra–Póros–Méthana–Aegina–Piraeus and Kósta (on the mainland). Private cars are banned, but noisy mopeds and motorcycles are permitted. An alternative (and expensive) means of transport for visitors are horse-drawn carriages.

Spétses (Σπετσες), the ancient Pityousa ("Island of Pines"), is a hilly island off the south-east coast of the Argolid (Peloponnese), three-quarters of whose area is covered by forest. The Aleppo pines that are such an attractive feature of the landscape were planted only at the beginning of the 19th c. by Sotirios Anargyros, a wealthy Greek emigrant. In recent years rich Athenians have built magnificent villas near the coast. From the end of the First World War tourism made a contribution to the island's economy when it began to attract prosperous middle class holidaymakers, and it is now the islanders' principal source of income. Many excursion ships put into Spétses harbour for a few hours.

History In antiquity Spétses was an island of no importance, and it seems to have been uninhabited for many centuries until the arrival of Albanian settlers in the 16th c.; their earliest settlement was in the Kastélli area. In 1760, after the Orlov rising, a rebellion against the Turks supported by Catherine the Great of Russia, the population was expelled from the island and Spétses town was laid waste. The inhabitants soon returned to their island, however, and commerce, seafaring and piracy brought them prosperity. Spétses was the home of Laskarina Pinotzis, known as Bouboulina, one of the great figures in the fight for liberation from the Turks. In 1821 it was the first island to take part in the war of independence: an event commemorated every year on September 8th by celebrations (including a firework display) in the Old Harbour.

Sights

★Spétses town

The only town on the island, Spétses (pop. 3600), is spaciously laid out, extending from the Palaío Limáni (Old Harbour) and Dápia districts, on the coast, to the upper town, Kastélli, and along almost half the north coast of the island. Particularly round the picturesque Old Harbour there are many handsome shipowners' and sea-captains' houses from the 18th and 19th c.

A good way to explore Spétses town – in a horse-drawn carriage

Above the Old Harbour, to the west, is the monastery of Áyios Nikólaos, where the Greek flag was hoisted in 1821. Here too the body of Paul-Marie Bonaparte, who died in 1827 on a warship lying off the town, was preserved in oil for several years.

The Mexis House, a fine late 19th c. mansion (signposted from the main square), houses a local museum, with relics of the war of liberation in 1821, including a casket containing the remains of Bouboulina, the heroine of the resistance to the Turks.

To the west of the Dápia quarter, with the New Harbour, is the historic Posidonion Hotel, built by Sotirios Anargyros in the 1920s, which still preserves something of the atmosphere of those early days of the island's tourist trade. In front of the hotel is a statue of Bouboulina. Her house can be seen in the Kounoupitsa quarter (to the south of the New Harbour, by the Town Hall). Opposite it is the mansion of Sotirios Anargyros.

Tour of the island

A road runs round the island for 24 km (15 mi.), though it can be followed only on a moped or motorcycle or on foot. At the very popular **Ayía Marína Beach**, south-east of Spétses town, are scanty remains of a prehistoric settlement. Off Cape Bísti, in the south-east of the island, is the islet of Spetsopoúla, which is owned by the shipowner Stavros Niarchos, with the luxurious mansion that he built on it.

Further west, on Cape Kouzouna, are remains of an Early Christian basilica of the 5th c. There are good and very popular beaches at **Áyii Anárgyri** and **Ayía Paraskeví**, where there is a pilgrimage church. Sailing yachts frequently anchor in Anárgyri Bay in summer. Near here, concealed by large rocks, is the Bekiri Cave, which served as a hiding place for freedom fighters in 1821 – and no doubt for other refugees.

From here the circuit of the island can continue either by way of the highest point on the island, Mount Profítis Ilías (244 m (801 ft)) and the monastery of Áyii Pantes (All Saints) to Ayía Marína or along a beautiful stretch of coast to Zongeria Bay at the north-western tip of the island, On the way back to Spétses are **Ligoneri Beach** (white shingle) and the Anárgyros and Koryialénios College, a school on the English public school model founded by Sotirios Anargyros in 1927.

★★Sými · M 7

Southern Sporades
Area: 63 sq. km (24 sq. mi.)
Altitude: 0–616 m (0–2021 ft)
Population: 2800
Chief place: Sými town (Yialós)

Shipping connections with Piraeus, Tílos, Rhodes and Kos. Hydrofoils to Rhodes and Kos daily in summer. Day trips to Sými from Rhodes (from Mandráki Harbour, Rhodes; 2 hours).

The island of Sými (Συμη), in the Dodecanese, lies 23 km (14 mi.) north-west of Rhodes at the mouth of Sými Bay (Sömbeki Körfesi) on the coast of Asia Minor, which is bounded on the north by the Reladiye peninsula and on the east by the Daraçya peninsula. It has an indented cliff coast-line – according to Homer it had eight good harbours – of 85 km (53 mi.). Its highest point is Mount Vigla (616 m (2021 ft)).

Sými harbour, with its landmark clock tower

Tourism Sými attracts many day trippers from Rhodes, and as a result Sými town tends to be crowded and noisy during the holiday season. It is quieter in the evening and outside the town centre.

One of the most picturesque islands in the Aegean, Sými – unlike other parts of Greece where fine old houses have been pulled down and replaced by faceless modern buildings – has retained and renovated its traditional houses.

History From ancient times the fortunes of Sými were closely linked with those of Rhodes. The island was occupied by the Turks in 1523, and after the Balkan War (1912) was held by Italy. It was reunited with Greece in 1947.

Economy From antiquity until modern times Sými was famed for its boat-building, and sponge diving also made an major contribution to its economy. Both of these activities have declined, and tourism has become an increasingly important source of income. Since the 1970s visitors have mostly been day trippers from Rhodes. Mass tourism, now developing, has some unfortunate consequences, but is the main alternative to emigration.

Sights

Sými town – one of the most beautiful towns in Greece, now protected as a national monument – lies at the head of a deep inlet, its white and ochre-coloured houses climbing up the slopes of a hill above the harbour.

★**Sými town**

A prominent landmark is the clock tower of 1881 at the entrance to the harbour. In the lower town round the harbour (Yialós) are numerous cafés, restaurants and shops, which in addition to the usual souvenirs sell spices and sponges. There are many fine old mansions (*arkhontiká*), now in course of renovation. From the town centre at the head of the harbour inlet a flight of some 500 steps, the Kalí Stráta, leads to the quieter upper town, from which there are fine views. On the summit of the hill was the ancient acropolis, later a castle of the Knights of St John and now the church of the Panayía. In the Khóra is a small folk museum displaying traditional costumes and local arts and crafts.

2 km (1¼ mi.) north-west of Sými (Yialós), in Nimborió Bay, are the remains of an Early Christian basilica, with fine mosaic pavements. To the south of this are catacombs, which in the 5th c. AD are believed to have housed a school of sculptors and icon painters.

Nimborió Bay

Almost all the excursion boats from Rhodes put into Panormítis Bay, at the south end of the island, for a visit to the monastery of the Archangel Michael Panormítis, one of the most important places of pilgrimage in the Dodecanese. It has a magnificent iconostasis with a much venerated icon of the Archangel Michael. Major festivals celebrated here are Whitsun (Pentecost) and November 8th (the feast of the Archangel Michael). The monastery has modest accommodation for large numbers of pilgrims or visitors.

Panormítis Bay

From the southern tip of Sými can be seen the islet of Sesklío (Σεσκλιο; lighthouse), which belongs to Panormítis monastery. Excursion boats from Yialós and Panormítis take visitors to the little island.

Sesklío

Sýros

I 6

Island group: Cyclades
Area: 86 sq. km (33 sq. mi.)

Altitude: 0–442 m (0–1450 ft)
Population: 20,000
Chief place: Ermoúpoli

Shipping connections with Piraeus, Rafína, Iráklion (Crete), Sámos and major islands in the Cyclades and Dodecanese. Bus services on the island.

The hilly island of Sýros (Συρος), lying roughly half way between Kýthnos and Mýkonos, is the principal centre of administration, commerce and fisheries in the Cyclades and a focal point of the shipping routes in the Aegean. The chief town, Ermoúpoli, is the seat of the Prefecture of the Cyclades and the see of both a Roman Catholic bishop and an Orthodox archbishop. Agriculture (market gardening, dairy products), shipbuilding and the textile industry are the major factors in the island's economy. Tourism plays only a modest role: Sýros is usually only a port of call on a tour of the islands. In the southern part of the island, which has good facilities, there are a number of beaches; the northern part is almost completely undeveloped and unspoiled.

History From 1207, after the Fourth Crusade, Sýros belonged to the Venetian duchy of Náxos, and since then it has had a substantial Roman Catholic minority. During the Turkish period, from 1537, it was under the

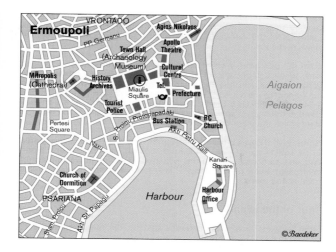

protection of France. During the war of Greek independence Sýros remained neutral, and as a result refugees from Smyrna, Chíos, Psará, Crete, Hydra and other islands were able to find sanctuary here. Close to the town of Áno Sýros, which was founded in the 13th c. and has remained predominantly Catholic, these new settlers established the town of Ermoúpoli ("City of Hermes") by the harbour, and during the 19th c., when Athens was little more than a small town of semi-Oriental type, this developed into the largest Greek port, an important staging post between Asia Minor and western Europe. It was only after the opening of the Corinth Canal in 1893 that the increased importance of Piraeus put a stop to its economic development. The population is now 40 per cent Catholic and 60 per cent Orthodox.

Sights

From ships entering the harbour of Ermoúpoli (Ερμουπολη; pop. 14,000), which is named after Hermes, the god of commerce, there is a striking view of the town, with the houses of the Ermoúpoli and Áno Sýros districts climbing up the slopes of two hills. To the right is Mount Vrondádo (105 m (345 ft)), crowned by the Orthodox cathedral, to the left the hill of Áno Sýros (180 m (591 ft)), with the RC cathedral of St George.

Ermoúpoli

The harbour front, as usual, is lined with cafés and tavernas, as well as shops selling *loukoumia* and *khalvadopitta*, two local specialities that will appeal to the sweet toothed. To the south-west are shipyards.

The central feature of this part of the town is the elegant marble-paved Miaoúlis Square, with good cafés and a monument commemorating Admiral Andreas Miaoúlis, commander of the Greek fleet during the war of independence. The imposing neoclassical Town Hall (by Ernst Ziller, 1876–81) contains a small archaeological museum with finds from Sýros and other islands in the Cyclades ranging in date from the Cycladic culture to Roman times.

Miaoúlis Square

To the north-east of the Town Hall is the Apollo Theatre (by the French architect Chableau, 1861–4), a scaled-down version of La Scala in Milan. Beyond this is the neoclassical church of Áyios Nikólaos (19th c.), with two tall bell towers. This is the select Vaporia ("steamships") district of the town, with handsome neoclassical mansions, many of them built by wealthy shipowners. On the hill above the Town Hall is the Orthodox Cathedral of the Anástasis (Resurrection), from which there are fine views of the town.

Áno Sýros

4 km (2½ mi.) north-west of Ermoúpoli, reached by way of a stepped lane, is the Catholic district of Áno Sýros (Ανω Συρος), established in Venetian times, which is the very picture of a typical Cycladic town. On the summit of the hill is St George's Cathedral (1834), and below this are a Capuchin friary (1633) and a Jesuit house. From Áno Sýros it is an easy climb to the highest peak on the island, Mount Pýrgos (442 m (1450 ft)), from which there are fine panoramic views.

Yiáros

North-west of Sýros is the arid and barren island of Yiáros (Γυαρος; area 37 sq. km (14 sq. mi.); alt. 0–489 m (0–1604 ft)). After the Second World War, and particularly during the military dictatorship, it was a place of internment and a penal colony. There are no shipping services to this uninhabited island.

Tour of the island

From Ermoúpoli a winding road runs west into the interior of the island, coming in 4 km (2½ mi.) to the convent of Ayía Varvára, where the nuns care for orphan children and produce hand-woven fabrics. The road continues by way of Kíni (pop. 250), a fishing village with a stony beach and fish tavernas, to the lively holiday village of Galissás (pop. 300), with a long sandy beach shaded by tamarisks. Other popular resorts are the fishing village of Fínikas (3 km (2 mi.) south), with a number of beaches in the surrounding area, and Posidonía, formerly called Santa Maria delle Grazie, near which is an ancient necropolis. Further along the coast road is the holiday resort of Vári (Βαρη) on the south-east coast, with good sandy beaches.

12 km (7½ mi.) of Ermoúpoli are the sites of a Bronze Age necropolis at Khalandrianí and the Cycladic fortified settlement of Kástri, now overgrown by vegetation. In Grammata Bay, on the west coast, archaeologists found Roman and medieval inscriptions expressing thanksgiving and offering prayers.

Thásos I 3

Islands of the northern and eastern Aegean
Area: 379 sq. km (146 sq. mi.)
Altitude: 0–1127 m (0–3698 ft).
Population: 15,000
Chief place: Thásos town (Liménas)

Ferries from Kavála to Skála Prínos and Liménas and from Keramotí to Liménas. Hydrofoils shuttle between Kavála and Liménas. Bus services on the island.

Thásos (Θασος), an attractive and fertile island, almost exactly circular in shape, lies in the northern Aegean, 8 km (5 mi.) off the eastern Macedonian coast. In spite of devastating forest fires in recent years it is still a green island. It is occupied by a range of hills, slashed by deep valleys, rising to 1127 m (3698 ft) in Mount Ypsári and well wooded at the north-eastern end of the range. The northern and eastern slopes of the hills fall steeply down to the sea; on the south and west sides they slope down more gradually. The most beautiful bays, with magnificent sandy beaches, are on the east coast, but along the 100 km (62 mi.) of the coast

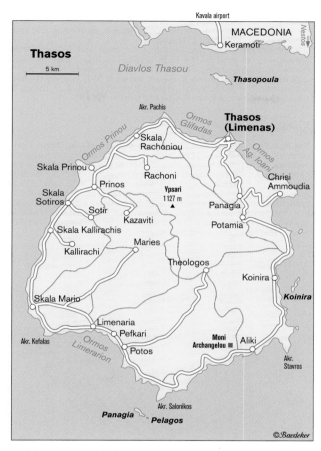

road that runs round the island there are numerous lonely little bathing coves and long sand and shingle beaches.

Economy The island's main sources of income are agriculture, mining (copper, zinc) and tourism, which has not yet taken over the whole island: even during the main holiday season the accommodation for visitors is not fully booked. The numerous camping sites are occupied by whole fleets of mobile homes. The white marble of Thásos was much prized in antiquity and is still quarried south of Liménas.

History 20,000 years ago red ochre (a type of haematite) was being mined at Limenária – the earliest known working of that mineral in Europe. About the middle of the 2nd millennium BC Phoenicians settled on the island, but were later displaced by Thracians. In the 7th c. BC Ionian Greeks from Paros captured Thasos from the Thracians and thereafter grew prosperous through gold and silver mining and trade.

The Greek painter Polygnotus, who decorated the Hephaisteion and the Stoa Poikile in Athens, was a native of Thasos. Between 464 and 404 BC the island was occupied, after fierce resistance, by Athens, and later became subject to Philip II of Macedon.

After periods of Roman, Byzantine, Venetian and Bulgarian rule Thásos was occupied by the Turks in 1455. In 1841 Sultan Mahmud granted it to Muhammad Ali, Khedive of Egypt, whose family held it until 1902. It was occupied by Greek forces in 1912, during the first Balkan War. The discovery of oil some 8 km (5 mi.) east of Thásos in 1994 led to tension between Turkey and Greece.

Sights

Thásos town

The island's chief town and port, known alternatively as Thásos town, Liménas or Limín (Λιμενας; pop. 2300), is almost an open-air museum: it occupies the western half of ancient Thásos, the size of which is evidenced by the walls enclosing the ancient naval harbour (now the fishing harbour), stretches of the town walls, originally 3515 m (11,535 ft) long, and the foundations of houses and temples. The ancient city brought to light by the French Archaeological School extends south-east from the harbour up the slopes of the ancient acropolis, now crowned by the ruins of the Kástro, a castle built in 1431 by the Genoese Gattelusi family, who held Lésbos and Samothrace.

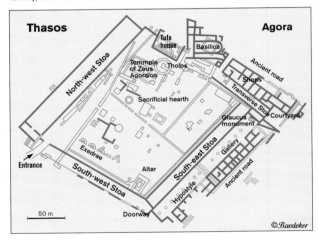

Inland from the ancient harbour is the ★**Agora** (4th c. BC to 1st c. AD), with the foundations of porticoes and stoas; some columns have been re-erected. Facing the Agora is the Archaeological Museum, which displays finds from ancient sites on the island. Its most notable exhibit is a 3.5 m (12 ft) high figure of a young man bearing a lamb on his shoulders. Outside the east corner of the Agora is the Theoria, a passage whose marble walls were decorated with reliefs of the late Archaic period (now in the Louvre in Paris). Further south-east is the sanctuary of Artemis Polo (6th c. BC).

To the south of the Agora are a paved court and, beyond a stretch of Roman road, the **Odeion** (2nd c. AD). South-west of this are the remains of a triumphal arch erected in honour of the Emperors Caracalla and Septimius Severus in AD 213–217 and a temple of Heracles (6th c. BC).

In the northern part of the ancient city, to the east of the old harbour, are **sanctuaries** of Poseidon and Dionysus (both 4th c. BC), a theatre of the 3rd–2nd c. BC, a sanctuary devoted to foreign divinities and, at the northern tip of the city, a sanctuary of the Patrooi Theoi ("Father Gods"; 6th c. BC). Further north, in the sea, can be seen remains of the breakwater of the ancient commercial harbour.

From the theatre (in which performances are given in summer) a path runs up to the Kástro, at the south-western tip of which is an ancient relief of a funeral meal, and to the foundations of a temple of Athena (5th c. BC) on the hill to the south-west. From the highest point of the **acropolis** there is a magnificent view of the town. From here a path runs down the slopes of a third hill, passing a recess containing a sanctuary of Pan, to return to the town.

A road runs round the island for some 100 km (65 mi.), running close to the coast, bringing all the villages and beaches within easy reach (bus services).

Panayía

From Thásos the road runs south-east by way of Panayía (Παναγια), a little town of slate-roofed, balconied houses that until 1912 was the chief place on the island, and along the eastern slopes of Mount Ypsári.

In Potamiá (Ποταμια) is a museum devoted to the work of the sculptor Polygnotos Vagis, a native of the village. From here there are beautiful views over the wooded valley to the sea and the 4 km (2½ mi.) long beach of Khrysí Ammoudiá (Golden Beach), the best sandy beach on the island.

Potamiá

The island of Thásos is covered by great expanses of forest, and its chief town, Thásos, is surrounded by lush vegetation

Tílos

Alikí peninsula

The road continues by way of Kínyra, which has a beautiful beach (Paradise Beach), to the Alikí peninsula, with two idyllic sandy bays. The one to the east is mainly favoured by nudists and backpackers. There is a route round the peninsula (signposted for the first part of the way) that leads to the remains of a sanctuary of the Dioscuri (5th c. BC) and two Early Christian basilicas. Beyond this are ancient marble quarries.

Potós

The road now runs high above the cliff-lined west coast to the former fishing village of Potós (Ποτος), now a tourist centre with a 2 km (1¼ mi.) long sand and shingle beach. On the way there is the Arkhángelou convent, which has an icon revered as wonder-working.

★Theológos

From Potós (or from Alikí) a side trip (10 km (6¼ mi.)) can be made to the unspoiled hill village of Theológos (Θεολογος; alt. 240 m (785 ft)), which in the 18th and 19th centuries was the chief place on the island. There are service buses to the village. The handsome old houses, most of them slate roofed and surrounded by walls, are protected national monuments.

Limenária

The road continues, passing the beautiful beach of Pefkári, to the second largest place on the island, Limenária (Λιμεναρια; pop. 1500), which was founded in 1903 by a German firm mining for ores and minerals here. On a hill above the harbour is a villa that belonged to the Krupp family. Limenária is now a popular bathing resort. Below the town can be seen disused and ruinous blast furnaces. Limenária has only a very narrow beach, but there is a good sandy beach 500 m west of the town.

Bathing resorts The pretty fishing villages of Skála Marión, Skála Kallirákhis and Skála Sotíras are still relatively unspoiled by tourism. From the last two there are pleasant trips to the hill villages after which they are named. Skála Rakhoniou, on the north coast, is now a popular holiday resort.

Tílos   M 7

Southern Sporades (Dodecanese)
Area: 63 sq. km (24 sq. mi.)
Altitude: 0–651 m (0–2136 ft)
Population: 300
Chief place: Megálo Khorió

Port: Livádia. Shipping connections with Piraeus, Sými–Rhodes, Nísyros–Kos–Kálymnos–Léros–Lipsí–Pátmos–Sámos, and Astypálaia. Hydrofoils to Kos, Sými and Rhodes (in summer). Bus services on the island.

Tílos (Τηλος) is a bare and rugged island in the Dodecanese (Southern Sporades), lying half way between Rhodes and Kos. The inhabitants make a modest living from farming, on terraces that have been laboriously built up over the centuries, and fishing. Tourism plays only a very small part in the economy, though it is now showing a rising trend. It offers good walking country, with varied and beautiful scenery, long inlets reaching deep inland and green wooded valleys. It also had pleasant sand and shingle beaches, some of them accessible only on foot.

Throughout the island's **history** its fortunes were closely linked with those of Rhodes and the Dodecanese Its Italian name was Piscopi. After the Second World War increasing numbers of the inhabitants emigrated overseas.

Megálo Khorió, the largest place on Tílos, with the hill of Áyios Stéfanos rearing above it

Sights

On the east coast of the island is the little port of Livádia (Λιβαδια), where the ferries put in. Almost all the hotels, pensions and tourist facilities are here. There is a shingle beach.

Livádia

From Livádia a concrete road runs north-west, climbing to a telecommunications tower from which there are wide views over the island. It passes the village of Mikró Khorió, which was abandoned in the 1970s. There are two churches, and in summer a bar (with music).

Mikró Khorió

2 km (1¼ mi.) north of Mikró Khorió are the ruins of the Venetian castle of Mesariá. Close by, to the west, is the Kharkadio Cave, where archaeologists discovered bones of dwarf elephants, a species that became extinct about 4500 BC.

Kharkadio Cave

Megálo Khorió (Μεγαλο Χωριο), the largest place on Tílos, with a population of just under 200, lies above Áyios Antónios Bay on the north-west coast of the island. It occupies the site of ancient Telos; there are some remains of walls. Above the village rises the rocky hill of Áyios Stéfanos (286 m (938 ft)), crowned by a castle of the Knights of St John. Here too, built on the foundations of an ancient sanctuary of Apollo and Athena, is a church of the Archangel Michael, now falling into ruin, which has fine 16th c. frescos.

Megálo Khorió

3 km (2 mi.) south of Megálo Khorió, on the south coast, is the sandy beach of Éristos, shaded by tamarisks.

Éristos

5 km (3 mi.) west, below a massive rock wall – hidden to view from the sea – is the uninhabited but well maintained monastery of Áyios

Áyios Panteleímon

Panteleímon, founded in the 14th c. The present buildings and the well-preserved frescos date from the 18th c.

1.5 km (1 mi.) north-west of Tílos is the islet of **Gaidouronísi**, with a lighthouse. 3 km (2 mi.) south-east is the little uninhabited island of **Antítilos**.

Tínos   I/K 6

Island group: Cyclades
Area: 194 sq. km (75 sq. mi.)
Altitude: 0–729 m (0–2392 ft)
Population: 8000
Chief place: Tínos town

Shipping connections with Piraeus, Rafína and other islands in the Cyclades. Bus services on the island.

Tínos (Τηνος), the south-eastern continuation of the mountain massif that extends from Euboea by way of Ándros, is the third largest island in the Cyclades, 30 km (19 mi.) long by 15 km (9 mi.) across. It is the "Greek Lourdes", a pilgrimage centre that on the great Marian feast days, particularly the Dormition on August 15th, draws many thousands of pilgrims, who fill all the accommodation for visitors, camp out in the open and picnic in the churchyard. Ordinary tourism is on a modest scale and the bathing resorts and beaches are never crowded. The island's main sources of income, apart from the pilgrimage trade (with half a million visitors every year), are the quarrying of marble and the growing of vegetables.

Tínos is famed for is famed for its **dovecotes** – elaborately decorated tower-like structures dating from Venetian times, many of them now renovated – of which there are around 800 scattered about the island. Particularly fine examples are to be seen at

The pilgrimage church of the Panayía Evangelístria, Tínos town

Kámpos and Tarambádos, to the north of Tínos town. The pigeons were valued for their tender flesh and for the droppings that were used as fertilisers.

History In antiquity, from the 3rd c. BC onwards, the sanctuary of Poseidon and Amphitrite on Tenos was a major religious centre, and in more recent times, since the early 19th c., the island has possessed a leading shrine of the Orthodox church. Held by Venice from 1207 to 1715, Tínos had the longest period of Frankish occupation of any part of Greece, and in consequence its population includes a considerable proportion of Roman Catholics. In 1822, during the war of liberation from the Turks, a nun named Pelagia, guided by a vision, found a wonder-working icon of the Panayía, which soon became the object of annual pilgrimages on the feasts of the Annunciation (March 25th) and Dormition (August 15th). The ecclesiastical and national significance of the island was increased when on August 15th 1940, two months before Mussolini's declaration of war, an Italian submarine torpedoed the Greek cruiser "Elli" that was lying in Tínos harbour for the feast of the Dormition.

★Tínos town

Visitors arriving in Tínos town (pop. 3000), the chief place on the island, can be in no doubt that this is a pilgrimage centre: commandingly situated above the town is the church of the Panayía Evangelístria, with a wide, steep pilgrimage way leading directly up from the harbour to the church. After the destruction of the Exómbourgo fortress by the Turks in 1715 this typical little Cycladic town, situated in a wide bay on the south coast, developed from a modest coastal settlement into the island's capital. This was the site of the ancient city, Asty. In Evangelístria Street, which runs up from the busy harbour parallel to the pilgrimage way, are shops selling all manner of devotional articles.

Panayía Evangelístria

The palatial church of the Panayía Evangelístria, the second largest church in Greece, was built in 1823–30, incorporating architectural elements from the Poseidonion (see below) and the Temple of Apollo on Delos. The interior contains innumerable votive offerings and valuable sacred objects. To the left of the entrance is the much venerated icon of the Panayía Megalokhori, over 800 years old, which is believed to have been painted by Luke the Evangelist and is credited with wonder-working qualities. Under the church are a mausoleum for those killed in the sinking of the cruiser "Elli" and the spot where the wonder-working icon was found. Here pilgrims draw holy water from the spring and children are brought from all over Greece to be baptised.

In a side wing are a Byzantine **museum** and a **gallery** displaying works by Tiniot artists, some of them (e.g. Yiannolis Khalepas) of international reputation. From the marble terrace there are fine views.

★Archaeological Museum

The Archaeological Museum, below the church, displays archaeological material from Tínos, and particularly from the two large sanctuaries on the island, the sacred precinct of Demeter (7th c. BC) at Tripotamos and the Hellenistic sanctuary of Poseidon and Amphitrite at Kiónia. Notable items are the huge storage vessels of the 7th c. BC, including a pithos with relief decoration, the main scene in which has been interpreted as the birth of Athena from the head of Zeus (who is depicted with wings). Open Mon., Wed.–Sat. 8.30am–3pm.

Other sights

Kekhrovoúnio convent

9 km (5½ mi.) north of Tínos town is the 12th c. Kekhrovoúnio convent in which the visionary nun Pelagia lived. It is still occupied by 50 nuns. Visitors are shown Pelagia's cell, a private place with a magnificent view.

Mount Exómbourgo

A few kilometres further north is Mount Exómbourgo (540 m (1772 ft)), a granite cone that is worth climbing for the sake of the wide views from the top. It is reached by taking a road on the left just before Falatados, leading to a church from which it is a short walk (20 min.). On this steep and rocky hill are the ruins of a Venetian castle and the island's medieval capital, Sant'Elena. In Loutrá, at the foot of the hill, is a convent of Ursuline nuns. Then by way of Kómi to Kolymbíthra Bay on the north coast, which has good and relatively unfrequented sandy beaches.

Kiónia

4 km (2½ mi.) west of Tínos town is Kiónia (Κιωνια), which has a long shingle beach. In front of the Tínos Beach Hotel, to the right, are the remains of the Poseidonion, the sanctuary of Poseidon and Amphitrite (open Tue.–Fri., Sun. 8.30am–3pm, Sat. 8.30–11am). To this sanctuary of the 5th c. BC, renovated in Hellenistic times, with a marble exedra, large numbers of people came for healing. The cult of Poseidon on Tínos went back to the 7th c. BC. He is said to have freed the island from a plague of vipers, after which he was worshipped as a god of healing. Associated with the cult of Poseidon from the 3rd c. BC was the cult of his wife Amphitrite, who was revered as the curer of women's diseases.

Around the idyllic **hill villages** of Kámpos, Tarambádos and Kardianí are numbers of particularly fine dovecotes. Kardianí is largely built of marble. Another pretty village, 4 km (2½ mi.) further north-west, is Isternia, which has marble-paved streets and a church with a tile-clad dome.

A few kilometres further on is the second largest place on the island, Pýrgos (Πύργος; pop. 500), also known as Pánormos, which is famed as a village of sculptors and painters. The house once occupied by the leading sculptor Yiannolis Khalepas (1851–1938) is now a museum. There is also a school of fine arts.

In the north-west of the island, to the south of Pánormos Bay, are a number of quarries in which green marble is still worked. There are few attractive beaches in this part of the island.

Zákynthos   E 6

Ionian Islands
Area: 402 sq. km (155 sq. mi.)
Altitude: 0–758 m (0–2487 ft)
Population: 32,000
Chief place: Zákynthos town

Airport 6 km (4 mi.) south of Zákynthos town (no airport buses). Air connections with Athens. Charter flights. Ferries Kyllíni (Peloponnese)–Zákynthos; in summer also Skinári–Pesáda (Kefaloniá) and Zákynthos–Nydrí (Léfkas). Bus connections with Patrás–Athens. Variable local bus services.

Zákynthos (Ζάκυνθος), the most southerly of the Ionian Islands, lies 16 km (10 mi.) off the west coast of the Peloponnese. It bears the mark of 300 years of Venetian history – when it was known as Fior di Levante, "Flower of the East" – and with its gentle green landscapes it has something of the air of Tuscany. The western half of the island is occupied by a karstic plateau rising to 758 m (2487 ft), the eastern half by a fertile and intensively cultivated alluvial plain. Among the island's products, in addition to olives and citrus fruits, are good white wines (Verdea, Delizia).

Zákynthos is famed as the island of the **turtles**. During the summer loggerback turtles (*Caretta caretta*) lay their eggs on the sandy beaches on the south coast of the island. But in recent years these beaches of fine sand have been attracting increasing numbers of holidaymakers, and this has steadily reduced the turtles' habitat. The 7 km (4½ mi.) long beach at Laganás in particular has been completely taken over by tourism. Argási on the Skopós peninsula and the bathing resorts on the east coast, in particular Tsiliví, are also major tourist centres. The beautiful beaches on the south side of the Skopós peninsula are still relatively unspoiled.

History The island has been known since the time of Homer by the name it still bears, said to be derived from the wild hyacinth (Hyacinthus orientalis L.). Settled at an early period by Achaeans and Arcadians, it soon developed into a trading and seafaring town whose influence in the western Mediterranean extended as far as the Iberian peninsula, where it founded the colony of Saguntum – or so at least the ancient historians say. In 455 BC the Athenian admiral Tolmides made the island, hitherto independent, a dependency of Athens. After the Peloponnesian War it became a member of the Attic maritime league. In 217 BC it was conquered by the Macedonians, in 191 BC by the Romans.

The finest view of Zákynthos is from Mount Bokháli on the west side of the town

Zákynthos was devastated by the Vandals in the 5th c. AD and conquered by the Normans in the 12th c. In 1209 it fell into the hands of an Italian noble family, the Orsini. It was occupied by the Turks in 1479 but recovered two years later by the Venetians, who called it Zante and held it until 1797. After brief Russian and French interludes Zákynthos became British in 1809; and finally in 1864 Britain returned it to Greece. From its long period of association with Venice the island has preserved a distinctly Italian stamp. In a devastating earthquake in 1953, however, almost all its old buildings were destroyed.

Zákynthos was the birthplace of the Italian poet Ugo Foscolo (see Famous People) and the Greek poet Dionysios Solomos (1798–1857), author of the Greek national anthem.

★Zákynthos town

The chief place on the island, Zákynthos town (pop. 10,000) extends in a wide arc round a bay on the east coast. It is a town of handsome buildings, spacious squares, picturesque streets and carefully groomed gardens. Almost all the buildings had to be rebuilt after the 1953 earthquake. The coast road is lined by hotels, restaurants and large numbers of shops. Its main shopping street is the busy Odós Alexandrou Roma.

Solomos Square

A good starting point for a tour of the town is Platía Solomou, a large square on the harbour front named after the poet Dionysios Solomos, who is commemorated by a monument in the square. (There is also a Solomos Museum in St Mark's Square). Near the seafront is the Venetian church of St Nicholas, originally built in 1561, whose bell tower once served as a lighthouse. Adjoining it is the Municipal Library, which also houses archives and a collection of pictures. It displays numerous photographs illustrating the devastating effect of the 1953 earthquake.

On the west side of the square is the Museum of Sacred Art (open Tue.–Sun. 8am–2.30pm), which has a rich collection of icons, iconostases, woodcarving, frescos, etc., from the Byzantine period to the 19th c. The development of the "Ionian school" of painting can be clearly seen on Zákynthos.

★Museum of Sacred Art

After the Turkish conquest of Crete in 1669 many Cretan artists fled to Zákynthos; and while Byzantine painting in general held strictly to standard patterns the Cretan artists were influenced by the art of the Italian Renaissance (Crete having been under Venetian rule since 1204). They depicted the saints not as celestial beings but as human beings concerned with the life of men. Among leading painters of the Ionian school were Parayiotis Doxaras (1662–1729), I. Strati Plakotos (1662–1728), Nikolaos Doxaras (1705–75) and Nikolaos Kantounis (1767–1834).

The museum also displays photographs and a relief model of the town showing what Zákynthos town looked like before the 1953 earthquake.

At the west end of the harbour is the church of Áyios Dionýsios (the island's patron saint), built in 1948, which survived the 1953 earthquake unscathed. The bell tower was modelled on the Campanile in St Mark's Square in Venice. It has numerous wall paintings of the 1980s, including

Áyios Dionýsios

scenes from the life of St Dionysius, who was born on Zákynthos in 1547.

★Bokháli

The road to the western suburb of Bokháli, which reaches up on to the hills ringing the town, passes the New Cathedral (Mitrópolis). Beyond this are the British Cemetery, laid out in the 19th c., and the abandoned Jewish Cemetery, which dates from the 13th c.

From the church of the Panayía Khrysopiyí there is a marvellous view over the town. It is a plain building with a richly carved and gilded iconostasis from the earlier church that was destroyed in 1953.

The road continues up to the Kástro, with the remains of walls dating from the Venetian period. Over the inner gate of the castle is the Lion of St Mark. The vaulting of the old prison can still be seen.

Southern Zákynthos

South-east of Zákynthos town is the Skopós peninsula, with a whole series of good and well-equipped beaches. Argási is a resort much favoured by British holidaymakers, though the beach is not one of the best.

Other popular resorts are Pórto Róma, with a small shingle beach, and Gérakas, with the longest sandy beach on the island. The beach at Gérakas is one of the numerous spawning grounds of the loggerhead turtle, which extend to the south end of Laganás Bay and include also the privately owned little islet of Marathonísi.

Laganás Bay

Thanks to the magnificent sandy beaches that run round Laganás Bay, Laganás (Λαγανας) is now the largest tourist development on the island. Until recently the bay was the most important breeding site of the log-gerhead turtle in the whole of the Mediterranean. Only a few years ago more than 1000 of these turtles, which are over a metre (40 in.) long and weigh anything up to 150 kg, were still depositing their tennis-ball-size eggs in the sand every year; then, after between 50 and 65 days, the young turtles, only 4 cm (1½ in.) long, would crawl down into the sea at night.

Now, however, as a result of the remorseless development of the tourist trade, the number of turtles coming here has been drastically reduced and the young turtles have only a slim chance of survival. For years various Greek and international agencies concerned with the protection of nature have been in conflict with local tourist interests, who seek to increase the number of visitors to the beaches by new illegal building and even use the turtles as a tourist attraction. Government plans to protect this endangered species have come up against strong resistance from local people, who fear that it will lead to a decline in the tourist trade. Surely there are enough beaches elsewhere on Zákynthos to satisfy the needs of holidaymakers.

Límni Kerioú

At the south end of Laganás Bay, where the road is lined by ancient gnarled olive trees, interrupted by vineyards, is the fishing village of Límni Kerioú (Λιμνη Κεριου), which has a shingle beach, with hotels, pensions and tavernas. A short walk away, in an area of marshland, are the pitch wells of Kerí, which have been famed since ancient times but are now almost covered by a growth of reeds. The pitch was used from antiquity to the 20th c. for the caulking of boats.

Zákynthos's Blue Grotto

Northern Zákynthos

Northern Zákynthos is, scenically, the most beautiful part of the island. It can be seen in a full day's drive – though this leaves little time for a boat trip along the bizarrely shaped rocky coast. **Alykés**

From Zákynthos town the route runs north, passing a series of tourist resorts on the east coast – Tsiliví, Plános and then Alykés (Αλυκες), one of the largest tourist centres on the island. The name means "salt pans"; and salt was indeed won here from the Middle Ages until the early 1990s.

Just to the south of Alykés, at the foot of Mount Vrakhionas (756 m (2480 ft)), Zákynthos's highest hill, is the largest village on the island, Katastári (Κατασταρι), which is dominated by the modern twin-towered church of the Panayía i Katastári. 2 km (1¼ mi.) further on a road goes off on the left to the idyllically situated walled monastery of Ioánnis Pródromos (John the Baptist). **Katastári**

The road (asphalted all the way) now follows a winding course along the coast, passing through increasingly lonely and barren but idyllically beautiful country, to Makrýs Yialós (Μακρυς Γιαλος). Only a few day trippers come to this little fishing village. From the little port of Áyios Nikólaos there are ferries to the neighbouring island of Kefaloniá (see entry). There are excursion boats to the Blue Grotto, a trip of about an hour. **Makrýs Yialós**

The boat sails north, passing bizarrely shaped rocks, to the Blue Grotto (Galazia Spilaia) that has been carved out by the surf near Cape **★Blue Grotto**

Skinári. The cave, discovered in 1897, has two chambers that shimmer in varying shades of blue. The play of colour is particularly fine in the early morning, with a spectrum of colour ranging from dark green to sky blue.

Cape Skinári

The route continues by way of the secluded village of Korithion to Cape Skinári, at the northern tip of the island. Boats from here take only 10 minutes to reach the Blue Grotto. There are also trips in larger boats to Shipwreck Beach (see below).

Áyios Andréas

At Volimes a track goes off to the abandoned monastery of Áyios Andréas, situated close to the coast. The bell tower bears the date 1641. Frescos and icons from the modest little church are now in the museum in Zákynthos town.

★Anafonítria

2 km (1¼ mi.) south of Volimes is one of the island's most popular destinations for excursions, the hill village of Anafonítria (Αναφωνητρια) with its winding lanes and whitewashed houses. It attracts many visitors to see the monastery of the Panayía Anafonítria to the south of the village. The tree-shaded precincts of the monastery, founded in the 15th c., are entered through an arched gateway, beside which are the remains of a defensive tower. The monastery's aisled basilica is believed to be the oldest church on the island. The silver-framed wonder-working icon of the Panayía is said to have been brought to Zákynthos from Constantinople after its capture by the Turks in 1453. The patron saint of Zákynthos, St Dionysius (see above), spent his last years as abbot of the monastery.

Pórto Vromí

From the monastery a road runs south-west to Pórto Vromí (Πορτο Βρωμη), located in an inlet reaching far inland that forms a natural harbour. From here there are excursion boats to Shipwreck Beach, which is accessible only from the sea. A few kilometres north-west, near the cliff-lined coast, is the abandoned 16th c. monastery of Áyios Yeóryios Krimnon, surrounded by whitewashed walls (access by way of Anafonítria).

A track running towards the coast from the Áyios Yeóryios monastery comes in 1.5 km (1 mi.) to a parking area from which a narrow path runs along the coast. 500 m along this path there is a fine view of ★**Shipwreck Beach**, in a sandy bay enclosed by high white cliffs. The beach is named after a freighter that ran aground here in the 1970s. The water in the bay is of a deep turquoise colour.

Kampí

From Anafonítria a road runs by way of Mariés to the village of Kampí (Καμπη), situated near the south-west coast amid vineyards, fields and olive groves. There are a number of tavernas, from which in the evening you can watch the sun sinking slowly into the sea.

Limniónas

A few kilometres further south is Limniónas (Λιμνιωνας), from which there are boat trips along the rugged coast, for example to the little offshore island of Karakonísi.

Loúkha
Gýri

From Áyios Leontas a road runs north into a lonely upland region. In the villages of Loúkha and Gýri (Λουχα, Γυρι), which both date from the 15th c., time seems to have stood still. Many of the inhabitants have left to seek better job prospects in the coastal resorts or in mainland Greece.

Makhairádo

The road from Koiloménos by way of Lagopóda runs past the convent of the Panayía i Eleftherotria, founded in 1961. Makhairádo (Μαχαιραδο) itself is dominated by the tall Venetian campanile of the church of Ayía Mávra, one of the most beautiful on the island, with particularly melodious bells. The church, whose exterior is entirely without decoration, has a richly decorated iconostasis. On a carved and gilded shrine in front of the iconostasis is a 16th c. icon of Ayía Mávra. From Makhairádo it is only 10 km (6¼ mi.) back to Zákynthos town.

**Practical
Information
from A–Z**

Practical Information from A to Z

Accommodation

See Camping, Hotels, Self-Catering

Air Travel

International flights

International charter flights and Greece's domestic airlines cater for air travel to all the Greek islands that have their own airports. All the scheduled services by the international airlines fly into either Athens, Thessaloniki or Kavala where passengers then transfer to internal flights. This means that to get to the islands in the peak season it is best to opt for a charter flight (see also Getting to the Greek Islands).

Internal flights

Greece has a dense network of internal flights, and all the major islands can be reached by Olympic Airways' daily domestic flights. There are also connections via Corfu. However, since the Greek domestic air timetables cannot always be relied on you should check in advance whether a particular flight will actually be operating at the scheduled time.

Island destinations from Athens: Astypalaia, Chania (Crete), Chios, Corfu (town), Ikaria, Iraklion (Crete), Karpathos, Kastoria, Kefallonia, Kos, Kythira, Leros, Limnos, Milos, Mykonos, Mytilini (Lesbos), Naxos, Paros, Rhodes, Samos, Santorini, Sitia (Crete), Skiathos, Skyros and Zakynthos.
Island destinations from Thessaloniki: Chios, Corfu, Crete, Lesbos, Limnos, Rhodes and Samos.
From Rhodes there are connections to Crete, Karpathos, Kasos, Kastellorizo, Kos, and Mykonos. There are also flights between Lesbos and Chios, Limnos and Samos, Kasos and Karpathos, and Kefallonia and Zakynos.

Olympic Airways

Head office: Syngrou Avenue 96, 11741 Athens; tel. (01) 9269111, fax 9267154
Booking office: 15 Filellinon St. (Syntagma Square), Athens
International flights: tel. (01) 9267555
Internal flights: tel. (01) 9267444

Ellinikon Airport, Athens
Information: (01) 9363363

Antiquities

The export of antiquities, including works of art such as icons, is strictly

◀ *Fishing harbour in Noausa on Paxos. One of the many romantic harbours which can be found on most Greek islands*

forbidden and subject to fines and imprisonment unless approval has been given by the Ministry of Culture and Science:

Ministry of Culture and Science, Odos Aristidou 14
10186 Athens; tel. (01) 3231693

Copies of antiquities in museum collections, such as frescoes, icons and jewellery can be bought and exported. These are available in shops as for example on Rhodes and from museum shops, including the National Archaeological Museum in Athens.

Beaches

The Greek islands have plenty of sandy beaches and lovely coves and bays where it is warm enough to swim from April to November. Between June and September the average water temperatures range between 19°C (64°F) and 23°C (73°F), but since the evening breezes off the sea can be decidedly cool you should also take some warm clothing.

Natural, unsupervised beaches have no facilities of any kind, and that includes warning signs, boundary buoys, nets, etc.

Natural beaches

The Greek National Tourist Organisation (Ellinikos Organismos Tourismou, EOT) maintains a series of supervised bathing beaches which in addition to the usual facilities (changing cabins, kiosks, play areas etc.) also have a range of sports facilities, restaurants, discos, etc.

EOT beaches

Beaches belonging to hotels are subject to strict government control and

Hotel beaches

Kambos Bay on Patmos: shingle beaches are common on Greek islands

are consequently well maintained and serviced, although they do not all necessarily have life-guards and first-aid stations.

Popular beaches

On the islands of Aegina, Poros, Hydra and Spetsai you can still find beautiful crowd-free bathing beaches. There are also good beaches for swimming on Kos, at Lindos on Rhodes, on Crete's Elunda beach, at Perama and Benitses on Corfu, and on Kefallonia.

Water quality

Many stretches of the Mediterranean coast are no longer as clean and unspoilt as they were only a few decades ago. This applies mainly to beaches close to the more densely populated areas and particularly to those on the Saronic Gulf where the water quality has suffered from the heavy shipping traffic and pollution by sewage outfalls from Athens. Swimming close to the city should therefore be avoided, and is actually banned in places.

Nude bathing

There are many beaches where going topless is not a problem. A few beaches also allow nude bathing but as a general rule this is forbidden, so if in doubt play safe and cover up.

Camping

Information

Panhellenic Camping Association
102 Odós Solonós, 10680 Athens
Tel. (01) 3621560, fax 3465262/5820353

A list of campsites is also available from the offices of the EOT, Greek National Tourist Organisation (see Information), and other sources of information include the local Tourist Police and the ELPA Automobile Club headquarters in Athens (see Motoring).

Camping anywhere except on official sites – by the roadside, on waste ground, etc. – is strictly forbidden.

Classification

Most Greek campsites are supervised by the tourist authorities. They are also classified according to their facilities:
Category A: very good facilities
Category B: good facilities
Category C: adequate facilities.
Besides the sites managed by EOT there are others run by the Greek Touring Club or privately owned. Some of these sites also have small chalets for rental.

Caravans

Caravans must comply with the following limits on size and weight: maximum height 3.8 m (12 ft 6 in.); maximum width 2.5 m (8 ft 3 in.); maximum length 12 m (39 ft); maximum axle weight 9 metric tons; maximum length of car and trailer 15 m (49 ft).

Car Rental

See Motoring

Chemists

See Health

Consulates

See Diplomatic Representation

Cruises

The main base for Mediterranean cruises is the port of Piraeus. Cruises that combine onshore excursions to the famous archaeological sites are particularly popular. There are also day-cruises from Piraeus to several islands, including Aegina, Poros and Idra in the Saronic Gulf. Other longer cruises call at, for example, Patmos and Rhodes in the Aegean, Crete, the Cyclades, Corfu, and Cyprus (including Limassol). They can also take in the whole of the Mediterranean, or visit ports on the Black Sea.

A list of the shipping companies that operate cruises can be had from the Greek Tourist Offices (see Information). Detailed information is also available from local travel agents.

The price of a day-cruise usually includes the return trip from the hotel to the port and a buffet lunch; the price of longer cruises includes full board as well as the travel costs (reductions for children on request). | Prices

Currency

The Greek unit of currency is the drachma (dr.). There are banknotes for 100, 200, 500, 1000, 5000 and 10,000 drs., and coins for 5, 10, 20, 50, 100 and 200 drs. | Unit of currency

Greece, though an EU member state, is not yet part of the European and Monetary Union since it failed to meet the entry criteria. The drachma is therefore its only official currency unit. | European and Monetary Union

As is usual in countries with weak currencies, it is best to change money in Greece rather than outside it. The simplest and most profitable way to get drachmas is to use one of the many bank cash dispensers. Complete with instructions in English, these are to be found in all the main island towns and tourist centres, and will take Eurocards and all the main international credit cards. | Changing money

Some hotels will change money at the reception desk, but the rate of exchange is likely to be less favourable than it would be from a bank.

Banks, besides issuing cash against credit cards, will also change Eurocheques, accompanied by a Eurocard, and traveller's cheques. Ordinary cheques will only be honoured after the bank has checked with your own bank, and this can take several days. Always keep the receipt for your traveller's cheques separate from the cheques themselves, and in the event of loss of any of your cheques or cards get them cancelled by calling the appropriate number immediately. Most large hotels, shops, top restaurants and car hire firms will take the major international credit credit cards. | Credit cards

Banks are usually open Mon.–Thu. 8am–2pm, Fri. to 1.30pm; some also open (at least during the holiday season) Sat. 8am–1pm. | Banking hours

Customs Regulations

The import of plants, walkie-talkies and firearms (other than sporting | Prohibited imports guns) is forbidden. Persons under 18 are not allowed to bring in tobacco products or spirits, and those under 15 may not bring in coffee.

Duty-free items

Member states of the European Union, and that includes Greece, form a common internal market within which items for personal use are generally free of duty. There are, however, certain guidelines on maximum amounts, and for Greece the upper limits for incoming travellers aged over 18 on items purchased elsewhere in the European Union are: 800 cigarettes, 400 cigarillos, 200 cigars, 1 kilo tobacco, 10 litres spirits over 22 per cent proof, or 20 litres less than 22 per cent proof, 90 litres wine (including no more than 60 litres sparkling wine), and 110 litres beer. If the Greek Customs and Excise officials carry out spot-checks you will have to prove to them that any imported goods are genuinely for personal use.

Entry from non-EU countries

The duty-free allowances for travellers (aged 18 and over) coming from non-EU countries are: 200 cigarettes or 100 cigarillos or 50 cigars or 250 g tobacco, 2 litres wine and 2 litres sparking wine or 1 litre spirits over 22 per cent proof or 2 litres spirits less than 22 per cent proof, 50 grams perfume and 1/4 litre eau de cologne, 500 grams coffee beans or 200 grams of instant coffee, 100 grams tea or 40 grams instant tea, plus duty-free are gifts up to a value of 45 ECU or 10,000 drs (children under 15: 23 ECU or 5500 drs.).

Vehicles

Private cars (and trailers, motorcycles, sidecars and mopeds) may be taken into Greece without payment of duty for up to 15 months but must be entered in the owner's passport. If a foreign car has an accident in Greece and becomes a write-off the customs authorities must be informed before the car can be scrapped.

Boats

Similar regulations apply to small motorboats and sailing boats brought in by road. Yachts (i.e. boats with cabin, galley, lavatory, etc.) must, on arrival in Greece, put in at a port with customs facilities and obtain a transit log (valid for six months, with the possibility of unlimited extension). They may bring in a Very pistol and flare pistol as part of their equipment.

Re-entry to other countries

Travellers from EU countries are permitted the same duty-free allowances as on entry, plus provisions for the journey up to a value of 50 US dollars and souvenirs to a value of 150 US dollars. For other English-speaking countries the duty-free allowances are as follows: Australia 250 cigarettes or 250 grams tobacco, 1 litre alcohol; Canada 200 cigarettes and 50 cigars and 400 grams tobacco, 1.1 litre spirits or wine or 8.5 litres beer; New Zealand 200 cigarettes or 50 cigars or 250 grams tobacco, 4.5 litres wine or beer and 1.1 litre spirits; South Africa 400 cigarettes and 50 cigars and 250 grams tobacco, 2 litres wine and 1 litre spirits; USA 200 cigarettes and 100 cigars and 2 kilo tobacco, 1 litre wine or spirits.

Diplomatic Representation

Canada

Embassy:
Odos Ioannou Yennadiou 4
11521 Athens; tel. (01) 7273400

United Kingdom

Embassy:
Odos Ploutarkhou 1
10675 Athens; tel. (01) 7236211

Consulates:
Leoforos Alexandras 2
49100 Kerkyra, Corfu; tel. (0661) 30055/37995

Odos Papa Alexandrou 16
71202 Iraklion, Crete; tel. (081) 224012

Odos Votsi 2
26221 Patras; tel. (061) 277329

Odos 25 Mariou 23
85100 Rhodes; tel. (0241) 27247/27306

Annetas
Laoumtzi 8, Kos; tel (0242) 21549

Akti P. Ralli 8
84100 Ermoupolis, Syros; tel. (0281) 82232

Embassy: United States
Leoforos Vasilissis Sofias 91
11521 Athens; tel. (01) 7212951/7218401

Electricity

Electricity is normally 220 volts AC; on ships it is frequently 110 volts AC.
Power sockets are of normal European type. Adaptors are necessary for
British or North American plugs. These can sometimes be borrowed in
hotels, but it is wisest to take your own.

Emergencies

The most useful source of help for tourists is the Tourist Police   Tourist Police
(Turistiki Astynomia). They have offices in many of the main centres
for tourism and can provide general information and advice about
where to stay.

Tel. (01) 171 (in Athens)

Tel. 100   Police
The police will direct all calls for assistance to the appropriate place.

Tel. 166   Ambulance
                                                                                   (Athens area)
Tel. 199   Fire service

Tel. 191 (national number for reporting forest fires)   Forest fires

Tel. 108 (throughout Greece)   Coastguard

Medical emergency service for sailors: see Sailing   Sailing
                                                                                   emergencies
See Motoring   Breakdown
                                                                                   assistance

Events

Feast days	Almost every place on the Greek Islands has its own patron saint whose feast day is celebrated with a festival. The festivities usually begin with a mass, sometimes followed by a colourful procession, ending up with a lively – and very secular – street party. The following list only includes the major saints' festivals.
January 1st	New Year's Day (feast of St Basil/Vassilios): cutting the "vassilopitta", a New Year's cake, often with a coin in it which brings a year's good luck to whoever finds it. In many places children, and sometimes adults too, go from house to house and are reward for their singing with money and/or cakes.
January 6th	Epiphany (Theophanie): blessing of the water commemorating Christ's baptism.
February	Carnival: the carnival festivities peak in the seventh week before the Greek Easter. There are grand parades particularly in the island main towns. On the Monday before Ash Wednesday (Kathari Deftera) the tone is set for Lent with unleavened bread, fish, seafood, salad and wine.
March 25th	Military parades on Independence Day.
April	Easter is Greece's most important religious festival (see Public Holidays; Facts and Figures, Religion). Mass is celebrated on the night of Easter Saturday/Sunday, culminating in the cry "Christos anesti!" (Christ is risen!). Bells peal, guns are fired, fireworks are let off, and Easter is also marked by a special soup, egg-rolling and an exchange of presents. Easter is particularly picturesque in Oia (Santorini) and Olympos (on Karpathos; Easter Tuesday).
April 23rd	Many places celebrate the feast of St George; special festivities on Limnos and Kos (horse-racing; songs and dances).
April–October	Son et Lumière every evening in the gardens of the Grand Master's Palace on Rhodes.
May 1st	Labour Day with parades, flower festivals, and a general exodus to the countryside.
Early May to October	Greek folk-dancing on Rhodes in the old town theatre and other performances, including events in the Grand Master's Palace.
May	Departure of the spongefishers at Kalymnos. Three-day festival in honour of the poet Homer (cultural and sporting events, art exhibitions, etc.) in Omiria on Ios.
Mid-May to end September	Son et Lumière in Corfu Town Citadel.
May 21st	Anniversary of the union of the Ionian Islands with Greece (1864); grand parades, especially in Corfu Town.
May 27th–29th	Dance Festival in Chania commemorating the battle for Crete. "Paleologina" festival in Mystra on May 29th.
June 21st	"Katakalo" midsummer bonfire on Rhodes.
End June	"Klidonas" fortune-telling game in the villages of Piskokefalo and Krusta (Lasithi, Crete).

Folk fair in Lefkimmi (Corfu).	Early July
Wine festival at Dafnes (Iraklion) and in Rethymnon park (for a week); raisin festival in Sitia (also Crete).	Mid-July
Literature and art festival in Lefkas town.	August
Corfu: celebration of feast of St Spyridon, patron saint of the island, whose relics are carried in procession through the town. This happens five times a year, i.e. also on Easter Saturday, Palm Sunday, the first Sunday in November and December 12th. Karya on Lefkas has a small annual festival in August; the highlight is the traditional Lefka wedding, enacted in national costume.	August 11th
International festival of medieval and popular drama in Zakynthos.	Mid-August
Assumption (Feast of the Mother of God; see Facts and Figures, Religion). Many Greeks return to their home villages for this festival, celebrated everywhere with gusto but particularly worth seeing in Tinos on Corfu, Lesbos, in Nepolis on Crete, Kyme and on Paros (fish and wine festival).	August 15th
Zakynthos: feast of St Dionysios, the island's patron saint, whose relics are processed through the streets of the island's capital, with the festivities culminating in a fireworks display. Another procession in honour of St Dionysius also takes place on December 17th.	August 24th
Santorini international music festival; classical music concerts by Greek and international groups.	August/September
Corfu Festival: concerts and the staging of ballet, theatre, and opera in Corfu Town. Also cultural festivals on Kefallonia (Argostoli and Lixouri: international music and folk-dance festival), Zakynthos (cultural festival in the island's capital) and on Paxoi (international classical music festival).	September
Church dedication and pilgrimage from all over Greece to Panagia Kanala, the church of the patron saints of the island of Kythnos.	September 8th
Naval festival in Spetses, commemorating victory over the Turks.	September 8th/9th
"Ochi" (No!) Day, commemorating Greece's defiance of the Italians in 1940; military parades (see Public Holidays).	October 28th
Commemoration of Arkadi Monastery in Rethymnon, Crete.	November 8th
Christmas Eve with children (and adults in many parts of the country) carol-singing from house to house; everywhere.	December 24th
On New Year's Eve the fisherfolk of Chios, carrying torches, parade through the streets with boats bedecked with lights, singing carols.	December 31st

Ferries

Visitors travelling by car to Greece can shorten their journey by using one of the many ferry services from Italy. These include scheduled services from Venice, Ancona, Trieste, Bari and Brindisi.

Annually updated maps and timetables for all Greek ferry services, including the international companies that operate services to Greece,   Timetables

Ferries

are obtainable from the Greek Tourist Office (see Information). The following list covers the main ferry services linking ports inside and outside Greece.

SERVICE	SHIPPING LINE, FREQUENCY

Between Italy and Greece

SERVICE	SHIPPING LINE, FREQUENCY
Ancona–Igoumenitsa	Minoan Lines, six times weekly Anek Lines, three times weekly in season, otherwise twice/three times weekly
Ancona–Igoumenitsa–Patras	Minoan Lines, six times weekly Anek Lines, five times weekly
Ancona–Corfu–Igoumenitsa	Strintzis Lines, three times weekly (in season), otherwise twice weekly
Ancona–Corfu–Igoumenitsa–Patras	Strintzis Lines, three times weekly (in season), otherwise twice weekly
Anacona–Patras	Superfast Ferries, daily
Bari–Igoumenitsa	Marlines, daily (in season), otherwise four times weekly Superfast Ferries, daily (in season)
Bari–Corfu–Igoumenitsa	Ventouris Ferries, four/seven times weekly
Bari–Patras	Superfast Ferries, daily
Bari–Sami–Patras	Ventouris Ferries, daily
Brindisi–Igoumenitsa	European Seaways, four times weekly (in season) Med Link Lines, daily (in season), otherwise once or twice weekly
Brindisi–Igoumenitsa–Sami–Patras	Med Link Lines, daily
Brindisi–Iraklion	Med Link Lines weekly (in season)
Brindisi–Corfu–Igoumenitsa	Adriatica, three times weekly Strintzis Lines, daily (in season), otherwise six times weekly Fragline Ferries, daily (in season), otherwise four/six times weekly Hellenic Mediterranean Lines, daily (in season), otherwise six times weekly Ventouris Ferries, daily (in season), otherwise four/six times weekly
Brindisi–Corfu–Igoumenitsa–Patras	Hellenic Mediterranean Lines, daily (in season), otherwise three/four times weekly Adriatica, three/four times weekly
Trieste–Corfu–Igoumenitsa	Anek Lines, four times weekly (in season), otherwise twice weekly
Trieste–Corfu–Igoumenitsa–Patras	Anek Lines, three times weekly (in season), otherwise weekly

Venice–Corfu–Igoumenitsa	Minoan Lines, daily (in season), otherwise three/four times weekly Strintzis Lines, three times weekly	
Piraeus–Chania	Anek Lines, daily Hellenic Mediterranean, daily	Ferries within Greece
Piraeus–Iraklion	Anek Lines, daily Minoan Lines, daily	
Piraeus–Iraklion–Rethymnon	Hellenic Mediterranean, daily	
Piraeus–Samos–Kusadasi Piraeus–Chios–Cesme	Hellenic Mediterranean, six times weekly Hellenic Mediterranean, five times weekly	Between Greece and Turkey
Bari–Cesme–Marmaris–Haifa	Poseidon Lines, weekly (in season)	To Israel
Piraeus–Rhodes–Limassol	Poseidon Lines, weekly	To Cyprus

Since the shipping companies accept no responsibility for losses, do not leave any items of value in your car during the crossing. It is also worth considering insurance cover against loss or theft while at sea.

Owners of caravans and motorhomes should check with the shipping line or with a travel agent that their vehicle is within the permitted size limits (see Camping). Some ferries have water and power points on their camper deck.

For ferry connections to and between individual islands see entries in the A to Z section of this guide (see also Island-Hopping).

Food and Drink

The aroma of herbs, mingling with meat or fish on the grill, and the flavour of olive oil bring back memories of any holiday in Greece. Basic Greek cuisine tends to be on the simple side, though, and, as its critics would have it, somewhat lacking in variety.

Greek dishes depend on a few basic ingredients: plenty of olive oil, tomatoes, garlic, onions, lamb, goat or chicken, sheep and goat's cheese plus whatever fresh vegetables are around, seasoned with, say, cloves, bay leaves or herbs to add that final flourish. Sauces made from egg and lemon juice are popular too. Cinnamon often features as well, particularly in desserts. Bread is a standard accompaniment to all meals. You just need to be aware that in Greece no one worries whether food is served piping hot.

For the Greeks breakfast is rather frugal, many of them settling for a cup of coffee plus bread and butter and jam or just a *koulouri* (white bread ring topped with sesame seeds). One legacy from the British is the English breakfast – eggs, sausage, bacon, tomatoes – served in many hotels but also in cafés and cafeterias. For many Greeks lunch is just a snack.

Eating habits

The main meal of the day is in the evening which, in restaurants at least, the locals seldom partake before nine or ten o'clock. This is not a problem for foreign visitors, though, since most restaurants serve meals from when they open. The Greeks never order a separate meal for each person. Starters, salads, fish and meat, all arrive on the table at the same time and everyone helps themselves from the many bowls and dishes. Dessert tends to be rather limited, often just fresh fruit and ice-cream. The table is only cleared when the guests have departed. Separate bills are not usually provided, with one person paying for everyone, although in tourist centres they are used to being asked for separate bills.

Food and Drink

Food

Starters
(*orektika*)

Before the main meal proper the Greeks usually take an aperitif (probably ouzo) with small appetisers (*mezes*) ranging between shrimp, mussels and other seafood, stuffed vine-leaves (*dolmades*; the cold variety are *dolmadakia*) and salads (*salates*). Then there are starters such as *tzatziki* (yoghurt and cucumber seasoned with garlic, salt and pepper), pureed aubergine (*melitzanes salata*) and *tarama* (cod's roe pureed and seasoned with olive oil, egg yolk and lemon juice), plus tasty little pastry parcels filled with cheese, spinach or minced meat.

Soups (*soupes*)

The soups are generally quite substantial and often thickened with egg yolk and lemon juice. They include *fasolada* (thick bean soup), *piperi soupa* (pepper soup, with meat and vegetables), and *sarosoupa* (fish soup). There is also *somos kreatos*, a clear chicken soup.

Meat (*kreas*)

Most meat arrives at the table grilled or fried. The most popular way of serving it is as *souvlaki*, little kebabs generally of diced pork but also chicken. Less frequently on the menu is *gyros* (the Greek version of spit-roasted doner kebab). Other favourites are lamb (*arnaki*) and mutton (*arni*). Kebabs of kidney, liver etc. are called *kokoretsi*. If you want grilled chicken ask for *kotopoulo*. One dish that you will find almost everywhere is moussaka, layers of minced meat, aubergine and potatoes, topped with a bechamel sauce.

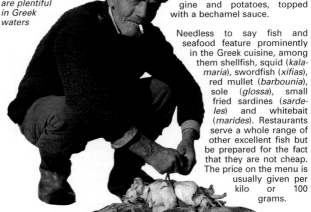

A fisherman with the day's catch. Octopus are plentiful in Greek waters

Fish (*psari*)

Needless to say fish and seafood feature prominently in the Greek cuisine, among them shellfish, squid (*kalamaria*), swordfish (*xifias*), red mullet (*barbounia*), sole (*glossa*), small fried sardines (*sardeles*) and whitebait (*marides*). Restaurants serve a whole range of other excellent fish but be prepared for the fact that they are not cheap. The price on the menu is usually given per kilo or 100 grams.

Vegetables, salads
(*lachanika, salates*)

The typical Greek vegetables are artichokes (*anginares*), aubergines (*melitzanes*), small squashes (*kolokitakia*), and peppers (*piperies*), mostly stuffed or cooked in oil.

Salads include green salad (*marouli*), tomato salad (*tomato salata*), asparagus salad (*sparanga salata*) and the ubiquitous archetypal Greek salad or "village salad" (*salata horiatiki*) of tomatoes, cucumber, black olives and feta cheese.

Cheese (*tyri*)

Greek cheese – feta is the most common – is mostly made from ewe's or goat's milk, and this is what is also used to make the delicious Greek yoghourt (*yaourti*)

Besides ice cream (*pagoto*) there is plenty of locally grown fruit as it comes in season, including water melons (*karpousi*), honeydew melons (*peponi*), peaches (*rodakina*), pears (*achladi*), apples (*milo*) and grapes (*stafyli*). Other favourite desserts are yoghourt with honey, and semolina pudding (*crema*). For anyone with a really sweet tooth there are typical Greek pastries such as *baklava* (flaky pastry with walnuts and almonds, dripping with honey) and *pitta me meli* (honey cake).

Desserts (*deser*)

Besides water (*nero*) and mineral water (*metalliko nero*, *soda*; usually uncarbonated) Greek soft drinks are mainly orangeade and lemonade (*portokalada, lemonada*) and fresh fruit juices (*portokalada fresca*).

Drink

The most common drink is wine (*krassi*). The Greeks produce both red wine (*mavro krassi*) and white wine (*aspro krassi*), which can be sweet or dry.

Wine

Some Greek white wines are treated with resin (*krassi retsinato*) so that they keep longer and this gives them a characteristic resinous taste which takes getting used to. It is a taste well worth acquiring though, since it goes very well with the local meat and fish. The Greek predeliction for resinating wine dates from the ancient world and traces of the pine resin (*retsina*) that is added during the fermenting process have been found in the very earliest amphora.

Retsina

There are also unresinated wines, both white and red, which meet European Community standards; they are identified by the letters VQPRD on the label.

Unresinated wine

The dry white wines and some red wines produced in the islands are usually not particularly outstanding, but the wines of Kefallonia (Robola), Zakynthos (Verdea) and Rhodes (Lindos) are worth trying. The white muscatel of Samos is excellent.

Wine-growing regions

The brewing of beer in Greece dates from the reign of King Otto, a native of Bavaria, and the popular Fix brand is still made to a Bavarian recipe. Otherwise lager and beer is brewed under licence by such well-known names as Heineken, Amstel, Carlsberg, Tuborg, and Löwenbrau. Draught beer is very hard to find.

Beer (*bira*)

The Greek national drink is ouzo, an aniseed-flavoured aperitif drunk either neat or with ice and water. The Cretan *raki* – not to be confused with Turkish aperitif of the same name – is a *marc*, quite strong, and usually without aniseed. *Masticha* is a liqueur made from the bark of the mastic tree. Another local liqueur is a Corfu speciality distilled from cumquats.Greek brandy (*coniac*) is fruity and fairly sweet.

Spirits (*pnevmatodi pota*)

Greek coffee (*kafe ellinikos*; never ask for a Turkish coffee!) is served in little mocca cups complete with the grounds. It comes in different strength and degrees of sweetness: *kafes glikis vrastos* (made with lots of sugar), *kafes varis glikos* (strong and sweet), *kafes elafros* (thin as opposed to thick). One popular version is the *metrios* (medium strong, medium sweet).Tourists can also get instant coffee (*nes*), which when served cold with ice is called a *frappé*. In tourist centres you can often also get cappuccino, topped with foamy milk.

Tea is always made with teabags. It comes as black tea (*mavro chai*), peppermint tea (*chai manda*) and camomile tea (*kamumillo*).

Coffee, tea (*kafes, chai*)

See Language

Menu

Getting to the Greek Islands

Since there are no direct scheduled international flights to the Greek islands the best way to get there by air is to take a non-stop charter

By air

Dining Greek Style

The aroma of herbs, meat from the grill, and the flavour of olive oil are essential ingredients of any Greek holiday. Although basic Greek cuisine tends to be on the simple side, its wonderful variety is usually only first revealed when you dine out in the evening since this, for the Greeks, is the food highlight of the day.

For most Greeks breakfast is often no more than a strong cup of coffee and a cigarette or two on the way to work, or, if they're really hungry, a *kolouri* (bagel of white bread topped with sesame seeds) or a *tiropita* (feta cheese pasty). Lunch is light, probably just a snack, often not taken until as late as four or five in the afternoon. In the evening, though, it's off to the taverna and if possible as one of a crowd. There you dine at around ten or eleven o'clock from a table groaning with bowls and dishes full of salads, starters and main courses. Everyone helps themselves when they feel like it: there is no question of ordering meals individually and when the bill comes it is usually for the group.

Whether or not eating such rich and usually oily food so late at night gives you indigestion will probably depend on what you are used to. In any case after a real Greek supper you are likely to understand the next morning why the locals go without breakfast. Dessert tends to be on the dull side – usually just halva or whatever fruit is in season – but there's a simple explanation for this. Many Greeks prefer, if they still fancy something sweet after their meal, to go elsewhere and drop in at a *zacharoplastia*, a pastry shop where even at night you can still get ices, sweet cakes and of course coffee.

Greek cuisine has a host of specialities, often varying according to the time of year. In summer along the coast and on the islands it's the season for fish and seafood: octopus, squid, shrimp (*garídes*) and lobster (*astakós*), mussels (*mídia*) and fish such as swordfish (*xifías*), red mullet (*barbounia*), small sardines and whitebait (*marides*), fried in oil.

There is also a whole range of other excellent fish but be prepared for the fact that they are not cheap; the price on the menu is usually given per kilo or 100 grams. You can, though, go into the kitchen and choose which fish you want.

Greek food essentially depends on a number of basic ingredients: plenty of olive oil, tomatoes, garlic, onions, lamb, goat or chicken, sheep and goat's cheese and seasonal vegetables such as broccoli, aubergines and artichokes. Then come seasonings like cloves, bay leaves and fresh herbs – parsley, chervil, occasionally mint – to give that finishing touch. Cinnamon often features as well, particularly in desserts. Sauces made from egg yolk and lemon juice (*avgolemono*) are also popular.

If you are already familiar with Greek food you will probably know which of its special features whet your appetite. It is worth bearing in mind, though, that a lot of oil combined with ice-cold water or beer does not go down particularly well – if at all – with an unaccustomed stomach. So it pays to settle just for, say, a glass of wine with your meal, at least to start with. You also need to be aware that in Greece no one worries whether or not food is served really hot. You will find that some salads, starters and dishes are exactly as you have them at home, but others will be different and some completely unknown to you. In any event a culinary voyage of discovery through the many local specialities is bound to be great fun. And of course there's no ignoring the fact that in the places popular with where there are no locals or even no one eating at all; check out the menu and prices in advance, and, if you can, look at what the other diners have on their plates. If you do not like what you see simply leave and head for the next taverna. For one thing is certain: for every gastronomical black sheep there are

Greek cooking is simple but hearty

visitors tourism has left its mark on the kind of food on offer. This often applies to eating establishments that are little more than "feeding stations" where you can expect neither friendly service nor good quality food. So be wary of places at least ten times as many good places to eat nearby. And these are tavernas where they still keep to the unwritten rule of Greek hospitality, that strangers should be well looked after and enjoy whatever is on offer.

flight. Otherwise you will have to fly into Athens, Thessaloniki or Kavala and transfer there, which in the peak season can mean having to spend hours waiting at the airport for a connection.

There are plenty of charter flights, mainly during to the summer, from London and other United Kingdom airports. Charter flights can be booked only as part of a package which also includes accommodation; some tour operators meet this requirement by issuing a voucher for cheap accommodation which you need not actually take up. Information about charter flights is available from travel agents and tour operators, who can also advise about the availability of reduced fares for scheduled flights (Apex, Super Apex, stand-by, etc.).

Apart from New York, Boston and Montreal there are few North American airports offering flights direct to Athens, which also makes it worth enquiring about charter flights and packages.

By rail

The best way of getting to Greece by rail so as to avoid the situation in the former Yugoslavia is either to make a detour through Bulgaria or travel from Paris via Brindisi, with the ferry crossing included in the fare. This only works out cheaper than a charter flight for holders of a cheap InterRail pass or a Eurotrain ticket.

By road

Given the unsettled situation in the Balkans travellers wanting to get to Greece by car from the rest of Europe are recommended to drive through Italy and take a ferry (see Ferries).

Greek Society and the Visitor

See Manners and Customs

Health

Greece is well supplied with doctors and many of them speak some English. Under European Community regulations British and Irish visitors to Greece are entitled to medical care under the Greek social insurance scheme on the same basis as Greek citizens. Before leaving home they should apply to their local social security office for form E111 and the accompanying leaflet.

Insurance

Since, however, these arrangements may not cover the full cost of medical treatment – and many Greek doctors only treat private patients – it is advisable, even for EU citizens, to take out short-term health insurance. Visitors from non-EU countries should certainly do so, especially since this should also cover the cost of transportation back home if necessary.

Police

Tel. 100; the police will direct all calls for assistance to the appropriate place.

Ambulance (Athens area)

Tel. 166

Chemists

Chemists are identified by a round sign with a red or blue cross over the door and a sign saying ΦΑΠΝΑΛΕΙΟΞ (farmakío, pharmacy).

Opening hours Mon.–Fri. 8.30am–2.30pm, 4–7.30pm, Sat. 8.30am–4pm.

Every chemist displays a notice giving the address of the nearest pharmacy that is open outside the normal hours.

Hotels

Although the Greek islands have quite enough hotel beds it can be difficult to find somewhere to stay at Easter and in the peak holiday months of July and August unless you have booked well in advance. EOT, the Greek National Tourist Organisation (see Information), keeps a list of hotels and further information (and reservations) can be obtained from the Greek Hotel Chamber:
Xenodochiako Epimelitirio (Hotel Chamber)
Odos Stadiu 24, 10564 Athens; tel. (01) 3310022/6, fax 3236962

Reservations

Greek hotels are officially divided into six categories. These range from L for luxury hotels, A, B, and C hotels (with different degrees of comfort, facilities, etc.) to D and E for budget accommodation. In the following selection the category appears in brackets after the name of the hotel.

Categories

During the peak season the room rates in Greece are on a par with those for holiday areas in the rest of Europe. Apart from luxury hotels the rates are government-controlled but they can be cheaper if booked through a tour operator, and will be considerably less outside the peak season.

Rates

Abbrevations: b. = beds, r. = rooms, bung. = bungalows

Hotels (selection)

Eginitiko Archontiko (B)
Odos Nikolaou 4; tel. (0297) 24968, fax 26716; 23 r.
Beautifully appointed 150-year-old villa, roof garden with bar.

Aegina

Galaxy (C)
Patitiri; tel. (0424) 65251, fax 65110
Right on the port, above the bay; large cool rooms with terraces. Good value for money.

Alonnisos

Kavos (B)
Patitiri; tel./fax (0424) 65083; 25 r.
With lovely shaded terraces above the port.

Aigialis (B)
Aigiali; tel. (0285) 73393, 73395, fax 73394/95; 30 r., 1 suite
At Aigiali between two sandy coves, the hotel is a complex of buildings in traditional Cycladic style with pretty rooms and a superb sea view; grand terraces provide a setting for quiet dinners with a view over the harbour and the villages.

Amorgos

Paradissos (B)
Chora; tel. (0282) 22187, fax 22340; 76 b.
All the rooms in this medium-category hotel have telephone, minibar and TV; with snack bar, cafeteria and poolside bar, plus minibus for transfers and excursions.

Andros

Karlos (C)
Astypalaia town; tel. (0243) 61330
Opposite the ferry jetty this hotel has clean rooms, little balconies and a lovely view of the castle.

Astypalaia

Hotels

★Saint George Lycabettus (L)
Kolonaki, Kleomenus 2; tel. (01) 7290711/19, fax 7290439; 278 b.
This most atmospheric and intimate of Athens' luxury hotels is on the slopes of the Lykabettos in the smart Kolonaki residental quarter, where it is very quiet yet close to the centre. From many rooms and the pool there is a magnificent view of the city; regulars include many artists and writers.

Electra Palace (A)
Nicodimu 18; tel. (01) 3241401/7, fax 3241875; 180 b.
Modern, quiet hotel – the best in the Plaka – with swimming pool on the roof terrace and a superb outlook over the Acropolis. The bustling old Plaka right on the doorstep is extremely picturesque, particularly in the evening.

Omiros (B)
Apollonos 15; tel./fax (01) 3235486; 60 b.
Quietly located small medium-class hotel in a hotel street in the heart of the Plaka; efficiently appointed, and roof garden with view of the Acropolis.

Aphrodite (C)
Apollonos 21; tel. 3234357, fax 3225244; 162 b.
Inexpensive well-appointed family hotel in a hotel street right in the busy Plaka; roof garden and top-floor rooms with a view of the Acropolis.

Chios

Chandris (B)
Chios town; tel. (0271) 44401, fax 25768; 156 r.

Markos' Place on Chios – a former monastery offers accommodation with style

This highly visible block on the south-western end of the bay has neat rooms and a swimming pool.

★Markos' Place (C)
Above Karfas beach; tel. (0271) 31990; 16 r.
This delightful little haven for individualists in search of that authentic Greek style is an old monastery leased 20 years ago and lovingly restored by Markos Kostalas, which has long since ceased to be known only to a select few. The former monks' cells may be simple with outdoor toilets and showers, but that hardly matters. Mostly visitors can lounge on the shady terraces and chat with the other guests or philosophise with Markos, the current hotelier and a former sea dog.

Sunset Hotel (B)
On Karfas beach; tel. (0271) 32420, fax 32343; 28 r.
If you prefer modern comfort and being close to the beach then opt for this well-kept hotel with its pool; relatively cheap outside the high season.

Corfu Palace (L)
Corfu

Odos L. Dimokratias 2, Corfu town; tel. (0661) 39485, fax 31749; 106 r.
The luxurious Corfu Palace caters mainly for business travellers and short-stay holidaymakers. Built in 1955 and much renovated this grand hotel in sight of the citadel is only a few minutes on foot from the old town. The nearest beach is a long way away but the hotel has its own pool; all the rooms have air-conditioning and a sea view.

Ermones Beach (A)
Ermones; tel. (0661) 94241, fax 94248; 200 bung.
The bungalows are stacked up on the slope running down to Ermones bay. To get to the topmost bungalows from the beach you have to clamber up lots of steps, unless, that is, you take the cable car.

Palaiokastritsa (B)
Palaiokastritsa; tel. (0663) 41207, fax 52234; 163 r.
Medium-class hotel with appealing, well-appointed rooms, some with sea view; the nearest shingle beach is a 5 min. walk, but you can also relax by the pool with its magnificent panoramic view.

Minos Palace (hotel and bungalows) (L)
Crete

Akti Illia Sotiru, Agios Nikolaos; tel. (0841) 23801, fax 23816; 142 r.
Grand hotel, surrounded by beautiful gardens on a little peninsula; the nine bungalows have a veranda with sea view.

★Doma (B)
El Venizelu 124, Chania; tel. (0821) 51772, fax 41578; 25 r.
This highly individual hotel is in a neo-classical villa in Chalepa, the old diplomatic quarter; from the restaurant you have an impressive view of the old town and the port.

Peninsula (hotel and bungalows) (A)
Agia Pelagia, Iraklion; tel. (081) 811313, fax 811291; 245 r.
This holiday complex is on cliffs close to the beach and has plenty of opportunities for water sports, plus tennis courts and entertainment programme.

Creta Palace (A)
Rethymnon; tel. (0831) 55181, fax 54085; 177 bung., 1 villa
Luxury hotel, 4 km (2½ mi.) from Rethymnon right on the wide sandy beach; Cretan architecture combined with modern design, large range of entertainment and sports facilities for the whole family.

Hotels

Sitia Beach (A)
Karamanli, Sitia; tel. (0843) 28821, fax 28826; 162 r.
Beach hotel on the edge of town with a view of Sitia harbour; entertainment programme and water sports.

Euboea   **Palirria** (B)
Odos El. Venizelou 2, Chalkida; tel. (0221) 28001, fax 81959; 55 r.
Modern hotel on the pedestrianised promenade.

Galaxy (C)
Karyston waterfront; tel. (0224) 22600; 72 r.
Large modern building; friendly staff.

Beis (C)
Kymi, in the northern part of the port; tel. (0222) 22604
Clean rooms with balconies; own taverna.

Folegandros   **Vrahos** (C)
Karavostasis; tel. (0286) 41450, fax 41304; 15 r.
Hotel on the beach in Cycladic style, close to the harbour; wonderful view from the veranda. Closed Oct.–Apr.

Idra   **Bratsera** (A)
Tombazi, Idra town; tel. (0298) 53971, fax (0298) 53626; 23 r.
Reckoned as one of the best hotels in the Aegean, if occupies a former sponge plant.

Idra (C)
Odos Voulgari 8; tel. (0298) 52102, fax 53330; 23 r.
On the slope close to the harbour; lofty rooms with wooden ceilings and lovely view.

Ikaria   **Evdoxia** (C)
Evdilos; tel. (0275) 31502, fax 31571; 8 r.
This modern hotel above the port (153 steps!) has small but well-appointed rooms with fabulous views.

Kastro (C)
Agios Kirikos; tel. (0275) 22474; 22 r.
Top hotel in the place; quiet, new, above the main square with a view of the port.

Ios   **Ios Palace** (B)
Milopotas; tel. (0286) 91269, fax 91082; 86 b., 14 bung.
Terraced Cycladic-style hotel on Mylopotamos beach (fine sand), the Ios Palace has good sports facilities plus a large garden terrace with sea-water pool and a jazz bar; the restaurant serves international and Greek specialities.

Philippo (C)
Chora; tel. (0289) 91290; 8 r.
This hotel, which can be noisy, has a pleasant lady proprietor and is in the centre of Chora near the National Bank of Greece.

Ithaki   **Mentor** (B)
Váthi; tel. (0674) 32433, fax 32293; 36 r.
Largest hotel on the island, 500 m from the beach; open all year.

Nostos (C)
Frikes; tel. (0674) 31100, fax 32293; 27 r.
Small well-kept family-run hotel at the entrance to Frikes; some rooms with balcony; bar and restaurant.

The one-time home of a rich ship owner: the Villa Themelina on Kalymnos

★**Villa Themelina** (B)   Kalymnos
Enoria Evangelistrias, Pothia; tel. (0243) 22682, fax 23920; 20 r.
This historic villa, with its pool and luxuriant garden, is on the north-east
edge of Pothia, and has been lovingly restored and tastefully furnished
with antiques by its owner. The best rooms have a large roof terrace
with a view over the whole town.

Plaza (B)
Massouri; tel. (0243) 47156, fax 47178; 60 r.
This hotel, right on Massouri beach, has a large pool; most rooms have
a lovely view of the little island of Telendos and the bay.

Miramare (B)   Karpathos
Karpathos town; tel. (0245) 22345, fax 22631; 43 r.
Modern medium-class hotel with pool and spacious rooms close to
the beach; best place in town, a short walk from the town centre.

Nikos (C)
Diafani; tel. (0245) 51410, fax 51316
Popular small hotel on the way out of town; small rooms with bath and
balcony, some with a fine view of the town and the sea.

Megisti (C)   Kassos
Megisti; tel. (0241) 49272, fax 49221; 17 r.
The island's only hotel; with wonderful sea view.

Anagenissis (C)   Kastellorizo
tel. (0245) 41495, fax 41036; 17 r.
Older but well-kept hotel; all rooms with bath and small balcony.

Hotels

Kea

Kea Beach (B)
Koundouros Joulis; tel. (0288) 31220/3, fax 31234; 80 r.
Simple medium-class hotel with pool and restaurant.

Kefallonia

Cephalonia Palace (A)
Lixouri; tel. (0671) 91111, fax 92638; 136 r.
The rooms in this quiet hotel (opened 1993) on the Paliki peninsula are in a number of two-storey buildings; there is a sandy beach nearby, and the closest large place is Lixouri, 6.5 km (4 mi.) away.

Mouikis (B)
Vironos 3, Lakithra; tel. (0671) 41562, fax 24528; 36 r.
Extremely smart apartment complex with lovely pool; overnight accommodation in studios (for 1–3 persons) and maisonettes (for 2–4 persons). The nearest beach is 5 km (3 mi.) away; many apartments have a sea view but also directly overlook Kefallonia's airport, which lies between Lakithra and the sea.

Kos

⋆**Kypriotis Village** (A)
Psalidi; tel. (0242) 27440, fax 23590; 502 r. and apartments
On the Agios Fokas road 4 km (2½ mi.) out of Kos town, this is probably the island's best holiday village, with everything the discriminating sports-loving visitor could desire; spacious concourse with several restaurants and bars, extensive pool area and sports facilities.

Platanista (A)
Psalidi, Kos; tel. (0242) 22400, fax 25029; 146 r.
A superb complex, with all the comfort of a first-class hotel, 2 km (1¼ mi.) out of Kos town and near the promenade, the Platanista is also impressive for the grand scale of its Venetian-cum-Mediterranean architecture.

An attractive hotel complex with Moorish charm – the Plantanista on Kos

The only drawback: the cuisine is not of the very best, so half-board is not recommended.

Paradise (C)
Bouboulinas St. 22, Kos; tel. (0242) 22988, fax 24205; 52 r., 5 apartments
This inexpensive medium-class hotel is highly recommended for anyone planning to spend only a short time on the island in the bustling centre of Kos town; friendly service and civilised atmosphere.

Anagenissis Xenia (C)   Kythnos
Loutra; tel. (0281) 31217, fax 31444; 50 r.
Modest rooms with view of the bay in a 19th c. house; lounge and large restaurant.

Karya Village (B)   Lefkas
Karya; tel. (0645) 41030; 22 r.
This relatively large modern hotel comes as something of a surprise in the island's hinterland; bar, restaurant and pool. Open Jul.–Oct. only.

Lefkas (B)
Lefkas town; tel. (0645) 23916, fax 24579; 93 r.
Most of the rooms (all with central heating) overlook the lagoon and the greenery of the square at the end of the causeway connecting the island to the mainland; conference facilities as well as a restaurant and bar.

Xenon Angelou (C)   Leros
Lakki; tel. (0247) 22514; 7 r.
This hotel with a family atmosphere is in a very quiet location north-east of the centre.

Erato (C)   Lesbos
Odos Vostani 2, Mytilini; tel. (0251) 41160, fax 27656; 22 r.
In the south of the town near the Olympic Airways office; friendly service; street noise but pleasant atmosphere with Greek guests.

Blue Sea (B)
Odos Koundourioti 91, Mytilini; tel. (0251) 23995, fax 29656; 58 r.
Near the ferry port, this large hotel with modern comfort is good for a short stay.

Delphinia (B)
Molyvos; tel. (0253) 71315, fax 71524; 125 r.
Large hotel and bungalow complex with its own beach; restaurant and sports facilities.

Akteon (C)   Limnos
Mirina, opposite the ferry quay; tel. (0254) 22258; 14 r.
Rooms with balcony, some with sea view.

Chronis Hotel Bungalows (C)   Milos
Adamas; tel. (0287) 22226, fax 22900; 24 bung., 46 b.
The bungalows in a garden setting are just above the harbour.

Clubhotel Kivotos (A)   Mykonos
Ormos bay; tel. (0289) 25795/6, fax 22844; 26 r., 4 suites
On Ormos beach, the hotel has individually designed rooms and many facilities including fitness centre and sauna, sea-water pool with poolside bar and squash court; free hotel shuttle to harbour and airport.

Zorzis (C)
N Kalogera; tel. (0289) 22167, 24168, fax 24169; 20 b.

In a quiet side street not far from the harbour, this town hotel with breakfast garden always has lots of regulars; the rooms have shower and telephone.

Naxos

Kavuras Village Bungalows (B)
Agios Prokopis (Stelida); tel. (0285) 25580, 25077; fax 25802, 80 r.
The terraced hotel complex on a slope not far from Agios Prokopis beach, with restaurant, sun terrace, pool and café bar, has rooms with a sea view from the balcony or terrace; Greek evenings once a week.

Iria Beach (C)
Agia Anna beach; tel. (0285) 24178, 24022/23, fax 24656; 14 apartments and four 2/3-person r., seven 4/5-person apartments
Pretty holiday complex, good for families with children, on Agia Anna's superb sandy beach; well-appointed apartments with kitchen, telephone, veranda or balcony.

Nisyros

White Beach (C)
Mandraki; tel. (0242) 31498, fax 31389; 48 r.
On the road to Pali, nearly 3 km (2 mi.) north of Mandraki, the terraced site slopes up from the beach; roof terrace with bar.

Patmos

★**Australis** (C)
Skala; tel. (0247) 31476; 21 r.
This very pleasant hotel, in the northern section of the bay, has large, cool, clean rooms; a friendly place, run by expat Australians, and has a fine view at night of the floodlit monastery of St John in Chora.

Paros

★**Astir of Paros** (L)
Naousa, on the beach; tel. (0284) 51797, fax 51985; 11 r., 46 suites
A luxury hotel, set in large gardens, the Astir, with its gourmet restaurant, offers every comfort for its discriminating guests, such as air-conditioned rooms with marble bathrooms, balcony or veranda; also a gymnasium, beach volleyball, golf, and water sports.

Sunsea (A)
Porto Paros, Aghios Ioannis Naousa; tel. (0284) 52010, fax 51720;
130 b., 46 bung., 15 suites
This large Cycladic-style hotel complex, 4 km (2½ mi.) out of Naousa and right on the beach, has several restaurants and bars, and a shopping mall; water sports and mountain bike centre, volley and basketball courts and five tennis courts (two of them floodlit).

Paxi

Paxos Club Apartments (B)
Gaios; tel. (0662) 32450, fax 32097
The holiday complex was built in 1993 in typical islands' style, incorporating an old stone house (1880) which is where meals are served when not on the terrace; guests can choose between studios and apartments (up to 5 persons).

Poros

Theano (C)
Poros town; tel. (0298) 22567; 24 r.
This guesthouse, opposite the naval school, has simple rooms, some with balcony, plus a restaurant.

Rhodes

★**Grecotel Rhodos Imperial** (L)
Leoforos Ialissu, Ixia; tel. (0241) 75000, fax 76690; 745 b.
The Imperial, a terraced hotel complex on the west coast, has well-tended gardens and a large pool area; its rooms are elegantly appointed and besides a shopping mall, restaurants and bars, it has plenty of sports facilities and an entertainment programme.

Steps of Lindos Village (A)
Lindos; tel. (0241) 31062, fax 31067; 168 r.
This pretty hotel complex, designed like a Greek village and set in wonderful gardens, has spacious rooms with balconies or terraces and a
view of Vliha bay; several restaurants and disco club.

Kava d'Oro (B)
Odos Kistiniou 15, Rhodes town; tel. (0241) 36980
Hotel with a friendly atmosphere in the old town, right by the city wall
and not far from the harbour.

Kerveli Village (B)   Samos
Kerveli; tel./fax (0273) 23006
Remote, quiet hotel complex on the east coast of the island, about 9 km
(6 mi.) from Vathy; you need to book in advance since this upmarket
venue is used by quite a number of tour operators.

Samos (C)
Sofouli 6, Vathy, Samos town; tel. (0273) 28377, fax 28482; 105 r.
The hotel's exposed location right on the street not far from the harbour
should not be offputting since the hotel not only has comfortable rooms
with balcony view of the gulf, but is also amazingly inexpensive. See
also Restaurants.

Proteas Bay (A)
1.5 km from Pythagorio; tel. (0273) 62144, fax 62620; 84 r.
Opened in 1997, the buildings of this first-class hotel, fairly close to the
Vathy road, slope down to the secluded shingle beach; taverna on the roof
terrace, pool, fitness suite, indoor pool, plus hotel bus to Pythagoreio.

Samaina (C)
Pythagoreio; tel. (0273) 61024, fax 61069
On the hillside above the harbour promenade, this popular little hotel
has a friendly atmosphere. It is far enough away from the hurly-burly of
the town, and has a panoramic view.

Niki Beach (C)   Samothraki
Kamariotisa; tel. (0551) 41561; 40 r.
On the beach to the north; small well-kept rooms with balcony and sea view.

Vedema (A)   Santorini
Megalohori; tel. (0286) 81796/7 and 81666, fax 81798; 106 b.
A member of the Small Luxury Hotels of the World chain, the Vedema is
5 km (3 mi.) from the airport and 1.5 km from its private beach; all
mod cons such as air-conditioning, marble bathrooms, restaurants,
bars, fitness club, art galleries, souvenir shop, laundry.

Panorama (C)
Thira; tel. (0286) 22271, 22481, fax 23179; 23 r.
Located on the rocky coast around the rim of the volcano and not far
from the centre, this has tastefully appointed rooms with verandas
offering a fabulous view over the neighbouring volcanic islands; the
same view can be seen from the restaurant with its bar and roof terrace.

Aster (B)   Serifos
Livadi; tel. (0281) 51191, 51789, fax 51209; 8 r.
Built in 1995, with bar, restaurant and TV lounge; all rooms have bath,
balcony with sea view, telephone and television.

Areti (C)
Livadi; tel. (0281) 51479, fax 51547; 13 r.

Hotels

Solitary inn on a rocky spur by the ferry quay; rooms with bath and balcony.

Sifnos **Alexandros** (B)
Platys Gialos; tel. (0284) 71333, fax 71303; 29 r.
Bungalow complex on the beach; open May–Sep.

Sikinos **Porto Sikinos** (B)
Tel./fax (0286) 51220; 37 r.
Beach complex with bar and restaurant; rooms with telephone and radio, some with air-conditioning.

Skiathos **Esperides** (A)
Ormos Achladias; tel. (0427) 22245, fax 21580; 162 r.
Luxurious hotel built in the older style with exceptional service, close to the sea.

Skopelos **Amalia** (B)
Skopelos town; tel. (0424) 22688, fax 23217; 50 r.
On the way out of town to Stafilos, the Amalia has clean, well-appointed rooms, all with shower and toilet en suite.

Skyros **Pension Karina** (D)
Tel. (0222) 92103, fax 93103; 7 r.
Traditional country house with lovely garden close to Skyros town; simple but well-appointed rooms and large shady terrace with wonderful view of the town.

Spetses **Possidonion** (A)
Spetses town; tel. (0298) 72006, fax 72208; 55 r.
Grand hotel (1914) on the beach promenade with palatial interior.

Symi **Albatros** (B)
Symi town; tel. (0241) 71707, fax 72257; 5 r.
South of the harbour; clean, bright rooms and friendly host.

Syros **Dolphin Bay** (A)
Galissas bay; tel. (0281) 42924, fax 42843; 138 b., 3 suites
Large hotel complex, 8 km (5 mi.) west of Ermoupoli, with restaurant, piano bar, disco and comfortable rooms; entertainment programme, facilities for children and sports activities such as table tennis, squash and tennis.

Ormiros (A)
Ormirou Metamorfosi 43, Ermoupoli; tel. (0281) 84910, fax 86266; 13 r.
This mid-19th c. classical villa is tastefully furnished with antiques; lovely view of town and harbour from the roof terrace.

Tilos **Marina Beach** (B)
Livadia; tel. (0241) 44293
On the eastern end of the bay; the rooms are small but clean, with shower and balcony.

Tinos **Tinos Beach** (A)
Kionia, on the beach; tel. (0283) 22626, fax 23153; 339 b.
One of the finest and most luxurious hotel complexes in the Cyclades, with restaurant, piano bar, snack bar and extensive sports facilities; rooms with modern comforts, balcony or veranda.

Thasos **Timoleon** (B)
Thasos town; tel (0593) 22177; 30 r.

Best place in town, with spacious rooms with balcony and sea view; quite noisy in the evening.

Best Western Zante Park (A)
Laganas; tel. (0695) 51948, fax 51949; 130 r.
Built in 1991 and extended in 1996, this Best Western has comfortable rooms with air-conditioning, telephone, TV, radio and minibar.

Zakynthos

Bitzaro Palace (B)
Kalamaki; tel. (0695) 45773, fax 23935; 87 r.
Modern, friendly hotel complex, particularly popular with Germans on package holidays; a short walk from the long sandy beach.

Information

Greek National Tourist Organisation

(Ellinikos Organismos Turismu, EOT)

Ellinikos Organismos Turismu (EOT)
Amerikis 2, 10564 Athens
Tel. (01) 3223111/19, fax 3224148

Headquarters
in Greece

Canada:
1300 Bay Street
Toronto, Ontario M5R 3K8
Tel. (416) 9682220

Offices abroad

1233 rue de la Montagne
Montreal, Quebec H3G 1Z2
Tel. (514) 8711535

United Kingdom:
4 Conduit Street, London W1R 0DJ
Tel. (020) 77345997

United States:
645 Fifth Avenue, New York, NY 10022
Tel. (212) 4215777

168 N Michigan Avenue, Chicago IL 60601
Tel. (312) 7821084

611 W 6th Street., Suite 2198, Los Angeles, CA 92668
Tel. (213) 6266696

EOT offices

Amorgos
Council offices in Katapoia; tel. (0285) 71246

Andros

Gavrion town hall; tel. (0282) 71282

Amerikis 2; tel. (01) 3310561; open Mon.–Fri. 11am–1pm.
Information booth on corner of Syntagma and Ermou
Ellinikon Airport East; tel. (01) 9694500, fax 9612722

Athens

Rizopaston Voulefton Iakovou Polyla, Corfu town; tel. (0661) 37520, 37638/39, fax 30298

Corfu

Information

Crete	Odos Kriari 40, Chania; tel. (0821) 92943, fax 92624
	Odos Xanthudidu 1, Iraklion Tel. (081) 228225, fax 226020
Ios	Ios municipal tourist office (May–Sep.); tel. (0286) 91028
Kea	Office in Korissia, Youlis–Kea; tel. (0288) 31256
Kefallonia	Argostoli, by the harbour; tel. (0671) 22248, fax 24466
Kos	Akti Miaouli, Kos town; tel. (0242) 29200, fax 29201
Kythnos	Council offices, Kythnos; tel. (0281) 31277
Lefkas	Lafkas town; tel. (0645) 23000, 24962
Lemnos	District offices; tel. (0254) 22996
Lesbos	Aristarchou 6, Mytilini; tel. (0251) 42511, 42513
Milos	Town Hall, Adamas–Milos; tel. (0287) 21370
Mykonos	Municipal office, Mykonos; tel. (0289) 23990
Naxos	Council offices, Naxos; tel. (0285) 22717, fax 23570
Paros	Paros (Parikia) town hall; tel. (0284) 51220
Piraeus	Zeas Marina, NTOG building, Piraeus; tel./fax (01) 44135716/30
Rhodes	Odos Archiepiskopu Makariu 5, Odos Papagu 31, Rhodes town; tel. (0241) 23655, 23255 and 27466, fax 26955
Lindos	Office in Lindos; tel. (0244) 31227
Samos	Odos Martiu 25; tel. (0273) 28582
Sifnos	Council offices; tel. (0284) 31977
Syros	Odos Dodekanis; tel. (0281) 86725

Reservations

The EOT offices do not make hotel reservations. To book a room in an establishment apply in writing to:

Xenodochiako Epimelitrio (Greek Hotel Chamber)
Stadiu 24, 10564 Athens
Fax (01) 3236962

Information can also be obtained from the local Tourist Police (Turistike Astynomia).; see Emergencies.

Island-hopping

Most of the Greek islands can only be reached by sea, i.e. by ferries (see entry) or hydrofoils (see below), but many of them are now also accessible by air (either by scheduled services or by air taxi: see below). For connections between individual islands see the entry in the Sights from A to Z section.

The main ferry services to the Aegean islands mostly operate out of Piraeus or in some cases Thessaloniki. Connections between the individual islands are less direct and it can sometimes be necessary to go back to Piraeus and start again. The mainland ferry ports for the Ionian islands are Patras and Igoumenitsa. See also Ferries

Ferries

With a speed of over 60 k.p.h. hydrofoils – or Flying Dolphins as they are known – are twice as fast as ferries, but also twice as expensive and they only take foot passengers. They operate, for example, between Piraeus and the islands in Argolis and the Saronic Gulf and the Sporades. In the summer months there are also express shuttle services between Rhodes, Kos and Samos, plus the islands of Nisyros, Kalymnos, Leros, Lipsi and Patmos.

Hydrofoils

Since boat departure times are often changed on account of, for example, wind and weather conditions, it is necessary to check with the operators beforehand, especially since delays – which can amount to days at a time – are not infrequent. If you are travelling with a vehicle, you should check in at least 2 hours before the ferry is due to depart. Further local information can be obtained from EOT offices (see Information).

Timetables

Olympic Airways operates daily flights from Athens to the main island capitals. Here too it should be stressed that the schedules for Greek domestic flights cannot always be relied upon (see Air Travel).

Flights from Athens

If you want to fly without having to rely on the scheduled services you can hire an air taxi in Athens. Information can be obtained from Olympic Airways and Aegean Aviation (Air Taxis) in the East Terminal of Athens Airport: tel. (01) 9950962, fax 9950655

Air taxis

Language

In most parts of Greece visitors are likely to come across local people with some knowledge of English or another European language; but in the remoter parts of the country it is helpful to have at least a smattering of modern Greek.

Modern Greek is considerably different from ancient Greek, though it is surprising to find how many words are still spelled the same way as in classical times. Even in such cases, however, the pronunciation is very different. This difference in pronunciation is found in both the divergent forms of modern Greek, dimotikí (demotic or popular Greek) and katharévousa (the "purer" official or literary language).
All official announcements, signs, timetables, etc., and the political pages in newspapers were formerly written in katharevousa, which approximates more closely to classical Greek and may be deciphered (with some effort, perhaps) by those who learned Greek at school. The ordinary spoken language, however, is demotic, which has been the officially accepted version of the language since 1975. This form, the result of a long process of organic development, had long established

Modern Greek

itself in modern Greek literature and in the lighter sections of news-papers. There are differences of both grammar and vocabulary between katharevousa and demotic Greek.

Greek alphabet

Greek	Name	English equivalent
A, α	alpha	a
B, β	beta	b
Γ, γ	gamma	g; y before e or i
Δ, δ	delta	d; as in "the"
E, ε	epsilon	e; as in "egg"
Z, ζ	zeta	z
H, η	eta	e; semi-long
Θ, θ	theta	th; as in "thin"
I, ι	iota	i
K, κ	kappa	k
Λ, λ	lambda	l
M, μ	mu	m
N, ν	nu	n
Ξ, ξ	xi	x
O, o	omicron	o; semi-long
Π, π	pi	p
P, ρ	rho	r; lightly rolled
Σ, σ	sigma	s
T, τ	tau	t
Y, υ	upsilon	u
Φ, φ	phi	ph
X, χ	chi	kh; as in "loch" ("kh/sh" before e/i)
Ψ, ψ	psi	ps
Ω, ω	omega	o; semi-long

There is no recognised standard system for the transliteration of the Greek into the Latin alphabet, and many variations are found.

Accents

The position of the stress in a word is very variable, but is always shown in the Greek alphabet by an accent. In the past there were three accents, but since there was no difference in practice between the three only the acute accent (´) is now used.

The diaeresis (¨) over a vowel indicates that it is to be pronounced separately, and not as part of a diphthong.

Punctuation

Punctuation marks are the same as in English, except that a semicolon (;) is used in place of the question mark and a point above the line (·) in place of the semicolon.

Numbers

Cardinals

0	midén
½	misós, -i, -ó(n), ímisis
⅓	tríton
¼	tétarton
⅒	dékaton
1	énas, miá, éna
2	dió, dío
3	tris, tria
4	tésseris, téssera
5	pénde

6	éksi
7	eftá
8	okhtó
9	enneá
10	déka
11	éndeka
12	dódeka
13	dekatrís, dekatría
14	dekatésseris, dekatéssera
15	dekapénde
16	dekaéksi, dekáksi
17	dekaëftá
18	dekaokhtó, dekaoktó
19	dekaënneá, dekaënnéa
20	íkosi
21	íkosi énas, miá, éna
22	íkosi dió, dío
30	triánda
40	saránda
50	penínda
60	eksínda
70	evdomínda
80	ogdónda, ogdoínda
90	enenínda
100	ekató(n)
101	ekatón énas, miá, éna
153	ekatón penínda tris, tría
200	diakósi, diakósies, diakósia
300	triakósi, -ies, -ia
400	tetrakósi, -ies, -ia
500	pendakósi, -ies, -ia
600	eksakósi, -ies, -ia
700	eftakósi, -ies, -ia
800	okhtakósi, -ies, -ia
900	enneakósi, -ies, -ia
1000	khíli, khílies, khília
5000	pénde khiliádes
1 m	éna ekatommírio

1st	prótos, próti, próto(n)	Ordinals
2nd	défteros, -i, -o(n)	
3rd	trítos, -i, -o(n)	
4th	tétartos, -i, -o(n)	
5th	pémptos	
6th	éktos	
7th	évdomos, evdómi	
8th	ógdoos	
9th	énnatos, ennáti	
10th	dékatos, dekáti	
11th	endékatos, endekáti	
20th	ikostós, -i, -ó(n)	
30th	triakostós, -i, -ó(n)	
100th	ekatostós, -i, -ó(n)	
124th	ekatostós ikostós tétartos	
1000th	khiliostós	

Expressions

Good morning, good day!	Kaliméra!	General

Language

Good evening!	Kalispéra!
Good night!	Kalí níkhta!
Goodbye!	Kalín andámosi(n)!
Do you speak	Omilíte
English?	angliká;
French?	galliká;
German?	yermaniká;
I do not understand	Den katalamváno
Excuse me	Me sinkhoríte
Yes	Né, málista (turning head to side)
No	Okhi (jerking head upwards)
Please	Parakaló
Thank you	Efkharistó
Yesterday	Khthes
Today	Símera, símeron
Tomorrow	Ávrio(n)
Help!	Voíthia!
Open	Aniktó
Closed	Klistó
When?	Poté;
Hotel	Ksenodokhíon
Single room	Domátio me éna kreváti
Double room	Domátio me dío krevátia
Room with bath	Domátio me loutro
What does it cost?	Póso káni;
Wake me at 6	Ksipníste me stis éksi
Where is	Pou iné
the lavatory?	to apokhoritírion;
a pharmacy?	éna farmakíon;
a doctor?	énas yatrós;
a dentist?	énas odondoyatrós;
Street?	i odós (+ name in genitive);
Square?	i platía (+ name in genitive);

Travelling		
	Aircraft	Aeropláno(n)
	Airport	Aerolimín
	Arrival	Erkhomós
	Bank	Trápeza
	Boat	Várka, káiki
	Bus	Leoforíon, búsi
	Bus stop	Stásis
	Change	Allásso
	Departure (by air)	Apoyíosis
	(by boat)	Apóplous
	(by train)	Anakhórisis
	Exchange (money)	Saráfiko
	Ferry	Férri-bóut, porthmíon
	Flight	Ptísis
	Information	Pliroforía
	Lavatory	Apokhoritírion
	Luggage	Aposkeví
	Luggage check	Apódiksis ton aposkevón
	Non-smoking compartment	Dya mi kapnistás
	Porter	Akhthofóros
	Railway	Sidiródromos
	Restaurant car	Vagón-restorán
	Ship	Karávi, plíon
	Sleeping car	Vagón-li, klinámaksa
	Smoking compartment	Dya kapnistás
	Station (railway)	Stathmós
	Ticket	Bilyétto
	Ticket collector	Ispráktor

Ticket window	Thíris	
Timetable	Dromolóyion	
Train	Tréno	
Waiting room	Ethousa anamonís	
Address	Diéfthinsis	Post office
Airmail	Aeroporikós	
Express	Epígusa	
Letter	Epistolí	
Letter box	Grammatokivótio(n)	
Parcel	Déma, pakétto	
Postcard	Takhidromikí kárta	
Poste restante	Post restánt	
Post office	Takhidromíon	
Registered	Sistiméni	
Stamp	Grammatósimo(n)	
Telephone	Tiléfono(n)	
Sunday	Kiriakí	Days
Monday	Deftéra	
Tuesday	Tríti	
Wednesday	Tetárti	
Thursday	Pémpti	
Friday	Paraskeví	
Saturday	Sávato(n)	
Week	Evdomáda	
Day	(I)méra	
Weekday	Kathimeriní	
Holiday	Skholí	
January	Yanouários, Yennáris	Months
February	Fevrouários, Fleváris	
March	Mártios, Mártis	
April	Aprílios	
May	Máyos, Máis	
June	Yoúnios	
July	Yoúlios	
August	Ávgustos	
September	Septémvrios	
October	Októvrios, Októvris	
November	Noémvrios, Noémvris	
December	Dekémvrios	
Month	Min, mínas	
New Year's Day	Protokhroniá	Holidays
Easter	Páskha, Lámbra(i)	
Whitsun	Pendikostí	
Christmas	Khristoúyenna	

Food

See also Food and Drink entry

Egg (soft)	awyo melato	Breakfast
Omelette	omeletta	
Fried egg	awya matya	
Egg and bacon	awya me bacon	
Bread/roll/toast	psomi/pso maki/tost	
Croissant	cruassan	
Rusk	friganyaes	
Butter	vutiro	

359

Language

	Cheese	tiri
	Sausage	lukaniko
	Ham	jambon
	Honey	meli
	Jam	marmelada
	Yoghurt	yaourti
	with walnuts	me karidya
	Fruit	fruta
Starters	Olives	elyes
	Goat's cheese	feta
	Aubergine salad	melidsana salata
	Stuffed vine-leaves (cold)	dolmadakya
	Cheese pasty	tiropitta
	Chicken soup	kottosupa
	Fish soup	psarosupa
	Fish roe	taramosalata
	Clear soup	somos kreatos
	Tomato soup	tomatosupa
	Vegetable soup	lachanosupa
	Oyster soup	mayiritsa
Salads	Potato-garlic puree	skordalya
	Tomatoes	tomata
	Cucumber	angurakya
	Greek salad	choryatiki
	Yoghurt with garlic and cucumber	tzatziki
	Herb salad	lachanosalata
	Potato salad	patatosalata
Fish	Lobster with oil and lemon sauce	astakos ladalemono
	Crab	garides
	Octopus	krake
	Grilled red mullet	barbounia scharas
	Fried sole	glossa tiganita
	Mussels	mithia
	Fried squid	kalamarakya tiyanita
	Baked cod	bakalyaros furnu
	Trout	pestroffa
	Salmon	solomos
	Bouillabaise	kakavya
	Scampi	karavides
	Mackerel	skumbri, kolyos
	Tuna	tonnos
	Swordfish	ksifias
Game and poultry	Chicken in lemon sauce	kota me supa avgolemono
	Roast chicken	kotopulo psito
	Roast turkey	galopula psiti
	Rabbit	kuneli
Meat	Lamb chop	paidakya arnisia
	Pork chop	brisoles chirines
	Sausage	sudsukakya
	Kebab	souvlaki
	Beefburger	bifteki
	Braised lamb	arni psito
	Roast lamb	arni sto furno
	Veal	moschari psito
	Mixed grill	mikst gril
	Roast sucking pig	gurunopulo
	Spit-roast/doner kebab	gyros

Beef fillet	vodino fileto psito	
Young goat	katsiki	
Stuffed vine-leaves (hot)	dolmades	Vegetables
Cabbage	lachano	
Artichokes	anginares	
Stuffed aubergine	melidsanes yemistes	
Stuffed tomato	tomates yemistes	
Stuffed pepper	piperyes yemistes	
Ratatouille	turlu	
Green beans	fasolakya	
Ochra	barnyes	
Fried pepper	piperyes tiganites	
White beans	fassolia	
Chips/French fries	patates tiganites	
Spinach with rice	spanakoriso	
Syrupy flaky pastry with nuts	baklavas	Desserts
Semolina pudding	crema	
Rice pudding	risogalo	
Grapes	stafilia	
Water melon	karpusi	
Honeydew melon	peponi	
Peach	rodakina	
Apple	milo	
Pear	achladi	

Drink

Aniseed aperitif	ouzo	Alcohol
White wine	aspro krassi	
Red wine	kokkino krassi	
dry	ksero	
medium-dry	imiglikko	
Resinated white wine	retsina	
Brandy	conyac	
Beer	bira	
Greek coffee	ellinikos kafes	Beverages
Coffee without sugar	kafe sketo	
Coffee with milk	kafe me yala	
Iced coffee	frappa	
Tea	chai	
Tea with lemon	chai me lemoni	
Herb tea	chai me apo votana	
Chocolate	sokolata	
Fruit juice	chimo frutu	
Orangeade	portocalada	
Lemonade	lemonada	
Water	nero	
Mineral water	mettaliko nero	

Manners and Customs

The people of Greece are courteous and helpful to strangers without being intrusive. They are passionately interested in politics and world events but it is probably wise for visitors not to get into any heated debate and above all to avoid thoughtless criticism of conditions in Greece.

Media

Clothing

As in many southern countries importance is attached to correct dress, although the growth of tourism has meant a more relaxed attitude in some respects (see Beaches).

Churches and monasteries

One situation where you will be expected to wear the right clothing is in churches and monasteries. That means no bare arms or bare legs, and wearing something on your head. Also no smoking, singing, whistling or photography. It is also considered inappropriate to be dressed in swimsuits or beachwear within sight of a monastery.

Media

ERT

Greece's state broadcasting company, ERT (Elliniki Radiophonia Teleorassi) incorporates Hellenic Radio (Elliniki Radiophonia, ERA for short) and Hellenic Television (three channels: ET1, ET2 and ET3).

ERA5

ERA5, the "Voice of Greece", broadcasts news bulletins in English on medium wave (Kavala 792 kHz) Monday to Saturday at 1.30, 3.40, 8.40, 10.40am and 12.35, 3.30, 6.40, 7.20 and 11.35pm, and on Sundays at around 8.40, 10.40am and 12.35pm.

Commercial TV companies

Commercial TV broadcasters include Mega Channel and Antenna TV. Hotels with satellite TV can get SAT 1, CNN, Euronews, etc.

Weather bulletins

See Sailing

Motoring

Car rental

As elsewhere, car rental has become an important part of the services sector in Greece. In addition to the international car-hire companies with reliable reservation systems, which are an important factor when booking a vehicle in advance for the peak holiday season, there are also local firms, particularly in the tourist resorts. Their rates tend to be lower but so also, very often, is the standard of their vehicles. If hiring a car on arrival, though, it is worth making the comparison, especially since the local rates can be negotiable.

The main rental companies have desks at Greek international airports. Arrangements for car hire can also be made through hotel reception desks.

The minimum age for hiring a car is 21. Although national driving licences are usually accepted the law calls for an International Driving Permit. A credit card is essential.

Driving conditions

Asphalt roads run between many of the larger places on the islands, but these can be very narrow and full of hairpin bends. Some of the remoter villages in the interior can only be reached by what as yet are little more than tracks.

As a general rule, avoid driving at night: there are usually no markings to show where the road ends, and often no verge, just a wide ditch, while even very good roads can have large, deep potholes. You will also have to contend with vehicles driving without lights and straying animals.

However large sums are being spent on upgrading the roads on all the islands, and many of the minor roads are due for asphalting in the near future.

Traffic rules and regulations

In Greece you drive on the right and overtake on the left. Road signs and traffic regulations are in line with the usual international standards. The police deal severely with any infringements, especially speeding and illegal parking, and can exact heavy fines, payable on the spot.

Seatbelts must be worn when on the move, and sounding the horn is forbidden in built-up areas. In well-lit places the rule at night is sidelights only. The blood alcohol limit is 0.5 per 1000.

Speed limits

The speed limits are: for cars (including cars with trailers) and campers 50 k.p.h. (31 m.p.h.) in built-up areas, 90 k.p.h. (56 m.p.h.) elsewhere, 110 k.p.h. (68 m.p.h.) on national trunk-roads, and 120 k.p.h. (75 m.p.h.) on motorways; motorbikes over 100 cc must keep to a speed limit of 80 k.p.h. (50 m.p.h.) outside built-up areas, and 90 k.p.h. (56 m.p.h.) on expressways and motorways; the speed limit for motorbikes under 100 cc outside built-up areas is 70 k.p.h. (43 m.p.h.) at all times.

Fuel

There are petrol stations in the main towns and resorts but they are not easy to find elsewhere. You can get 95 and 98 octane unleaded super, plus leaded super and diesel. On safety grounds you are not allowed to take full spare petrol-cans on ferries.

Motorist assistance

Foreign motorists can get assistance through ELPA, the Greek Automobile and Touring Club, which has offices throughout Greece. The address of its head office in Athens is: Messogion Street 2/4, 11527 Athens; tel. (01) 7488800, fax 7786642.

OVELPA breakdown service

OVELPA is a breakdown service operated by ELPA for the benefit of foreign motorists. Its yellow patrol cars are marked "ASSISTANCE ROUTIERE" and if you need their help prop the bonnet of your car open or wave something yellow.

OVELPA has local centres which are on call round the clock. To call them dial the area code followed by 104. There is a charge for their services but members of some motoring organisations are entitled to special rates. ELPA also keeps a list of lawyers in various Greek towns and cities who can give free legal information.

Police

Tel. 100

Ambulance (Athens area)

Tel. 166

ELPA tourist phoneline

ELPA in Athens operates a special phoneline for visitors which gives out tourist information in English, French and Greek on a daily basis (inc. Sun. and pub. hols) between 7.30am and 10pm.
The number to call is: (01) 174.

Nightlife

The Greek night-life most popular with foreign visitors is an evening at a typical taverna or bar where you can enjoy bouzouki music and/or folk-songs, or somewhere with a full programme of Greek songs and dances. Many of the big hotels also have night clubs and piano bars, while in the tourist resorts there is certainly no shortage of discos.

Casinos

There are casinos on Rhodes and Corfu. The casino (and night club) on Rhodes is in the Grand Hotel, in the centre of Rhodes town, and on Corfu it is in the Hotel Palace, south of Corfu town. In both places you can try your luck at blackjack, chemin de fer, roulette and fruit machines.

Opening Hours

There are no official opening times for shops in Greece, so shopkeepers can open and close when they like. In tourist resorts they sometimes stay open round the clock, even on Sundays and public holidays. There are no longer any official opening hours for bars and other licensed premises. See also Public Holidays.

Shops

As a rule many of the shops in towns and tourist centres are open Mon.–Fri. 8.30am–3pm, 5–7pm, or 8/9pm, Sat. 8am–3pm.

Museums

Since the opening times of museums and archaeological sites are constantly changing, enquiries should be made before visiting. As a rule museums are closed on Mondays and open Tue.–Sun. 8.30am–3pm.

Half-day opening only on feast-days and public holidays, including January 6th, Monday before Ash Wednesday, Easter Saturday and Monday, May 1st, Whit Sunday, August 15th and October 28th.

Most museums close on January 1st, March 25th, Good Friday and Easter, May 1st and over Christmas.

Restaurants

Restaurants usually open from noon to 4pm and 8 till midnight; some stay open all night.

Chemists, see Health; Banks, see Currency.

Photography

Most museums allow photography with a hand-held camera but will charge extra for the use of a tripod or flash. The amount they charge depends on whether the photographer is amateur or professional, and on the size and type of the photograph. The special permit must be requested and paid for in advance; for information, apply to the Greek National Tourist Organisation.Photography of military installations is not permitted.

It is advisable to check that your travel insurance covers valuable film and photography equipment. Since film is quite expensive in Greece make sure to take enough with you.

Post

Official Greek post offices (Ellinika Tachidromia, ΕΛΤΑ) are generally open Mon.–Thu. 8am–2pm, and Fri. until 1.30; some post offices in Athens stay open until 8.30pm. Post-boxes are yellow and are emptied daily. Mail for general delivery should be marked "poste restante".

The postage to elsewhere in Europe for a postcard or an ordinary letter (up to 20 grams) is 120 drs. The best place to buy stamps is a post office; you may pay more in other places such as hotels, souvenir shops.

Public Holidays

Set dates

January 1st	New Year's Day
January 6th	Epiphany
March 25th	Independence Day

May 1st	Labour Day
May 21st	Unification Day
August 15th	Assumption
October 28th	"No" Day, commemorating rejecting the Italian ultimatum in 1940
December 25th, 26th	Christmas

Easter: unlike the Catholic and Protestant churches, which use the Gregorian calendar, the Orthodox Church calculates the date of Easter according to the Julian calendar. This means that the Greek Easter only coincides with that of the other western churches once in every four years, and is between one and four weeks later in other years. In Greece both Good Friday and Easter Monday are public holidays. In 2000 Easter Monday falls on April 30th, in 2001 on April 15th, and in 2002 on May 5th.

Movable holidays

The same applies to other movable holidays linked to Easter, namely the Monday before Lent (49 days before Easter) and Whitsun (Whit Monday is also a public holiday) which comes 50 days after Easter.

On the Greek islands the feast-days of saints and their churches play an important part in the islanders' lives (see Events).

Feast-days

On January 2nd and 5th, the Saturday before Carnival, Maundy Thursday, Shrove Tuesday, Easter Saturday, Easter Monday, May 1st and Whit Sunday most public offices and shops are either closed or only open in the morning (see Opening Hours).

Opening hours

Radio and Television

See Media

Restaurants

Restaurants are classified in categories, and the prices they charge are monitored by the market authorities. Hotel restaurants in Athens and the large tourist resorts normally offer the standard international cuisine, and the smaller restaurants and tavernas concentrate on Greek specialities.

Tavernas are the traditional Greek places for eating out. The interior will be simple, especially since in summer you invariably eat outdoors, sitting at plain wooden tables. In the tourist centres, though, there is a growing tendency for restaurants to adopt a more sophisticated style, complete with tablecloths and candles for that intimate atmosphere. This does not mean, however, that the quality of the food will be any better than in an ordinary taverna. Many tavernas serve food from midday to midnight, and it will usually be warm rather than piping hot, since this is how the Greeks like it. If you prefer not to eat with other tourists then wait till after 10pm when the locals have their evening meal. Unless you expressly ask to have your food served in a particular order everything will be dished up together. It is also customary in Greece to be presented with one bill for the whole table, although in tourist resorts it has increasingly become possible to ask for separate bills.

Tavernas, restaurants

Hotel breakfasts (*proyevma*) are of the usual continental type and normally served between 8 and 10am. Lunch (*yevma*) is normally eaten between 12 noon and 3pm and dinner (*dipno*) is served between 8 and

Mealtimes

11pm, though in summer many restaurants are open until midnight, and the Greeks themselves only sit down to eat around 10pm (see Food and Drink; Baedeker Special p. 340).

Menu

The menu is often in Greek and English or another European language, though in the more modest establishments it is likely only to be in Greek (and often handwritten). Only in the very traditional restaurants and tavernas is it still possible to go into the kichen and choose for yourself.

Coffee houses,
pastry shops

The coffee house (*kafenion*, see Baedeker Special p. 23) plays an important part in Greek life and is much more than a place where you can get a cup of coffee. To some extent it has assumed the role of the ancient agora, where the locals meet to exchange the latest news, gamble and do business. Coffee is served with a glass of water (*nero*) and ouzo is often accompanied by olives, cheese and other appetisers (*mezes*).

Every town also has its pastry shop (*zacharoplastia*) where tea and coffee, as well as the great variety of delicious sweet pastries that are such a Greek speciality, are available.

Restaurants (selection)

Aegina

Kafenion Agora
Behind the covered fish market in Aegina town
In the street parallel with the port, a popular meeting place for the fishermen; excellent fish at acceptable prices.

Alonnisos

Paraport
Alonnisos town
Always busy, with delicious grilled dishes; wonderful view from the terrace.

Amorgos

Vizentsos
Katapola, in the Xilokeratidi district
On the other side of the harbour; excellent food, with a pleasant atmosphere inside and out.

Lakki
Aegiali beach; tel. (0285) 73253
Lovely location in a pretty garden with seaview; Greek dishes, including fish, with fruit, salads and vegetables from the garden, great moussaka, sweet lukumades, and grill specialities.

Andros

Archipelago
Andros town; tel. (0282) 24430
This elegant restaurant's specialities include its fish.

Scirocco
Batsi; tel. (0282) 41023
High above Batsi, with a superb view of the beach and the sea; Italian and Greek menu.

Astypalaia

Kikis Corner
Astypalaia town, on the port
Always busy in the evening; some dishes highly recommended.

Athens

★**Bajazzo**
Tyrteous Street 1/corner Anapafseos Street 14; tel. (01) 9213012
The top place in town, in a stylishly restored neoclassical patrician villa close to the Acropolis; gourmet Greek cuisine.

A taverna on the shady Platia in Mesta (Chios)

★Gerofinikas

Kolonaki, Pindaru 10; tel. (01) 3636710
Highly regarded classic Greek restaurant at the end of a long arcade; popular with visitors and business people; special Greek dishes found nowhere else, and oriental specialities such as exceptional desserts.

Xynos

Plaka, Odos Geronda 4; tel. (01) 3221065 (open Mon.–Fri.)
One of the oldest and finest garden tavernas in Athens, with frescos typical of the Plaka.
   This inexpensive establishment, with good food and a big choice of dishes, has many local regulars; musical accompaniment, a large shady courtyard for eating outdoors in summer.

Tsekura

Plaka, Odos Tripodon 3
Long established, highly ethnic taverna, with retsina from the cask; lots of regulars, simple but very tasty cuisine; specialities *stifado* and octopus salad.

Two Brothers

Odos Livanou 36, Chios town
Near the Hotel Chandris; Greek and international cuisine and a quiet courtyard.

Chios

Zorbas

Karfas; tel. (0271) 32340
Well-run shady taverna serving good grilled meat and fresh fish.

O Morias

Mesta; tel. (0271) 76400

367

Restaurants

Popular taverna with good plain fare on the shady Platia; the cook lets you look in the pans and put your own meal together; free *masticha* brandy as a digestif.

Corfu

Aegli
Odos Kapodistriou 23, Corfu town; tel. (0661) 31949
This smart café restaurant has been located for 40 years in the Liston colonnade on the Esplanade; international menu.

Nausikaa
Odos Nausikas 11; tel. (0661) 44354
The Nausikaa is one of the town's best restaurants; international and Corfiot specialities are also served in the lovely garden. The stuffed courgette flowers and the dolmades are outstanding, and there are plenty of treats for anyone with a sweet tooth.

The Venetian Well
Corfu old town, by the Kremasti fountain; tel. (0661) 44761
Greek haute cuisine and good wine list, but the best thing is the location on the most-picturesque square in the old town.

Crete

Tamam
Odos Zambeliou 49, Chania
Substantial good plain fare at moderate prices in former Turkish baths.

Kiriakos
Odos Dimogratias 51, Iraklion
Smart restaurant – one of the best in town – with pleasant atmosphere, somewhat away from the centre and popular with Greek business people.

La Rentzo
Radamanthiu 9, Rethymnon
Smart restaurant in an historic crypt, stylishly furnished with fine antiques; Greek and international cuisine.

Euboea

La Fiamma
Chalkidikekida, on the quayside north of the bridge
Italian food but Greek personnel; steak as well as pizzas.

Oinomageirion To Ovreika
Karystos
Just the place for sheep's testicles or goat soup!

Folegandros

Kritikos
Folegandros town; tel. (0286) 41218
Garden restaurant with Greek cuisine and grills a speciality.

Ikaria

Taverna T'Adelfia
Agios Kirikos, between the main square and ferry terminal
Value for money with waterfront terrace.

Ios

Blue Lotus
Ios town, on the main street; tel. (0286) 91430
English-run Chinese restaurant.

The Mills
Ios town; tel. (0286) 91284
Beautifully located hilltop taverna, with windmills close by; Greek dishes and pasta.

Ithaki

Gregori

Vathi, at the east end of the promenade
Specialities are lamb and fish, but you also pay for the lovely view; popular with the yachting fraternity.

Uncle Petros   Kalymnos
Diamanti Square, Kalymnos town
In this unassuming restaurant at the eastern end of the waterfront, you can get really good fresh fish as well as Greek specialities.

Kokkinidis
Massouri, opposite the Massouri Beach Hotel
With a terrace high above the road; large choice of Greek dishes.

Mayflower   Karpathos
Diafini
Rather unpretentious; good food but the portions could be larger.

Lazarakis Taverna   Kastellorizo
Megisti port
One of the many waterfront tavernas that are famous for their fish. Other speciality: *revithikokeftedes* (chickpea burgers).

To Steki   Kea
Joulis; tel. 22151
Pretty terrace restaurant with Greek cuisine.

Il Camino   Kefallonia
Platia Kentriki, Argostoli
If you want a change from Greek food, try this restaurant on Argostoli's main square for its Italian specialities; you obviously pay for the elegant ambience but the prices are reasonable, very friendly service.

Kalafati
Argostoli fruit market
Simple place, popular with the locals; good Greek food at moderate prices.

Limnos   Kos
Kos town, harbour promenade
Near the harbour taxi rank, this popular taverna has a wide choice of Greek dishes.

Select
Kos town.
Right by the Agora, this street restaurant is a quiet oasis in the busy nightlife of the town; fine Greek cuisine and good value for money.

★Old Pyli Taverna
On the road from Amianou to Old Pyli; tel. (0242) 41659
Reckoned by the locals to be one of the best and most-inexpensive fish restuarants on Kos, the taverna only serves fish caught that day; book in advance.

Reganto   Lefkas
Odos Dimarkou Venioti (near Agios Spyridonas church), Lefkas town
Taverna with good plain fare, particularly popular with the locals.

Achiwada
Varia suburb, 5 km (3 mi.) from Mytilini centre, on the quayside   Lesbos
Elegant establishment with excellent food and high prices.

Restaurants

One of the last ethnic tavernas on Kos lies in the mountain village of Zia

Milano Pizza
Odos Pavlou Koundourioti; tel. (0251) 21110
Pasta and pizzas on the waterfront.

Melinda
Odos Agora, Molyvos
Australian-run restaurant, quite expensive, with Greek, Italian and Indian menu.

Limnos **Gregories**
Platy bay, in the north
Grill dishes; shady terrace, always busy.

Lipsi **Kali Kardia**
Menu with plenty of choice.

Milos **Ouzeri**
Adamas; tel. (0287) 22660
Ouzo bar with serves Greek main courses as well as *mezes*.

Mykonos **Philippi**
Odos Kalogera, Mykonos town; tel. (0289) 22294
Exceptional cuisine and elegant ambience with prices to match; Greek and international menu, very pretty garden. Reservation recommended.

Naxos **To Kastro**
Naxos town, overlooking the castle
Excellent restaurant in superb setting.

Nisyros **Sunset**

Mandraki waterfront
Second taverna up from the harbour; specialises in generous fish dishes.

Lalula   Paros
Naousa, by the post office
Greek, French and Spanish cuisine; menus changed daily, can be expensive.

★Old Harbour   Patmos
Skala harbour, middle of the waterfront; tel. (0247) 31170
Probably the best restaurant on the island; the most popular tables are on the terrace with its superb view of the floodlit Monastery of St John and the harbour. Attentive service and very good food; not unduly expensive.

Nautilus   Paxoi
Lakka harbour
Solid medium-priced Greek cuisine, though fish is expensive; very pleasant dining in the shade of ancient olive trees.

Manolis Dinoris   Rhodes
Platia Musiu 14A, Rhodes town; tel. (0241) 25824
Universally appreciated for its seafood, this restaurant in the old town is in former stable buildings.

Piano Restaurant La Rôtisserie
Rodos Palace Hotel, Trianton, Ixia; tel. (0241) 25222
One of the island's best restaurants; particularly good snails, smoked salmon, and lobster, fine desserts.

Samos Hotel Roof Garden   Samos
Sofouli 6, Vathy; tel. (0273) 28377
In the roof-garden restaurant of this hotel (see Hotels) you can get a snack during the day and dine elegantly at night, but its best feature is the excellent view over the roofs of the town and the bay.

Museum Café
Platia Pythagora, Vathy
Below the archaeological museum you can get breakfast or a simple meal in the large garden and recover in the shade from the exertions of a visit to the museum.

★Lakis
Odos Polykrates (road to Vathy), Pythagoreio
The best way to eat out in this *ouzeri*, with its friendly service and good food, is to join a group and order a variety of starters and main courses for the whole table; lovely view of the old town and the harbour, popular with locals after 10pm.

★Selene   Santorini
Thira; tel. (0286) 22249
Santorini specialities and international cuisine; expensive.

Petros   Skiathos
Oia, opposite Hotel Fregatta; tel. (0286) 71263
Popular taverna, with fish and vegetarian dishes; always busy.

Kanapitsa
On Kanapitsa peninsula
Plenty of choice, always busy; one of the peninsula's best and most expensive tavernas.

Sailing

Skyros	**Skyros Pizza Restaurant** Skyros town Outstanding pizzeria; the monster pizza is big enough for two.
Skopelos	**Ouzeri Finikas** Skopelos old town This cheery *ouzeri*, with terrace, has a large choice of meat and fish; cheese croquettes a speciality; friendly service.
Spetses	**Klimataria** Spetses town, near the gymnasium Large choice of traditional dishes, retsina from the cask.
Symi	**Georgios** Chorio main street Acceptable prices for good food; with terrace.
Syros	**Medousa** Odos Androu, Ermoupoli In an alley close to the harbour; delicious starters and grilled dishes.
Thasos	**Chrisi Amoudia** Thasos town, on the beach Good choice; brisk and friendly service, terrace.
	New York, New York Thasos town, by the old harbour Large but not unduly cheap pizzas; smart taverna.
Tilos	**Irina** Livadia beach Excellent cuisine with a wonderful view of the bay.
Tinos	**To Kutuki** Odos Georg L. Gafu, Tinos town Small but plenty of atmosphere.
Zakynthos	**Sarakino** About 0.6 km (1 mi.) out of Laganas Greek and international menu in the grounds of the ruined mansion of the same name; music and dance in the evening.
	Panorama Bochali, Zakynthos town Smart taverna; shady terrace with superb view, wine from the cask.

Sailing

Entry formalities

Foreign yachts wishing to cruise in Greek waters must first put into a port with authorised facilities for customs clearance. Since the passengers and crew of any such yacht are officially classified as visitors in transit the craft has to be issued with a transit log. This entitles it to free passage in Greek waters for up to six months and allows passengers and crew to go ashore provided their nights are spent on board. Anyone wishing to stay ashore or leave Greece by some other means must have official entry and exit stamps in their passport.

During the yacht's stay in Greece the transit log must be kept on board and presented to any port authorities that ask for it. After the first six months the yacht's owner can ask the customs authorities for a 12-month extension. Pleasure craft brought in by road are subject to broadly the same import regulations as private cars; they are allowed to stay in Greece free of duty for four months. For further details see Customs Regulations, Travel Documents.

All the main ports and harbours have marinas – and ancillary services – run by the Greek Tourist Organisation, local authorities or private sailing clubs, and more are planned.

Greece has more to offer sailing enthusiasts than almost anywhere else, especially in the Aegean which is ideal for sailors. Sailing schools include those in Athens, on Corfu, Syros, etc. For further information (including harbour dues and canal tolls) contact the Greek National Tourist Organisation (see Information) or one of the following:

Athens Sailing Association
15A Xenofontos Street, Athens
Tel. (01) 4121211

Hellenic Yachting Federation (HYF)
Akti Navarchu Kunturioti 7, Kastela, 18534 Piraeus
Tel. (01) 4137351, fax 4131191
The HYF can also supply information about sailing regattas.

Piraeus Port Authority: tel. (01) 4511311

Charter boats sailing within Greek territorial waters must be registered under the Greek flag and be officially authorised to charter. A copy of the charter contract and a list of the passengers and crew must be lodged with the port authorities at the port of departure, and the person in charge of the boat must carry copies of both. A boat may only be chartered if the charterer and another member of the party can produce a sailing certificate or prove that they have the necessary skills.
    Boat charter

Further information about chartering (charter firms, types of boat, rates, etc.) can also be obtained from the Greek National Tourist Organisation (see Information).

Special weather bulletins and gale warnings (6–7 on the Beaufort scale) are broadcast several times daily on Hellas Radio (ERA) on VHF channel 16 in Greek and English.
    Weather bulletins

There are also weather reports for shipping, in English, on medium wave (729 kHz) and VHF at 6.30am Monday to Friday.

Tel. 148 for weather conditions.   *24-hour hotline*

Tel. 108 (throughout Greece)   *Coastguard*

Besides weather bulletins and storm warnings Greek radio also gives advice on medical assistance. The medical emergency service transmits in English round-the-clock on:
    Medical emergency
    Athens Radio, call-sign SVN, 2182 kHz, medium wave.

Self-catering

Self-catering houses and flats can be rented on all the Greek islands, and you will find letting agencies for them in your own country and in Greece. Properties for let include patrician villas and even cave-dwellings (e.g. in Oia on Santorini) that have been restored by the Greek National Tourist Organisation.

Farm holidays are ideal for anyone who enjoys the simple yet friendly atmosphere of staying in a farmhouse; this kind of accommodation is available on several islands, including Lesbos and Chios, and features in
    Farm holidays

a leaflet available from the Greek National Tourist Organisation (see Information).

Shopping

The Greek islands offer good opportunities for acquiring souvenirs, although with the growth of mass production good quality items have become harder to find.

Pottery

Pottery and ceramics can be found at all prices, and range from poor copies of ancient vases to the finest products of Paros. Lindos, on Rhodes, is famous for its plates and Archangelos, also on Rhodes, for its vessels, while Sifnos produces its own characteristic decorated pottery. A word to the wise: since the colours in the designs are not always glazed some Greek ceramics need to be washed with great care.

Textiles

Handwoven articles particularly worth mentioning include the folk art of Skyros, Karpathos and Rhodes, although anything with ancient motifs is aimed exclusively at the tourist market. The shaggy woollen flokati rugs, either in natural wool or a wide range of colours, are also very popular. Other buys in the textile line include Greek costume, embroidery (embroidered tablecloths, handkerchiefs, slippers, etc.), lace, and leather goods (especially handbags).

Marble, pewter, carvings, etc.

Items made of marble, onyx and alabaster, copper and pewter ware, and carvings from olive wood are also popular purchases.

Jewellery

A wide range of gold and silver jewellery – often reproducing the

Sponges and shells are popular souvenirs from the Dodecanese

designs of ancient Greece and Byzantium – is on sale in the main resorts and cruise ports.

Although genuine antiquities may not be taken out of Greece (see Antiquities), you can get very good replicas in official museum shops. **Museum copies**

Icons are much prized by art-lovers, and you can commission your own hand-painted icons from local artists. **Icons**

The best place to get natural sponges is on Kalymnos (see Sights from A to Z, Kalymnos) or in the neighbouring Dodecanese. The most expensive ones are those with a uniform texture. **Sponges**

The choice of local delicacies ranges from aromatic honey, fig cakes drenched in ouzo, chocolate, nut-spread, dried fruit, hazel nuts, almonds, pistachios and of course various wines and spirits. Cheese, olive oil and herbs can make good souvenirs as well. **Food and drink**

Sport

The more active holidaymakers will find plenty of sporting outlets for their energy while on the Greek islands.

The conditions for angling both offshore and from the shoreline are ideal; boats and fishing gear can be hired in almost all the coastal resorts. **Angling**

There are plenty of mountain huts, provided by the Greek Alpine Climbing Association, mostly on peaks between 1000 m (3282 ft) and 2000 m (6564 ft) such as Dirfys, on Euboea, and Psiloritis in the White Mountains of Crete. For information about mountain huts contact the Greek National Tourist Organisation (see Information). **Climbing**

Scuba-diving – as distinct from snorkelling – is forbidden in order to protect the marine habitat. There are some exceptions, however, but anyone diving in those particular waters must keep strictly to the regulations issued by the relevant department of the Ministry for Culture. A list of these areas and their current restrictions, which fish may be caught, and where cylinders can be refilled, is available from the Greek National Tourist Organisation (see Information). It is always advisable, in any case, to check on the local situation first with the relevant port officials. **Diving**

Golf is a relative latecomer to Greece, so the following courses are all the more welcome for golfing visitors: **Golf**

Corfu:
Corfu Golf & Country Club (on the Ropa plain, 17 km (10½ mi.) from Corfu town); 18 holes
Tel. (0663) 94220/1, or Athens (01) 6922809, fax 6923028

Rhodes:
Xenia Golf Afandou (19 km (12 mi.) from Rhodes town); 18 holes
Tel. (0241) 51255/57

Walking and hiking on the Greek islands is becoming increasingly popular, and some tour operators offer special packages for walking holidays on several islands in the Aegean. For a list of local hiking clubs and walking itineraries contact the Greek National Tourist Organisation (see **Hiking**

Information). The walk through Crete's Samaria Gorge in summer is a particular favourite.

Cycling and mountain biking is gaining in popularity on several islands, and in many places you can hire cycles and mountain bikes, plus helmets and other accessories.

Riding — Information about horseback-riding is available from the Greek Riding Club, Paradisu 18, Marussi; tel. (01) 6826128.

Rowing — Rowing boats can be hired from most rowing clubs or marinas; regattas are usually held Apr.–Sep.

Sailing — The main holiday resorts have water sports centres where you can hire boats and take sailing courses. For further information see Sailing.

Swimming — Swimming from a secluded beach is one of the real pleasures of Greece (see Beaches). A list is also obtainable of the network of maintained beaches set up by the Greek National Tourist Organisation. These are good for swimming and have proper facilities for changing, boat hire, children's play, eating out, etc. (see Information).

Tennis — Many hotels have their own tennis courts and there are tennis clubs close to the beach on, for example, Corfu (Chania), Crete (Iraklion), and Rhodes.

Water-skiing — Many places rent out water-skiing equipment and have water-skiing schools; islands where this applies include Chios, Corfu, Crete, Kythira, Lesbos, Mykonos, Patmos, Poros, Rhodes, Skiathos and Spetses.

Windsurfing — Windsurfing boards can be hired at all the Greek National Tourist Organisation beaches.

Taxis

Taxi fares in Greece are lower than in most other European countries. In the island capitals there are taxi ranks on the main squares, and at the ports and airports. Taxis can be ordered by phone or hailed on the street, and sharing a taxi with other passengers is quite usual, although the fare will not be any lower as a result.

Special charges — There are additional charges when a taxi is hired at a railway or bus station, airport or seaport, for any piece of luggage over 10 kg, and for journeys between 1 and 5am. There are also special surcharges at Christmas and Easter.

Communal taxis — The communal taxis which ply in many holiday centres provide an even cheaper alternative; they will carry on picking up passengers for so long as there is room for them.

Long trips — For longer trips, such as excursions, you should settle on the fare in advance.

Telephone

Most places in Greece have international direct dialling. There are no public telephones in post offices; to make a call or send a telegram you have to use one of the offices of OTE, the Greek telecommunications organisation. In main towns these are often open daily from 6.30am to midnight, and elsewhere from 7.30am to 10pm Monday to Friday. Most public payphones take phonecards (tilekartes); these can bought from OTE offices, kiosks, etc.

For Greece: tel. 151
For abroad: tel. 161

Directory enquiries

From United Kingdom to Greece: 0030
From Greece to United Kingdom: 0044
From Greece to United States/Canada: 001

International dialling codes

When telephoning to Greece or abroad from Greece the initial zero of the local dialling code should be omitted.

Within Greece: tel. 155
Abroad: tel. 165

Telegram

Time

Greece is on Eastern European Time (2 hours ahead of Greenwich Mean Time).
   Summer Time (3 hours ahead of GMT) is in force from the end of March to the end of September.

Tipping

In hotels, restaurants and cafés the service charge is included in the price, although an additional tip of 5 to 10 per cent – by way of rounding up the bill, for example – will always be welcome.

Hotels, restaurants, cafés

It is customary to round up the fare by around 10 per cent. At Easter and Christmas taxi drivers, hairdressers, etc. expect a "present", currently in the order of 100 drs.

Taxis

Travel Documents

Since October 1997 passport controls at the frontiers of EU countries are no longer necessary for non-commercial vehicles and visitors. Citizens of EU countries only require an identity card or a passport, whichever is applicable. For visitors from the United Kingdom, Commonwealth countries and the United States, all they need is a valid passport for a stay of up to three months. If they wish to stay longer than three months they must apply to the local police authorities for an extension, and do so at least 20 days before the end of the three months. Children under 16 must have their own passport or be entered in the passport of one of their parents. Anyone with a new passport who is entering Greece with a vehicle must also have their old passport with them.
   Visitors whose passport contains any stamp or other entry by the authorities in (Turkish) Northern Cyprus may be refused entry into Greece.

Identity papers

British driving licences and registration documents, and those of other EU countries, are accepted in Greece. Nationals of most other countries must have an international driving licence (see Motoring).
   An international insurance certificate (green card) valid for Greece is required, and although third party insurance is compulsory in Greece, it is also advisable to take out temporary comprehensive insurance.

Vehicle papers

On entry into Greece details of the car, which must bear the usual oval nationality plate, will be entered on the owner's passport.

Vaccinations

No vaccinations are required for visitors from Europe and North America.

Ship's papers

See Sailing

When to Go

The best time of year to visit the Greek islands, with their Mediterranean climate (see Facts and Figures, Climate), is in the spring – from around the second half of March till late May or early June – and autumn, during the months of September and October, and sometimes also early November. The summer months – mid-June to early September – are very hot and this is when insects such as mosquitoes are at their worst. From mid-November to late March it tends to be rainy.

Spring

In the months of March, April and May the weather is mild and pleasant, and everywhere is in bloom. Easter, which also falls within this period, is the most colourful of all the Greek festivals, too, and is celebrated with processions, etc. on all the islands.

Summer

The summer months are extremely hot, particularly in the towns, although the dryness of the air, and the *meltemi*, the prevailing wind from the north, make the heat tolerable. The summer conditions are also ideal for visiting the many festivals and folk events, not to mention the wine tastings and wine festivals.

Even in summer it is advisable to take a sweater or something warm to wear in the evening since it can get quite cool on the coast and up in the hills; if any boat trips are planned take a waterproof, and walkers and climbers will need stout footwear. Sun cream and insect repellent are essential, and avoid heavy meals during the day.

Autumn

In October the temperature starts to cool down and the first rain appears, but the fine weather often continues into November.

Glossary (Art and Architecture)

Abacus The upper part of the capital of a Doric column, a square slab above the echinus.

Abaton, Adyton The innermost sanctuary of a temple, to which only priests were admitted.

Acanthus A spiny-leaved plant used in the decoration of Corinthian and Byzantine (Justinianic) capitals.

Acropolis The highest part of a Greek city; the citadel.

Acroterion A figure or ornament on a roof ridge or the top of a pediment.

Agora The market place of a Greek city, the main centre of public life.

Amphiprostyle Temple with columned portico at both ends.

Amphora A two-handled jar of bulbous form.

Anathem Dedication gift.

Annulus A ring round the shaft of a Doric column below the echinus.

Anta A pillar-like projection at the end of the side wall of a temple.

Antetemple Temple with pillars between the anta walls on the narrow front side.

Apsis Usually semicircular room at the end of a temple cella or a church.

Archaic art Art of the 7th and 6th c. BC in Greece.

Architrave A horizontal stone lintel resting on the columns of a temple.

Basilica 1. Originally a royal hall, usually divided into aisles, used for commercial or judicial purposes. 2. The standard form of Christian church developed in the 4th c., with three or five aisles.

Basis Pedestal of statues and of Ionic and Corinthian columns.

Bema 1. A platform used by orators. 2. The sanctuary of a Christian church.

Bomos A square altar.

Boss 1. Roughly hewn stone in a wall. 2. Ornamental projection covering an intersection and carved in situ.

Buleuterion Council chamber; the meeting-place of the council (bule) of a Greek city.

Capital Topping or head of a column or a pillar.

Caryatid Clothed female figure used as a column to support an entablature.

Cathedra A bishop's throne.

Glossary

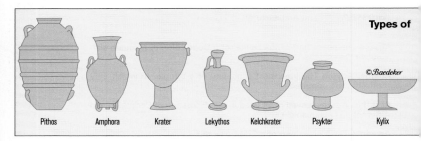

Types of
Pithos Amphora Krater Lekythos Kelchkrater Psykter Kylix

©Baedeker

Catholicon The principal church of a monastery.

Cavea The auditorium (seating) of a theatre.

Cella The windowless inner chamber of a temple where the image of the god is kept.

Chiton A pleated linen garment worn with a belt, mostly in Ionia.

Chlamys A short cloak.

Choregos Choir leader: a person who financed the choir performing in a tragedy.

Classical Art in Greece from around 480 to 330 BC.

Conch Semicircular niche surmounted by a half-dome.

Cross in square Byzantine church plan, with large domed central bay at the intersection of four arms of equal length.

Cyclopean masonry Masonry of large irregular blocks of stone in pre-classical architecture; attributed to the Cyclops.

Demos Community, people, popular assembly, place.

Diaconicon A room in the right-hand lateral apse of a Byzantine church.

Dimini culture Culture of the first half of the 3rd millenium BC on the Greek mainland, named after the place near Volos where it was discovered.

Dipteros Temple surrounded by a double row of columns.

Dipylon A double gateway.

Double anta temple A temple with antae at both ends.

Dromos A passage; specifically, the passage leading into a tomb.

Echinus A convex moulding under the abacus of a Doric capital.

Entasis A swelling in the lower part of a column.

Epistyle Another name for architrave.

Exedra A recess, usually semicircular, containing benches.

Greek Vessels

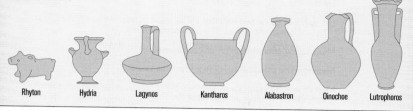

Rhyton   Hydria   Lagynos   Kantharos   Alabastron   Oinochoe   Lutrophoros

Exonarthex The outer narthex of a church.

Frieze A decorative band above the architrave of a temple; in the Doric order made up of metopes and triglyphs, in the Ionic order plain or with continuous carved decoration.

Geison The cornice of a temple.

Geometric style Named after the geometric ornamentation of the style between 1050 and 700 BC.

Gorgoneion Head of the Gorgon, to ward off evil; under the aegis of Athena.

Gymnasion A school for physical training and general education, consisting of a square or rectangular courtyard surrounded by colonnades and rooms of varying size and function.

Halle Long building, usually with solid back wall and open columns in front, often double aisled; since the 3rd century BC with two storeys.

Hellenism Age from Alexander the Great to Augustus (330–30 BC).

Heraion A temple or sanctuary of Hera.

Herme A square pillar with a head of Hermes or some other god; later with a portrait head.

Hippodrome An elliptical course for chariot races.

Hypocaust An underfloor heating system.

Iconostasis A screen in a Byzantine church between the sanctuary and the main part of the church, bearing tiers of icons.

Intercolumnium Space between columns measured in diameters.

Isodomic Horizontal courses (masonry).

Kantharos A drinking cup with two handles.

Kore Girl, maiden; also name for Persephone.

Kouros Statue of a naked youth.

Krater A two-handled jar for mixing water and wine.

Lekythos A narrow-necked oil-flask.

Lesche Assembly room, clubhouse.

Lutrophoros Large two-handled vessel used to fetch water for the bridal bath; often in the graves of the unmarried dead.

Maeander A continuous fret or key pattern.

Megaron The principal room in a Mycenean palace.

Metope A rectangular panel between the triglyphs in the frieze of a Doric temple, either plain or with relief decoration.

Minoan culture Culture on the island of Crete from 2600 to 1100 BC.

Monopteros Temple without a naos, usually circular.

Mycenean culture Greek mainland culture from 1580 to 1150 BC named after Mycene where it was discovered.

Naiskos A small temple.

Naos Temple, temple interior.

Narthex Entrance hall of a Byzantine church.

Necromanteion Oracle of the dead.

Necropolis Cemetery ("city of the dead").

Nymphaeum Fountain-house; precinct of the nymphs.

Octagon Eight-sided building.

Odeon, Odeion A hall, usually roofed, for musical performances, etc.

Opisthodomos A room corresponding to the pronaos behind the naos (cella) of a temple.

Orchestra A circular or semicircular area between the stage and the auditorium of a theatre in which the chorus danced.

Orthostat A large block of stone, set vertically, in the lower part of a temple wall.

Panayia "All Holy"; the Mother of God, the Virgin.

Pantokrator "Ruler of All"; Christ.

Parados Side entrance to the orchestra of a theatre.

Pastophoria The two side apses (diaconicon and prothesis) of a Byzantine church.

Pendentive A triangular section of vaulting forming the transition from a square base to a circular dome.

Peripteros Temple surrounded by colonnades.

Peristyle Range of columns surrounding a building.

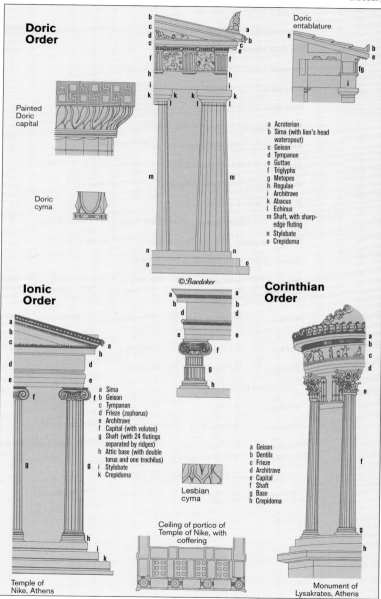

Doric Order

Painted Doric capital

Doric cyma

Doric entablature

a Acroterion
b Sima (with lion's head waterspout)
c Geison
d Tympanon
e Guttae
f Triglyphs
g Metopes
h Regulae
i Architrave
k Abacus
l Echinus
m Shaft, with sharp-edge fluting
n Stylobate
o Crepidoma

©Baedeker

Ionic Order

a Sima
b Geison
c Tympanon
d Frieze (zophorus)
e Architrave
f Capital (with volutes)
g Shaft (with 24 flutings separated by ridges)
h Attic base (with double torus and one trochilus)
i Stylobate
k Crepidoma

Lesbian cyma

Ceiling of portico of Temple of Nike, with coffering

Temple of Nike, Athens

Corinthian Order

a Geison
b Dentils
c Frieze
d Architrave
e Capital
f Shaft
g Base
h Crepidoma

Monument of Lysakrates, Athens

Pithos A large storage jar.

Polychromia Polychromatic colouring of classical sculpture and temples.

Porticus Entrance hall with columns.

Pronaos Vestibule at the entrance to a temple.

Propylaia A monumental form of propylon.

Propylon Gateway.

Proskenion Apron stage in the theatre.

Prostylos Temple with columned portico in front.

Prothesis A room in the left-hand lateral apse of a Byzantine church.

Prytaneion Official seat of the prytanes (city councillors).

Pyrgos Tower, bastion.

Rhyton A drinking vessel, often in the form of an animal's head.

Sima The gutter of a building, with lion-head water spouts.

Skena Multi-storied stage in the theatre.

Stadion 1. A measure of length, 600 feet. 2. A running track of the same length. 3. A stadium, with a running track and embankments or benches for spectators.

Stele An upright stone slab (often a tombstone), usually with an inscription and frequently with relief carving.

Stoa A portico; a hall with columns along the front.

Stylobat The top step of the base of a column.

Temenos A sacred precinct.

Thesauros Treasury.

Tholos A circular building, rotunda; a domed Mycenean tomb.

Triglyph A projecting member, with two vertical channels, between the metopes of the Doric order.

Tropaion Trophies; victory or votive memorial.

Tympanon Gable of a Greek temple, decorated with reliefs.

Volute Spiral scroll on an Ionic capital.

Index

Achilleion 128
Adámas 230
Aegina 75
Aetós 176
Afántou 266
Agathonísi 281
Air Travel 328
Aiyiáli 82
Aíyina 76
Akrotíri 292
Álinda 217
Alónnisos 79
Alónnisos town 80
Aloprónia 297
Alykés 323
Amárynthos 166
Amnisós 147
Amorgós 80
Amorgós town 81
Anáfi 83
Anáfi town 83
Anafonítria 324
Anávatos 119
Ándros 73, 83
Ándros town 85
Anemómylos 126
Angelókastro 129
Angístri 78
Áno Merá 235
Áno Sýros 310
Anoyí 177
Anóyia 145
Antikýthira 207
Antimákhia 204
Antíparos 245
Antípaxi 253
Antiquities 328
Ántissa 226
Apéri 186
Apikía 86
Apíranthos 240
Apolakkiá 266
Apóllonas 240
Apollónia 230
Apollonía 295
Áptera 136
Argostóli 194
Arkádi Monastery 140
Arkása 185
Arkesíni 82
Arkhánes 146
Arkhángelos 267
Arkí 251
Armenistís 172
Art and Architecture 46
Artemísio 164
Asklipío 267

Ásos 196
Astypálaia 88
Astypálaia town 88
Athens 89
Avlémonas 206
Avlonári 167
Ayía Ánna 164
Ayía Galíni 140
Ayía Marína 78, 187, 217
Ayía Pelayía 206
Ayía Rouméli 138
Ayía Triáda 149
Ayía Triáda 136
Ayía Varvára 147
Ayiásos 227
Áyii Theodóri 77
Áyios Andréas 196, 324
Áyios Efstrátios 216
Áyios Isídoros 227
Áyios Kýrikos 171
Áyios Nikítas 212
Áyios Nikólaos 83, 87, 149, 164
Áyios Nikólaos
    Gountoukli 265
Áyios Panteleímon 315
Áyios Pétros 87
Áyios Stéfanos 165
Áyios Yeóryios Bay 129
Áyios Yerásimos 195

Batsí 88
Beaches 329
Bear's Cave 136
Benítses 128
Blue Grotto 323

Camping 330
Cape Fanári 172
Cape Lefkáta 212
Cape Skinári 324
Cave of the Nymphs 176
Chíos 113
Chios town 116
Chloe 216
Climate 14
Corfu 70, 122
Corfu town 123
Crete 130
Cruises 331
Culture 46
Currency 331
Customs Regulations 331
Cyclades 18

Delos 73, 153
Diafáni 187

Diplomatic
    Representation 332
Dodecanese 17
Dokós 170
Donoúsa 161
Doryssa Bay 276
Dreros 151
Drogaráti Cave 197
Dryopís 208
Dystós 166

Economy and Transport 25
Elafónisos 207
Electricity 333
Eloúnda 151
Émbonas 266
Emergencies 333
Emporió 120
Emporiós 183
Environment 21
Eresós 227
Erétria 165
Erimonísia 161
Éristos 315
Érmones 129
Ermoúpoli 309
Euboea 161
Évdilos 172
Events 334

Facts and Figures 10
Faliráki 266
Famous People 41
Faneroméni convent 271
Farmakonísi 218
Fauna 20
Ferries 335
Filóti 240
Fiskárdo 196
Flora and Fauna 19
Fódele 144
Folégandros 167
Folégandros town 167
Folk Traditions 60
Food and Drink 337, 359, 361
Fountain of Arethusa 177
Foúrni Islands 172
Frangokastéllo 139
Fry 187
Fylakopí 230

Gáios 251
Galanádo 240
Gávdos 139
Gávrio 87
General 10

Index

Geology 11
Getting to the Greek Islands 339
Glóssa 300
Glossary 379
Glyfáda 130
Górtyn 147
Gourna Bay 218
Gourniá 151
Gouvernéto 136
Greek alphabet 356
Gýri 324

Health 342
Heraion 277
Heroon 297
History 29
Hotels 343
Hydra 168
Hydra town 169

Idaean Cave 145
Ierápetra 151
Ikaría 170
Imbros Gorge 139
Information 353
Inoússai Islands 121
Ionian Islands 15
Íos 73, 172
Íos town 174
Iráklia 161
Iráklion 140
Island Groups 15
Island-hopping 70, 355
Istiía 164
Itanos 152
Ithaca 174

Kalami 129
Kálamos 213
Kallithéa 266
Kalloní 225
Kálymnos 72, 177
Kálymnos town 180
Kamáres 147, 295
Kamári 292
Kameiros 266
Kamíros Skála 266
Kampí 324
Kanála 208
Kanóni 127
Kántanos 137
Kardamaína 204
Karfás 118
Karlovási 281
Kárpathos 183
Kárpathos town 185
Karthaia 192
Karyá 212
Kárystos 166
Kásos 187
Kassiópi 129

Kastélli Kíssamou 137
Kastellórizo 188
Kastellórizo town 189
Kástro 196, 296, 299
Katápola 81
Katastári 323
Katavóthres 194
Katharón Monastery 177
Katholikó 136
Káto Zákros 152
Kattaviá 267
Kávos 128
Kéa 190
Kéa town 191
Kefaloniá 70, 192
Kéfalos 204
Kekhrovoúnio convent 318
Khalépa 136
Khálki 240
Khalkís, 162
Khaniá 132
Kharkadio Cave 315
Khóra 249
Khóra sfakíon 139
Khorió 182
Khrysí 152
Kímolos 198
Kióni 177
Kiónia 318
Kipouríon 195
Knossos 142
Kokkári 281
Kontopoúli 216
Korissía 191
Korission Lagoon 128
Kos 72, 199
Kos town 201
Koufonísi 161
Kounópetra 195
Kranioi 194
Kremastí 264
Kritiniá 266
Kritsá 149
Kými 167
Kýthira 205
Kýthira town 206
Kýthnos 207
Kýthnos town 208

Laganás Bay 322
Lake Kournás 140
Lakhaniá 267
Lákithra 196
Lákka 252
Lakkí 217, 242
Langáda 121
Language 355
Lassíthi plain 150
Lefkás 70, 209
Lefkás town 211
Lefkímmi 128
Lemnos 214

Léntas 148
Lerikos 212
Léros 216
Lésbos 218
Levíta Islands 82
Limenária 314
Limín Khersonísou 151
Límni 164
Límni Kerioú 322
Limniónas 22, 324
Linariá 304
Lindos 267
Lion of Kéa 192
Lipsí 228
Lipsí town 228
Lissós 137
Livádi 293
Livádia 315
Livádia valley 89
Lixoúri 194
Lóngos 252
Loúkha 324
Loutrá 208, 242
Loutrá Aidipsoú 164

Makhairádo 324
Makry's Yialós 194, 323
Máleme 137
Mália 151
Málonas 267
Mandráki 241
Manners and Customs 361
Mantamádos 224
Marmári 166
Mátala 149
Media 362
Megálo Khorió 315
Meganísi 213
Mégas Lákos 195
Melissáni Cave 197
Melos 229
Menetés 186
Mérikhas 208
Mesara 147
Mesariá 87, 291
Messongí 128
Mestá 121
Metaxáta 196
Mikró Khorió 315
Mílos 230
Minoa 81
Mókhlos 151
Mólyvos 224
Monastery of St John 250
Monastery of the Apocalypse 249
Monastery of the Taxiarchs 294
Moní Khristou Thassou 244
Moní Tsambíka 267
Monólithos 266
Moraítika 128

Moriá 223
Motoring 362
Moúdros 215
Mount Aínos 195
Mount Dírfys 163
Mount Exómbourgo 318
Mount Filérimos 264
Mount Ida 146
Mount Kérkis 281
Mount Kolóna 76
Mount Krikelo 82
Mount Pantokrátor 128
Mount Profítis Ilías 78, 136, 265, 291, 296
Mount Yioúkhtas 146
Music 60
Mýkonos 73, 232
Mýkonos town 233
Mýkonos, Delos 73
Mylopótamos 206
Mýrina 215
Myrtiá 146
Myrtiés 182
Myrtiótissa 130
Mýrtos 196
Mýli 166
Mytilíni 222, 274

Naoúsa 244
Náxos 73, 235
Náxos town 237
Néa Artáki 163
Néa Moní 118
Nightlife 363
Nikiá 242
Nimborió Bay 307
Nísyros 72, 240
Nydrí 213

Oía 291
Oinoë 172
Olýmpi 120
Ólympos 186, 227
Opening Hours 364
Oreí 164
Ormos Korthíou 87
Othonian Islands 130
Óthos 186
Otziás 191

Palaío Pýli 204
Palaiokastrítsa 129
Palaíokastro 137, 152
Palaiokhóra 77, 137, 206
Palaiópolis 88, 230
Panayía 294, 313
Panayía Kalamiótissa 83
Panayía Khozoviótissa 82
Panayía Myrtidíon 206
Panormítis Bay 307
Pánormos 182

Páros 73, 242
Páros town 243
Patitíri 79
Pátmos 72, 245
Paxí 251
Pédi 307
Pélekas 130
Perakhóri 176
Veríssa 293
Petaloúdes 245
Petaloúdes Valley 264
Pétra 225
Phaistós 148
Photography 364
Piraeus 253
Písses Bay 192
Plátanas 148
Platáni 203
Platýs Yialós 194
Plomári 227
Polikhnítos 227
Poliókhni 215
Pólis 177
Politiká 163
Pontikonísi 127
Population 22
Póros 196, 213, 255
Póros town 256
Pórto Katsíki 212
Pórto Vromí 324
Post 360
Potamiá 313
Potós 314
Practical Information 328
Praisós 153
Prasonísi 267
Préveli Monastery 140
Prokópi 164
Psakhná 163
Psará 122
Psérimos 204
Public Holidays 364
Pýrgos 319
Pyryí 120

Quotations 63

Religion 24
Restaurants 365
Rhodes 72, 256
Rhodes town 258
Rhodopos peninsula 137
Róda 129
Roviés 164

Sailing 372
Salamína 271
Salamis 270
Samariá Gorge 138
Sámi 197
Sámos 72, 271

Sámos town 273
Samothrace 282
Samothráki 282
Sanctuary of the Cabiri 283
Santoríni 73, 285
Sariá 187
Saronic islands 16
Self-catering 373
Sérifos 293
Sérifos town 294
Sesklío 307
Shopping 374
Sidári 129
Sífnos 295
Sights from A to Z 75
Sígri 226
Síkinos 296
Síkinos town 297
Sitía 152
Skála 196, 248
Skála Kallonís 226
Skhinoússa 161
Skíathos 297
Skíathos town 299
Skópelos 299
Skópelos town 300
Skýros 301
Skýros town 303
Soúda Bay 136
Soúyia 137
Spétses 304
Spétses town 304
Spinalonga 151
Sporades 16
Sport 375
Stavrós 177
Steniés 86
Stýra 166
Sými 72, 306
Sými town 307
Sýros 307
Sykaminéa 224

Taxis 376
Télendos 183
Telephone 376
Temple of Aphaia 77
Temple of Artemis 127
Temple of Poseidon 256
Thásos 310
Thásos town 312
Theológos 314
Thera 291
Thérma 171, 285
Thermí 223
Thíra/Firá 289
Thirasía 293
Tilos 314
Time 377
Tínos 73, 316
Tínos town 317

Index

Tipping 377
Tomb of Phocus 77
Toploú Monastery 152
Transport 27
Travel Documents 377
Tríon Patéron 119
Tris Boukés Bay 304
Tsoungriá 299
Týlisos 145

Vái Beach 152
Variá 223

Vasilikí 212
Vaterá 227
Vathý 176, 183
Vlakherna Monastery 127
Vóri 148
Vourkári 191
Vourliótes 281
Vrontádos 121

When to Go 378

Xi 195

Xirókampos 217

Yéni 213
Yiáros 310
Ypapanti caves 252
Ypsiloú 226

Zagora 87
Zákynthos 71, 319
Zákynthos town 320
Zía 204
Zipári 204
Zoodókhos Piyí 83, 256

Source of Illustrations

Front cover: Tony Stone Images.
Back cover: AA Photo Library (J.A. Tims)

Abend: 101, 110, 112.
Archiv für Kunst und Geschichte: 36, 41, 42, 43 (2x), 44 (3x), 45, 179, 135, 231, 258.
Borowski: 176, 178, 213, 323.
Galenschovski: 154.
Megaro Gyzi, Santorin: 287.
Feltes-Peter: 3 (top), 5, 6 (bottom right), 7 (2x), 13, 17, 28, 55, 57, 115, 116, 121, 181, 182, 199, 201, 202, 205, 217, 228, 247, 248, 250, 272, 273, 275, 279, 278, 329, 370, 344, 347, 348, 363, 366.
Hackenberg: 12, 78, 89, 169, 186, 189, 146, 268, 305.
HB-Verlag, Hamburg: 87, 235, 294, 341.
Henseler: 23, 150.
Hicker: 123, 127, 320.
IFA: 8, 24, 62, 159, 171, 224, 238, 260, 263, 264, 301, 317, 326, 338.
Janicke: 105.
Kramer: 283.
Krause: 191.
Cyclades Museum, Athens: 47.
laif: 61, 98, 100, 241, 254.
Mauritus: 6 (bottom left), 22, 68, 157, 313.
Kai U. Müller: 3 (bottom), 6 (centre), 92, 106, 175, 198, 245, 296.
W. Otto: 76.
Pasdzior: 210.
Schapowalow: 126, 220, 225, 226, 257, 298, 306, 315.
Schumann: 138.
srt: 119.
Storto: 59.
Strobel: 82, 168.
Strüber: 142, 143.
ZEFA: 195, 197, 207, 214, 290.

Imprint

136 illustrations, 76 maps and plans, 1 large map at end of book

German text: Dr Bernhard Abend, Achim Bourmer, Birgit Borowski, Dr Katja David, Astrid Feltes-Peter, Carmen Galenschovski, Wolfgang Liebermann, Helmut Linde, Reinhard Strüber, Andrea Wurth.

Consultant: Axel Kramer

Editorial work: Baedeker Redaktion (Astrid Feltes-Peter)

Cartography: Franz Huber, Munich; Christoph Gallus, Hohberg-Niederschopfheim; Mairs Geographischer Verlag GmbH & Co., Ostfildern (large map)

General direction: Rainer Eisenschmid, Baedeker Ostfildern

English translation: James Hogarth

5th English edition 2000

© Baedeker Ostfildern
Original German edition 2000

© 2000 The Automobile Association
English language edition worldwide

Published by AA Publishing (a trading name of Automobile Association Developments Limited, whose registered office is Norfolk House, Priestley Road, Basingstoke, Hampshire RG24 9NY. Registered number 1878835).

Distributed in the United States and Canada by:
Fodor's Travel Publications, Inc.
201 East 50th Street
New York, NY 10022

All rights reserved. No part of this publication may be reproduced, stored in a retrieval system or transmitted in any form by any means – electronic, photocopying, recording or otherwise – unless the written permission of the publisher has been obtained.

The name *Baedeker* is a registered trade mark.

A CIP catalogue record of this book is available from the British Library.

Licensed user:
Mairs Geographischer Verlag GmbH & Co.
Ostfildern

Typeset by Fakenham Photosetting Ltd, Fakenham, Norfolk, UK
Printed in Italy by G. Canale & C. S.p.A., Turin

ISBN 0 7495 2266 6

Principal Sights of Tourist Interest

★★

Aegina: Temple of Aphaia
Athens
Chíos: Néa Moní
Corfu
Crete
Delos

★

Amorgós
Ándros
Chíos
Euboea
Hydra
Ikaría
Íos
Kálymnos
Kárpathos
Kéa
Kefaloniá
Kos
Kýthira
Lefkás
Lemnos
Lésbos
Melos

★★

Kos: Asklepieion
Mýkonos
Pátmos
Rhodes
Santoríni

★

Náxos
Nísyros
Páros
Sámos
Samothrace
Sérifos
Sífnos
Skíathos
Skópelos
Skýros
Spétses
Sými
Sýros
Thásos
Tínos
Zákynthos

The places listed above are merely a selection of the principal sights – places of interest in themselves or for attractions in the surrounding area. There are of course innumerable other sights in the Greek islands, to which attention is drawn by either one or two stars.

Notes

Notes

Notes

Notes

Would Ra...

mutua...

3 4028 08197 8026
HARRIS COUNTY PUBLIC LIBRARY

Quinn
Quinn, Tara Taylor
The truth about Comfort
   Cove

WITHDRAWN $6.50
                    ocn823745842
                    01/14/2013

Lucy had never seen him outside of his professional capacity. Never even had a drink with him.

He'd b... she'd a... else. P... Ramsey...

Ramse... he was... places... With someone.

Not her. With Lucy, he was always in control. But would he loosen up after a glass of champagne? Did he drink beer? Or dance? People danced at weddings. With their arms around their dance partners.

Ramsey's shoulders were broad. His arms would be strong. And warm.

It was so long since Lucy had been held....

Her phone was ringing. Grabbing the cell from her nightstand, she expected to see either her work number or her mother's on the caller display.

It was neither. "Hello?"

"Did I wake you?" The deep tenor of Ramsey's voice shook her and she welcomed the darkness that had been closing in on her just seconds before.

"No, I was awake."

He couldn't possibly know she'd been thinking about his fingers on her skin....

Dear Reader,

Welcome to Comfort Cove! You're in for an intense reading experience here. We have a cold-case detective who refuses to give up without finding all the answers.

And a family that could be blown apart by the truth.

There's another detective in Aurora, Indiana, who's working on the case, too. At the same time, she's searching for her own truths.

We have a wedding and a death in the culmination of a trilogy that takes us to a small coastal town in Massachusetts. But *The Truth About Comfort Cove* also stands alone—connected to, but apart from, the first two books in the series, *A Son's Tale* and *A Daughter's Story*.

I can guarantee that this is as emotionally gripping a read as any of the stories I've written for you over the years—and yet it's not like them at all. I don't know what sets this book apart. I didn't consciously change, or learn anything new, or go about my craft in a different way. I just know that in *The Truth About Comfort Cove,* everything that is me, everything that defines my writing, came together in a nearly perfect way. Or maybe it's just these particular people and their story that make it different.

So many times when I write, I watch my characters grow up. I think that in this book, as a writer, I grew up.

And so I give you this promise: *The Truth About Comfort Cove* is a book you will not regret buying.

Tara Taylor Quinn

P.S.—I love to hear from my readers. You can reach me at staff@tarataylorquinn.com.